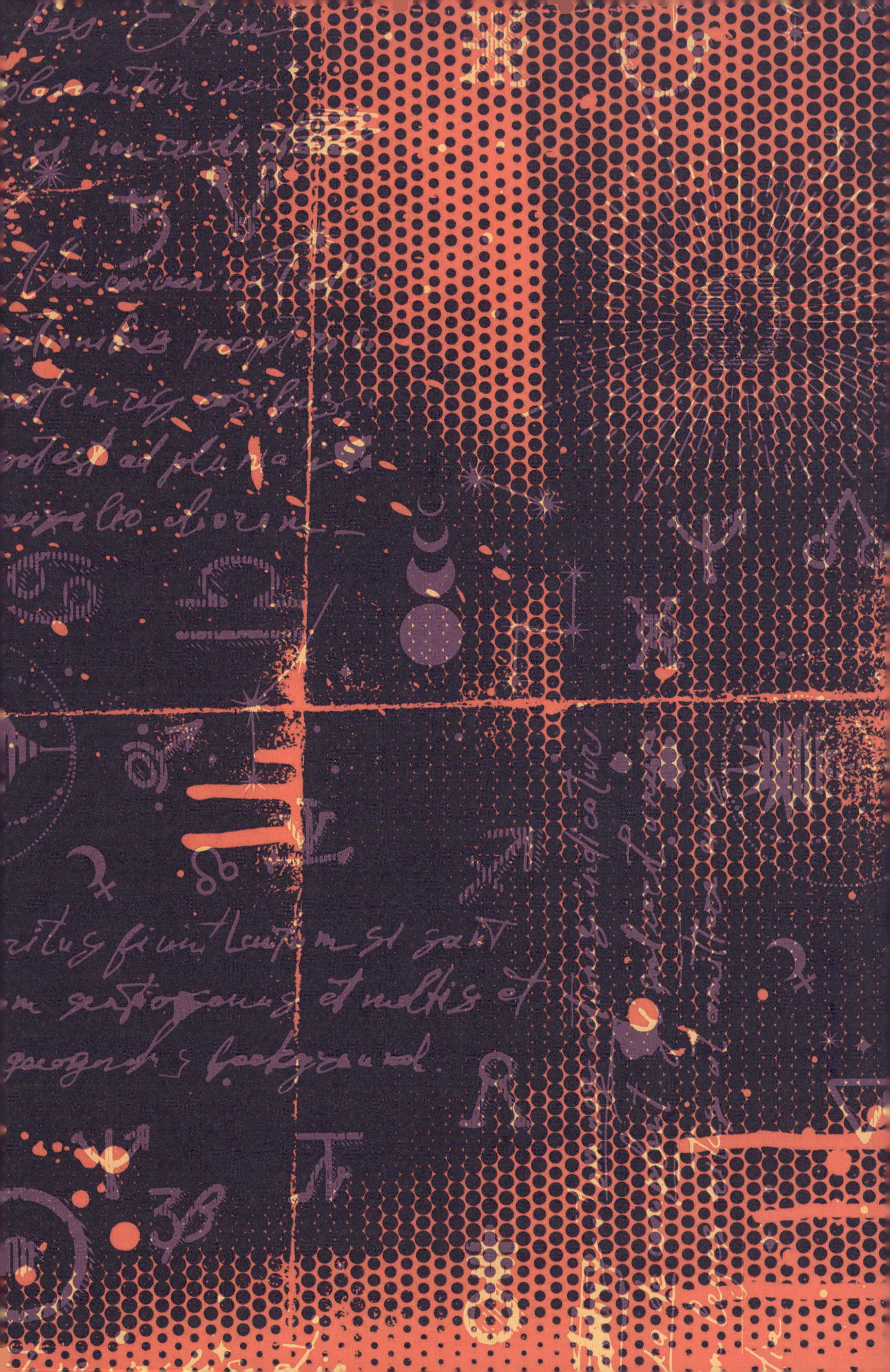

TOUCHED BY THE PRESENCE

"In these pages, we learn what has secretly driven Gary Lachman all these years—from rock music, through Nietzsche, a near electrocution, Faculty X, and Silver Age comics, to endless insights into magic, the occult, the evolution of consciousness, and superhuman powers. We learn what it means to be 'touched by the presence.' This is a profound read by a real reader and a real writer."

JEFFREY J. KRIPAL, AUTHOR OF *HOW TO THINK IMPOSSIBLY*

"Gary Lachman is one of the world's foremost historians of esoteric culture, having written seminal books about Blavatsky, Steiner, Swedenborg, Jung, Ouspensky, Colin Wilson, Aleister Crowley, and many others. His newest book, *Touched by the Presence,* is a deep dive into his mind—and his incredible journey. This book describes an amazing transformation from an abusive childhood, to becoming a near-homeless vagabond, and then a Rock and Roll Hall of Fame inductee, to his present career as an intellectual of high standing. While the book is a tribute to Lachman's creativity and his humanity, what stands out to me is his unwavering curiosity about the deepest philosophical problems facing contemporary humans."

JEFFREY MISHLOVE, PH.D., HOST OF THE *NEW THINKING ALLOWED* YOUTUBE CHANNEL

"In this compelling autobiography, Gary Lachman, former iconic pop musician turned author, vividly describes his inner and outer odyssey and the key people, movements, and books that have influenced him. He tells a riveting personal story that is full of fascinating observations on life, literature, culture, books, places, and more."

CHRISTOPHER MCINTOSH, AUTHOR OF *OCCULT GERMANY*, *OCCULT RUSSIA*, AND *THE CALL OF THE OLD GODS*

"In *Touched by the Presence*, former Blondie rocker Gary Lachman has written a zestful and inspirational memoir. A late baby boomer who grew up in a dysfunctional New Jersey family, he discovered music as a path of escape during the vibrant 1970s counterculture that spurred his life pivot to writing lucid books on spirituality and consciousness. Highly recommended!"

EDWARD HOFFMAN, PH.D., AUTHOR OF *PATHS TO HAPPINESS*

"Fluid and articulate, *Touched by the Presence* is at heart a bibliophile's memoir, delivering wide-ranging assessments of 20th-century philosophers and literary thinkers by an avid young reader who devoured them while undergoing a major life transition from being a member of a world-famous band to a prolific writer on distinctly off-the-grid metaphysical subjects. Spanning twenty years from the 1970s through the 1990s, the story is as much about the books Lachman encounters on this journey as the people. And the satisfying Act I–style ending leaves him and us poised on the brink of this new life, wondering what comes next."

VICTORIA NELSON, AUTHOR OF *ON WRITER'S BLOCK*

TOUCHED BY THE PRESENCE

From Blondie's Bowery and Rock and Roll to Magic and the Occult

GARY LACHMAN

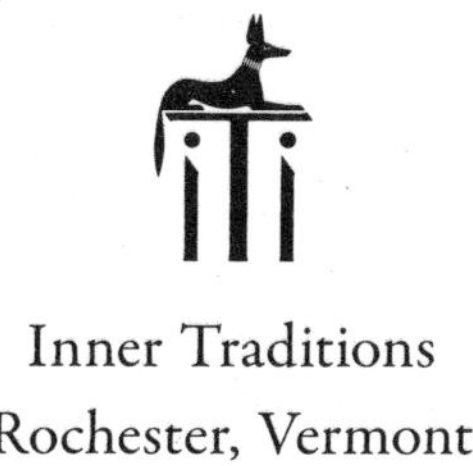

Inner Traditions
Rochester, Vermont

Inner Traditions
One Park Street
Rochester, Vermont 05767
www.InnerTraditions.com

Cataloging-in-Publication Data for this title is available from the Library of Congress

ISBN 979-8-88850-311-9 (print)
ISBN 979-8-88850-312-6 (ebook)

Printed and bound in India by Replika Press Pvt. Ltd.

10 9 8 7 6 5 4 3 2 1

Text design and layout by Debbie Glogover
This book was typeset in Garamond Premier Pro with Garamond ATF Subhead and Lulo used as display typefaces
All photos © Lisa Jane Persky

To send correspondence to the author of this book, mail a first-class letter to the author c/o Inner Traditions • Bear & Company, One Park Street, Rochester, VT 05767, and we will forward the communication, or contact the author directly at **gary-lachman.com**.

Contents

1 Faster Than a Speeding Bullet 1

2 Pulp Fiction 30

3 The Journey to the East 58

4 No Exit 83

5 Blood of the Poet 106

6 Touching the Presence 128

7 Knowledge Is a Funny Thing 152

8 Do the Work 181

9 Looking for the Miraculous 201

10 The Love of Wisdom 233

11 Into the New Age 268

12 Living in the Real World 298

13 The Crack Up 322

14 London Calling 350

✷

Acknowledgments 375

Was it destiny?
I don't know yet.

For Clem Burke, drummer extraordinaire, 1954–2025.
We were all touched by his presence.

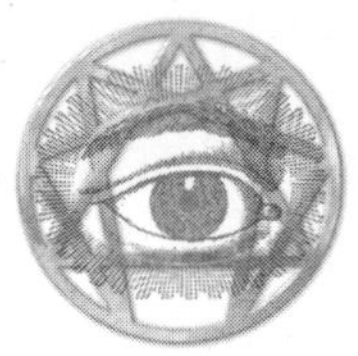

1
Faster Than a Speeding Bullet

I am often asked how I went from being a "rock star" (although I never was a star, more of a satellite, and one with an eccentric orbit) to a writer on esotericism and the history of consciousness. This memoir is an attempt to answer that question. I was a musician from 1975 to 1982, performing on guitar and bass with Blondie, Iggy Pop, and my own band, The Know—the name inspired by my interest in Gnosticism. I returned to music for a few years in the late 1990s, from 1996 to 2000, stopping with the birth of my second son and the beginning of my career as a writer. I received a contract for my first book, *Turn Off Your Mind*, a revisionist view of the 1960s, in 1998—the year my first son was born—and by 2000 was working on my second, *New York Rocker*, an account of, as the subtitle says, "my life in the Blank Generation." In recent times, I returned to playing music, once again, for several months in 2022. All told, I worked as a musician, songwriter, and performer for roughly ten years.

I became a full-time writer in 1996, when I moved to London, and I have been one ever since. I had written some articles and book reviews in the early '90s in Los Angeles, but was not yet making my living as a writer. If I count my years growing up in New Jersey, just across the Hudson from Manhattan, I lived in the New York area for roughly twenty-four years; five of those were spent in NYC proper. I lived in

Los Angeles for a total of sixteen years. The rest of my life—at least, up until now—I have spent here in London, aside, of course, from periods of travel. I came to London shortly after I turned forty; the anniversary of my arrival here recently passed. I am now sixty-seven. I have been a writer for twenty-seven years and have twenty-five books to show for it.

I should mention that, along with being a musician and a writer, I worked for several years in retail, first at a video rental shop, then at a metaphysical bookstore, both in Los Angeles, in the 1980s and '90s. After this, I started a PhD track in English Literature at the University of Southern California, but dropped out after a year. I found academia severely limiting and by then the "political correctness" craze, now well established, had begun and I saw that as a white male of a certain age who had no interest in deconstructing anything, I would most likely never get a job.

I then worked for a year as a science writer for the University of California, Los Angeles. Given that I have no background in science, this was a position I should never have occupied. Yet I did so on the strength of my writing and ability to transmute dry, unappetizing scientific reports into readable prose, singing the praises of the molecular biology department and the great advances made by our astrophysicists to alumni and foundations targeted for donations and grants. I got the job after my wife saw an advertisement for it in the *Los Angeles Times* and insisted I apply. I left it after the collapse of our marriage, which lasted from 1992 to 1995—the marriage, not the collapse, although it, too, was protracted. It was following the breakup of my marriage that I left Los Angeles and moved to London. As should be obvious, my sons are the product of a later relationship.

From 1984 to 1990, I earned a degree in philosophy from California State University, Los Angeles. I had intended to carry on and eventually teach philosophy, my career move after rock and roll, something my professors found incomprehensible. But my marriage—to a colleague at the bookstore—got in the way.

I should point out that I am not an academic and that I hold no academic position, although I have taught online courses based on some of my books for the California Institute of Integral Studies. As an independent thinker, however, I have lectured quite a bit in the UK, Europe, the US, and as far afield as South America and Australia.

For some reason that remains obscure, I've always wanted to be a writer. I was always fascinated by and interested in words—I read the dictionary when I was young, and English was my best subject in school, with history and art close runners-up. I did well in philosophy in later years, and won awards while studying it, but my interest was always in what is known as "continental philosophy," the European variety that brought literature and art into the discussion—think of existentialism—rather than the Anglo-American analytic tradition of logical positivism and linguistics analysis, which I found rather dull and superficial. I remain abysmal at any math more complex than adding up a grocery bill. This meant I did not do that well in symbolic logic, which is a kind of philosophical algebra. Aside from astronomy, I was bored by science.

Comic books were my introduction to reading, and early on I wanted to be a comic book artist and write and draw my own comic. I did have a character, The Raven, and did draw a few panels and fill in the speech bubbles. But, although I could draw, this didn't get very far. I did continue to draw intermittently in later years; when on tour as a musician I brought along a Rapidograph pen and a sketch book, and some tattered sketches from that time remain in a box in a closet. My last attempts at graphic art were some woodcuts I made during my marriage in the early '90s.

Later, when I started reading science fiction and fantasy—I was a great fan of H. P. Lovecraft and the *Weird Tales* set—I wrote stories. These, with much else, have vanished in the void. Actually, my first attempt at writing was a school play for Thanksgiving. In it, students working on a school play about Thanksgiving share a collective dream in which they are all transported back in time to the first Thanksgiving, an early sign of both the interest in dreams and the strange character of time that would inform my later work. This was in 1964, and I was in the third grade; I would have been eight going on nine.

But something happened in my adolescence. It was then that I began to want to be a poet. I can't say why. The lyrics to rock tunes—Bob Dylan's, John Lennon's—no doubt played a part in this. I was yet to learn how to play guitar—when I did, I was self-taught—and I can remember coming across a paperback at a school book fair, which was an attempt to encourage my fellow students to read, something not needed in my case. I was—am—an unrepentant obsessive reader, having picked up the habit by the age of five, possibly earlier. The worst torture I can think of would be to lock me in a room bereft of anything interesting to read.

The book I found at the fair had song lyrics on one page and poetry on the other. So, the lyrics to Procol Harum's "Homburg," written by Keith Reid, were on one page, and T. S. Eliot's "Love Song of J. Alfred Prufrock" were on another. The opening line of that poem still sends a shiver down my spine. "Let us go then, you and I . . ." (A similar frisson accompanies Coleridge's "In Xanadu did Kubla Khan . . .") Similarly, there were lyrics to, say Lennon and McCartney's "A Day in the Life" facing something by e e cummings or Ezra Pound or Yeats. I was twelve at the time.

Pop music was all the rage and I must have felt that if I couldn't play I could at least write lyrics.

For a time, I rewrote the lyrics to pop tunes.[1] The melody would come into my head and I would accompany it with stream of conscious-

---

1. I can remember bringing 45s into gym class in the third grade and dancing to Chubby Checker's "The Twist." Among his many jobs my father was a caterer, and he would often bring 45s home from the jukebox at the tavern where he worked. Gary U.S. Bonds's "Quarter to Three," Frankie Vaughan's "Tower of Strength"—both hits in 1961—and various girl-group numbers made up my early listening. Later, following the British Invasion which brought The Beatles, Dave Clark Five, Zombies (a favorite), Herman's Hermits, and many other British pop groups to America's shores, on Friday afternoons, just before the end of class, our teacher allowed us to perform a kind of karaoke to their songs, strumming the pretend guitars we had cut out of plywood in shop class.

ness impromptu lyrics of my own. I did write these down in a notebook that, again, like much else, has since disappeared. Years later, when, at eighteen, I left home and started living in New York, I began writing songs on a broken-down piano that made up part of the furniture in the storefront-turned-studio on East 10th Street, where I lived. Any poetry I was still writing turned into songs, and soon after this I joined a band and became a musician.

I had no musical training. In high school many of my friends were musicians; one of them later went on to become the drummer in the very successful band of which I, too, was a member. This, of course, was Blondie. There were guitarists, bassists, keyboardists, drummers, and singers among these friends. Aside from myself and my drummer friend, I don't think any of them made it to a professional level. It is ironic that I did, given that I wasn't a musician and was more or less tolerated and allowed to hang out with those who were.

How did it happen that I was part of a musical movement—the New York CBGB scene—that, as the cliché goes, "changed the face of pop music"? That I recorded albums, went on tours, met and worked with some big names in the business, wrote a hit song, earned gold records, and was inducted into the Rock and Roll Hall of Fame, while the friends who were much better musicians than I was didn't? That's a good question. Writing this memoir will, with any luck, go some way to answering it. But here I'll just say that I was willing—eager—to take the risk involved, as Joseph Campbell used to say, in "following your bliss." I was happy to give up safety and security—i.e., living at home and staying in college—and, as Nietzsche advised, "live dangerously," by throwing myself into an adventure that, 99 percent of the time, ends in failure and disappointment, if not drug addiction, alcoholism, or worse.

Even with the success I've had—modest but not negligible—failure and disappointment have not been foreign to me. Neither, for that matter, have drugs and alcohol. I have had to deal with the failure of my own band to secure a recording contract as well as with the fact that songs of mine which are just as good as the ones that were successful will most likely remain known only to the relatively few people who came to my performances—that is, they will remain unknown. One of these songs, "Amor Fati," became our signature tune and my own life's motto. I borrowed it from the philosopher Nietzsche, who was a powerful influence on me then, and remains so, although at sixty-seven I have a somewhat different appreciation of his work than I did when I came across it at sixteen. *Amor fati* means "love of fate." It was Nietzsche's "formula for greatness." It means more than an acceptance of life—it is an affirmation of it, even in its most painful, tragic, and uncertain forms.[2]

This, of course, is easier said than done. I have certainly had quite a bit of fate to love. One such portion is the fact that the song in which I express this sentiment is among those that most likely will remain unknown. If I were superstitious I might think that fate itself arranged this as a test, to see if I really could love a fate that included a large helping of disappointment. Fate and its fellow traveler, destiny, turned up in more than one of my songs, as they later did in my books. They will also make more than one appearance here.

I'VE MENTIONED MY LOVE OF BOOKS AND READING. I am writing these notes in the British Library, where I have researched and written practically all of my books. I first learned of the British Library from reading the work of a British writer who has been a powerful influence on me. This is Colin Wilson, whom I first read when living with my bandmates in a rundown illegal loft space on New York's Bowery in 1975, when I had been playing in the then-unknown band Blondie for only a few months.

Wilson is best known for his first book, *The Outsider*, an existential study of creative individuals suffering from the lack of meaning in the modern world, which was first published in May 1956.

2. Versions of the song are available on YouTube.

When it appeared, I would have been six months old, having been born on Christmas Eve, 1955, smack in the middle of the baby boom. Eisenhower was president, the Korean War and Joe McCarthy had only recently become old news, America still had only forty-eight states, and the Iron Curtain was firmly in place, although Khrushchev's "thaw" had begun, following the death of Stalin. The Cold War, however, was as frigid as ever.

Had I known what they were, and had my blue-collar parents, who were not readers, purchased copies, I could have seen photographs of Wilson in articles in *Time*, *Life*, and other magazines. He was, in a phrase he would later use of celebrity thinkers, the "intellectual flavor of the month," although his practically global fame at the age of twenty-four would soon dissolve when the critics who had at first sung his praises changed their tune to something more of a funeral dirge. I write about this in my book about Wilson.[3]

I didn't read *The Outsider* until late 1977, by which time I had left Blondie and begun my first stint as a resident of Southern California, and was on my way to forming The Know. But in the summer of '75, amidst the debris of the previous hippie generation—which would soon make way for the punks—I came across a copy of *The Occult*, Wilson's "comeback" book, published in 1971.

Up until then, the only interest I had in anything "occult" came in the form of the weird fiction I devoured—I've mentioned Lovecraft and *Weird Tales*—and the 1930s and '40s horror films I had grown up watching on television. But something about the book attracted me, and once I had started reading it I was hooked. Another factor in my conversion to occultism, if I can call it that, was the flamboyant gay biker artist who had the lease on the building and who rented us our floor. He was a devotee of the notorious dark magician Aleister Crowley, who had found a place for himself in the pop world after being among the

---

3. *Beyond The Robot: The Life and Work of Colin Wilson* (New York: Tarcher Perigee, 2016).

people The Beatles "liked" and presented on the cover of their album *Sgt. Pepper's Lonely Hearts Club Band*, released in 1967, when I was eleven.

The artist gave impromptu readings with Crowley's then rather rare *Thoth Tarot Deck*, painted canvases based on the trump cards, and often read aloud from Crowley's books, especially *The Diary of a Drug Fiend*, a work popular in my crowd for obvious reasons. In this setting, I found myself becoming more and more fascinated with the occult and with the people, like Crowley, who had made it their life. Later, this early, naïve, enthusiastic fascination with the mysterious world of magic and mysticism would slowly and with much effort be transformed into a fairly serious attempt to understand its place and meaning in human history and consciousness.

I DIGRESS. I mention Wilson here—there will be more about him further on—because it was through reading about his life that I came to know about the British Library. Not the British Library where I am sitting at a desk at the moment, writing these notes in mid-January 2023, but its original form as the Reading Room of the British Museum.

Before the success of *The Outsider* had him in newspapers and on television, in order to save money, for a time Wilson slept in a waterproof sleeping bag on London's Hampstead Heath, a vast, open swath of land, much of which remains as it did when Keats and Constable tramped over its hills in the nineteenth century. Wilson was often woken up by a dog or a policeman, after which he cycled downhill to the British Museum in Bloomsbury—famous for Virginia Woolf and her set—where he worked on his first novel until closing time in the famous Reading Room, with the shades of Marx, Ruskin, H. G. Wells, George Bernard Shaw, and other famous habitués hovering in the background.[4] In 1997, most of the books housed in the Reading Room were

4. Colin Wilson, *Ritual in the Dark* (London: Gollancz, 1960).

transferred to their new home at the British Library, a monstrous work of postmodern architecture, grotesquely mirroring the Victorian pile of St. Pancras station. The old Reading Room was refit as a tourist attraction and has been closed since 2013.

I got my first card to the Reading Room in 1983. This was at the tail end of a "mini search for the miraculous" that had me in Chartres Cathedral, Stonehenge, Glastonbury, the site of Gurdjieff's "Institute for the Harmonious Development of Man" in Fontainebleau, just outside of Paris, and other spots, such as Gorran Haven, the tiny village in Cornwall, in the far west of England, that Wilson had left London for in 1957. I went there on a pilgrimage to meet Wilson. I did and began a friendship that lasted until his death in 2013, at the age of eighty-two.

During 1996, my first year in London, I went to the old Reading Room until it closed. And I have been coming to its new incarnation since it opened a year later. I have by now spent more time in the library and on Hampstead Heath than Colin Wilson, my inspiration for frequenting both, ever did. It is often the fate of true fans to be more royal than the king, although I've yet to spend a night rough on the Heath in a sleeping bag.

LIBRARIES HAVE ALWAYS BEEN SPECIAL places for me, as they are for any inveterate reader, and it is sad that with the advent of the "information age" they have steadily lost their literary character and are now seen as "knowledge centers" or multi-purpose community facilities, mostly given over to computers. At least, the ones I have access to in London have taken on this character. I guess things must change with the times, although I've never understood exactly why.

My love of libraries began during my school years. I've often remarked that I got an education by skipping school and going to the library. I spent many hours wandering among the stacks, reading poetry and books about art and film, science fiction and horror stories. To this day, my most "archetypal" powerful dreams, in which I experience a happiness more intense than anything in waking life, involve my discovering a secret bookshop filled with old paperbacks and magazines.

My parents did not share my passion, and I once received what I will call a "severe reprimand" when I returned home late from school with a stack of library books. That I was punished for wanting to read gives some idea of the atmosphere at home during my childhood.[5] But this censure was not limited to home. The first novel I read was *The Scarlet Pimpernel* by Baroness Orczy, in the third or fourth grade. I must have liked it because the title character was a kind of superhero—at least, he wore a mask and had a secret identity. (The 1934 film version with Leslie Howard remains a favorite.) The teacher reprimanded me because I read it straight through in a few sittings, rather than plodding through it piecemeal each week, as the rest of the class did. This was an early example of my habit of striking out on my own and not sticking to the schedule or remaining with the group.

I suspect that my mother was positively frightened by books, in the sense that uneducated, uncultured people—neither of my parents finished high school—fear what they don't understand. They find it threatening. On one occasion my mother tossed a collection of books I had been hiding from her—as much for the sexy covers as for the content—down the stairs in our house.[6] Others, she tore up.[7] As you might suspect, books were not the only things I hid. There was, for example, my journal.

---

5. Among my father's several jobs—at least during the summer—was that of an umpire at softball games. He would bring me along, hoping I'd develop a taste for sports; I didn't, aside from a brief interest in basketball in my late adolescence. I would smuggle a paperback or a comic with me, and would find a quiet spot where I could read. When he saw me, he said, "Put the book down and watch the game."

6. One was the Bantam paperback edition of D. H. Lawrence's *Lady Chatterley's Lover*. The cover, a sexy illustration of the lady in question, topless but with her back to the reader, was I believe by the same artist, William A. Edwards, who did the covers for Bantam's paperback editions of Hermann Hesse's novels.

7. This was the fate of my paperback copy of Hunter Davies's *The Beatles: The Authorized Biography*. This was in 1970. Although I had been a casualty of the mid-1960s British Invasion, I went through a phase of personal Beatlemania just before and after the group broke up.

One afternoon—I would have been around fifteen or sixteen—on my way home from school, my mother took me by the hand and marched me to the local police station. At the time she was working as a traffic warden, and had become friends with the sergeant, who was there, sitting at his desk. A notebook in his hands looked awfully familiar. Looking up from it, he stared at me and said, "So you think you're a genius, eh?"

He was looking at my journal, in which I had written some poems and had filled a page with an immodest assessment of my talents, writing "I am a genius" several times. Coming upon this—which could not have been by accident, as I had hidden it—my mother could think of no better course of action than to show it to a policeman. I wasn't happy that my private, inner life had been exposed so rudely, and made my feelings clear. I can't remember whether I got the journal back, but to this day I am not one for journaling or keeping a diary.[8]

Such chastisement, however, only increased the appeal of the printed page. In my late teens, when the friction between myself and my parents reached injurious levels, psychologically and physically, the local library was a haven for me—what today we would call a "safe space"—and I would spend hours there during temporary extended absences from home. I liked nothing better than to find a desk in a quiet corner and huddle behind a stack of books. I must admit, though, that, like many "library cormorants"—a more eloquent sobriquet than "bookworm," coined by the poet Coleridge—I have not always followed the rules. One infraction serves to give an idea of at least some of my taste in reading at the time.

As did thousands of other American adolescents in the early 1970s, I fell under the spell of Hermann Hesse, who was metaphorically enjoying

---

8. The psychologist Abraham Maslow, father of "humanistic psychology," whose work has been an important influence on me, had a similar relationship with his mother, whom he called a "horrible creature." An account of Maslow's difficult childhood can be found in Edward Hoffman's *The Right to Be Human: A Biography of Abraham Maslow* (Los Angeles: Jeremy P. Tarcher, 1988).

a posthumous best-selling success—he died in 1962—with the paperback editions of his novels, published by Bantam Books, with their often sexy covers.[9] My introduction to Hesse came when a hippie girl I had a crush on—I remember her flannel shirt, braless breasts, and patchouli oil—gave me a copy of *Siddhartha* in 1970, when I was fourteen.

There will be more on Hesse further on. I mention him here because it was through reading Hesse that I came across the name Jung—C. G. Jung, that is. I can't remember exactly where I saw the reference. I suspect it was on the back of *Demian* or *Narcissus and Goldmund*, along with other names, such as Dostoevsky and Nietzsche, both of whom I later went on to read. In any case, it led to a criminal act. I saw that my high school library had a copy of Jung's autobiography, *Memories, Dreams, Reflections*, published after Jung's death in 1961, and, not bothering to check it out with the librarian, I simply walked out with it. This would have been 1970 or '71. I am sorry if I deprived any other students of the opportunity to read the book, although, to be honest, I would be surprised if any of my classmates then would have wanted to.

I read the book and can't say that I made much of it or really understood what Jung was saying—it would take my writing a book about Jung to do that.[10] But he talked about dreams, about his inner life, something I was becoming aware of in my own life, and, as Hesse did, about becoming an individual, about finding your "true self," not the one you were when dealing with school or your parents or your friends. None of my friends were readers or "poetic" or "sensitive," at least, not in the way that I thought of myself as being, and I was made fun of because of this. It was this self that I was beginning to feel when I read poetry or tried to write it, when I read Hesse, and when I fantasized and dreamed about my future as a poet or artist or musician.

---

9. The covers were the work of William A. Edwards. See J. P. Williams, "The Mystery Artist Behind Hermann Hesse's Paperback Covers in the 70s," Medium website, April 20, 2022.

10. *Jung the Mystic* (New York: Tarcher/Penguin 2012).

I held on to that copy of *Memories, Dreams, Reflections* for some time. I can remember the plastic protecting the book cover, with its photograph of Jung smoking his pipe and paging through a manuscript, with his Gnostic ring visible on his finger—this photo has been used for some paperback editions—and the library call letters in black print on a white square on the spine. I hadn't discovered Nietzsche as yet, but with first Hesse and then Jung, my love of German literature and thought began. (Yes, I know Jung was Swiss, but he wrote in German; Hesse, too, was German-Swiss.) Even the name "Jung" sounded strangely mysterious, at least, after I learned how to pronounce it correctly. Another name long mispronounced was Goethe's, which I mangled into the crude monosyllabic "Goeth." Later, Proust suffered under "Prowst."

I didn't know it then, but I suspect that Jung himself would have said I was responding to the archetype of the "wise old man," the sage, the teacher. I am not a Jungian—for that matter, neither was Jung—and readers of my book about him know that I can be critical of Jung and his work. But because of this early exposure to the challenge to "become who you are," I can only say that at bottom I have a love of what Jung and Hesse stood for and meant to me then that overrides any later criticism.

Yet one day, many years later when I had moved to Los Angeles, going through my books—which by then I had shipped back and forth across the country more than once; they have even traveled across the Atlantic—I picked this copy out, looked at the jagged remains of the page that had borne the library's stamp and which I had torn out, and felt a sudden pang of guilt. I put the book in a padded Manila envelope, addressed it to my high school, and put it in the mail. I didn't include a return address and could only wonder what the late fees might have been.

I'VE MENTIONED THAT I LEARNED HOW TO READ from comic books. I don't remember the first comic I saw or the process of learning how to read, although of course I do remember "See Dick and Jane" and "Run, Spot, run!" from the early Dick and Jane "see and say" reading books by Zerna Sharp and William S. Gray, which were used to teach reading to my generation. But I am sure that I started reading before starting school, which I must have done in late 1960, at the age of four, given that I graduated from grammar school in 1969, when I was thirteen.

The first comic that I remember was *Atomic Rabbit*, a creation of the artist Al Fago, which started in 1955, the year of my birth. I must, however, have gotten hold of the character's later incarnation as *Atomic Bunny*, the change happening in 1958, when the artist Pat Masulli took over, although I distinctly remember "Rabbit," not "Bunny."

Why "Bunny" seemed a preferable alternative to "Rabbit" I can't say, except perhaps that the change was a result of the comic book scare created by the publication, in 1954, of the psychologist Frederic Wertham's fear-mongering work *The Seduction of the Innocent*. This best-selling text of social psychology argued that the violent imagery in comic books had a deleterious effect on children and should be banned, rather like similar concerns raised by video games today. The comics Wertham mostly had in mind were the admittedly often gory volumes put out by EC (Entertaining Comics) in the early 1950s, titles such as *Tales From the Crypt*, which served as the inspiration for the Amicus 1972 horror film of the same name, as well as the later television series. Wertham included superheroes in his sweeping indictment too, claiming that *Superman* promoted fascism, *Batman* homosexuality (exactly what was his relation to his sidekick Robin?), and that *Wonder Woman* was rife with sadomasochism (her magic lariat was a bondage fetish, no? And besides, she had large breasts and an ample décolletage . . .).

These DC Comics reigning stars were just hanging on to their spots on the magazine racks following the superhero—actually, "mystery man"—popularity slump post-WWII. Wertham's attack—later discredited—did not help their sales. Indeed, *Batman*, now a multibillion-dollar franchise, was nearly discontinued. I can hazard a guess that "Bunny" was thought more cuddly and kid-friendly than "Rabbit"—too explicitly animal?—

although one wonders if Wertham ever saw or analyzed the effect of the often explosively violent scenes in the Warner Bros *Bugs Bunny* and *Looney Tunes* cartoons, or the even more madcap *Daffy Duck*, which I watched practically every day on television.

I doubt if my mother ever heard of Frederic Wertham or *The Seduction of the Innocent*—she certainly wouldn't have read the book—but I suspect that the trickledown effect of Wertham's profitable paranoia must have reached her at some point, and that it had lodged in her mind that comic books were bad. This censure extended even to the innocuously-renamed *Atomic Bunny*. I can remember carrying a copy of the uranium-fueled lagomorph's adventures—the creature got its superpowers after eating a uranium enriched carrot—back from the candy store where I got it, and my mother shaking her head and voicing some displeasure. Whatever her dismay, it didn't deter me, and for the next several years—until my late teens, when I sacrificed my collection to fund my relocation to New York—comics were among the most important and influential things in my life.

I know that I was reading at age five because I can remember surviving a crisis that, at the time, rocked my world. I was staying with my maternal grandmother—the only one of my grandparents that I can say I knew—my mother having deposited me with her for some reason.[11]

---

11. I didn't know my father's parents. His father died before I was born. I had a vague idea of his mother as an old woman whom he visited in the "home" (mental?) where she was, although I never went with him and don't remember ever meeting her. I knew my mother's father, but have only vague memories of him being ill in bed at the "projects" (social housing) where my grandmother lived, and of my father shaving and cutting his hair. He spoke little or no English; my father spoke a little Polish and I remember hearing him speak it with my grandfather. He called me "Sputnik," after the Russian satellite, because of the "John Glenn haircut"—a crew cut popularized by the astronaut—I sported then. My mother's father and my father's mother came from the same region, Galicia, in Eastern Europe, which had gone back and forth between Polish and Ukrainian control over the years. My mother's mother was from Ireland; my father's father from Prussia—at least according to my father, who said it in the same breath as "Cracow." This could have meant the buffer zone between Poland, Austria, and Russia, established after the defeat of Napoleon. Lachman is a German name, perhaps of German-Jewish origin.

My sister, four years older than me, was not with us. I had asked my grandmother, an old Irish battle-ax, for a dime—ten cents—so I could buy a comic book at the local candy store. It was difficult getting this from her, and to her reluctance she added the caution that I didn't buy one that I already had. There was little chance of that, although it does suggest that I was already gathering a collection. Yet, when I got to the candy store, it seemed I might not get one at all.

Comic books had cost ten cents from the beginning.[12] But in late 1961—November, in fact—they went up in price. I only discovered this when I got to the candy store and picked up a copy of *The Flash*, which was one of my favorites—mostly because of the artwork by Carmine Infantino, who did the art for another favorite character, Adam Strange. I'm not suggesting that at five I knew who Infantino was; I only learned this, and the names of other artists, some years later. For some arcane reason I have never understood, the publication calendar of comics and magazines is always at least a month ahead of the workaday one. So, a July issue comes out in June. In this case, it was the December 1961 issue, #125, which came out in November, in which Flash and his sidekick, Kid Flash, race back in time and far into the future—Einsteinian relativity came in handy here—to defeat some menace.

I must not have seen the difference in price on the cover, because when I handed the copy along with my dime to the man behind the counter, he told me that the price had gone up to twelve cents and that if I wanted to buy it I needed two more pennies. I had a difficult time getting the extra two cents from my grandmother, who hadn't wanted to give me the dime in the first place, but I persevered.

Comics remained at twelve cents until the end of the '60s, when they increased to fifteen cents, which marked the start of the decline of my own interest in them, which became official when Jack Kirby, my favorite artist, left Marvel to join its rival, DC, in 1970. Like most

12. David Hadju's excellent account of the comic book paranoia of the '50s is titled *The Ten-Cent Plague* (London: Picador, 2008).

comic readers of my generation—children of the Silver Age, which began in 1956, practically when I did—I started out reading DC's line up, *Superman*, *Batman*, *Green Lantern*, *The Atom* (I've already mentioned *The Flash*) and my favorite, *Justice League of America*. But I became a Marvel fan when I came across a copy of *Fantastic Four*—issue #18, September 1963—in which they battle the practically unbeatable Super-Skrull, an alien who possessed all the FF's individual powers. My allegiance to DC began to quaver at that point.

I discovered this issue, with Kirby's explosive artwork, while we were on a family summer holiday on the Jersey shore. A shop in Surf City—not the one immortalized by Jan and Dean—sold packs of six comics at a discount price.[13] They were discounted because their titles had been clipped off. I had no idea why the covers were mutilated, and it was always a gamble exactly what you would get because only the covers of the copies at the front and back of the pack could be seen through the plastic wrap. The others were obscured, so it was something of a lucky dip. But at six comics for a quarter, who's complaining?

Selling these copies was actually illegal, because the shops that had originally stocked them—candy stores or drug stores—had cut the top quarter off their covers to send to the publisher as proof of unsold copies, for which they were refunded. This saved on shipping the actual copies, and the publishers believed that the issues were rendered damaged and therefore unsellable. They were wrong, and I for one was glad that they were.

Back then, there weren't specialty comic shops nor were comics seen as collectable; that only started up in the late '60s, and the notion that early issues of *Spider-Man* would fetch millions of dollars was still well in the future. Many comics would simply get thrown out after they were read, just like yesterday's newspapers. I remember finding a few

---

13. Jan and Dead were a successful pop duo in the early '60s, with a "surf sound" rather like the Beach Boys. "Surf City" (1963), where there are "two girls for every boy," was a No. 1 hit.

that way, and for a time afterward I kept an eye on the neighbors' garbage. Years after I had sold my collection for a pittance, I would feel a pang of deep regret and loss every time I walked into a comic shop and saw issues I'd had: #1's of *Spider-Man*, *Fantastic Four*, *Avengers*, *X-Men*, and others, hanging on the walls. This wasn't because had I held on to them I could have got a better price—they were never an investment. It was more like how Marcel feels in *Remembrance of Things Past*, when the taste of madeleine "recaptures the past" for him.

This poignant sense of a lost world came to me often in the mid-2000s, when my young sons and I became fans of the *Justice League* animated series on Cartoon Network. My sons never became real comic readers, or readers of any sort—victims of the digital age—but they loved the series, *Batman* and *Superman* too. We would haunt comic shops here in London, searching for the superhero action figures that they collected and which today are stored in a box in a closet in my flat, the young boys who coveted them now young men in their twenties.

I CAN SAY THAT THE BEGINNING OF MY INTEREST in the sort of things I've come to write about started with comics. The Legion of Superheroes didn't have their own comic—at least, they didn't when I first came across them. They were the second feature in *Adventure Comics*, whose main character was Superboy. Aquaman and Green Arrow shared its pages too. The Legion of Superheroes was made up of teenagers from the future who possessed superpowers. Some of them came from other planets. The strip started in 1958 and predates Marvel's *X-Men*, another team of superpowered teens, which began in 1963.

I followed the Legion's adventures, although I can't say they were one of my favorites. But one of the Legion led to a question. His name was Cosmic Boy and his power was magnetism, like the Marvel super-villain Magneto. He had a pink and black costume, anticipating chav fashion by decades, and was one of the three main characters, along with Saturn Girl and Lightning Lad. But why was he called "Cosmic Boy" instead of "Magnetic Boy"? "Lightning Lad" was obvious; he shot lightning bolts. But "Saturn Girl"? What did Saturn have to do with her power—telepathy—even if it did mean she sported a nifty Saturn emblem, rings and all, on her costume? It didn't make sense.

In search of a solution to this mystery, I asked my sister what "cosmic" meant. She didn't know. I then asked my mother, who didn't know either. I didn't bother to ask my father, who I imagined would also draw a blank. You might say that I've been looking for the answer to that question ever since.

The Silver Age in comics, from 1956 to 1970, saw the return of the superhero after the big slump in sales of comics of this type following the end of WWII. It was at that point that publishers frantic to plug holes in a sinking market turned to the violence, gore, horror, and sex that had kept the pulp magazines afloat, and which EC served up with relish. The return of *The Flash* in 1956, in the September issue of *Showcase*, #4, is generally seen as the start of the era. Ironically, this enormously creative and productive period in comics—a true and meaningful Renaissance, arguably comics' most fertile time—came about precisely because of the impact of Frederic Wertham's scathing attack on EC's gruesome titles.

One result of Wertham's *The Seduction of the Innocent* was the establishment of the Comics Code Authority, a system of self-regulation initiated by publishers in 1954 to avoid a government censor. It served a similar purpose as the Hays Commission, which started in 1934, did for the movies. With the white stamp in the upper right-hand corner of the cover, parents could be assured that the comics their sons were reading (aside from *Archie* and the romance titles, most comics were a "boy thing") would not give them nightmares or predestine them to a life of crime—although, of course, there were no guarantees.

The Flash that appeared in *Showcase* was a modern age refit of the original Flash, a superhero from the Golden Age of Comics, the pre-Wertham 1940s. *Showcase* was an anthology title that featured characters some of whom would move on to comics of their own; a similar tryout title was *The Brave and the Bold*. The Flash made the grade, with the first issue of his own comic appearing in 1959; in it he fights the Mirror Master, one of a retinue of inventive super villains the "scarlet speedster" battles. It was numbered 105 to establish a continuity with the original *Flash* comic, whose last issue, #104, had appeared in 1949, when superheroes were being defeated more soundly by changes in popular taste than by any of their archenemies. By the late '50s, with EC going under and the Comics Code overseeing creative output, the appeal of modernized, intelligent, graphically sophisticated, and on the whole healthy adventures with heroes kids could see as positive role models grew. DC began to revive a whole slew of mystery men who had succumbed to the comic slump in the late '40s.

Green Lantern, The Atom, Hawkman, Aquaman—all of whom had popular incarnations in the Golden Age—now appeared in highly stylized, sleek, and very modern guises. Another space-age refit transformed the Golden Age Justice Society of America into what became my favorite DC title, *Justice League of America*. In recent incarnations of the Justice League, the nationalist tag has been dropped; but as every fan of the *Superman* television series starring the tragic George Reeves knew, Superman and his fellow superheroes fought for "truth, justice, and the American way."

One of the few things I ever talked about with my mother were the comics from when she was growing up in the 1930s and '40s. She didn't have much to say about them and really only remembered *Wonder Woman*, but hearing her mention them somehow made them alive, and I believe that my interest in history and the past began with my fascination with the comic heroes from the Golden Age.

One of the odd things about the popular culture of the 1960s and early '70s was that a great deal of it was a revival of the popular culture of the '30s and '40s. Comics may have spearheaded this revival, and I'm sure there must be academic treatises about it. Television, too, must have played its part.

Along with comics, television, of course, was a central part of my adolescence. I've mentioned my interest in the horror films of the 1930s and '40s. I watched Universal's series of *Frankenstein* (1931) and *Dracula* (1931) films, as well as *The Wolfman* (1941), *The Invisible Man* (1933), *The Mummy* (1932), and others religiously. To this day, RKO's original *King Kong* (1933) is probably my all-time favorite film.[14] These, as well as '50s sci-fi and monster films (*Earth vs. the Flying Saucers* [1956] and *Creature from the Black Lagoon* [1954], for example) made up several hours of Saturday morning television time, along with the many cartoon shows, like *Johnny Quest* and *Space Ghost*, which were popular then.[15]

But other figures from decades earlier were revived on television and, by my last year in high school—1973—had become appropriated by the '60s hippie generation. As a kid, I first watched the Marx Brothers, W. C. Fields, and Humphrey Bogart on television on Sunday afternoons. By the time I was seventeen, I was watching *A Night at the Opera* (1935) or *The Maltese Falcon* (1941) in a college auditorium, filled with smoke rising up from the joints that practically everyone in the place were smoking, myself included.

---

14. Francois Truffaut's *Fahrenheit 451* (1965), based on the Ray Bradbury novel about a dystopian future where reading is banned, is a very close second—not surprisingly, given my love of books.

15. I can only mention here the profound impact that genius of special effects, Ray Harryhausen, who created the effects in *Earth vs. the Flying Saucers* and dozens of other films, had on my growing consciousness. Like many other sci-fi and fantasy film fans of my generation, the battle between the Argonauts and the skeletons in *Jason and the Argonauts* (1963) set a singular high-water mark for animation. Nothing served up by CGI these days comes anywhere near to the undeniable sense of the "uncanny" that Harryhausen's stop action work achieved. This is precisely because Harryhausen never aimed to be "realistic"—the bugbear of unimaginative minds—but *convincing*, something entirely other.

Although it was the most modern decade to date, the '60s saw the beginning of a fascination with the past, especially in the form of its popular culture. In the back pages of comics, collectors posted advertisements for their catalogues of back issues of current titles, but also for issues of Golden Age comics, many of them featuring characters I had never heard of. People today who see old comics as investments would find the humble prices asked for comics from the '40s or '50s back then unbelievable.

I became fascinated with these catalogues and, whenever I could, sent away for them. I couldn't afford to buy anything, but I loved looking at the titles and the occasional illustration of a forgotten Golden Age character—Doll Man, say, or the Blue Beetle, who would, in fact, be revived by Charlton Comics, which ran a poor third to DC and Marvel throughout the '60s.[16]

DC wasn't the only comic book publisher digging into its past in search of bankable resurrections. Marvel entered the superhero Silver Age with issue #1, November 1961, of *The Fantastic Four*. Priced at ten cents, the title didn't increase to twelve cents until the third issue. The series was inspired by the success of *Justice League of America*, which, with its seven heroes for the price of one, was doing very well. Superman, Batman, Wonder Woman, and the Silver Age versions of Flash, Green Lantern, and Aquaman were joined by J'onn J'onzz the Martian Manhunter, one of the few new superheroes created in the '50s and the second alien in DC's lineup.[17] Martin Goodman, Marvel's pub-

---

16. I should add, though, that while the production values on Charlton's comics were low relative to DC and Marvel, they did produce some interesting characters. Along with the revived Blue Beetle, there was Captain Atom, drawn by Steve Ditko, one of Marvel's top illustrators until he left in 1967—thus ending my interest in Spider-Man. Another Ditko/Charlton creation was The Question. In the 1980s, DC purchased the rights to Charlton's action heroes.

17. He first appeared in *Detective Comics* #225, for November 1955. He was brought to Earth from Mars through an experiment with a teleportation machine. Unable to be sent back, he adopted a human appearance—like the Hulk, he had green skin—and remained in his secret identity as a detective, John Jones.

lisher, directed Stan Lee to come up with something similar. Lee collaborated with Jack Kirby, and the Fantastic Four were born.[18]

One member of the team, Johnny Storm, the Human Torch, was a revived Golden Age character. The original Human Torch, a flame-producing android, was one of Timely Publication's (Marvel's Golden Age ancestor) most popular characters. By *Fantastic Four* #4, May 1962, Lee and Kirby revived another sleeping superhero, this time as a villain. Prince Namor, the Sub Mariner, emperor of Atlantis, was Marvel's version of Aquaman, although his character was more complex, as befitted a Byronesque anti-hero. Namor was, like the Human Torch, one of Timely's most successful characters. The success of *Fantastic Four* inspired another team effort, this one more strictly along the lines of the Justice League.

In the wake of the FF, Marvel spawned several other super characters, all of whom enjoy phenomenal success these days as the subjects of films. Iron Man first appeared in the March 1963 issue of *Tales of Suspense*, a science fiction title in the tradition of EC's *Weird Science*, which was making the switch to featuring superheroes. Ant Man made his debut in *Tales to Astonish* #27, January 1962, a similar title making the same switch. The Mighty Thor debuted in *Journey Into Mystery* #83, August 1962. The Hulk was the only one to start off with his own comic, starting in 1961; this folded after the sixth issue, in March 1963, but he would later return with the Sub Mariner in the pages of a refitted *Tales to Astonish*, and would eventually get his own title back. Thor, the Hulk, Iron Man, and Ant Man (with his curvaceous sidekick, the Wasp) would appear in *The Avengers* #1, September 1963. As with the

18. Like many comic book artists, Kirby moved back and forth between DC and Marvel, as well as working for other publishers such as Red Circle, who also published the *Archie* series. Kirby developed *Adventures of the Fly* (1959) for Red Circle. Before co-creating the Fantastic Four, Kirby created an earlier team series for DC, the *Challengers of the Unknown*, who, like so many Silver Age characters, got their start in *Showcase*, appearing in issue #6 for February 1957. The Challengers were four non-superpowered adventurers who battled a variety of sci-fi and monster-based menaces.

Justice League, each of these characters had their own strips in other titles—the members of the Fantastic Four didn't—and would eventually receive comics of their own.[19]

It was in *The Avengers* that Marvel made the most spectacular return of a Golden Age great. In *The Avengers* #4, March 1964, Timely's most popular—and most timely—hero returned. Captain America had a run in the 1950s as "Captain America, Commie Smasher," whose title tells us all we need to know about it. This was during Timely's incarnation as Atlas Publications. During the '40s, Captain America smashed "Nazis and Japs," and when Marvel decided to revive him in the '60s, they forgot about his brief tenure in the McCarthyite '50s. He was said to have been stuck in a frozen suspended animation, caught in a block of ice ever since he deflected an experimental Nazi drone plane into the Arctic Ocean. Revived, he became a new member of the Avengers.

In a short time, though it hadn't pulled the market out from under DC, Marvel had certainly become its most robust challenger. In a sense, had Marvel kept the name Timely, this would have been apt. What made Marvel different from DC was that the adventures its comics depicted seemed to take place in the contemporary world in which its readers lived. The stories took place in New York, not fictional locations like Superman's Metropolis or Batman's Gotham City.

The Fantastic Four had a skyscraper, the Baxter Building, in midtown Manhattan. Given that they all lived in the same city, it made sense that characters from one comic would turn up in another, making cameo appearances because they were "in the neighborhood." This didn't happen with DC. Another difference is that the FF didn't have "secret identities," although, of course, many Marvel characters did. The tone of the writing was hip, street-smart, funny, and often referred to

---

19. I should perhaps mention that my first published piece of writing was a letter appearing in issue #63, April 1969, of *The Avengers*. In it, I complain about the many member changes that had taken place by then.

events in the news. I first learned about Tolkien's *The Hobbit* and *Lord of the Rings* from references to them in Marvel comics—"Frodo lives!," something of a hippie catch phrase, turned up in a number of issues. And their heroes had problems, something that just didn't seem to be the case with Superman or Batman, although later incarnations of these characters brought out their own neuroses.

The Hulk had anger management issues. The Thing, from the Fantastic Four, was almost as strong as the Hulk, but he would have gladly given up his power if he could return to being normal Ben Grimm and not the lumpy, orange rock monster cosmic rays had turned him into. That his girlfriend was blind says it all. Spider-Man was a thoroughly mixed-up teenager when mixed-up teenagers—introduced by James Dean—were still the rage. *The X-Men* featured teenagers whom people feared because they were mutants, a reflection of the growing animosity toward youth culture and a symbol of the widening generation gap.[20]

Although DC tried to mimic Marvel's approach, there was always something distant about the world in which their characters lived, just as there was something distant about the writers and artists producing the comics. Marvel always provided credits for the writer and artist, but also for the inker and the lowly letterer, the person spelling out the characters' words and thoughts in the speech balloons. DC never did this—or, only did later, after Marvel had made it standard procedure. This created a feeling that you, the reader, *knew* the people creating your favorite title. They even had nicknames: Stan "the Man" Lee, Jack "King" Kirby. This quasi-intimacy was promoted in the fan club Marvel established in 1964, the Merry Marvel Marching Society, of which I

---

20. In *Turn Off Your Mind*, I note the parallels among various expressions of a growing fear of "dangerous" youth—such as in *The X-Men* and also the film *Village of the Damned* (1963), based on John Wyndham's novel *The Midwich Cuckoos* (1957), about children born with strange mental powers who shared a group mind—with the rise of the hippies in Haight-Ashbury, who by 1966 had taken to calling themselves "mutants."

was a member. Like thousands of other mixed-up adolescents, I felt I had found a home, and in a sense, I had.

EARLIER I MENTIONED ADAM STRANGE, a character who appeared in one of DC's science fiction titles, *Mystery in Space*, which was following the trend toward hero-oriented content. Adam Strange was technically not a superhero. He didn't have powers (neither did Batman, for that matter, but he did wear a mask and cape). But Adam Strange did sport a rocket pack and a nifty ray gun, and a striking red-and-white uniform and helmet. He was the creation of Julius Schwartz, Gardner Fox, and Mike Sekowsky, and first appeared in *Showcase* #17, for November 1958.

I mentioned that Carmine Infantino later took over the artwork, his sleek, angular, modern style well suited to a "space-age" hero. I also mentioned earlier that the Adam Strange adventures became a favorite, and in recent time I think I discovered why. I spelled this out in a talk I gave at the Deus ex Machina conference, held at Masaryk, Brno, in the Czech Republic in 2021. The conference was about the links between esotericism and technology, and the title of my talk was "Superhuman, Transhuman, Fully Human: Whose Future Is It?"

The talk examined the similarities and differences among three different ways of looking at "transcending" what in the talk I call the "only human"—our everyday, "normal" state and way of being. "Superhuman" refers to comic book figures like Superman, who had "powers and abilities far beyond those of mortal men." "Transhuman" speaks for itself—it is the sensibility informing the increasingly popular "transhumanist movement," which seeks to go beyond our flesh-and-blood humanity by merging with machines and computers, rather like the Borg in *Star Trek: The Next Generation*. "Fully human," is a coinage of the humanistic psychologist Abraham Maslow, and refers to our possibilities of "self-actualizing," of realizing our potentials so that we "become who we are" rather than remaining as muted, inferior versions of ourselves.

I argued that superheroes present models of self-actualization appropriate for youth, but that a kind of literalizing of these exemplars is behind the transhumanist movement.[21] Its adherents literally want to be "men of steel," immune to disease and even death—an aim they share with the early twentieth-century Russian Cosmist school, which I write about in *The Return of Holy Russia*. But this, I suggest, isn't transhuman at all, in that the goals aimed at here are merely extensions of our everyday, "only human" desires. Being "fully human" in Maslow's sense means transcending our usual wants and desires, sprouting from what he calls our "deficiency needs," which are concerned with what we *lack*: food, shelter, sex, love, self-esteem—the lower rungs on Maslow's well-known hierarchy of needs. Our need to self-actualize is a higher need, a meta-need in that it stems not from what we don't have but from our creative possibilities—our need to *use* our powers, to "give" of them.

I tried to illustrate what this meant by contrasting two versions of a "superman": the comic book hero, and the aim of Nietzsche's philosophy, the *Übermensch*, which is often translated as "superman," but really means "overman," a term that emphasizes the transcendent character of what Nietzsche had in mind. The technology the transhumanists look to as the means of their transcendence could very well one day enable humans to fly or see through walls, or even make them invulnerable. But it could never produce the sense of "well-being and zest" that comes to Nietzsche's "self-revolving wheels," an image he uses in *Thus Spake Zarathustra* to illustrate the experience of inner freedom that comes to those who manage to tap the wellsprings of their creativity. They are self-motivated, not requiring a stimulus from outside. We can see these "self-revolving wheels," who experience a psychological version of "perpetual motion," as examples of what Maslow meant by being "fully human."

---

21. In 2006, when my sons and I were bonding over our love for superheroes, I wrote an article about their positive influence for the *Times Educational Supplement*. See Gary Lachman, "Caped Crusaders Teach Us Tolerance," Tes Magazine website, May 26, 2006.

I also suggested that my first introduction to a form of Romanticism came through comic books. I spelled this out in an article I wrote based on the talk.[22] "Comic books," I wrote, "were my earliest introduction to romanticism, not as a school of literature and thought—that wouldn't happen for another few years—but as a hunger for *something more* than what I later learned the philosopher Heidegger called 'the triviality of everydayness.'" I went on: "This hunger for *something more* than everyday life, which is the essence of romanticism, is also the essence of our 'evolutionary appetite,' our innate urge to transcend ourselves, to self-actualize."

It struck me that the Adam Strange stories captured the essence of Romanticism and its sense that human beings are the inhabitants of two worlds: the everyday world of getting and spending, of work and all the necessities of life, and an "other" world, one of possibilities beyond the everyday, of magic and mystery. They did this because they took the notion of humans as the inhabitants of two worlds literally.

Adam was an archaeologist, and on a trip to the Andes something remarkable happened: he was hit by a weird ray of light coming from outer space—he later learns it is called the "zeta beam"—and finds himself transported to the planet Rann, an Earth-like world orbiting Alpha Centauri, some twenty-five trillion miles away. There, he meets a beautiful woman, has adventures, saves the planet, and becomes a hero, all the while sporting his rocket pack and ray gun. But the effect of the zeta beam wears off and he finds himself back on Earth. He discovers where and when the zeta beam will appear again, and for the rest of the series he is off, heading into the jungle or up a mountain to intercept the zeta beam and return to Rann, only to be sent back to Earth once again. But he is determined to become a citizen of this new world and to find a way to remain on Rann forever . . .

Many Romantics have shipwrecked in their attempts to "remain

---

22. See Gary Lachman, "Superhuman, Transhuman, or Fully Human?," Gary Lachman blog, February 3, 2023.

on Rann forever," to, that is, maintain their occupancy of the "other" world. Others, failing in the attempt, reject the idea altogether, deny the reality of any "other" world, and remain satisfied with the rewards of this one while casting a cynical eye on inexperienced youth still hungering for magic. Yet some, a small proportion, are able to retain a taste, an awareness of the *reality* of this "other" world and remind themselves of it when the brute presence of *this* world threatens to obliterate all remembrance of it. For them it isn't a question of escaping Earth and settling on Rann forever, but of being able to *transform* their life here into something more like what it is on that alien but poignantly familiar planet.

Comic books, then, introduced me to a world rather different than the one I knew—a much wider, deeper, more *interesting* world in which anything was possible. The everyday world of parents, siblings, school, friends, and relatives was implacably there, and would become more so as time went on. As Wordsworth says, "the shades of the prison house" close in as we move from the paradise of childhood into the dreary world of adults. But there was an escape, a portal into *another world*, in which one could travel in space and time to other planets and meet remarkable people and have amazing adventures, and in which one felt *more at home* than at the dinner table or in the classroom.

As you might suspect, I availed myself of this escape hatch as often as possible.

2 Pulp Fiction

The past that the Silver Age revival of Golden Age superheroes introduced me to was not limited to comics. I've mentioned films. One result of the remarkable popularity superhero comics enjoyed in the 1960s was a revived interest in the action serials of the 1930s and '40s, many of them featuring heroes from the Golden Age. By today's standards, these cliff-hangers, early versions of our contemporary addictive Netflix series, seem incredibly primitive, although some of the best, like the *Flash Gordon* serials, had impressive production values and made up in set design and atmosphere what they lacked in cinematic finesse.

They were short, action-packed features, generally about twenty minutes long, that warmed an audience up for the main attraction. They ended with the hero falling off a cliff—hence the name—or about to be hit by a train or with some other seemingly inescapable doom about to overtake him or her. The audience would be urged to return to the theatre next week to discover what happened. Would the hero escape from the collapsed mine, burning building, or ferocious beast? Of course he would, otherwise the remaining chapters of the serial, of which there were many, would be disappointing. Everyone knew that the *Masked Marvel* or *Spy Smasher* or the *Green Hornet* or *Commando Cody* (a late entry in the serial market, appearing in the '50s) would avoid destruction and eventually defeat the villain. But realism wasn't essential nor was it wanted. The audience wanted thrills and the satisfaction that comes with good triumphing over evil.

Sex was generally not on the menu; when it was, it was usually associated with the bad guys, with a femme fatale among their company having an itch for the hero who, more times than not, resisted her charms. In the *Flash Gordon* serials, Princess Aura, the seductive and provocatively dressed daughter of the evil Ming the Merciless, has the hots for Flash, who has eyes only for the more modest but faithful and wholesome Dale Arden. But in general, the erotic took a back seat to ray blasters, winged aliens, and wonky space ships. There could be a romantic interest. The hero's girlfriend was routinely captured by the villains and set as bait in a trap, much as Lois Lane was for Superman, in countless comics and episodes of the television show. But the relations between the two were always fairly chaste.

Some serials, like *Flash Gordon* and *Commando Cody*—who, like Adam Strange, got around via a handy rocket pack—were shown on television, usually on Saturday mornings, with the separate episodes edited together to make a "full-length feature." Others were brought back to the big screen. When the 1960s *Batman* television series was at its height, the original *Batman* serials of the '40s were released to theatres.[1] I was among the many young fans at Saturday matinees who were disappointed in the low-budget production with ill-fitting costumes, a non-descript black limousine for the Batmobile, and an unimpressive basement room with clearly artificial bats for the Batcave, all in black and white.

Years later, when I showed some scenes to my sons, the serials having come out, like practically everything else, on DVD, they laughed. But even with all its drawbacks, there was something about this crude attempt at portraying the mysterious figure of the night that captured my imagination, as did the other serials that turned up on television.

Call it the aura of the past. But of what did that aura consist? I

---

1. *Batman* (1943) and *Batman and Robin* (1949).

didn't ask myself this question then. I am reflecting now, many years later—more than I'd like to admit—on my experience then, and trying to understand what it was about these cheaply made artifacts of trashy pop culture that evoked such a powerful response in me. Time had to do with it, and perhaps an adolescent outbreak of what the German Romantic poets called *Sehnsucht,* a word with no exact English translation but which is usually said to mean "inexpressible longing," and which I later defined for myself as "nostalgia for a place I've never been." I would also later identify it as a form of what Colin Wilson (whom I had yet to read) called "Faculty X," our ability to grasp "the *reality* of other times and places." Not merely the *fact* they existed, which merely knowing about them would provide. I *knew* that these creaky films had been made years before I was born. But this was knowledge of a different kind. Somehow, I got a taste of their *reality*—again, as Marcel does when he tastes the madeleine and is suddenly and vividly taken back to his childhood.

Of course, none of this entered my mind then, when I watched these serials. I was merely caught up in them, carried away, as their original audience had been decades earlier. But the habit of seeking out more information, more knowledge about something I was interested in, which later served me in my writing, had started. I tend to be obsessive, as most writers are. If I become interested in a subject, I want to know all about it; and if I become interested in a writer, I read everything of theirs I can find. I wanted to know more about these fifteen-part expeditions into the imagination and the world they were from. Luckily, there were sources I could turn to.

The interest in Golden Age comics which had sparked a nascent comic book collecting culture had also given birth to the comic book fanzine. Fanzines were magazines put out by fans, hence the name. I imagine they have a link to the amateur journalism of the early twentieth century, which I became aware of because of my interest in

H. P. Lovecraft, who got his start in it. I began to see advertisements for comic fanzines in the back pages of comics, where I had discovered the collectors' catalogues. One in particular became a favorite. This was Larry Ivie's *Monsters and Heroes*. This was a more professional, slicker production than most fanzines. It was sold on the newsstands, but it had the fanzine's do-it-yourself character.

Along with being a comic collector and authority on popular culture, Ivie was a professional artist; among his credits is the co-creation, with EC artist Wally Wood, of *T.H.U.N.D.E.R. Agents*, a 1960s series published by Tower Comics that combined superheroes with the '60s obsession with secret agents, started by the popularity of the James Bond films. *Monsters and Heroes* was self-published by Ivie. If it wasn't entirely a one-man show, it was pretty close.[2]

Monsters and Heroes combined superheroes, monster films, action serials, 1940s radio shows, and fantasy literature in a remarkable blend. Ivie had done some work for *Castle of Frankenstein*, the rival of Forrest J Ackerman's more popular *Famous Monsters of Filmland*, both magazines devoted to horror films. In *Monsters and Heroes*, he brought in the monsters from that medium and introduced them to the heroes from another. Articles on *King Kong*, superhero serials like 1944's *Captain America*, radio series like *The Shadow* (who knew what evil lurked in the hearts of men), pulp heroes like *Doc Savage*, and art by upcoming names like Berni Wrightson, creator of *Swamp Thing*, filled its pages. Ivie contributed most of the original art, writing and illustrating his own superhero fantasy series, *Altron Boy*. Ivie was also a great fan of Edgar Rice Burroughs, creator of Tarzan, and John Carter of Mars (an early twentieth-century *Star Wars*), and he devoted much of his magazine to Burroughs's legacy. One artist, of whom I became a devotee and who for me was more than any other associated with Burroughs, was Frank Frazetta.

---

2. Another remarkable underground publication of the time was Wally Wood's *witzend*, which featured comical, often bawdy strips as well as horror and science fiction stories with work by Wood and others from the EC days. It also included the "Mr. A" stories by Steve Ditko, which were inspired by the objectivism of Ayn Rand.

Frazetta, who had also worked for EC, did the covers for *Creepy* and *Eerie*, graphically adult black-and-white comics devoted to horror. They were published by Warren Publications, which put out *Famous Monsters* and also *Blazing Combat*, a war comic, and *Vampirella*, which featured an impossibly curvy female member of the undead—the covers again by Frazetta. Their magazine format (they were priced at thirty-five cents) enabled them to avoid coming under the Comics Code restrictions, and they had inherited the EC tradition, even using artists like Wally Wood, who had worked for EC. Steve Ditko, who created Spider-Man and Doctor Strange at Marvel, also worked for them, among many other great comic artists.

Frazetta, whose work today is highly collectable, illustrated film posters, did a stint with Al Capp of *Li'l Abner* fame, and even illustrated a few episodes of *Playboy*'s bawdy comic strip—in more ways than one—*Little Annie Fanny*. He also did the covers for Donald A. Wollheim's Ace Books paperback editions of Burroughs's *Tarzan* books, which I began to collect at the time.

I've written about Ace Science Fiction Classics—as their sci-fi and fantasy list was called—in *Turn Off Your Mind*, and how they were in many ways responsible for the phenomenal success of Tolkien's *Lord of the Rings* when a pirated edition of the trilogy put out by Ace became a surprise best-seller on 1960s college campuses. It is arguable that, without that early unauthorized edition read mostly by members of the youth culture Tolkien disdained, Middle Earth and its hobbits would not have become the very profitable modern myths they are today.

Priced at forty cents, and slightly smaller than standard mass-market paperbacks, Ace published practically all of Burroughs's enormous backlist, as well as a slew of other writers, such as Andre Norton, Otis Adalbert Kline, and Philip K. Dick—one of the few writers from their list still read today. Their Burroughs list included the John Carter of Mars series; the Pellucidar books about a world at the Earth's core; the books set in Caprona, a land rather like that in Sir Arthur Conan

Doyle's *The Lost World*, where prehistoric animals thrive; the Carson of Venus series; and other works.

Roy G. Krenkel, another EC veteran, did many covers for the Carson of Venus and Mars books. I liked his work, but it was softer, more subtle—classical, I would say—than the powerful, visceral, and frankly sexy lines of Frazetta, whose covers often included a scantily clad, voluptuous female. Before I discovered my father's pornography collection—modest by today's standards, made up of copies of *Playboy*, *Penthouse*, lesser known girly magazines, and assorted paperbacks—my introduction to sex came from the alluring female figures in Frazetta's illustrations. His time with *Little Annie Fanny* and *Li'l Abner* (if anyone remembers Daisy Mae, you'll agree) was later put to good use.

I GREW UP IN WHAT WAS, and is even more today, effectively another borough of New York, even though it was across the Hudson in New Jersey. New Jersey is called the Garden State, but Bayonne, where I grew up, was not a part of the state where this title applied. It was urban, but without the attractions that a big city provides. There were, for example, no bookstores in Bayonne, which meant I had to look elsewhere when my need for books grew beyond what the paperback racks at the drugstores could offer. Manhattan's skyscrapers were only a short bus ride away, or one could take the PATH train under the Hudson from Jersey City. One reason why I started to make the journey in my later teens was to visit the Barnes & Noble bookshop on Fifth Avenue.

If there were no bookstores in Bayonne, there was little nature there either. Aside from the occasional family drive, I did not see much of it, and I certainly did not grow up with it. I grew up with television. My access to nature was the rubbish-strewn shoreline of the polluted New York Bay, along which I often strolled and meditated on the future, or the trees in the city park. It wasn't until I moved to Los Angeles and took drives of my own outside the city and into the mountains that I began to have any real experience of nature. But even this was mediated by the images of nature I came to know through art. And the art that first did this—at least, the art that I remember doing this—were the covers Frazetta did for the Tarzan books.

As I think of this, one cover in particular stands out. Tarzan is standing on a moss-covered tree limb in a clearing in the dense, tenebrous jungle, wearing only a scant leopard skin, his long, dark hair flying back. His own outstretched limbs are striped by bands of sunlight cutting through the trees. From above, a savage ape is hurtling toward him.[3]

Why this image always comes to me when I think of being in nature, I can't say, although I do associate it with climbing trees in the city park. Something about the rich colors, the dappled light, the shade, and overall sense of a living, dynamic scene struck me. Even now, I have a great fondness for the simple contrast of a blue sky, white clouds, and green trees which I seem to trace back to this illustration. I became a collector of the Tarzan series and the other Ace Burroughs editions as much for the covers as for the stories, and used to rummage through the overstuffed paperback racks of one luncheonette in particular, where the copies they had seemed to have been there for years.[4]

But even more than the Tarzan books, or perhaps simply in another way, Frazetta's magic captured me in the covers he did for the Lancer paperback editions of Robert E. Howard's Conan stories. Perhaps it was because, with the Conan stories, a darker element, sorcery, had entered the scene. This was the time of "sword and sorcery," of warriors, wizards, and willing wenches—and I was an early casualty.

Robert E. Howard was one of the three musketeers of *Weird Tales*, the other two being H. P. Lovecraft and Clark Ashton Smith. I became a confirmed reader of all three. For a time, Smith was my preferred favorite. He was a poet and an aesthete; along with the long-forgotten

---

3. Edgar Rice Burroughs, *Jungle Tales of Tarzan* (New York: Ace Books, 1963).

4. Ace was famous for their "Ace Doubles," which featured two separate novels bound back-to-back, in a format known as *tête-bêche*, French for "head to tail"—what one might call a publishing version of "*soixante-neuf*."

George Sterling, Smith was part of the pre-Beat San Francisco literary scene, a young contemporary of Jack London. Smith was "decadent"— or, at least, affected a kind of decadence, incongruous as it was to the log cabin he lived in for most of his life in Auburn, California. It was through Smith that I came to know the French Romantics, Gautier, de Nerval, and Baudelaire, to whom I was devoted for a time and whom I learned about through Enid Starkie's brilliant biographies of Baudelaire, Rimbaud, and a remarkable figure, the poet Petrus Borel, known as "the Lycanthrope," a member of the notorious nineteenth-century bohemian set, the Bouzingo.

But Howard was the first one I read, having come across the collection of stories Lancer titled *Conan the Usurper*, which appeared in 1967. Frazetta's cover featured the incredibly muscular Conan straddling an enormous snake, which is about to strike. His hands are chained to a dungeon floor, while dark figures loom in the shadows and the bones of previous victims litter the cell. When I saw that the cover was by Frazetta, I was sold and went on to collect the entire series and the other collections of Howard's stories Lancer published. I read them obsessively, seeking out Lancer's distinctive purple-edged pages, inhabiting Howard's tales of a civilization that existed after the sinking of Atlantis (Howard's earlier and more introspective King Kull stories were set in that lost time) and before the beginning of recorded history. When I "grew up" and my science fiction and fantasy collection suffered a similar fate to my comic books, the few Lancer copies I later found in secondhand bookshops brought this time back to me. They remain powerful talismans that trigger that poignant retrieval of the past I have already spoken of.

Smith never enjoyed a revival in the way that Howard and Lovecraft did; his lapidary, by contemporary standards overwritten prose was not quite as accessible to adolescent readers as was the work of his colleagues. He did, however, outlive them, dying in 1961, just as the Lovecraft revival was getting underway and the Beat scene in North Beach had taken off. Howard never knew the success of his barbarian, who not only spawned contemporary "sword and sorcery" characters such as Michael Moorcock's albino swordsman Elric and Fritz Leiber's Fafhrd and the Gray Mouser, but also later films and video games. He also gave birth to one of the most artistically sophisticated comic books, Marvel's *Conan the Barbarian*, drawn by Barry Smith. Along with Jim Steranko—famous for his work on *Nick Fury, Agent of S.H.I.E.L.D.* and *Captain America*—Smith was one of the great second-generation Silver Age comic artists to arrive at Marvel.

Howard lived a lonely existence in Cross Plains, Texas, and was fixated on his mother. In 1936, when he heard that she had entered a coma from which she would not recover, at the age of thirty he blew his brains out with a pistol he carried to protect himself from imaginary assailants. Today I find it hard to read more than a few pages of either Howard or Smith, to whom I nevertheless return when fits of nostalgia overcome me, which happens fairly often. Lovecraft fares better—some of him, at least. But if it wasn't for Howard and his tales of the Hyborian Age, I wouldn't have been led to Lovecraft, Smith, or *Weird Tales*.

ALONG WITH THE REVIVAL OF GOLDEN AGE HEROES and the old serials many of them featured in, another large part of this remembrance of things past through popular culture was my introduction to the pulp magazines of the time. The pulps, as they are generally called, got their name from the cheap wood-pulp paper their stories were printed on, unlike the slick pages of the more prestigious "glossies." Pulp magazines started up in the early twentieth century and were the successors to the "penny dreadfuls" and dime novels of the late nineteenth century. The first pulp was *Argosy* magazine, which featured stories by Edgar Rice Burroughs, Abraham Merritt (who became a favorite), as well as Western writers like Zane Grey—but also more mainstream ones like Upton Sinclair. By the 1920s, the medium was a roaring success and had spawned a variety of pulps dedicated to specific genres.

The most famous detective pulp was *Black Mask*, which began in 1920 and featured the hard-boiled fiction of Dashiell Hammett, Raymond Chandler (whom I prefer over Hammett), Earl Stanley Gardner, and others. Hugo Gernsback's *Amazing Stories*, which started in 1926, was the first magazine devoted exclusively to science fiction. Others, like *Famous Fantastic Mysteries*, *Startling Stories*, and *Planet Stories*, to give a few examples, soon followed. Early issues of *Amazing Stories* featured reprints of tales by Edgar Allan Poe, Jules Verne, and H. G. Wells, but it soon spawned a whole generation of pulp sci-fi writers, among whom was Lovecraft. But Lovecraft, who was really a writer of horror fiction and only turned to a form of science fiction in his last days, was associated with one pulp in particular, which has become almost more popular today than it was when it was in circulation. This was *Weird Tales*.

Weird Tales, which started in 1923, called itself "the unique magazine," and it did cater to a more peculiar—what we today might call transgressive—taste than the science fiction pulps. Although there was, of course, a lot of what was called "space opera" in the sci-fi pulps, with E. E. "Doc" Smith's Lensman and Skylark series defining the genre, science fiction writers increasingly aimed to make their stories plausible within the context of science fact. Ray guns and bug-eyed monsters—the sort of adventures John Carter or Carson Napier would have had on Mars or Venus—were abandoned for more intelligent, sophisticated scenarios and, in a later development, for the use of the genre as a means of social critique, something that H. G. Wells had been doing with novels like *A Modern Utopia* (1905) and *Men Like Gods* (1923), and Aldous Huxley and George Orwell would do with *Brave New World* (1932) and *1984* (1949). By now, there is a whole genre of dystopian science fiction, both in literature and film, and it is almost impossible today to depict a future society that either isn't a dystopia or hasn't passed through a catastrophic breakdown and reverted to some pre-technological state.

Weird Tales and the other pulps dedicated to horror and fantasy (*Terror Tales*; *Strange Detective Mysteries*, which combined genres; and the economically titled *Horror*, to name a few) did not bother about this adult concern. They wanted to elicit and evoke a certain sensation in the reader. In that sense they were unabashedly sensational. One could see that from their covers, which blended sex with horror in the same way that pulps like *Spicy Detective Stories* or *Detective Story Magazine* (a favorite, by the way, of the philosopher Ludwig Wittgenstein) blended sex with crime. Many of these striking, risqué covers, featuring half-nude females in provocative poses recoiling from some diabolical threat, were the work of Margaret Brundage, one of the few women artists defining the pulp aesthetic. Other artists associated with *Weird Tales* were Hannes Bok, who also wrote fantasy fiction; Frank R. Paul; and Virgil Finlay. Finlay became another of my favorites, and I tried unsuccessfully to approximate with pen and ink his meticulous black-and-white "scratchboard" style. All of these artists brought a sophisticated charm to what was usually considered unsophisticated trash.

On the raw, gross side, *Weird Tales* simply aimed to scare the reader. As was the case with some of EC's more dubious efforts, often this aim prompted something closer to disgust than fright—rather as the increasingly gory and bloody "splatter" films popular in the 1970s and '80s did. But on a higher—for sake of a better word—level, it aimed at something more than a shiver up the spine, even if its editor, Farnsworth Wright, was probably not aware of this. This was a sense of awe, of the sublime, which, as the philosopher Edmund Burke pointed out long ago, always carries a charge of terror. As the poet Rilke wrote, "Beauty is the beginning of a terror which we are just able to bear." (Rilke also knew that "every angel is terrible.")

Today we say "awesome" and call something "sublime" if we like it, without having a sense of the true meaning of these terms. We use "tremendous" in a similar way, not realizing that in its original meaning it referred to that which made us tremble. If something is awesome we should be awestruck by it, literally stopped in our tracks. If something is sublime, it isn't beautiful. It can even be ugly, outside the accepted standards of beauty. We think of mountains and waterfalls as beautiful, but this is because we have become inured to them, desensitized to their power through their domestication in travel brochures and nature calendars. Rocky, craggy cliffs aren't beautiful in the classical sense; their irregular form falls outside the canons of harmony and proportion. Yet, in the late eighteenth century, poets like Goethe, Wordsworth, and Coleridge began to *see* them as sublime, and as I point out in some of my books, this strikes me as evidence of an evolution of consciousness, a shift not only in our ideas about the world, but an actual change in how we perceive it.

Heady stuff, perhaps, for a pulp magazine like *Weird Tales*. But it reminds us that there is a difference between horror and terror. Most of the films that are placed in the horror category these days are really terror films—for this same reason, we are plagued by numerous political "terrorists" but never hear of any "horrorists." As my spell-check has just informed me, we don't even have a word like horrorist. Terror, I would say, always implies some straightforward physical violence or threat, such as Norman Bates presents in Hitchcock's film *Psycho* (1960), which, incidentally, is based on the novel by Robert Bloch, a contributor to *Weird Tales*. In a number of films, a knife-wielding maniac terrorizes a group of teenagers. We may feel horrified at this, especially when we see it as a segment on the news—real life, as Oscar Wilde said long ago, imitating art. But the horror we feel doesn't stem from a physical threat to us, but from our reflection on that state of things today, when such things happen.

Horror has a metaphysical aspect which can have nothing to do with a physical threat. Think of the 1932 film *The Mummy*, directed by Karl Freund and starring Boris Karloff. It remains one of the great horror films, but there is little if any physical threat in it—unlike the 1959 Hammer remake with Peter Cushing and Christopher Lee (or the ridiculous blockbusters of the 2000s). The audience barely sees the mummy itself. Nevertheless, the film succeeds in creating a genuine atmosphere of horror—Freund's background in German expressionist cinema saw to that.

Horror can arise from something as unphysical and immaterial as knowledge, and as every Lovecraft fan knows, this is precisely what he presents as the source of the overwhelming horror that engulfs the unfortunate protagonists in his stories. The most well-known of Lovecraft's tales, "The Call of Cthulhu," begins with the most well-known quotation from his work: "The most merciful thing in the world, I think, is the inability of the human mind to correlate all its contents." Doing so would, Lovecraft believes, "open up such terrifying vistas of reality" that we would either be driven mad or forced to seek out the "peace and safety of a new dark age."

Although he did not think much of *The Waste Land*, Lovecraft, in his stories but also in his life, agreed with T. S. Eliot that "humankind cannot bear very much reality," as Eliot states in *Four Quartets*. Reality in Lovecraft's case included the existence of aeons-old extra-terrestrial alien beings, loathsome entities such as the maddening squid-faced Cthulhu, who once dominated our world and was set to return to reclaim it.

But, although Lovecraft populates his world—his mythos—with such unspeakably malign agents, what is truly terrifying in his work is his cosmic vision, in which humanity is a negligible participant in a universe as indifferent to its fate as it is unaware of it. (In my book *The Caretakers of the Cosmos*, I point out the similarity of much of Lovecraft's vision with that of the contemporary social philosopher John Gray, another misanthropist.) It is this existential character of Lovecraft's vision that sets him apart from the aestheticism of Smith or the blood and thunder of Howard. It is essentially the same vision as Eliot's, without the poet's appeal to religion as a comfort and guide in the darkness.

As many of my generation did, I came to Lovecraft and the other *Weird Tales* writers first through Poe and other authors of classical science fiction, horror, and adventure. In this, I was aided by the editions of Poe, Jules Verne, H. G. Wells, Sir Arthur Conan Doyle, and H. Rider Haggard published by Airmont Books. Airmont was a kind of *Classics Illustrated* of paperbacks—safe comic versions of classic works of literature—and I collected them as I did the Ace Burroughs and the Lancer Howard books. They weren't sensational in the way the others were. Their covers were tame by comparison, and had a distinct nineteenth-century feel, an aesthetic I came to enjoy—especially that of the *fin de siècle*, my love of Sherlock Holmes and "gaslight London" contributing much to this. There was a particular drug store in town that stocked these titles, and as I think of them now, I can catch a brief taste of the atmosphere of the place, a certain coolness and pharmaceutical smell mixed with that of perfume.

I never read children's books, and must admit to a distinct aversion to Dr. Seuss. There was nothing like the young adult market of today, no *Harry Potter*, of which, I also must admit, I was unable to get through more than a few paragraphs when I attempted to read it. Along with classics like *Robinson Crusoe* and *Treasure Island*, the literature I first read after *The Scarlet Pimpernel* were the tales of adventure and wonder read by adults in the previous century. *She* and *King Solomon's Mines* by H. Rider Haggard; Sir Arthur Conan Doyle's *The Adventures of Sherlock Holmes* and *The Lost World*; *Twenty Thousand Leagues Under the Sea* and *Journey to the Center of the Earth* by Jules Verne; Poe's *Selected Stories and Poems*; *The War of the Worlds*, *The Time Machine*, *The Island of Dr. Moreau*, and all the rest of H. G. Wells—I read all of these and more in the Airmont editions. I went on to write about Poe and Wells and, although by now I have read the stories more times than I remember, every few years or so I return to Conan Doyle and follow Holmes and Watson on their adventures. Having lived in London now for many years—I live not far from Baker Street—I can now place myself in the city and join them even more when "the game's afoot."

I read a great deal of contemporary science fiction as well; writers like Robert Heinlein, Arthur C. Clarke, Isaac Asimov, A. E. van Vogt, and Ray Bradbury, who was a favorite for a time. I was among the many adolescents captured by *The Martian Chronicles*, *The Illustrated Man*, and *The Golden Apples of the Sun*. Today I find Bradbury sentimental and have not read Heinlein or Clarke for some time; a recent attempt at Asimov's *Foundation* series was aborted soon after liftoff. Yet, a year or so ago, I did read with great interest and delight John Wyndham's series of very sophisticated and intelligent science fiction novels—*The Midwich Cuckoos*, *The Trouble with Lichen*, *The Day of the Triffids*, and the rest—which I hadn't before, and which were a happy discovery.

I was a fan of later science fiction magazines like *If* and *Galaxy* that had taken the place of the pulps. But for some reason that I am doing my best to pin down, I was more drawn to the fantastic than to the scientifically plausible, a preference which some of my more critical readers might agree is in evidence in my own books. And when I discovered Lovecraft, sometime around the age of twelve, I plunged into his Cthulhu Mythos as gleefully as the gill-necked characters of his stories dive into the terror-ridden waters off the coast of Innsmouth (along with Arkham, this is one of the fictional New England towns infested with Lovecraft's morbidly fascinating imagination).[5]

I can't say exactly why I was drawn to Lovecraft and to horror, and "weird fiction" in general, more than to science fiction—which I nevertheless loved. Odd to say, but it seemed somehow more *human*, less technologically oriented than science fiction, although Lovecraft's cosmic fiction—which relegates humanity to an existential nullity—is today adopted by adherents of a posthuman philosophy eager to jettison the anthropomorphic past. Lovecraft's materialist view denied any significance to human existence—or to existence in general—and the only meaning he derived from life was an aesthetic one. (It may be that my love of sunsets has as much to do with Lovecraft's description of them casting their magical glow over gabled rooftops as it does with

---

5. Lovecraft fans might be interested in my map of his homes and haunts in Providence, New York, and along the Eastern Seaboard. See *Facts Concerning H. P. Lovecraft and His Environs* (Herb Lester Associates, 2024).

Wordsworth.) He wrote about ancient, eldritch horrors and supernatural beings, yet his worldview was that of nineteenth-century scientific materialism. He was a quirky eccentric, an Outsider both from Colin Wilson's perspective and the title of one of Lovecraft's early stories. With Poe, Lovecraft—and many a sensitive adolescent, myself included—could say, "From childhood's hour I have not been / As others were—I have not seen / As others saw—I could not bring / My passions from a common spring . . ."[6]

Lovecraft "identified," as we would say today, as an English gentleman of the eighteenth century, with a profound disgust for the modern world and a loathing of its non-white, non-Aryan inhabitants. He was fixated on the past, the colonial days of his beloved Providence, Rhode Island; his brief tenure as a husband of a Jewish woman—remarkable given his anti-Semitism—in the ethnically mixed Brooklyn of the 1920s drove him to what he would most likely call "paroxysms of unspeakable loathing."[7]

By the time of his death from cancer at the age of forty-six, in 1937, Lovecraft had effectively stopped writing. Unlike Howard, who was much more the pulp professional, hammering away at his Underwood typewriter in a number of genres, Lovecraft never bothered to rewrite work an editor had rejected, or even thought to send it to another editor. He was too much the "gentleman" to think of himself as a "professional" writer, and lived in poverty, surrounded by the furniture of his idealized childhood, mollycoddled by his aunts. His entire life was a determined attempt to ignore the practical world and immerse himself in the "aura of the past," the colonial years of the original English Yankee stock. As Colin Wilson has pointed out, Lovecraft's "mythos," which evokes the sense of some unspeakable evil separated from human consciousness by a thin, easily perforated veneer of "civilization," can be

---

6. From Poe's poem "Alone."

7. I write about Lovecraft's time in Brooklyn in "The Horror of Clinton Street: Lovecraft in Brooklyn," *Fortean Times* #396, September 2020.

read as an assault on modernity. It is a kind of Romanticism gone sour.

Lovecraft was a poet—as were both Howard and Smith—and even if his verse, inspired by Addison and Pope, rejects the vision of Coleridge and Wordsworth, he was as much a Romantic as they were. Although I read Lovecraft's poetry, making my way through *Fungi from Yuggoth* and his other macabre verse—much as I would later do with the poetry of Aleister Crowley, who also didn't care for Eliot's *Waste Land*—I do not go back to it. (Nor, for that matter, do I go back to Crowley.) Yet one early poem of Lovecraft's does, I think, express the essence of his vision, for sake of a better word.

In "Phaethon," from 1918, Lovecraft writes: "Why should I fret in microcosmic bonds / That chafe the spirit, and the mind repress / When through the clouds beam beckoning beyonds / Whose shining vistas mock man's littleness?"

Why indeed? Lovecraft may have felt that the "shining vistas" and "beckoning beyonds" he evokes have only an aesthetic significance. Yet, what he is speaking of here is the *Sehnsucht* of the Romantics, that "nostalgia for a place they've never been" but in whose existence they indubitably if often tragically believed.

I believe this "nostalgia" is something more than a debilitating yearning for some inaccessible "never-never land," although, in the lives of some Romantics, this is in fact what it was. It is an expression of our human appetite for meaning, the very meaning that Lovecraft, the arch-materialist, denies. But this materialism, with its militant rejection of any meaning or significance, human or otherwise, to existence can be seen as part of Lovecraft's assault on the despicable modern world. We think we are so important, with our "progress" and technological achievements. Fools! We are nothing—negligible results of blind forces operating in a pointless universe, the same forces that, in a different time and place, produced the unutterable horrors of Yog-Sothoth, Nyarlathotep, Azathoth, and the other mind-shattering members of Lovecraft's Cthulhu Mythos. Yet I, Lovecraft, who *knows* this, can rise above the common herd who embrace the illusion of modernity, can recognize their stupidity, and can take delight in scaring the bejesus out of them . . .

Although he would not admit it, Lovecraft the poet has a different perception. The "shining vistas" and "beckoning beyond" that mock man's "littleness" are at the same time testament to his—our—greatness.

WHEN I THINK OF THIS PREFERENCE NOW, for the "weird" let us call it, over the scientific, it seems obvious that, given my later interest in magic and the occult, I would be drawn to that element in Lovecraft and other writers with a taste for the strange and supernatural. Until that summer of 1975 found me playing in a rock band and living on the Bowery, I had no conscious interest in magic or witchcraft or anything like that—aside, as mentioned, for my love of weird fiction and horror films. But is it too much to wonder if a latent predilection for the occult was making itself known? I could just as easily say my taste for weird pulp fiction primed me for my later interest in the occult. But where did that taste come from in the first place? I have often wondered if some relation a few generations back, a Kabbalist or alchemist from Eastern or Central Europe, where most of my genes are from—at least, according to the DNA test I invested in—is the source. Who knows? Wherever it came from, it was there and blossomed in my late adolescence and early teens.

Reading Lovecraft, I became fascinated by his Cthulhu Mythos and the pantheon of ancient entities at work in his fiction. I was introduced to this idea—which runs throughout Lovecraft's stories and to which Smith, Howard, and other *Weird Tales* writers, such as Frank Belknap Long, contributed—through the work of August Derleth. Derleth has acquired a bad reputation these days, mostly through the efforts of Lovecraft purists who want to prune the master's oeuvre of any material that is not *echt* Lovecraft. This purge has produced a body of hair-splitting exegeses—the kind common in academia—that will keep any anorak happy. But without Derleth and Arkham House, which saved

Lovecraft from publishing oblivion, Lovecraft's legacy would not have survived. Derleth may have taken liberties with that legacy, as some critics maintain, but it was through Derleth that readers of my generation learned of it in the first place.

Reading Derleth led, in my obsessive way, to discovering other writers. Some would reappear later, when my interest in magic and the occult led me to Crowley and the Hermetic Order of the Golden Dawn. Two members of that most famous secret occult society of the late nineteenth century were writers of weird fiction, and both were powerful influences on Lovecraft, who writes of them in his essay *Supernatural Horror in Literature*. Yet, in different ways, Arthur Machen and Algernon Blackwood were believers in the very supernatural reality that Lovecraft denied.

Machen's most powerful work, *The Great God Pan*, caused a scandal during the *fin de siècle* because of its decadent blend of sexual evil and atavistic horror; among its defenders were Oscar Wilde, whose *The Picture of Dorian Gray* is itself a work of weird, supernatural fiction. Lovecraft incorporated earlier writers' work into his Mythos, such as the sardonic Ambrose Bierce and Robert W. Chambers, author of the eerily disturbing *The King in Yellow*, and from Machen he took the theme of a malign nonhuman race that civilization has forced into hiding but which every now and then emerges from its subterranean shelter, with devastating results. His story "The White People" is about such an appearance, and in it Machen speaks of the "Aklo letters," an alphabet of an ancient lost language with occult powers that Lovecraft later referred to in his mythos stories.

Like Lovecraft, Machen abhorred modernity and—again like Lovecraft—he was a figure out of time, an anachronism, although a much more cheerful one, a character of gaslight London among the reporters and hacks of 1920s Fleet Street. In recent years he has been rediscovered as an early proponent of "psychogeography," a loose mashup of psychological, occult, and sociological ideas relating to the effect of urban cityscapes on the consciousness that moves through them. Think of Walter Benjamin's *flaneur* as a practiced psychometrist who can perceive the strata of past time and experience as he saunters along the city's boulevards—which, come to think of it, is more or less how Benjamin understood himself, but with a Marxist twist. Psychogeography has its roots in surrealism—think of Andre Breton's *Nadja* and Guy Debord's *dérive* ("drift")—and has been popularized by Iain Sinclair, a writer alive to London's occult past. Machen's account of his marathon expeditions through the unfrequented spaces of an endless London, *The London Adventure* (1924), is a recognized classic of the genre. Machen was a member of the Hermetic Order of the Golden Dawn during Aleister Crowley's controversial tenure, but he later rejected magic and moved toward a kind of religious mysticism.

Algernon Blackwood joined the Golden Dawn after Crowley's initiation led to the fracture of the original group, but his interest in the occult and esoteric had been established well before that. Like W. B. Yeats, another celebrated member of the Golden Dawn, Blackwood pursued Madame Blavatsky's Theosophy before taking on magic. Lovecraft singled out Blackwood's eerie tale of a strange journey along the Danube, "The Willows," as his personal favorite—no small honor, coming from such a connoisseur of weird fiction. Yet while Blackwood, like Lovecraft and Machen, wrote of atavistic horrors—in his story "Ancient Sorceries," for example—he was more drawn to a kind of "cosmic" mysticism than to horror, a vision that presented a rather different picture of mankind's place in the universe compared to Lovecraft's darker view.

Blackwood was fascinated by what at the time was called "higher space," the idea that human consciousness could access other dimensions of space than the three we are usually occupied with. In many of his stories, his protagonist has experiences of "cosmic consciousness," a sense of being aware of and participating with the cosmos as a whole. "Cosmic consciousness" became a catch phrase of the psychedelic hippies of the 1960s, when it was popularized by Timothy Leary. Leary got it from a book published in 1901, *Cosmic Consciousness* by the psychiatrist R. M. Bucke. Bucke believed that humanity was evolving into a higher form of consciousness, one that could embrace the entire cosmos, and he argued that evidence for this could be found in great religious and creative individuals of the past. From his writing, one gets the impression that Blackwood had more than a glimpse of this new form of consciousness, and it filled him with a cosmic vision antipodal to Lovecraft's.

Blackwood's interest in "higher space" led him to the Russian philosopher P. D. Ouspensky, who wrote about it in his early metaphysical masterpiece *Tertium Organum*. In 1921, Ouspensky was saved from a White Russian refugee camp in Constantinople—having been deposited there by the Russian Civil War—when a wealthy and enthusiastic reader of the book brought him to London, where he lectured to a select group of writers and intellectuals, Blackwood among them. I tell the story in my book about Ouspensky.[8]

Ouspensky had crossed a collapsing Russia, first as a student of the enigmatic Armenian esoteric teacher G. I Gurdjieff, then as a teacher of Gurdjieff's system, known as "the Work." Gurdjieff's system, which starts with the depressing recognition that one is a machine devoid of free will, had no place for "higher dimensions" or "cosmic consciousness," although, in *Tertium Organum*, Ouspensky wrote a philosophical bestseller about both. Yet Blackwood was interested enough in Gurdjieff's ideas to spend time at his Institute for the Harmonious Development of Man in Fontainebleau, outside of Paris, before deciding that, in the end, it wasn't for him. It is curious to reflect that Blackwood was attending Ouspensky's lectures and putting himself through Gurdjieff's rigorous regime of psychological and physical exercises while Lovecraft was experiencing his paroxysms of loathing and disgust during his brief stay in Brooklyn.

I would come across Machen and Blackwood again, some years later, when, as mentioned, my interest in magic brought them back on my

---

8. *In Search of P. D. Ouspensky* (Wheaton, IL: Quest Books, 2004).

radar. At the time, a more immediate result of my interest in Lovecraft's mythos was my introduction to what was then called "adult fantasy."

Anyone familiar with Lovecraft's aversion to sex will know that this doesn't refer to what we might think it does. "Adult fantasy" in this context doesn't mean wild erotic perversions or a session of sexual cosplay; it refers to a genre of literature that was popular in the late nineteenth and early twentieth century but which had gone out of fashion in modern times. It was brought back to readers' consciousness and made popular again through the success of Tolkien's *Lord of the Rings*, which, as mentioned, was helped in no small part by the huge sales of the Ace "unauthorized" paperback edition.

The "authorized" paperback edition of *Lord of the Rings*, with Tolkien's imprimatur, was published in 1965 by Ballantine Books, who brought out a paperback of *The Hobbit* in the same year. I was nine and wouldn't read Tolkien for another few years. Ballantine soon saw they had a bestseller on their hands and that the student audience for Tolkien's "whimsy," as one critic of the books called it, was huge. Although it had yet to reach me, the Hermann Hesse revival had started, and he and Tolkien would soon be corralled together on more than one hippie bookshelf. Was there anything like Tolkien they could add to their list, Ballantine asked? Yes, there was. Quite a bit, in fact.

In 1967 Ballantine published a paperback edition of E. R. Eddison's Elizabethan fantasy, *The Worm Ouroboros*, originally published in 1922. As I point out in *Turn Off Your Mind*, the ouroboros, or snake swallowing its own tail, is an ancient hermetic symbol. Its appearance in a classic of fantasy literature is an example of the frequent cross-fertilization between the occult and that literary tradition, a point I make in *A Dark Muse*, which includes essays on many of the authors I mention here.

Ballantine followed *The Worm Ouroboros* with Eddison's Zimiamvian trilogy, *Mistress of Mistresses*, *A Fish Dinner in Memison*, and *The Mezentian Gate*. Next came Mervyn Peake's *Gormenghast*

Trilogy, released in 1968, the year of Peake's death. The logic evidently was that if one trilogy was a success, others would be too. They were. By the late '60s, a full-scale fantasy boom was in swing. Copies of Eddison and Peake hit the hippie trail—there were even bands named H. P. Lovecraft and Titus Groan, the main character of Peake's epic. The "psychidyllic" character of the British LSD scene—think of The Beatles' "Strawberry Fields Forever" or the Small Faces' "Itchycoo Park," with their evocations of lost childhood—blended well with the fairy-tale tone of much of the reading material '60s psychonauts were absorbing.

By this time, the publishing levees had broken and a fantasy flood was let loose. In 1969, Ballantine decided to republish a whole catalogue of forgotten fantasy classics. To this end they enlisted the aid of the contemporary sword and sorcery writer Lin Carter, a prolific yarn spinner in the Burroughs–Howard tradition, whose paperbacks featuring his hero Thongor of Lemuria (another lost continent, this time in the Pacific) sported their own Frazetta covers. Other publishers had picked up on the *Weird Tales*/Lovecraft revival and were issuing paperback reprints of stories in the genre. Veteran pulp editor Leo Margulies collected classics for Pyramid Books under the titles *Weird Tales* and *Worlds of Weird*. L. Sprague de Camp, who, with Lin Carter, had edited and completed some of Howard's unfinished Conan stories for Lancer, did the same for Pyramid, producing *The Spell of Seven*, *Swords and Sorcery*, and *The Fantastic Swordsmen*. All of these collections sported covers by Virgil Finlay. The pulps may have been gone, though cheaply produced digest-size magazines, like R. A. W. Lowndes's *Magazine of Horror*, which I read, reprinted stories and art from the Golden Age. Yet, if the pulps were gone, the paperbacks seemed to be filling their place.

If August Derleth was responsible for reviving Lovecraft's literary existence, Lin Carter deserves the credit for reestablishing fantasy as a serious literary genre. In 1969, Ballantine started its Adult Fantasy series, edited by Carter. It ran until 1974, which was about the time my interest in fantasy began to diminish, its place being taken by fantasies of another sort. Before then, however, I was a dedicated collector of these titles, whose covers by Gervasio Gallardo, George Barr, and Robert LoGrippo, rivalled in eerie, otherworldly beauty the best of Margaret Brundage or Virgil Finlay, although without any of the pulp eroticism. Sex was not part of the other worlds to which these now highly collectable paperbacks delivered me and the thousands of other readers who enjoyed them. This was more a world of "m'ladies" and "m'lords," not the buxom willing wenches of Howard's lusty tales.

Under the sign of the unicorn, the distinctive logo each title in the series carried in the upper right corner of the cover—a marking as recognizable as Lancer's purple edges or Ace's three-quarter size—Carter brought back to imaginative life a remarkable number of forgotten authors. James Branch Cabell, George Macdonald, Evangaline Walton, H. Rider Haggard, William Hope Hodgson (whose uncanny *The Night Land* is an unrecognized classic), Ernst Bramah, C. J. Cutliffe Hyne, Hope Mirless, and H. Warner Munn were only some of the writers of fantastic fiction Carter repackaged for a generation itching to expand—if not blow—their minds, do their own thing, and drop out of an increasingly mechanized, "disenchanted" society. (I was as yet too young to do any of these things, but was eagerly awaiting the time when I could.)

Lovecraft found a place among these forgotten writers, as did Clark Ashton Smith, whose tales of lost Atlantis, futuristic Zothique (the last civilization of mankind), ancient Hyperborea (a polar land often evoked by occultists), and weird Xiccarph somehow seemed to fit the jeweled, ornate landscapes of these works more than the often more graphic horrors of *Weird Tales*. Another work in the series with more than a touch of exoticism was William Beckford's classic *Vathek*, a tale of Oriental mystery from the eighteenth century that Beckford, famous for the orgies put on at his celebrated folly, Fonthill Abbey, is said to have written in a weekend following one such revel.

Vathek is soaked in the exoticism of the *Arabian Nights*, a book which was an important influence on Lovecraft. It was also an influence on Arthur Machen, whose still-chilling horror-mystery *The Three Imposters*, another classic brought back to life by Carter, aimed to make at least fictionally real Robert Louis Stevenson's characterization of London as "Baghdad on the Thames."

WERE HE ALIVE TO HAVE SEEN THESE EDITIONS—and had he taken better care of his health, he very well could have been—Lovecraft would certainly have been pleased to see many of the writers of the fantastic fiction that he loved, as well as his own work, getting this kind of serious and popular attention. No doubt, though, he would have been most pleased to see one writer in particular, whose work Lovecraft's own early efforts clearly emulated, being brought back to a new, appreciative readership. This was the Anglo-Irish author Edward John Moreton Drax Plunkett, better known as Lord Dunsany, appropriately pronounced "done zany."

Before his resurrection by Carter, Dunsany—whose full name could be that of a character in one of his stories—was in a long literary limbo, his books unread and most of them out of print. During the Edwardian era, he was one of Britain's most popular authors, in the same league as George Bernard Shaw and H. G. Wells. Aside from his fantasy stories, Dunsany was also a poet, a playwright, an essayist, a politician, and the possessor of one the oldest baronial seats in the country. He was fabulously wealthy, and when not in London, Paris, or another capital, he lived in a thirteenth-century Norman castle in Ireland, which his ancestor had erected centuries earlier. Because of his association with Lovecraft, for a time Dunsany's fantastic tales acquired a new audience. But none of his other works enjoyed a revival, and today pretty much all of it has once again returned to obscurity.

Although they both helped to create the genre of serious fantasy literature, Dunsany was in many ways the polar opposite of William Morris, who we can say originated the tradition with his classic *The Wood Beyond the World*, published in 1890, and which Ballantine brought out in 1969. Morris was the original arts-and-crafts off-the-grid bohemian. His early work, *News from Nowhere*, depicted an aesthetic utopia, a dream that later British socialists, like the Fabian Society, tried to make concrete, losing a great deal of the aestheticism along the way. The delicate watercolored atmosphere of Morris's fantasies, like *The Well at the World's End*, helped to spread the attraction of a preindustrial civilization which would inform many a commune that sprouted up in the quest for the "alternative society" in the '60s and '70s. Yet, while Dunsany's fantasies are equally limpid and precious, there is no redeeming social message to be found in them, no call for the kind of aesthetic "homespun" that would have readers designing their own furniture and wallpaper, and which could be found in Morris. Like Morris, Dunsany had a love of beauty; but, unlike many drawn to socialism, he also had the money to enjoy it. And, for most of his life, that is what he did.

Lovecraft, one of Dunsany's readers, didn't have Dunsany's good fortune, and had to satisfy his appetite for beauty with cost-cutting marathon coach excursions along America's Eastern seaboard in search of prerevolutionary colonial remains—or with the productions of his own imagination. But, before Lovecraft's imagination led him into the dark spaces of the Cthulhu Mythos, he devoted himself to writing in the style of Dunsany. Dunsany's tales of ancient gods and lost cities, heroic battles and quests for magical treasure, of "The Fortress Unvanquishable, Save for Sacnoth"—said to be the first-ever tale of "sword and sorcery"—and *The King of Elfland's Daughter*, are conveyed in an opulently jeweled narrative style informed with a world-weary irony, a kind of Schopenhauerian pessimism, what used to be called "Oriental fatalism." The tone appealed to Lovecraft's aesthetic nihilism. The language makes as much music as sense—sometimes more—with sonority and rhythm often taking over from meaning, as it does in the poetry of Swinburne. It is a language that evokes more than it can say, which we might understand as the peculiar trait of symbolism or, in fact, of poetry in general.

The titles of some collections of Dunsany's stories that appeared "under the sign of the unicorn," *At the Edge of the World* (1970) and *Beyond the Fields We Know* (1971), tell us that Dunsany's world is as much one of escape from dreary reality as the cruder pulp fiction that would follow. Gods die, pantheons crumble, kingdoms tumble, but it is all a dream, not a Wagnerian *Götterdämmerung*, but a series of gentle idylls spun out in a peaceful reverie. They are brief, beautiful but pointless respites from the necessities of what Baudelaire called "implacable life." It is no wonder that W. B. Yeats, another Irishman, whose early work expressed a hankering for fairy lands, would find Dunsany's tale, "Idle Days on the Yann," about a voyage through a dream landscape, one of the most moving stories he ever read. Lovecraft felt much the same, and in his early work did his best to capture the style of the master.

Lovecraft's early novella, *The Dream Quest of Unknown Kadath*, one of the later releases in the Adult Fantasy series, appearing in 1973, is written in Dunsany's highly self-conscious, rarefied aesthetic style. For readers used to the more traditional terrors of "The Rats in the Walls" or the cosmic horrors of the Cthulhu Mythos, it can be an acquired taste. If Lovecraft's literary legacy ended with his Dunsany pieces—think of "The Cats of Ulthar"—it is doubtful he would be remembered and read at all today. One could, in fact, see him as another of the forgotten fantasists that Lin Carter briefly resuscitated in the early 1970s. And, although I do go back every now and then to the best of the Mythos stories, wanting to recapture the atmosphere of dread Dunwich or abominable Arkham, to visit the forgotten plateau of inhospitable Leng or sunken and unpronounceable R'lyeh, for me, at least, Lovecraft's early excursions into an ethereal dreamland simply don't hold up. There is something insubstantial about them, something too precious, like pieces of fragile porcelain or delicate cloisonné. I don't return to Dunsany for the same reason, although there was a time when I read him avidly, and devoured as much fantasy as I could find. But then, I don't read much fantasy these days, having simply outgrown it.

I also imagine that the glut of films, literature, television shows, and other popular culture media saturated with fantasy today has led to a resistance to it in me—and, I must say, similarly with "the occult." The "fantastic," the "weird" have their effect because they are something *different* from the everyday, the ordinary. They are most effective when they break into the everyday and lead us to challenge its dominance, to ask questions about reality. (And if we ask enough questions, often enough, we run the risk of becoming philosophers, not to mention alienating our friends.) This may result in a sense of wonder or one of horror—or, as Lovecraft managed to achieve in some of his later work—a combination of both. This, if we remember, is the formula for the *sublime*.

When the fantastic is the norm, when wizards and warlocks and spirits and sorcerers overcrowd our forms of imagination, they become the new "everyday" and "ordinary," and quickly become as banal as the humdrum world they had hitherto transcended. We can see something similar in the way that surrealism, originally a powerful shock to rational bourgeois complacency, soon devolved into fashion, with shopping bags and T-shirts sporting images that initially were scandalous, but at which no one today bats an eye. We see this in the history of art and literature, when a movement toward realism overdoes it and prompts a resurgence of romanticism, or too much idealism incites an urge to bring the dreamers down to Earth. Some kind of compensatory mechanism is at work. But, while the ideal would be a creative, fruitful union of the two, an alchemical *coincidentia oppositorum*, what usually happens is the pendulum swings from one extreme to another. But the union is possible, and occasionally it does happen.

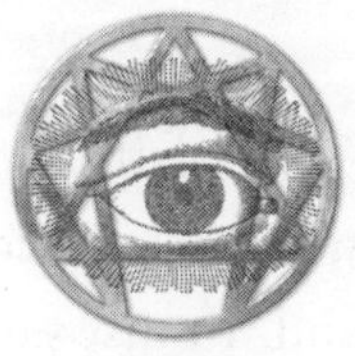

3
The Journey to the East

By the time the hippie girl I had a crush on handed me a paperback copy of Hermann Hesse's *Siddhartha*—the one with the blue cover and a statue of the Buddha, which Bantam had put out—Hesse had been dead for eight years. He died in 1962, just as the various revolutions that would rock the '60s were getting started. By 1970, the year I first read him, Hesse's books were as much a part of the counterculture as marijuana and rock and roll, and sold as well as, if not better than, both. Had Hesse lived until then—and it is possible he could have, although at ninety-three he would have been pushing it—he no doubt would have been surprised, if not baffled, by his enormous success. He once said that he would never be popular in America, and that he was understood there by at best ten people. Either Hesse underestimated the ability of Americans to understand his work, or millions of adolescents and members of the love generation were reading him avidly but without comprehension.

Yet, Hesse, who lived long enough to be aware of the rising American interest in his work, had reason to wonder if his new readers across the Atlantic were getting his point. Except for a brief spell in the 1920s, he had never really been popular with Anglophone readers.[1]

---

1. My hardcover copy of *Steppenwolf*, published by Henry Holt and translated by Basil Creighton, was published in 1929.

In German speaking countries, he was, of course, very well known—in fact, he was quite an established figure. He had two distinct periods and achieved a wide readership in both.

Peter Camenzind (1904) established the mold of most of Hesse's early novels, with the hero rejecting conventional life and taking to the high road in search of adventure. It expressed the sort of sensibility familiar to the *Wandervogel* generation, the "wandering birds" German youth movement of the late nineteenth and early twentieth centuries. These were young people who abandoned bourgeois security and took to the roads, getting "back to nature" and singing and playing guitar along the way, much like the hippies who read Hesse did. Unfortunately, many of these "wandering birds" later found their way into the National Socialist Party, while much of what was left of the younger *Wandervogel* entered the ranks of the Nazi Youth.

Peter Camenzind put Hesse on the literary map and made his name, but in the aftermath of WWI and Hesse's own psychological crises, Hesse produced a book so unlike his earlier romances that he published it under a pseudonym—that of Emil Sinclair, the book's protagonist—and the reading public could not tell it was him. It was only after the book won a prestigious and lucrative prize as the best first novel of the year that Hesse returned the prize money and made it known that he was the author. The book, *Demian* (1919), was the product of the chaos of the war and of the confusions of Hesse's own soul, to clarify which Hesse had undergone extensive analysis first with Jung and then with Josef Lang, one of Jung's disciples.

Yet, by the late 1940s, Hesse had stopped writing novels. His last, *The Glass Bead Game* (published by Bantam as *Magister Ludi*), appeared in 1943 but had been written during the '30s and, although awarded the Nobel Prize for literature in 1946, for the postwar generation he was decidedly passé. Romantic novels about "inwardness" and the "search for the self" were of little interest in a Germany levelled by the war and split by global politics. Hesse wasn't troubled, and enjoyed his withdrawn and quiet life in Montagnola, in the hills above

Lake Lugano in Ticino, the Italian-speaking part of Switzerland, which he would depict in his novella, *Klingsor's Last Summer* (1919). In 2008, I visited Hesse's Casa Camuzzi while working on my book on Jung, and drank a glass of wine in his honor.

Hesse was always a solitary character, and he protected his solitude, erecting a notice at the entrance to his home letting potential visitors know that he was not available and wished to be left alone.[2] One suspects that the readers he had in his last years were courteous, polite, and considerate, and would have respected his wishes. But, by the mid-sixties, a flock of wandering birds from the United States, eager to let it all hang out, would most likely have ignored it. It may have been just as well that, by then, Hesse had left the building.

HESSE'S AMERICAN SUCCESS STARTED IN 1951, when Henry Miller—a favorite writer of mine during my early days in New York—suggested to his publisher, New Directions, that they put out an edition of *Siddhartha*, translated by Hilda Rossner. They did, and the paperback that appeared in 1957 was the edition that adorned beatnik bookshelves until Bantam acquired the work. Miller praised the book far and wide, suggesting it to friends and urging it on correspondents. Another Hesse promoter was Colin Wilson, who included Hesse in his study of alienation in the modern world, *The Outsider.* Wilson's extended analysis of Hesse's work in this surprise existential bestseller brought the reclusive German romantic into many American and British homes.[3]

One spot in the New World that seemed very interested in Hesse was the North Beach area of San Francisco. This was the West Coast stomping ground of the Beat generation, just getting started around

2. One visitor Hesse did enjoy meeting was T. S. Eliot, who sought him out after reading his little book about Dostoevsky, *A Glimpse into Chaos* (1919), and referred to it in the founding modernist poem *The Waste Land* (1922).

3. It did the same for G. I. Gurdjieff. *The Outsider* is one of the first books in which someone outside the Gurdjieff Work writes about it at any length.

the time New Directions issued their paperback edition of *Siddhartha*. Although the Beats were eager to take their own journeys to the East—the title of a novella by Hesse—it was Hesse's at the time more shocking and "transgressive" novel, *Steppenwolf*, that was making the scene. We can say that the Beat generation was born at the famous reading of Allen Ginsberg's *Howl* at the Six Gallery in San Francisco in 1955. Lawrence Ferlinghetti's City Lights would publish the poem the next year—in its trademark plain wrap, black-and-white cover—and Jack Kerouac's *On the Road* would follow in 1957. Given a founding poetic text entitled *Howl*, it's not surprising that the wandering birds nesting in North Beach would be taken with a novel about a man who believes he is a "wolf of the steppes."

Yet, in 1961, a year before his death, when word of *Steppenwolf*'s popularity among the Beats and at least one angry young Brit had reached Hesse's retreat, Hesse added a note to a new edition of the book. Hesse pointed out that of all his books, *Steppenwolf* was the one that was "more often and more violently misunderstood than any other." Hesse regretted that it seemed only one side of Harry Haller's (the book's protagonist) character was appreciated—that of the "wolf of the steppes." But behind Haller's torment and suffering lay a different, more detached world, a "second, higher, indestructible world . . . a positive, serene, superpersonal and timeless world of faith."

This was the world revealed when, at certain moments, Harry is suddenly reminded of "Mozart and the stars," moments when his heart stands still "between delight and sorrow" and he sees "how rich was the gallery of my life and how thronged the soul of the wretched Steppenwolf with high eternal stars and constellations." These are moments of *remembrance*, as are the moments when Marcel in Proust's novel "recaptures the past."

When I first read *Steppenwolf*, I was not aware of the importance of this phenomenon, nor that it would form the heart of Colin Wilson's insights into what he calls "Faculty X," our inherent but little understood—or even recognized—ability to grasp "the *reality* of other times and places." Yet, when I first read *The Occult*, one reason I was taken with it was that Wilson often referred to Hesse, as well as to Nietzsche and Sartre, two thinkers whom I would meet, at least through their work, soon after reading Hesse. And when I later read *The Outsider*—at the start, I might say, of my tenure as one—I was well prepared for Wilson's extended look at Hesse's work, having by then read everything of his I could find.

But the book of Hesse's that had the greatest effect on me in my teens wasn't *Siddhartha* or *Steppenwolf*, but *Demian*, the work that emerged after Hesse's analysis with Jung and Josef Lang—although, an earlier work, *Beneath the Wheel* (1906), was another favorite. Both *Demian* and *Beneath the Wheel* are about adolescence and coming of age and the difficulties that sensitive youth have in a world geared toward the practical business of making a living, something with which I and others like me could identify. Both books depict characters caught in a system that has no place for poetry or inwardness. Both are in the mold of the *Bildungsroman*, the "novel of education."

Hans Giebenrath, the intellectually brilliant but emotionally starved protagonist of *Beneath the Wheel*, is crushed by the system, the "wheel." Whatever spark of creativity and imagination he may have possessed is drummed out of him by his parents and teachers; in the end, he drowns after a night of carousing after spending time, as Hesse did, in an asylum.

But Max Demian is a different story. He is the idealized portrait of a character who has "individuated," in Jung's term. We can see him as an expression of the archetype of the Self, someone who has "become who he is." He acts as a model and mentor for Emil Sinclair, a sensitive youth, like Hans Giebenrath, who has had the good fortune to meet Demian, who appears at different times in his life, helping him to surmount certain difficulties in his development. If Hesse's earlier *Bildungsroman* concerned youth's encounters with the world and its education—along the lines of Goethe's *Wilhelm Meister's Apprenticeship*—in *Demian*, the protagonist's education concerns an encounter with his Self.

LIKE *STEPPENWOLF*, *Demian* is a happy hunting ground for Jungian symbols and archetypes; they are all there: the Shadow, the Anima, the Self. And, although I read and reread *Steppenwolf*, and was particularly fascinated by Harry Haller's adventures in the Magic Theatre—entrance to which is "for madmen only" (my friends and I at the time relied on marijuana to get us in)—it wasn't until I was older that I began to identify with its themes more seriously. It is really a book for older readers, those who have entered midlife, which, as Jung tells us, is when the task of individuating really begins. This becomes clear when we recognize that the Steppenwolf's problem is not so much that he is a divided soul—a man and a wolf—although a central theme running through all of Hesse's work is the need to reconcile the polarities in human nature, a theme he shared with Jung and which informs his medieval fantasy, *Narcissus and Goldmund* (1930). Harry Haller's real problem is one I would become aware of when I began to read Sartre and Camus: the problem of freedom.

Haller is free, but he doesn't know what to *do* with his freedom, and his lack of purpose turns his freedom into such a burden that he considers escaping it by slitting his throat. What we can call the "Mozart and the stars effect" happens when the *reality* of his freedom comes back to him, and he is reminded of life's infinite potential.

Demian is a different story. Although Hesse wrote it when he was in his forties, *Demian* is a young person's book. The Bantam edition I read and reread obsessively, with the cover image of Frau Eva holding Demian and Emil Sinclair close to her breast, and the hawk, a symbol of the Self, hovering in the background, begins with this statement: "I only wanted to live in accord with the promptings that came from my true self. Why was that so difficult?"

Why indeed? Why is it so difficult to follow the promptings of our true self? That was a question I asked myself repeatedly throughout my teens, and sought the answer to in my reading. Nothing should be easier than to be oneself. But, as anyone who has ever tried it knows, nothing can be so difficult, especially when you make your first attempts. Being oneself is difficult at any age. But those first steps taken in that direction often precipitate considerable chaos and confusion.

"He who would be born must destroy a world"—this is the message that miraculously appears on Emil Sinclair's school desk after he has sent a picture he has drawn to Demian, of a hawk emerging from an egg that he had seen in a dream. This is the hawk depicted on the book's cover. "The bird is struggling out of the egg. The egg is the world." The bird must destroy the world in order to fly to the Gnostic god, Abraxas. Abraxas, the cock-headed god, is an antinomian figure. He is beyond society's conventions, beyond good and evil. He unites the opposites and is associated with individuation and the Self. Demian learns about Abraxas through his conversations with the church organist Pistorius—who, I later learned, was based on Hesse's analyst, Josef Lang.

Hesse was one of the few people to whom Jung sent a privately printed copy of his strange work of "spiritual dictation," *The Seven Sermons to the Dead*, that came to him during his "descent into the unconscious" following his breakup with Freud. It emerged with the same material that Jung recorded in his *Red Book*, and is fundamentally concerned with the process of "differentiation"—of separating from the undifferentiated Pleroma (read: unconscious) and achieving one's own individuality.[4] Abraxas figures largely in Jung's *Seven Sermons*, and this strange text was included in that edition of Jung's *Memories, Dreams, Reflections* that I stole from my high school library.

It was clear that the *Seven Sermons* and *Demian* were about the same thing, and in a very real sense I can say that after reading *Demian* I became a Gnostic. Not in the sense of embracing the doctrines of the

4. An excellent exploration of Jung's *Seven Sermons* can be found in Stephan Hoeller's *The Gnostic Jung and the Seven Sermons to the Dead* (Wheaton, IL: Quest Books, 1982).

ancient Gnostic sects, about which I knew nothing at the time. But in the more fundamental and vital sense of wanting *gnosis*, the kind of inner knowledge that Hesse and Jung spoke of, and which also involves a kind of remembering, a reexperiencing of what we already know but have forgotten.

But these reflections were far from my consciousness when I first read *Demian*. More to the point was the reality of having to "destroy a world" in order to be born. "World" in my case meant my family life at home. Depending on your point of view, it was either a blessing or a burden that I came of age during the tail end of the '60s, when the challenge not to conform, and to "do your own thing," still had currency.[5] The generation gap had opened and was widening. The alienation from my family I experienced because of my love of reading now escalated into more or less open warfare. The war in Vietnam was one reason. My father fought in WWII, and had been decorated for bravery. He was not taken with the hippies, draft dodgers, and anti-war protesters while I, all of fourteen and of course knowledgeable about these things, took their side.[6]

It was a generational conflict played out in millions of American homes. My sister, who was a few years older than me, should really have

---

5. A favorite television program at the time was *Then Came Bronson*, about a disillusioned journalist who travels across the states on a motorcycle, in search of the meaning of life. It lasted one season, from 1969 to 1970.

6. Years later, when I came to write my first book, *Turn Off Your Mind*, about the sixties, I was surprised to discover how antipathetic I came to feel toward the popular "revolutionary" figures of the time—characters like Abbie Hoffman, Jerry Rubin, Angela Davis, et al.—whom I had unreflectively considered heroes back then. They struck me as presumptuous, self-righteous egoists, more concerned with power, self-aggrandizement, and celebrity than anything else. In saying this, I am not suggesting that Richard Nixon and Spiro Agnew, *bêtes noires* of the sixties radicals, were preferable or that the war in Vietnam was justifiable. But I could understand how my father and others like him, who had risked their lives in WWII, would feel less than sympathetic to these individuals. My political sympathies today are neither right nor left, conservative nor liberal, and I am of the firm conviction that the most important questions about human existence cannot be answered through politics.

been more involved in this than I was, but she was not rebellious and by this time we really had little to say to each other. Civil rights were another thorny topic. The discord erupting at home was accompanied by the same breaking out at school. I can remember one occasion when, after getting into some trouble—a frequent occurrence—the principal asked what was bothering me. I began to say something about the way the world was, how people were treated, about their rights and so on. He looked at me and said, "But you're much too young to be bothered by this. Forget about it. Mind your own business." Sage advice, no doubt. But I was never able to profit by it.

In *Demian*, Hesse portrayed an encouraging, successful attempt at following the promptings of one's true self, but other sources were less sanguine. J. D. Salinger's *The Catcher in the Rye* was a must read. While I enjoyed it and identified with much of it, in the end Holden Caufield struck me as something of a bore. Perhaps by this time I had become "Europeanized" through reading Hesse, and Salinger was too American for me. I didn't read any of his other books and to this day, with a few exceptions, I am not attracted to American writers. The ones I used to like, such as Henry Miller, I now find impossible to read. The Beats, too, no longer hold any attraction, and haven't for some time. Readers of *Turn Off Your Mind* will know that I am critical of both.

Another big book at the time was Joseph Heller's *Catch-22*. I don't know what I would think of it now, but back then I appreciated its absurdist comedy, something that informed the novels of Kurt Vonnegut, whom I also read avidly. Going back to Vonnegut recently, I was surprised to discover what a nihilist he was—"existential," the critics said—something that would not have troubled me at the time. I remember reading *Cat's Cradle*, *The Sirens of Titan*, *Slaughterhouse-Five*, *God Bless You, Mr. Rosewater*, and Vonnegut's other novels in high school, finding them hilarious and thoroughly enjoying them. As many teenagers did, I identified with his depiction of an absurd, meaningless universe and our pathetic attempts to impress some purpose on the inescapable randomness of life—at least, this is what I think I felt at the time.

Meaninglessness and absurdity seemed liberating. They undermined the solid, oppressive world of my parents and my teachers and supported my growing conviction that life was about *something else*, even if at the time I had little more than a vague idea of what that something else might be. It also helped my self-esteem to think that, unlike my parents and teachers, and practically everyone else, *I* saw the truth about life and was not taken in by its deceptions. Such thoughts are a tonic when faced with a world devoid of interest in your true self. I should mention that Vonnegut, too, did not hold up under a recent reading.

Unlike Peter Camenzind or Emil Sinclair, at fourteen I wasn't able to take to the high road and leave the claustrophobic, suffocating atmosphere of home for more spacious climes. There I was, at least for another few years. And although I tried to follow the promptings of my true self, most times all that amounted to was trouble and the constant arguing that had by then become a regular feature of my teen years. My mother, who had a frustrating childhood spent taking care of her older siblings' children, did everything she could to prevent me from having anything to do with my true self. My father, who most likely was not happy being married to my mother (hence his pornography collection) was, if not distant—he had more than one job and worked most of the time—generally called on only when the conflict became serious. He liked to keep to himself and became angry if drawn into the fray. It may go without saying that neither parent nor my sister ever talked with me about anything—a not uncommon feature of dysfunctional families.

I don't blame my parents; I was difficult and they didn't know what to do with me. But it was a struggle, an uphill battle all the way. Freud said that a man who "has been the indisputable favorite of his mother keeps for life the feeling of a conqueror, that confidence of success that often induces real success." Freud was such a man. Yet he did not say that the opposite was true, that lack of such favor invariably leads to defeat. It does not. It does, however, place before the unfavored man some additional hurdles.

KAFKA'S GREGOR SAMSA, who wakes up one morning to discover he has been transformed into a cockroach, often seemed a better depiction of my life at home than anything Hesse offered. *The Metamorphosis* seemed to be written for me especially, an identification I shared with many of its adolescent readers. Today I find Kafka overrated and have not gone back to him for many years, but I could say that back then I read the Modern Library *Selected Stories of Franz Kafka* "religiously." I certainly read "In the Penal Colony" and others of his stories many times. I remember once sitting in the backyard of my parents' house reading *Selected Stories*, when the older, grown son of our downstairs neighbors, whom he was visiting, saw me and said hello. When he saw what I was reading, he said, "Kafka? You're reading Kafka?"—impressed that it wasn't science fiction and surprised that I would even know who Kafka was.

A similar surprise was felt by my high school gym teacher when he asked about my hobbies. The school was taking some kind of survey of the students and for some reason the gym instructor, a friendly, muscular, slightly overweight black man whose name I cannot recall, was given the job of asking the boys to tell him about themselves—what they liked to do, what their favorite sport was, and so on.

Aside from a brief interest in basketball, I had no interest in sports. When it was my turn to be interviewed, I told the gym instructor about my reading. I mentioned the writers I've talked about in these notes and when I got to Kafka, he gave me a strange look. I wasn't sure what that meant and, thinking it best to keep the promptings of my true self under wraps, I covered my tracks and tried to appear '"just like everybody else"—that is, "normal." I said something like, "A lot of other students must be reading these books too," wanting to avoid any suggestion that I was "different." He looked at me, shook his head, and said, "No, they aren't. No one else mentioned them. Do you know how different you are?" I smiled, mumbled something, and moved on.

Yes, I was different and knew it. So did my friends—or, at least, the people that I thought of as my friends. This difference, though, afforded no advantage. Quite the opposite. Hesse was right. Following the promptings of your true self was difficult.

Literature wasn't the only avenue through which I tried to find a way to myself. I've already mentioned Jung. Another important work of psychology came to me not through reading, but through music. One vivid memory of my teens is of being in my room, listening to the disc jockey Alex Bennett play John Lennon's first solo album, *John Lennon/Plastic Ono Band*, on WMCA radio one evening. This raw, at times disturbing record, whose stripped-down sound presaged the "punk rock" that was on its way, was released in December 1970, just before my fifteenth birthday. The record was a response to the breakup of The Beatles and an expression of Lennon's psychological pain. Some tunes, like "Love" and "Look at Me," were gentle and melodic. Others, like "I Found Out," were more aggressive. And others, like "Mother" and "Well, Well, Well," erupted with volcanic emotion—in them, Lennon simply screamed. This should not have been surprising given that Lennon, who was something of an intellectual impulse buyer, was at the time absorbed in his latest fad, the "primal scream" therapy of Arthur Janov.

Janov was a psychotherapist and, during one session, he heard one of his patients emit "an eerie scream welling up from the depths of his soul." The pain prompting this scream didn't derive from some current problem or condition but was a gut-wrenching outpouring of the repressed pain of his childhood. Janov believed he had discovered a new therapeutic technique. He encouraged his patients to return to and relive painful experiences from their past, and to express the pain that at the time they had stifled. Lennon took to this avidly. He certainly had a lot of pain, most of it about the loss of his mother.[7]

I found a copy of Janov's *The Primal Scream* and read it. I could not afford psychotherapy and, at fifteen, most likely would have found it difficult to find a therapist specializing in Janov's technique, especially in New Jersey. I did the next best thing and, alone in the park one day, I let out a few howls of my own. I can't say it did much good, and in any case, there was so much screaming going on at home, there was probably not that much unexpressed pain to well up from the depths of my soul anyway.

Arthur Janov wasn't the only celebrity shrink in the early '70s. At a time when various self-help and therapeutic techniques and gurus sprouted like mushrooms after a rain, the ideas of one aggressively self-promoting individual seemed especially suited to the psyches of young people. This was the Scottish "anti-psychiatrist," R. D. Laing. If, in *The Metamorphosis*, Kafka had presented an extended parable about alienation and the loss of self, we can say that, in his once-bestselling books, Laing presented a phenomenological-existential-psychological analysis of why such alienation and loss are inescapable in modern society.

Laing's central theme can be easily formulated: madness—especially schizophrenia—is a "sane" response to an insane world. In the way that neo-Marxist thinkers such as the Frankfurt School, whom I would encounter years later, argue that we are all inescapably trapped within the meshes of "late capitalism," Laing argued that we are all

---

7. I was a fan of Lennon in my teens and, not long after his murder in 1980, I sang his songs "Instant Karma" and "Cold Turkey" at a performance for one of his charities at Hurrah, the club in New York where my band The Know often played. I have to say, I think it a shame that he is remembered for his song "Imagine," which strikes me as not only a rather sentimental work but an oddly nihilistic one. Lennon's vision of a world without "countries," "no religion," and with "nothing to live or die for" is a child's world, not an adult's. Lennon seemed never to grow up—hence, perhaps, his attraction to Janov's therapy.

inescapably trapped within our schizoid psyches, fashioned by our upbringing in the modern nuclear family. Because of this, we are all guilty of the crimes we accuse others of; according to Laing "we are all murderers and prostitutes—no matter to what culture, society, class, nation one belongs, no matter how normal, moral or mature one takes oneself to be."

Laing argued that, in order to protect the "mad" from hurting others or themselves, we lock them away in asylums, while at the same time we allow politicians and generals and arms manufacturers to kill thousands in wars—and they remain free and are considered sane. Hence, the "sane" world is one in which violence and destruction turn a neat profit. There was a "catch-22" here of considerable proportions. By the end of the decade, such logic would be used by Charles Manson and his "Family" as justification for the Tate-Labianca murders that shocked Los Angeles in the summer of 1969. When asked why they killed the actress Sharon Tate and four others, Manson's Family replied by asking why the US government napalmed peasants in Vietnam.

Radical leftist groups, like the Weathermen, who emerged from the SDS (Students for a Democratic Society), and later the SLA (Symbionese Liberation Army), who would kidnap Patty Hearst, made similar allowances for their excesses, claiming they were "at war" with an oppressive, imperialist society. Many people otherwise opposed to violence, stricken with guilt because of their "privileged" First World status, felt sympathy for such justifications.

Laing had taken the "double bind" theory of the polymath Gregory Bateson and ran with it. The "double bind" appears when we are given mixed messages—mutually exclusive injunctions that cancel each other out—and are not able to explain to the person making these requests our difficulty in fulfilling them. A perpetual "tilt" sign goes off in our psyche. Or we are placed in a situation in which, in order to comply, we must go against ourselves. So, when one is desperately trying to follow the promptings of one's true self, but is confronted with a parent from whom one wants love but who inhibits our following of those promptings, one is placed in a "double bind." One wants to be "authentic," but one still also wants love. One wants both but can only have one, because embracing one eclipses the other. Or, take the mother who stifles her child and suppresses anything creative and original in him, but who nevertheless says to him, "You do know that I love you, don't you?" The confusion that sets in, to which the young are especially subject, can be painfully disorienting.

In more contemporary times, we call such behavior "gaslighting," after the film *Gaslight* (1944), in which suave but treacherous Charles Boyer slowly drives the beautiful but trusting Ingrid Bergman mad. In the film, Gregory Anton (Boyer) does this purposefully, for his own nefarious reasons. But it can happen in the family without any conscious purpose, because the people perpetrating it have been subject to the same treatment, as had their parents, and so on, right back to Adam, Eve, and the kids. One might even say the doomed Hans Giebenrath of Hesse's *Beneath the Wheel* is a victim of the double bind. This is why Laing argued that, rather than having an organic base, treatable with drugs, schizophrenia is produced by the family and, by extension, society.

Where Janov urged his patients to let out a primal scream about the pain of their childhood, Laing argued that even the most loving family environment is little more than an incubator of madness. Technically, the family is "schizogenic," a producer of schizophrenia.[8] This does not mean, as is often thought, that it produces split personalities, little Jekylls and Hydes, although in extreme cases of parental mistreatment, multiple personalities might result. It means a "split" between the person and their external reality, or one within themselves. The outer world becomes so impossible to navigate through that one withdraws into one's subjective world; in extreme cases, this leads to a state of catatonia. Or one is reduced to a perpetual battle with oneself, and incessant "yes and no" with a resultant paralysis.

---

8. Oddly enough, this was a term that Abraham Maslow applied to his mother.

In *The Politics of Experience* (1967)—a title pre-echoing his contemporary, Timothy Leary's, *The Politics of Ecstasy* (1968)—Laing told his readers that "from the moment of birth, when the stone-age baby confronts the twentieth-century mother, the baby is subjected to these forces of violence, called love . . ." For someone like myself, caught in a stifling family atmosphere with no immediate way out, such radical views seemed rather appealing, at least, for a time.

Laing had hoped that his first book, *The Divided Self* (1960), would make him an overnight sensation in the way that *The Outsider* had put twenty-four-year-old Colin Wilson on the literary map. Laing's ascent was less sudden, but his celebrity, once achieved, was longer lasting and more influential, at least during the '60s and '70s; as Wilson once told me, he "sat out the sixties" and made a "comeback" only in 1971, with *The Occult*.

Laing started out as a proponent of "existential phenomenology," a psychotherapeutic method that sought to understand the ravings of psychotic patients as clues to their "being-in-the-world," rather than as "symptoms" of their illness. As I would later learn, this was, in fact, an approach that Jung had pioneered during his time at the Burghölzli Clinic in Zürich, under the direction of Eugene Bleuler, who coined the term "schizophrenia." With Jung, it eventually led to his "discovery" of the "collective unconscious." With Laing, it led to rather different results.

By the mid-sixties, Laing had found a place for himself in the upper echelon of the counterculture, rubbing radical elbows with Leary, Allen Ginsberg, Alan Watts, and political gurus like Herbert Marcuse. He advocated the legalization of cannabis (marijuana) in the UK, and had indulged liberally in what had become the accepted sacrament of the mystic decade, lysergic acid diethylamide 25 (LSD or "acid"), suggesting that others do the same. Like Leary, Watts, Ginsberg, and countless other less notable pilgrims, he would make the "journey to the East," spending time in an ashram in India, even living for weeks in a cave in the Himalayas with a holy man.

But for all his cries for the need for love, Laing was not really a proponent of flower power. He had a tough Scots' "hard man" character that led to more than one fracas. On one occasion, he was arrested for throwing a bottle of wine through the window of a Bhagwan Shree Rajneesh center in North London. His drinking was on the monumental scale associated with his countrymen; one of his daughters once remarked that the only way she could get close to him was by sharing a bottle of whiskey with him. And Laing's idea of "letting it all hang out" was rather more disturbing than a clutch of hippies engaging in the group therapy made fashionable by the Gestalt therapist Fritz Perls, one of the house gurus at the Esalen Institute, the hot tub spiritual retreat on California's Big Sur coast, which opened in 1962.

In 1965, Laing and his fellow anti-psychiatrist Joe Berke started the Philadelphia Association, a collection of various doctors and therapists who shared a disdain for mainstream psychiatry. That year, Laing acquired a lease on Kingsley Hall, a community center in East London, and turned it into a laboratory for the study of madness as a sane reaction to an insane world. It was in some ways a UK version of Leary's Castalia—the name Leary gave to the massive Millbrook estate in upstate New York which a supporter had given the good doctor for his use—although on a less lavish scale. (Castalia is the name of the utopian society depicted in Hesse's *The Glass Bead Game.*)

When word got out about it, Kingsley Hall became a popular stop on the counterculture trail. Radicals, poets, artists, hippies, bohemians, and other members of the "alternative society" soon made the pilgrimage to its door. Behind it, one could, it was believed, throw off the conditioning imposed by the schizoid "sane" world, and embrace the liberating effects of madness. The process was often facilitated by the use of LSD and other drugs. Laing's fellow Scot Sean Connery stopped by and took acid with Laing to help relieve the tensions of playing James Bond. Syd Barrett, leader of the psychedelic band Pink Floyd, had, by the time of his visit, taken more acid than was good for him, and was already sliding into madness.

Unlike Leary, Laing was still a practicing doctor, and his main interest was in providing a safe space in which to carry out an experiment in what we might call "controlled schizophrenia." The subject was Mary Barnes, a nurse, who had come to Kingsley Hall not to help Laing with his patients, but to become one. Under a regime of twenty-four-hour therapy, Mary regressed to infancy. She retreated into the basement, where she smeared the walls with excrement, shouted obscenities—a feather from Janov's cap—and was generally not only allowed but encouraged to descend into madness. Laing saw this descent as a form of existential rebirth, much as Leary saw his LSD soirees as a means of deconditioning their participants, freeing them from the "imprinting" inflicted on them by straight society. How successful both were is debatable.

I wouldn't know about Kingsley Hall until many years later, but I had found a copy of *The Divided Self* and read it. By the time I did, the Kingsley Hall experiment had ended, after two patients threw themselves off the roof. I can't say I understood much of it at the time, although I identified with Laing's remarks about schizophrenia and how behavior that might seem aberrant to others—especially one's parents—could really be a way of trying to communicate. My reflections on this found their way into the journal that my mother took to the police sergeant. Having a member of Bayonne's finest page through my intimate thoughts struck me as confirmation of Laing's ideas about family relations. If my assertions of genius had not set off alarm bells, I suspect the pages in which I discharged my sense of isolation and fear of madness certainly would.

But the book of Laing's that had the most impact on me was his collection of schizoid poems, Zen *koans*, existential dialogues, and solipsistic monologues entitled *Knots* (1970). It was Laing's way of presenting the confusing, paralyzing, and ultimately depressing state of non-communication in which we were all inescapably enmeshed. The book's opening gives an idea of what the reader will find inside. It expresses the paralysis that accompanies the extreme self-consciousness endemic to youth, which in me had by then reached a particularly sensitive state.

"They are playing a game. They are playing at not playing a game. If I show them I see they are, I shall break the rules and they will punish me. I must play their game, of not seeing I see the game." Laing continues: "They are not having fun. I can't have fun if they don't. If I get them to have fun, then I can have fun with them. Getting them to have fun is not fun. It is hard work . . ." You get the picture.

As I had with Vonnegut, I went back to *Knots* recently, a book I hadn't looked at since I first read it sometime in 1971. It did not hold up—but then, I no longer am a confused fifteen-year-old, suffocating in a claustrophobic family atmosphere of pettiness and triviality, seriously considering madness as a possible escape hatch.

It is easy to see Laing's approach as merely another set of radical ideas that fizzled out as the '70s progressed. By 1975, Laing himself was drinking heavily and finding it difficult to get his work published; he died in 1989 at the age of sixty-two. Yet I can appreciate and sympathize with the frustration and disgust that accompanies attempts to speak the truth in a world resistant to it. And it is not only in our naïve teens that we are faced with such a world. At sixty-seven, I have been battered, bruised, and around the block several times, but I still find myself at a disadvantage when dealing with people for whom truth is whatever they can get away with, and who have a distinct aversion to the genuine article. One often wishes for an impatient Alexander to cut through the knots such individuals tie in our lives.[9]

It was around this time that I first started experimenting with drugs. At fifteen, they were easier to get than alcohol—although that,

9. Reference is to the Gordian Knot. Legend has it that this was a knot so complicated, whoever could undo it would become the conqueror of Asia. Alexander the Great undid it by cutting through it with his sword.

too, was often enough not a problem. Cigarettes, as well. I gave up smoking in 1980. I was never a confirmed smoker, but it was part of the image as a rebellious teen, and later as a musician. Today tobacco makes me ill and I consider the British habit of smoking cannabis mixed with the stuff an aberrant waste.

I won't bore the reader with tales of drunkenness. Like other teenagers, I drank—usually whatever was available—got drunk, got sick, and wound up in situations the memory of which even now produces pangs of embarrassment. Today I drink wine in occasional immoderation. I am no connoisseur, but I do prefer Merlot, Malbec, and Cabernet Sauvignon—and in the summer, Chardonnay and Pinot Grigio. I live in London, city of pubs, but am, alas, not a fan of ale. I prefer cafés to pubs—that's the European in me—and coffee to beer. I will have a cold lager on the infrequent hot day, though the hops make me sleepy. Wine is poetry in a bottle—a very different effect.

But, by drugs here I mean marijuana and psychedelics, both of which, it will come as no surprise, were very popular among my friends; I've already mentioned using marijuana as an entrance ticket to Hesse's Magic Theatre. My first experience of marijuana, though, was not very promising. I cut class with an older student and smoked a joint with him. It was not a success. I became ill—a not uncommon experience with virgin smokers—and had to stay out of my other classes too. This later required some explanation. What I remember most about the experience is hearing the Cat Stevens song "Moonshadow" playing constantly in my head.

This seems reason enough never to touch the stuff again. But I persevered. Like many others at the time, I had been reading the works of Carlos Castaneda, about his adventures with Don Juan, the Yaqui Indian who taught him the secrets of various mind-altering plants so that Castaneda, too, would become a *brujo*, a sorcerer, and "walk a path with heart," open to the mysteries of the world.

For a fifteen-year-old stuck in a dull New Jersey town, cramped in a small second-floor flat with a family impervious to understanding him, such a prospect seemed tempting. It was, of course, difficult to secure the peyote, datura, jimson weed, and other "power plants" that Castaneda, under Don Juan's tutelage, encountered. But, with a nickel- or dime-bag of grass (five or ten dollars' worth), we did our best.

Castaneda's books weren't the only ones about drugs that came my way. Along with the occult boom of the 1960s, the products of which I would discover a few years later, there was also a boom in drug literature. Some works were even considered literary classics, such as DeQuincy's *Confessions of an English Opium Eater.* Another was Baudelaire's *Artificial Paradise,* first published in 1860. I had already come across Baudelaire, as mentioned, brought to him and the other French Romantics by Clark Ashton Smith. I discovered that marijuana, in the form of hashish, had been popular among them. They had all belonged to something called the Hashish Club, a group of writers and artists and doctors and other interested individuals who gathered together in Paris to dine and entertain themselves by eating large portions of the stuff. That sounded like fun.

Equally popular were books about "the psychedelic experience." There was, of course, Aldous Huxley's *The Doors of Perception* (1954), about his experiences with the drug mescaline. Mescaline, I discovered, was the active substance in the peyote that Castaneda had eaten—it was what got him high—and under its effects, he met the spirit Mescalito and was taken on an extraordinary adventure. Huxley didn't meet Mescalito, but his description of "seeing as Adam saw on the first day of creation" seemed equally exciting. Yet if peyote was difficult to come by, mescaline was no easier. I subsequently discovered that synthesizing mescaline from peyote is a tedious business, making it unprofitable for popular use.

But there were other substances widely available, and books describing the effects of LSD found their way to me. Among them was Alan Watts's *The Joyous Cosmology* (1962); Robert S. de Ropp's *Drugs and the Mind* (1957); and Charles Tart's *Altered States of Consciousness* (1969), a classic anthology covering marijuana, LSD, dreams, meditation, and other non-ordinary states.

These books and others went into scientific and philosophical detail about various drugs' effect on the brain and consciousness, and were much more informative and helpful than the anti-drug films we were shown at school. Those ludicrous propaganda efforts usually depicted some poor soul descending into madness and being plagued by nightmarish hallucinations, such as looking in the mirror and seeing his face turn into that of a monster. These attempts to scare us away from drugs were laughable; if anything, they led to disappointment when the sort of shock effects we expected from the drugs, based on the films, didn't occur.

As with my first experience with marijuana, my first LSD trip was not a success. And while I soon came to enjoy smoking grass, I never grew fond of acid. Had my first encounter with it been more pleasant my appreciation of it today might be different. I'm willing to accept this. Nevertheless, I've taken LSD a few times, but on no occasion was the experience enjoyable—though this does not mean I had a "bad trip"—nor have I ever experienced the kind of "ego death" and immersion in the One that many devotees have reported. I've taken "magic mushrooms" on several occasions and did enjoy those experiences. But on these trips, too, nothing particularly mystical or spiritual occurred, and I have never experienced a hallucination—at least, not knowingly.

I suspect that at fifteen I was too young to take the sacrament, but an opportunity arose and I did. I can still recall the slight prism effect the flake of what was called "window pane acid" gave off when I first saw it under a street lamp. It was a tiny square of what looked like mica, about the size of a small SIM card. Leary had advised on the importance of the proper "set and setting" when casting off on a trip, and I imagine that at least on this account he was right. Roaming the streets of Bayonne, New Jersey, on a Friday night, filled with a high-octane hallucinogen was most likely not the best milieu in which to "turn off my mind, relax, and float downstream," but it was what was available.

I can recall the peculiar sensation when the stuff came on, an odd tingling accompanied by a strange glow surrounding everything that until that moment had remained unnoticed. There was a kind of "sizzling" going on in the background, like a mild electrical current. But, rather than finding myself on the outskirts of a "separate reality," as one of Castaneda's books calls it, what seemed to be taking place was that the everyday reality I wanted to escape instead became even more real. Not in the way that it had for Huxley but, as I later came to understand, in the way that reality overwhelmed Roquentin, the protagonist of Sartre's *Nausea*, which I had yet to read. Everything was *too* real and I suspect what I experienced was an attack of existential angst, the "dread," as Kierkegaard, whom I had also yet to read, called it, of "being" itself. It seems I was an existentialist before I knew it.

At one point as we roamed the streets, we bumped into someone we knew. When told what we were doing, he laughed. For some reason, he put his hand on my chest and felt my heartbeat. He made a face and said, "Man, your heart is beating fast!" and shook his head. It was common practice to "mess with people's heads" when they were stoned and I don't think he meant to mess with mine in particular. But he had, and the idea that I was going to have a heart attack took hold and stayed in place for the rest of the evening. Another friend we bumped into, more experienced with the stuff, sat with me on the steps of the post office and talked me down. That helped.

I stayed out quite late that night, wanting the stuff to wear off before I went home. At one point I found myself watching as the traffic lights down the length of Broadway, our main drag, changed at the same time. I had the odd idea that if the traffic lights were conscious, intelligent, and if they didn't want us to know they were, they would act precisely as they were acting, like machines . . . It was an insight I decided to keep to myself. I stayed out that evening until well after midnight. Even so, the effects hadn't yet worn off, and only did after I had been home for some time.

The next day, I had to help my father, among whose several jobs was catering for small affairs, weddings and such. I spent much of the time washing dishes and reading Lovecraft—the Ballantine Beagle edition of *The Lurking Fear* (1971)—feeling fairly shattered. I tried the stuff once or twice again, determined to see if I could enjoy it. After all, Laing had said, "If I could turn you on, if I could drive you out of your wretched mind, if I could tell you I would let you know," and I figured I would give the drug a few chances of doing that. But I preferred grass, which could set me adrift on poetic daydreams and seemed to add a gentle background music to everything. LSD made me feel as if I had my finger stuck in an electric socket for several hours, and had the peculiar effect of making everything look as if it was made of tinsel, and sweating.

Later, I came to know several people who were into psychedelics, both during the resurgence of interest that happened in the late '80s and early '90s when I lived in Los Angeles, and during my time in London. With few exceptions, I've found that their conversation tends to be about their drug experiences or matters relevant to them. Like a recently converted believer, they have little interest in anything other than their new faith, which they are eager to share with you. Again, with a few exceptions, I've also found little of interest in the large body of drug literature that has grown up over the years. As DeQuincy pointed out long ago, drugs do not make one poetic or even interesting. Given opium, he said, a man who spends all day with oxen will dream of oxen. DeQuincy had fantastic dreams under opium because he was a poet. People who have written about their drug experiences—such as Huxley, or Baudelaire, or Walter Benjamin (a writer I would encounter years later)—are worth reading because they are interesting in the first place. It's their intelligence and ability to express themselves that makes their account of their experiences interesting and therefore profitable. At best, drugs can release what we already have inside us. As William James said of alcohol, they can release our "yea-saying" faculty and induce a mystical affirmation of life. It all depends on what we have inside us.

But drugs cannot be substituted for the hard work of "bringing forth what is within you," as the Gnostic Gospel of Thomas urges us to do—with good reason. Failure to do so, it warns, will "destroy you." Dreams remain dreams until they are *pressed* into reality by creative effort. Drugs can show us possibilities and potentialities of which we might otherwise remain ignorant. They may even be able to give us an idea of "who we are." But the difficult task of *becoming* ourselves remains in our hands.

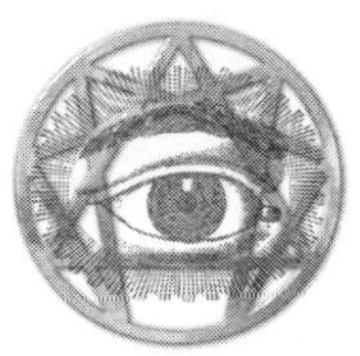

4

No Exit

In my senior year of high school, circa 1972–73, when I was sixteen and seventeen, my reading attracted the attention of someone who would have a very positive effect on my future, although he would not know how influential he was nor what that future would be. Before this, my obsession with books and ideas met with incomprehension and resistance from my parents and was the source of mild ribbing from my friends. Some of them did read, to keep up appearances, but nothing like I did. I wrote poetry too. Most of this I kept to myself, but I did show some friends, mostly girls, some poems. Sometimes we would gather at one of the hippie girls' homes after school, smoke pot, and someone would strum a guitar while someone else recited a poem. My interest in these gatherings was not solely literary but, although the girls liked me, they were not sexually attracted, so relations remained frustratingly platonic. Nevertheless, we were kindred spirits, people for whom the lyrics to a song were important. A popular book at the time was Leonard Cohen's *A Spice Box of Earth*, in the Bantam paperback edition circa 1968. Another was Lawrence Ferlinghetti's *A Coney Island of the Mind*, in the 1958 New Directions edition; oddly enough, Ferlinghetti didn't publish it under his own City Lights imprint.

I never met Leonard Cohen, but I did meet Ferlinghetti many years later, after I moved to London. At the time, I knew the London poet

Michael Horowitz, who was part of the 1960s London poetry scene, and Ferlinghetti was in town to take part in an event Michael had organized. When I met him, I told Ferlinghetti how important *A Coney Island of the Mind* was for me in my teens. "Yes," he said with a sigh. "That's what everyone tells me."

ALTHOUGH I WAS KEEN ON POETRY, this did not mean I necessarily got along with the English teachers, and a lacuna in my education appeared at the start of my senior year because of this. I don't remember her name, but because of some unruly behavior on my part, I was exiled from class by my English teacher and, for a week or two, spent that hour of the day in the library. This was no punishment, but it meant that I missed getting an introduction to Shakespeare. By the time I got a place in another class, the Bard was old news—if, indeed, he had been taught at all. I expect that my minimal appreciation of Shakespeare today stems from that week or so of exile. A loss, no doubt. But getting into that other class was worth it.

It was taught by a young teacher, Mr. Daler. I don't remember his first name, if I knew it. But he was what we would call "progressive." He was in his twenties and looked a bit like Bobby Kennedy. He listened to rock music. He was a fan of the Grateful Dead, and I remember him saying that the Moody Blues sounded like they had "read half of *Siddhartha*," which is conceivable. He obviously knew Hesse. He was also familiar with Lovecraft. When studying poetic forms, we came to the couplet and were asked to give an example. I submitted this from Lovecraft, which he attributes to the "mad poet, Abdul Alhazred," author of the aptly maddening but mercifully nonexistent *Necronomicon*: "That is not dead which can eternal lie / And with strange aeons even death may die."

That scored high marks with Mr. Daler, and one afternoon, when, with one or two other students—as well as another teacher—I went back to his flat to smoke pot, I saw he had quite a few Lovecraft and Ballantine Adult Fantasy paperbacks on his bookshelves. I can't remember what it was, but there was another assignment and, in answer to it, I wrote a line from William Blake's *Jerusalem*, "I must create a system, or be enslaved by another man's. My business is not to reason and compare; my business is to create." This went over well too.

Mr. Daler was keen on modern literature and once remarked that if he suggested teaching *Ulysses*, the school principal would probably think he meant Homer, not Joyce. It was in his class that we read *Catch-22* and also William Golding's *Lord of the Flies*. There was much discussion about the latter, and the class got to talking about how they would react if they found themselves, like the schoolboys in the book, stranded on a deserted island. Students identified with different characters and, when it came to me, Mr. Daler said I would be Piggy, the chubby, spectacled, brainy one who tries to keep up some semblance of civilization while the rest of the group descends into barbarity.

I didn't care for the physical traits—I did wear glasses but wasn't chubby—but was gratified at being recognized as an intellectual. I had also received some less than friendly treatment by my less-intellectual friends, but nothing as severe as Piggy had. Yet, even if this identification was less than ideal, it meant that here was at least one individual who saw the positive side to my bookishness, and recognized it as an asset and as an indication of some future life beyond the expectations of my peers.

This recognition was the first positive response from an older male I had received, and it was the first time I felt some kind of approval. It was also the first time I recognized that this approval was something I wanted. No double bind here. I won't say Mr. Daler became a role model, but he certainly became someone whose approval I sought and more importantly could receive by "being myself," something that up until then had not been the case.

I CAN'T SAY EXACTLY WHEN, but at some point during the school term Mr. Daler started giving me books to read. And while he taught the rest of the class the standard curriculum, he tested me on the reading he had given me. I suspect this was not following official procedure, but he was very likely bored and may have gotten a kick out of being a kind of mentor to me. So, he taught me one thing and the rest of the class another.

I talked with him about existentialism, which, along with the other fads making up the potpourri of early '70s pop philosophy, was all the rage. I had come across the term in my reading of Hesse, and R. D. Laing had talked about it. But I still wasn't sure exactly what it was. Mr. Daler helped clarify things by pushing me into the deep end. One of the books he gave me was Jean-Paul Sartre's *Existentialism is a Humanism* (1946). I later came to know this was an important work that established a significant difference between Sartre and Heidegger, who for me at the time was little more than another foreign name I mispronounced. What Sartre's famous postwar lecture amounted to for me then was at first a compound mystery—now I needed to know not only what existentialism meant, but also humanism.

It is in this lecture that Sartre formulated what became a defining insight of his brand of existentialism, the notion that in human beings "existence precedes essence." In a nutshell, this means that, unlike chairs or other man-made objects, we exist before we know why we do.[1] We turn up here without a *Rough Guide*—God did not create us; there is no reason for our existing at all. We are, as Heidegger said, "thrown into existence." This means we are free to create ourselves but absolutely responsible for our choices and decisions. We can't blame anyone else.

---

1. For Sartre, a chair, a book, an automobile, and other man-made objects have an "essence," a reason for existence before they are brought into being. But this is not the case with us. We exist before we know *why* we do—if, indeed, we ever find this out. This is the "essence," if you will, of our *freedom*. We decide on our reason for existing, we take responsibility for it. Those who avoid this are "inauthentic," and embrace some reason given to them by society, religion, or politics.

Trying to do so was a rejection of freedom. One form of doing this was being like everyone else.[2]

A lot of this no doubt went over my head (I reread the lecture recently, for the first time in decades), but this idea of "creating oneself" was not very different from "following the promptings of your true self." And both were about being who *you* were, not the person others (your parents, your teachers, even your friends) wanted you to be. I did my best, and wrote an essay about it—which may have been where I referenced the Blake quotation mentioned above. It must have been adequate, because Mr. Daler continued sending other books my way.

One book he gave me made a powerful impact at the time, and I've gone back to it often over the years. This was *Irrational Man* (1958), by William Barrett. Barrett was a professor of philosophy at New York University, remaining there until he retired in 1979. He had been something of a prodigy, starting at New York City College when he was fifteen. He was an editor at *Partisan Review* and a literary critic for *The Atlantic Monthly.* All of this, of course, I didn't know at the time, and found out only later. Barrett was part of a New York intellectual scene that included the poet Delmore Schwarz and the critic Philip Rahv. But he's best known for making the not-always-accessible philosophy known as existentialism, coming over from the Parisian *rive gauche*, available to the non-technical but interested reader.

Most people who had heard of existentialism associated it with berets, beatniks, jazz, and black turtlenecks—an image imported from the Café des Deux Magots and other Left Bank haunts that had become fashionable among the avant-garde in New York and San Francisco.

---

2. My chronology may be a bit off here. One important event for me during this time was a broadcast on the local PBS (Public Broadcasting Service) television station of a BBC dramatization of Sartre's *Roads to Freedom* trilogy. This was broadcast in the UK from September to December 1970. I can't remember exactly what year I watched it, but it may have been 1971, and I would have to have been already aware of Sartre and existentialism in order to have wanted to. It was rebroadcast in the UK in the summer of 2022. I watched it and found it as gripping as when I first saw it.

But Barrett took existentialism seriously. *Irrational Man* was the first book to introduce Kierkegaard, Nietzsche, Heidegger, Sartre, Camus, and other figures associated with existentialism to a wide American audience, an introduction Barrett had started with essays he'd written a decade earlier for *Partisan Review*, and which were later published as *What Is Existentialism?* (1964). Barrett went on to write other books addressing the theme of the loss of meaning in the modern world, a staple of existential thought, all of them very readable, as well as a memoir of his years on the New York cultural scene, *The Truants* (1982).

The Doubleday–Anchor paperback of *Irrational Man* that Mr. Daler put in my hand had a blue cover with the striking image of one of the sculptor Alberto Giacometti's tall, attenuated figures, suspended in space as if floating in a void. This spare, slender form symbolized the equally thin "being" of modern man—and, as I came to learn, "being" was a central concern of existentialism.

It is difficult now, fifty years later and after much time reading many books about existentialism in particular and philosophy in general, to capture the sense of excitement but also the mystery and sheer strangeness I felt just holding the book. My familiarity with it now makes recapturing that early ignorance almost impossible. Yet, if I try, I can get a taste of that first thrill, that sense of stepping out of the ordinary world and into one more real—even if, at the time, I didn't understand much of what Barrett said and wasn't aware of the historical context in which he placed existentialism. All that would come later. What I felt then was that I was being introduced to a whole world of people who saw things as I did, or who would at least understand me when I tried to tell them how I saw it.

A few years later, when I read *The Outsider*, a book that predated Barrett's *Irrational Man* by two years, I learned, among other things, that the Outsider "sees too deep and too much and what he sees is chaos." It is difficult to avoid anachronisms and to not project what I came to understand and feel some years later onto the less self-aware consciousness of my late teens. But I can say that this characterized my state at the time. I did see things others didn't—or, if they did, they seemed not to grasp their significance. More accurately, I can say that I saw through much of what everyone else seemed to accept as given and unquestionable.

The Gnostics, whom I later came to study through my interest in Jung, claimed that we live in a false world, that the universe of space and time and matter was the work of a kind of idiot god who believed he was the true creator but who had really usurped power from his master. They associated the Jehovah of the Bible with this false demigod, and I came to know that the poet William Blake felt much the same, and called that God "Old Nobodaddy."

Blake, too, knew that the world around us was more than it appeared to be, and that if we "cleansed" our "doors of perception," we would see it rightly. Huxley had taken Blake's phrase for the title of his book and many people I knew, myself included, were following his cue as to how our doors of perception could be cleansed. But the clarity of vision I experienced then wasn't prompted by taking a hallucinogen but by an increasing sense that, as the Gnostics believed, the world around me was false. Not in a metaphysical sense, although I would soon come to see that the world of space, time, and matter we inhabit is not all it seems to be. It was, as I was beginning to understand, false in an *existential* sense.[3]

One notion Barrett brought home in *Irrational Man* was the idea of "authenticity." Being "authentic" meant having an unavoidable confrontation with reality, seeking it out even, rejecting the illusions and stories we tell ourselves in order to give what is at bottom meaningless chaos some sense of necessity. The world around me seemed to be rife with falsehoods, untruths, pretense, with lies that everyone knew were lies but which no one admitted to aloud. It was rather like living in the fairy tale of *The Emperor's New Clothes*, but a version in which, even

3. It wouldn't be until some years later that I read Hans Jonas's work relating Gnosticism and existentialism, *The Gnostic Religion* (Boston: Beacon Press, 1958).

when the truth is pointed out, it makes no difference and the pretense is continued. If being "existential" meant recognizing this and rejecting it, I was all for it.

The austere form of Giacometti's sculpture was an expression of this rejection, and it linked modern art to what I took to be the "existential style." I became an indiscriminate devotee of everything modern: surrealism, expressionism, Dadaism, cubism—anything that seemed in some way to reject the normal world within which I was supposed to find a place for myself. That this all came from Europe helped, and my later journeys were not to the East but to the West. For a time I was very keen on the *art brut* of Jean Dubuffet, simply because it was so striking, raw, and unaesthetic. I remained a devotee of the surrealists for many years, and still have a nostalgic liking for André Breton, whose poetry I read at the time.

Around this time, I used to haunt the "Art and Music" room of the city library, looking through art books at reproductions of Picasso, Braque, Dali, Max Ernst, and Kandinsky—in the way I had indiscriminately read through books of modern poetry—stored in what were called the "stacks." I was also keen on foreign films, most of which I first became acquainted with not by seeing them but by reading their scripts. There was a wonderful series of books, whose title and publisher I've been unable to track down, that published the scripts along with stills from the films of Fellini, Bergman, Truffaut, Cocteau, and other avant-garde foreign filmmakers.

I became a great fan of Bergman's films, especially *The Seventh Seal* and *Wild Strawberries*, and also of Cocteau's *Testament of Orpheus* and *Blood of a Poet*. There was a television program broadcast late on Sunday nights, I think by NBC, called, I believe, *The Sunday Night Film Festival*, that played dubbed versions of foreign films. Before I started going to New York and seeing these films at places like the St. Marks Cinema or the Bleecker Street Cinema, whose ads I would see in the *Village Voice*, New York's underground newspaper, I first saw them on an old black-and-white television set in my room with the sound as low as possible, so my mother wouldn't come in and shut it off. One memorable event from this time was a screening the library held of Luis Bunuel and Salvador Dali's film *Un Chien Andalou* (1929), with its infamous scene of a woman's eye being sliced by a razor (I subsequently learned that a cow's eye had been used). Everyone who made up the "hip" contingent in school turned up at this, and much marijuana-inspired discussion followed.

Another book that made a powerful impact on me then was Sartre's novel *Nausea*, in the New Directions paperback edition that was published in 1959. I've already mentioned how my first experience of LSD induced in me a perception of things rather like how Roquentin, the protagonist of the book, sees the world. I later came to have a different idea of what Sartre's vision of *la nausée* means and what it tells us about the peculiarities of human consciousness. But, at the time I was impressed with Sartre's description of seeing the world without all of the comfortable illusions we cast over it to keep its absurd truth at bay. I made a habit at times of repeating a word over and over until it no longer carried any meaning but was simply a sound emitted from my mouth. I had already rejected religion; I was brought up Catholic but had already stopped going to church a few years earlier. (My mother continued to go, to pray for me, and eventually had a priest talk to me.)

Sartre's play *No Exit* was of course another existential must-read, as were Albert Camus's *The Stranger* and *The Myth of Sisyphus*, published in the Vintage paperbacks brought out in the 1960s, with the fantastic absurdist covers. His earlier novel, *A Happy Death*, with a cover featuring a Sannyasi wrapped in a yellow robe, was another favorite. Camus's "absurd" was the equivalent of Sartre's "nausea," and while these themes are generally associated with a nihilistic, pessimistic view of life, for me at the time they were a source of excitement and creativity. I was experiencing the breathtaking sense of freedom that came with the revelation that the explanations and reasons given for the "way things were" were no explanation at all, but merely arguments to maintain the illusions and to keep people like me from *finding out*. Later I would learn that such demolition work is only the first step in the process of arriving at some true relation to things—a necessary clearing away before the difficult task of creating new values begins.

I COULD SAY THAT A DIM AWARENESS of the need for that task of creating new values—or, at least, for a more positive approach to these existential insights—began when Mr. Daler suggested yet another book. As the end of term drew near, everyone at school talked about what they were doing next. Most of the people I knew were, like myself, going on to the state college in nearby Jersey City. My mother wanted me to attend a Catholic college, as my sister had, but I refused. When Mr. Daler asked what I intended to study, I mentioned Eastern philosophy. Like existentialism, this was also very popular at the time; unlike existentialism, it has remained so.

William Barrett had edited a selection of D. T. Suzuki's lectures; Suzuki was the leading exponent of Zen Buddhism, and Barrett's collection did for Zen what *Irrational Man* had done for existentialism.[4] I read this and a short book of Suzuki's called *What is Zen?* published by Harper and Row's Perennial Library series. The Beats were also interested in Zen; I had read and enjoyed Kerouac's *The Dharma Bums* (1958) more than I had *On the Road*. And I had read Alan Watts's *Beat Zen, Square Zen, and Zen* (1958) and his *The Way of Zen* (1957).

I had by then tried to sit and meditate, and it seemed that at times I could "see" whatever I was concentrating on rather like when I had taken acid, but in a much milder, gentler way and without the paranoia. Years later I would learn that what I was seeing was the thing's "is-ness," its "being," without the definitions we automatically place on our perceptions. Although I did not know it, I was practicing what I would later learn was the phenomenological technique of "bracketing," a kind

4. D. T. Suzuki, *Zen Buddhism: Selected Writings of D. T. Suzuki* (New York: Doubleday, 1956).

of conscious, purposeful *forgetting* of what we think we know about something, trying to see it fresh, without presuppositions.

This way of seeing was rather like Sartre and Camus's "nausea" and "absurd," respectively, but without the negative side effects, as it were. It was more like how Huxley had described his perceptions under mescaline. It was also, I believe, how poets see the world and why Blake could write of seeing "heaven in a wildflower." Again, I am looking back on early experiences and insights, and doing my best not to infect them with how I understand things now. But this way of seeing would, years later, become a central theme in some of the books I would write.

WHEN I MENTIONED MY INTENTION to study Eastern philosophy, Mr. Daler said, "Really?" and suggested I wait before deciding. Perhaps he thought I had a talent for Western philosophy—after all, I had been reading Sartre and Camus—and didn't want me following the current fashion of seeking "wisdom from the East." He then asked if I had come across a particular philosopher yet: Friedrich Nietzsche. I said I had.

On one of my increasingly frequent trips to the Barnes & Noble bookshop in New York (Mr. Daler had said Manhattan was the center of human consciousness at the time, and I took him at his word), I had picked up a paperback selection of Nietzsche's writings, translated by Oscar Levy, a German-Jewish scholar who first translated him into English. I hadn't got that far with it, but I had a vague idea that Nietzsche said that "God is dead," something with which I agreed at the time, and that he talked about some higher type of individual called the "superman." Supermen I of course knew about from the comics, and at the time there were religious advertisements on television telling viewers that God, in fact, wasn't dead.[5] But so far, I hadn't been gripped by what I had read of Nietzsche in the way that I had by Sartre or Hesse. (It's no secret that much of the appeal of existentialism was that it was

5. Years later, I would see bus hoardings in London telling me that he never existed.

as much a literary as a philosophical movement—also, to some extent, a fashion statement—which makes perfect sense, as it was a philosophy about life, not the classroom or study.)

I brought my copy of Nietzsche into class and showed it to Mr. Daler. He shook his head. "No," he said. "This is a bad translation. You need to read Nietzsche in the translations by Walter Kaufmann. Find some Nietzsche translated by him and read it before you decide on studying Eastern philosophy." So I did.

Walter Kaufmann was born in Freiburg, Germany, in 1921, just as the nascent National Socialist movement was getting started. He was brought up Lutheran, but at the age of eleven converted to Judaism; he subsequently learned that his grandparents were Jewish. Converting to Judaism and discovering you were part of a Jewish bloodline were not the most promising career moves in the Germany of the 1930s, and in 1939, just before the start of WWII, Kaufmann emigrated to the United States. There, he would eventually earn an MA and a PhD in philosophy from Harvard. He became a professor of philosophy at Princeton University, a haven at the time for *émigré* German intellectuals, attracting not only Einstein but the cultural philosopher Ernst Kahler and the Austrian novelist Hermann Broch, both of whom I would read in later years.

Early translations of Nietzsche into English suffered from a tendency to treat him as a prophet. More times than not, this led to turning his lucid, mobile, agile prose into bombast and portentous rhetoric. It is unfortunate that if there is one book Nietzsche is known for by Anglophone readers, it is *Thus Spoke Zarathustra*. This presents Nietzsche at his most poetic and prophetic, but it is also full of more than one lapse of taste. The mock-Biblical tone Nietzsche adopts in this book is unlike any of his others, and many of his readers did not grasp that Nietzsche was using it ironically. It was this orotund, oracular approach that his early English translators aimed at and unfortunately achieved.

German is not the most fluid language, and German philosophy is notoriously difficult, as I discovered years later when I studied Kant and Hegel. Nietzsche is one of the few philosophers who can write, and he is one of the even fewer German philosophers whom one can enjoy reading—Schopenhauer, his erstwhile mentor, is another. Unfortunately, Nietzsche's mastery of prose was lost on his early English translators, and the selection of his work I had tried reading was the work of one of the worst offenders. Whatever his value as a scholar, Oscar Levy's English rendering of Nietzsche achieved what today one might think impossible: it made him unreadable.

This was not the case with Walter Kaufmann. Perhaps the fact that Kaufmann was himself a poet made the difference. He was also a philosopher. Nietzsche wrote poetry, and although he is not as well-known to English-speaking readers in this capacity, his sensitivity to language makes him one of those difficult characters that academic scholars dislike. Is his work philosophy or literature? Nietzsche himself didn't care about these distinctions, but the same question was raised about figures like Sartre and Camus, and often used by Anglo-American philosophers to dismiss them. For analytical philosophers, the kinds of questions existentialism raised, about freedom and meaning, were frankly absurd—not in Camus's sense, but in the sense that they were considered meaningless. (Such hath Wittgenstein wrought.) One of the odd things about Kaufmann's rendition of Nietzsche is that he presents him as one of the forerunners of existentialism, but at the same time as a kind of forerunner of the analytical philosophy that existentialism rejected.[6] As one of his later French interpreters, Gilles Deleuze, said of Nietzsche, his thought is "nomadic," mobile, crossing boundaries, and not fixed to one school.

Nietzsche had also suffered under the Nazis—not personally, he was long dead by the time Kaufmann had to leave Germany to escape Hitler, but his reputation did after his work fell into Nazi hands. One of

6. This was an approach taken by Arthur Danto in *Nietzsche as Philosopher* (New York: Columbia University Press, 1965).

the tragic ironies of Nietzsche's life—as well as of the history of ideas—is that after his collapse into madness, in Turin, Italy, in 1889, control of his work passed to his sister, Elizabeth Förster-Nietzsche, a virulent anti-Semite, Aryan supremist, and later supporter of Hitler. (Nietzsche himself wrote about the "great race swindle," and once called for all anti-Semites to be shot; he was also a great critic of German militarism.)

Nietzsche lingered on, suffering general paresis (general paralysis of the insane) until his death in 1900. During that decade, his sister used to dress him in a toga and seat him at a window, where she would introduce prestigious guests to her famous brother, who was oblivious to everything around him. (When I later wrote my book about Rudolf Steiner, I came to learn he was one of these visitors.)

At the time of his mental collapse, Nietzsche was practically unknown. By the time of his death, he had become a worldwide phenomenon, influencing an entire generation of writers, artists, thinkers, and musicians—practically everyone on the A-list of early twentieth-century culture. When Hitler came to power, Elizabeth offered her brother's work to the Nazis on a platter, and hack Nazi scholars and editors published mutilated versions of his books, edited in such a way as to make him sound like a precursor of national socialism. One of the books thus appropriated was *Thus Spoke Zarathustra*.[7] In his last days, Nietzsche had a premonition of what would happen after his death. In his poignant autobiography, *Ecce Homo*, a book about how "one becomes who one is," Nietzsche pleaded that he not be confounded "with what I am not." Sadly, this was a recurring fate in Nietzsche's posthumous life.[8] He

---

7. Possibly the worst example of this editorial mutilation was the edition of Nietzsche's notebooks published under the Nazis as *The Will to Power*, and presented as a grand metaphysical opus, the culmination of his work. It is nothing of the kind. It is what it is: Nietzsche's notebooks, brilliant as anything else he wrote, but not a book, and certainly not one presaging the philosophy of national socialism. The later edition edited by Walter Kaufmann and R. J. Hollingdale clarified this.

8. See my essay that looks at the history of Nietzsche's various misappropriations: Gary Lachman, "Trickle Down Metaphysics: From Nietzsche to Trump," Gary Lachman blog, February 11, 2023.

also wished that he had not written *Thus Spoke Zarathustra* in German.

Kaufmann had a double task: to improve on the earlier, clumsy English translations and to rehabilitate Nietzsche's reputation.[9] These two birds were dispatched with a single stone. Kaufmann's translations turned what had been stentorian rhetoric into clear, lively thought, and made unmistakable the fact that Nietzsche, while no angel (he said he'd rather be a satyr than a saint, and a buffoon best of all), would have had no truck with Nazi thugs. The thought was difficult, yes, dangerous even, certainly challenging. But the language that expressed it was vital. As Nietzsche said about the only god he could believe in: his prose "danced." Nietzsche said he had not written his books with ink but with blood. This was not abstract philosophy conducted in the study or classroom, to be put aside when the lesson ended. It was living thought engaged with the question of how to live, and to be alive even more, the "life more abundant" announced in the Gospels that Nietzsche so eloquently rejected. It was, as Kaufmann and William Barrett had both argued, existential thought.

Today, I'm not sure what work of Nietzsche's translated by Kaufmann I first read. He had edited a collection of excerpts from writers and thinkers considered part of the existential tradition, *Existentialism from Dostoevsky to Sartre* (1956), and the selections from Nietzsche's work he included here may have been the first I read. Mr. Daler may have given me a copy of this, or I may have found it at Barnes & Noble (I had by that time discovered their secondhand branch) or the city library. Depending on how far back one wished to go, existentialism could be seen to have its roots in figures like St. Augustine and Pascal. Or rather,

9. Along with Kaufmann, R. J. Hollingdale was the other translator to rehabilitate Nietzsche's standing in the English-speaking world. He was not a philosopher, as Kaufmann was, but he did write an excellent introduction to Nietzsche's life and work, *Nietzsche: The Man and His Philosophy* (Cambridge: Cambridge University Press, 1999 revised edition). Hollingdale also translated Goethe, Schopenhauer, and E. T. A. Hoffmann in the beautiful old Penguin editions with classic paintings on their covers.

an existential sensibility can be found in these figures—even in Plato, in the early dialogues, in which Socrates explores the question of the "good life."

Kaufmann's selection provided my first acquaintance with the work of writers I had so far only read about, but hadn't read. Barrett's *Irrational Man* had provided an analysis and historical context, but Kaufmann's selection gave me small helpings of thinkers with whom I would become better acquainted over the years. Some I had read, like Sartre, Camus, and Kafka. But I had yet to read Kierkegaard (credited with getting the modern existential ball rolling), Rilke (a poet), Dostoevsky, Jaspers, Heidegger, and Nietzsche. I would later become familiar with them all—Rilke's *Duino Elegies* would become a kind of sacred text for me at one point. But then, it was Nietzsche who made the most impact.

Why was that? When I look at the selection from Nietzsche's work in Kaufmann's collection today, I see that he starts with an excerpt from Nietzsche's early essay "Schopenhauer as Educator," from his book *Untimely Meditations*. Nietzsche asks what traits are shared by all people of all lands, and he concludes that men everywhere are timid and lazy. Their timidity is displayed in their aversion to stand out in a crowd, their desire to remain part of the herd, and to so avoid the acrimony of their neighbors, who also do their best to be like everybody else. (I would later learn that such herd-mentality is shared by those whom Heidegger referred to as "they.") Their laziness is expressed in their desire to avoid the effort involved in breaking free of the herd and in their taste for comfort.

Sadly, this is still true today, the present writer being no exception. But what of those who are not so timid and not so lazy? "The human being who does not wish to belong to the mass must merely cease being comfortable with himself; let him follow his conscience which shouts at him: 'Be yourself! What you are at present doing, opining, and desiring, that is not really you . . .'"

This is the message I had heard from Jung, from Hesse, from Sartre, and now here it was again. All three, I had learned, had read Nietzsche and been influenced by him. Perhaps it was time I did the same.

KAUFMANN HAD TRANSLATED and edited *The Portable Nietzsche* for Viking Press—with its purple cover sporting a woodcut of Nietzsche with his enormous moustache—and somehow a copy of this fell into my hands. Having written what I have above, about how *Thus Spoke Zarathustra* in some ways gives a wrong impression about Nietzsche's style, I must admit that, like many others who came across him at an impressionable age, it was this book that made me a Nietzschean, insofar as anyone could be a Nietzschean. In his poem "Out of the High Mountains," which closes *Beyond Good and Evil*, Nietzsche's nomad character is affirmed. "Only those who change stay akin to me," he tells his readers.

The apparent paradox is emblematic of his thought. To be the same as Nietzsche, you must be different. That is, you, too, must change, must *become*. To be a Nietzschean does not mean to follow Nietzsche, but to become who you are, although, to be sure, many faux Nietzscheans and much vulgarization of his ideas came in the wake of his death—and not only Nazis were responsible. Like all good teachers, Nietzsche can help show you the way to yourself; but once the path is clear, you must walk it alone, even if it means walking away from Nietzsche. (Bad teachers show you the way to *them*.)

The same is true of Jung and Hesse, or Sartre. Zarathustra himself tells the disciples that have gathered around him to leave him, to mistrust him, and to follow their own path. "You had not yet sought yourselves and you found me," he tells them. Now it was time for them to lose him and find themselves. I had been in the process of finding—or creating, the difference is often difficult to distinguish—myself for a while by then, and now I, too, had found Nietzsche.

It is impossible for me to relate in any chronological order how I came under Nietzsche's spell. The best I can try to do here is to give a general impression of the effect he had on me. Again, I repeat, I was no young genius, absorbing Nietzsche's philosophy easily. There was much I didn't understand and, like many who rejected Nietzsche, much of what he said did seem bizarre, and I would only understand it some years later—if, indeed, I do understand it. But there was some powerful immediate attraction. There was something in his voice that made me feel he was speaking to *me*, something I had felt when reading *Demian*, which is the most Nietzschean of Hesse's novels.[10]

This, of course, is a common phenomenon with writers who mean something to us, but in Nietzsche's case, it had a peculiarly seductive, or I should say persuasive, power. This is because so much of his rhetoric spoke of the future, and I couldn't help but think that the future he had in mind was the one in which I lived. In *The Antichrist*, written in the last firework display of his brilliance before the madness set in, Nietzsche tells his readers that he wrote not for today, nor even for tomorrow, but for the "day after tomorrow." Again, at the time he was writing, Nietzsche's books went mostly unread. He did not believe anyone alive at the time could understand him, and this gives his writing an *intimate* quality for the readers who did come to him—the feeling, illusory as it may be, that you are part of a small group, perhaps one of the future readers he hoped and longed for.

The future Nietzsche had in mind was one in which the figure he called the *Übermensch* would play a great part. Kaufmann went against the standard translation of this as "superman," instead sticking to the original German and offering "overman." It is unfortunate that the Nazi tar still sticks to popular definitions of the *Übermensch*, who is not some muscular Aryan, lording it over the lesser beings around him. Readers with any familiarity with Nietzsche soon discover that his overman has nothing to do with any master race. Nietzsche was emphat-

---

10. In 1919, Hesse published an essay, "Zarathustra's Return," in which Nietzsche's prophet calls for German youth to not give in to bitterness and resentment following their nation's defeat in WWI.

ically not racist, and spoke well of the Jews, nor was the overman in any way a biological concept. In his notes, he points out that humanity is an end, meaning that no new species of human would supplant *homo sapiens*. The overman is not a product of biology or blood—nor, as is often thought today, of technology—but of culture. The question isn't what new species will humanity give way to, a query that excites proponents of current transhuman and posthuman philosophies, but what type of human should we aim at being?

Needless to say, this is a question with a long history. Race has nothing to do with it, and going by Nietzsche's remarks about his fellow Germans, he certainly didn't believe they were overman material. The overman for Nietzsche meant, as he remarked in *Ecce Homo*, "a type that has turned out supremely well." Such types could appear in any race, any nation, and under the most diverse conditions. In the same breath, he repudiated the "scholarly oxen" who suspected him of Darwinism—the idea that "natural selection," whatever that might be, will produce overmen in the way that, so Darwinists believed, it produced us.

What was needed, Nietzsche said, was the "great and rare art" of "giving style to one's character." This required discipline—not the discipline of a doctrine or a belief, but that of art. This was the exact opposite of the hippies' ethos of "letting it all hang out" and "getting back to nature." As Jung had said about individuation, and as I later learned about esoteric teachings, this was a work *against* nature. This was a conscious molding of one's self, an education of one's self, as in the tradition of the *Bildungsromane* that Hesse had written. It was an attempt at self-evolution, and it was through Nietzsche that I first became aware of the idea of a creative evolution, the notion that I could *aim* at becoming something more than myself, which, as I would later understand, was at the same time a process of becoming fully myself.

Years later, I would come across a formula for self-creation offered by the early English Nietzschean, A. R. Orage, who later became a student of Gurdjieff, himself a proponent of a conscious evolution. "Evolution is altogether an imaginative process: you become what you have been led to imagine yourselves to be." I might not have been able to formulate this as lucidly and concisely then, but in some way, I intuited that this was what Nietzsche was about.

One other idea that Nietzsche put forth in *Zarathustra* excited me: this was what he called "eternal recurrence." This is the at first somewhat disheartening notion that the life one has led, and all of the history that led up to that life, will repeat itself exactly as it has been, eternally, and has already repeated itself endless times over. If we think of eternal recurrence as reincarnating, not into a new life, as a different person, but into the same life and as exactly the same person, we can get an idea of what Nietzsche means (think of the film *Groundhog Day*). The phenomenon of déjà vu, the feeling that some event has happened before, is a psychological taste of eternal recurrence. For Nietzsche, it was linked to his "formula for greatness"—*amor fati,* the "love of fate"—that would have nothing different, not in the past nor the future. Such a love would not only endure such a fate, but even will it.

At first this strikes us as a monstrous prospect, and I can't now say exactly why I was attracted to the idea and didn't reject it as mad. Perhaps I was attracted to it precisely because it was so unpalatable; it seemed to put the full weight of existence on me, and I was determined not to turn away from reality, however unpleasant it was. Years later, when I lived in Los Angeles and worked at a metaphysical bookshop, I used to scandalize Buddhists and other proponents of reincarnation by adhering to this ostensibly grim doctrine. But there was a logic behind the idea.

Nietzsche tells us that if we have ever felt a moment of happiness, of beauty, of love for life, we must know that it is linked to all the other moments of life. If we say "yes" to that moment, we must say "yes" to all that had gone before, as well as to all that will come. Nietzsche tried to work out a mathematical proof for recurrence, but his attempts at this in *The Will to Power* are not convincing. More important than such proof was seeing eternal recurrence as a thought experiment. In *The Gay Science,* the book that preceded *Zarathustra* and in which Nietzsche first proposes recurrence (as well as the death of God), this is how he presents it: as a monumental "what if?" He asks how we would respond if a demon came to us and told us that recurrence was true. Would we "gnash our teeth" at such a horror? Or have we experienced a "tremendous moment" that would make such a prospect desirable? Could we say not only "yes" to life—our life exactly as it has been—but "encore"?

It is a considerable question. Who but those "who had turned out well" could consider such a possibility with anything but misgiving? For Nietzsche, accepting recurrence was a test of one's overman potential.

My seeing the "isness" of things—their "being"—led to a sense of the poignancy and preciousness of existence. The sheer fact that anything existed when there could just as easily be nothing gave everything a strangeness, as if being—existence itself—was the rarest of things. This blended with what I was beginning to feel after reading Nietzsche. Being seemed delicate, fragile, and in need of protection. Although he "philosophized with a hammer," Nietzsche was a gentle, even timid character who famously asked a friend to propose to the woman he loved because he was too shy to broach the subject. As I later came to learn, this existential preciousness, in fact, is the insight that Rilke expresses in the *Duino Elegies*, in which he charges mankind with the task of saving existence from oblivion by drawing it *inward*, making it "invisible," an idea I later drew on in my book *The Caretakers of the Cosmos*.

I became a life-affirmer then, one of Nietzsche's "yea-sayers." It was a more positive stance than the absurdist one I had been taking. It seemed a step forward. It was also apolitical. Nietzsche had no interest in politics, but, as I soon came to learn, Sartre and the other Parisian existentialists were tripping over themselves to be *engagée*. I had no interest in Marxism or any of the other radical political ideologies the French seem to enjoy so much. I also had no interest in the Freudian-Marxist mélange offered by the New Left philosopher Herbert Marcuse, a popular '60s campus figure, and would only years later read some of the Frankfurt School. Nietzsche had set himself the task of overcoming the nihilism that had become routine by the time I became aware of it. Kurt Vonnegut may have written funny, absurd books about it, and Sartre gripping drama, but Nietzsche saw the need to go beyond such black humor and to take the question seriously. I agreed with him.

A READER OF THESE AUTOBIOGRAPHICAL REFLECTIONS may wonder if all I did during my high school years was read books and immerse myself in abstruse questions of existential philosophy. That did take up quite a bit of my time, but of course I was also involved in the usual life of the average teenager, at least, of my generation. Anyone observing me then would not have noticed anything particularly remarkable or different about me; the one exception to this was Mr. Daler. I in no way stood out as someone "most likely to succeed"—quite the opposite, which made my later musical success something of a surprise. I was not particularly popular, and the girls I was interested in weren't interested in me. I was sexually frustrated and made use of my father's pornography collection. I was not a brilliant student; in some courses, like math and foreign languages, I did so poorly I had to attend summer classes. I wanted to study German—a nod to Hesse and Nietzsche—but was forced to take Spanish and French, and failed both.

I listened to rock music. I argued with my parents and took drugs. I was depressed and fantasized about getting as far away from New Jersey as possible—something I did manage to do, having lived in Los Angeles and now London. I was painfully self-conscious, unhappy with my looks, and hated having photographs taken of myself. I was at different times utterly convinced of my genius, which had yet to produce any evidence of itself other than my indiscreet journal, and filled with the corrosive self-loathing peculiar to one's late teens. Like many others at that age, I was filled with the teenage angst that makes nihilism and an absurd, meaningless universe appealing prospects.

I don't know if it is the case with other cultures—I think not—but Americans seem to see their high school years as the best time of their life. This may be a relatively recent development, brought about by the nostalgia industry in popular culture (Steven Spielberg's films, for example) and the romanticism about the 1950s that took root in the 1970s—all that Americana about having sex in the backseat of a car that Bruce Springsteen tapped into.

Did my parents pine for their teenage years—the 1930s and '40s, during the Depression and WWII? In more recent times, through the miracle of social media, people from our school days with whom we might otherwise not be in touch, either through chance or by design, now "like" our Facebook posts and expect us to like theirs regularly. I also have a sense that, since my generation (I was a late boomer), there has been a progressive infantilization of the population—an obsession with youth linked to an avoidance of the responsibilities of adulthood. This may be what the '60s hath wrought. Of course this is all subjective and I could be mistaken, but when I look at photographs of earlier times, say the 1930s or '40s, everyone looks a bit more adult—not to mention better dressed.

I don't share this American *Sehnsucht* for my teens. Nietzsche said the major difficulty he had in accepting eternal recurrence in his own life—which was a peculiarly miserable one filled with illness, loneliness, and lack of recognition—was that it would mean his sister would recur too. There are, of course, greater evils—think of all the catastrophes, man-made and natural, that would be repeated. But the idea of going through high school again—now, that is a consideration.

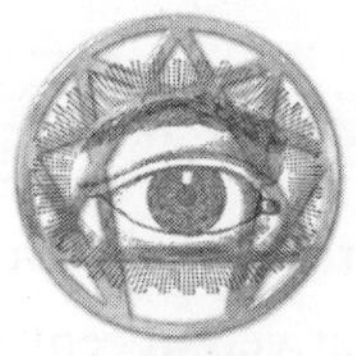

5
Blood of the Poet

I graduated from high school in June 1973. I was seventeen. I started college in September that year, and so was about a year younger than most of the other students. College was not radically different from high school. The campus was larger and there were more students, most of whom I didn't know. Some friends from high school did attend, but we were rarely in the same class. What I remember most about the campus was that the college radio station played Pink Floyd's *Dark Side of the Moon* in the quad practically continuously. That, and the smell of marijuana that lingered in the air. Today, I would not find this appealing, but back then it was. It may have been the tail end of the hippie days, but you would not have thought it.

I would return to university in California a decade later and earn a degree, but my first experience of college was brief. I left sometime in 1974, during my second semester, and entered my life of crime. That is too romantic a way of putting it, to be sure, but the truth is that until I wrote about this time in *New York Rocker*, my memoir of my rock and roll years, I didn't realize that I had been a juvenile delinquent.[1] "Juvenile," though, is not quite correct, as I had by then turned

1. Gary Valentine, *New York Rocker: My Life in the Blank Generation* (London: Sidgwick & Jackson, 2002). The title comes from *New York Rocker* magazine, published by Alan Betrock, who in early 1975 produced the first Blondie recordings that I play on.

eighteen—a fact that led to consequences. At the time, I thought of them as a necessary part of my life as a poet—the need for a wide range of experience, to break the rules and cross the boundaries that the less bold remain within. In a word, to pay my dues. Today I am not so sure.

During my short stay at college my academic performance remained on par with my high school work. I did well in courses that interested me, and poorly in what bored me. Even though Mr. Daler had advised otherwise, I did take a course in Eastern religions, and enjoyed it. One of the books assigned was Huston Smith's *The Religions of Man* (1958); years later, in California, when working at the Bodhi Tree Book Shop, I would meet Smith, who gave a talk there. Oddly enough, I took a course in philosophy, but it bored me and I didn't do well in it. It was a course in critical thinking, and didn't encourage reflection on the big questions I had spent much time pondering. "What is the meaning of life?" did not turn up on the exam. I managed to get by in the science courses that were mandatory, but just barely, and avoided math. I enjoyed and did well in an esthetics course, in which we read Dewey's *Art and Experience*, although today I have no idea what his esthetic theories are. A course in mythology had us reading Ovid's *Metamorphosis*. I enjoyed it but remember some friction between the teacher and myself. Over what, I can't recall.

The class I did best in was English. I continued to write poetry. In my last year at high school, a poem and an essay of mine were published in the school magazine. I don't remember much of either, and if I retained a copy of the magazine it was fairly soon lost in the wreckage. I also remember the ritual of spending the last days of high school having my yearbook signed by classmates, and my signing theirs. I remember writing a poem for the occasion and inscribing it in various yearbooks. If I had a persona then, it was that of the poet. The poetry did not live up to the persona, but at that point this didn't matter. As I came to learn during my musician days, the right attitude and look can make up for a great deal.

The English instructor at college recognized my interest in poetry and encouraged it. He also suggested that I try other forms of writing—fiction and essays. He wasn't a guide in the way that Mr. Daler had been, but he did think I had writing potential and that I should develop it. I did—at least, I filled a notebook with poems and ensured that this time it would not be discovered. Eventually, I decided that I had to *do* something with them. That an English teacher thought they were worth writing was good. But what would other people think?

During that year, I gave my first solo performance, reading my poetry at the college café. It was an evening of music, with guitars and bongo drums and singing, and somewhere in the middle of this, I took to the stage and read a few poems. I had a sheaf of poems in one hand and a cigarette in another. I was nervous. At that stage, I was not a good reader, and my performance that evening left much to be desired. At one point someone in the audience asked if I could speak louder. I replied "I don't think so," and carried on mumbling and puffing on my cigarette.

But, if the poetry was bad and my performance no better, I at least looked like a poet—in my eyes, if in no others. My hair was long. I wore an old corduroy jacket and a turtle-neck top, and baggy jeans and sneakers. I had taken to wearing tinted glasses. My eyesight was bad, and had been since I was young. I hated wearing glasses and, in order to salvage some self-respect, when I got older I insisted on getting ones with a tint. Later, this self-consciousness about my appearance led to my wearing dark glasses practically all the time.

I CONTINUED MY INDISCRIMINATE READING while in college. Now it is all something of a blur, but I know I read the Beats, books on Zen and other Eastern religions, and books about drugs and altered states of consciousness. I was quite interested in these and, to be honest, much of my time I spent getting high and cutting class and listening to music. Other influences informed a drift away from my studies. In my last year at high school, I became friends with three sisters, and it was through knowing them that I would leave college.

I came to know them through an older student I had become friends with—the one, in fact, who had introduced me to marijuana. He was the first of a few friends who subsequently showed signs of mental instability. For some, this developed into a full-blown mental breakdown—at least three friends from that time spent time in mental hospitals. With others, it was less extreme.

The sisters came from a troubled family. The oldest was my age, the others were a year and two years younger. The story was that their mother had left their father and run away with their marriage counsellor. They were not exactly feral but they were wild, and gave off a scent of sex. Their father was Czech and their mother Turkish, and the combination gave them an exotic character.

I had an immediate crush on the oldest sister. She wore an "Enjoy Coca-Cola" T-shirt without a bra, and I liked seeing her nipples poking up from under it. She once did an impromptu belly dance in it, in a diner we hung out in, and impressed the clientele. Her hair was in Little Orphan Annie ringlets, and she had a pouty, slightly indecent smile. She knew I was smitten, but she was with my older friend and she saw me as a brother, and treated me like one. I became "part of the family" and started to hang out with the three of them. On one occasion, we took acid; what I remember from that "trip" was hearing the Emerson, Lake & Palmer track "From the Beginning" ("It's all very clear / You were meant to be here / From the beginning") going round in my head and thinking the puddles we were walking through were clouds.

It was all pretty harmless. But when their parents separated, the two older sisters went to live with their father, who moved out of Bayonne to a neighboring city. He worked nights, so they had the big flat to themselves. It took an effort to get out there—it was a long bus ride away—but their place soon became party central.

I went there often, with different friends. We smoked pot, drank, listened to rock music, with the usual fumbling and groping occasionally leading to private matters behind a bedroom door. The older teen who had turned me on to pot came, but he soon showed signs of becoming odd. He would drift off into dissociative states, or start telling us about Jesus. After a while he stopped showing up. The sister who had been with him didn't mind. By that time, different boys were competing for her attentions and receiving them. I was then interested in the middle sister, who was near my age, but she didn't share my interest.

The youngest lived with her mother, but she would come for weekends, and on one of these she decided to take me to bed. She was sixteen and experienced. I was older and not. Having failed to score with her sister, and having enough alcohol and marijuana in me to inhibit any resistance, I did not object. I liked her and thought she was cute, but wasn't interested in her sexually. But she was in me, and made that clear. She took me in hand, led me to the bedroom, and that was it. I lost my virginity. I can't say that I remember much about it now, and I suspect it was over fairly quickly. But that didn't matter. *That* it had happened was more important than how it had.

For some reason, after that, I didn't see the sisters for some months. I had by then started college and, one afternoon while I was walking near the campus, a bus stopped and I saw two girls get off. It was the two older sisters. They had seen me from the bus. They were happy to see me and I was glad to see them. They explained that their father had passed away—I don't remember from what but I do remember them saying that he had taken to drinking heavily—and they'd had to leave their old flat. But they had gotten a new one now in Jersey City, near Journal Square, where the PATH trains to New York were. They were living there; their younger sister was still living with their mother, but she visited often. Did I want to see it? It was just a short ride away. And their sister would be coming soon and would love to see me.

I describe the flat in *New York Rocker*. It was, as you might expect, a crash pad. When their sister arrived, we wound up having sex again. I was too passive to say no, and too affection starved to want to. To hit myself over the head about it now would be pointless. Yes, I was stupid. But relations at home were at their worst and, whatever one might think about the repercussions, these sisters provided me with more of a sense of belonging than I had with my family. They accepted me and provided an approval I didn't get anywhere else. But this family reunion wasn't without its surprises. Before I left, I discovered that my "girlfriend"—it was now official that this was who she was—was pregnant.

I might as well have been told she could fly or that she was an alien. I don't think any of us really understood what it meant that she was pregnant. We were still kids ourselves. Although, as I would come to understand, in the eyes of the law some of us were not.

I must have stayed there for some time, because by the time I got home it was late. My mother wasn't happy about this, and another argument started up. That was it. I'd had it, and I suspect the news I had just received must have added to my state of mind. I threw some things into a backpack—my notebook being one of them—and headed out the door. The sisters had given me their telephone number, and at a phone booth I called and asked if I could come there. Of course I could. So, I did.

At that point, I started living there. For a while I tried to keep up with my classes but circumstances were against me. Soon enough I gave it up and dropped out of college.

Around this time, I also came into the orbit of two other friends I talk about in detail in *New York Rocker*. One would earn a place for himself in the more obscure annals of rock trivia—as well as some considerable royalties—as the lyricist to some songs Blondie would record. The other would go from being something like the William S. Burroughs Jr. of Bayonne, New Jersey, to becoming a born-again Christian. The first passed away some years ago, after many years of being restricted to a wheelchair, having lost his legs after falling onto a subway track. He was a labile, unstable character who took too many drugs than was good for him, and he would spend more than one stretch in a mental home. The last I heard about the other is that he was leading a flock of the faithful in Manchester, England. If this is true, that the two of us wound up living in the UK by very different paths seems one of those odd coincidences that life occasionally throws up.

Like my late unfortunate friend above, whom I'll call "R," this other, whom I'll call "P," also took drugs—many of them. I'm not sure how I became involved with him. I had heard about him from other friends—one was the musician who became the drummer in Blondie. He, the drummer, was always ahead of the curve in what would be the "next big thing," and when everyone else was listening to the Grateful Dead, he had picked up on David Bowie and what would be called "glitter rock." P was another glitter devotee, and among the stories I had heard about him was one about how he and R had dressed up as "droogs" from Kubrick's film *A Clockwork Orange*, and made it to the television news when they crashed a Halloween bash at the Waldorf Astoria hotel in New York at which the New York Dolls, a local glitter band, were playing.

P had a striking look. He was tall and thin, wore sleeveless black T-shirts, dark "granny glasses," a Chairman Mao cap and jacket, heavy army boots, tight black jeans, mascara, rouge, lipstick and—as Alex in Kubrick's film did—false eyelashes on one eye. He had a reputation for violence and was said to have nearly killed someone who had called him a faggot. He worked for the Port Authority in New York, had his own flat, and his father was a cop. He was not an intellectual but he had read Nietzsche and was keen on the *Übermensch*. In one of his songs, during his ersatz fascism phase, Bowie sang that we "gotta make way for the *homo superior*," and P identified with this. He certainly felt he was, in Nietzsche's much-abused phrase, "beyond good and evil." He was a dominant type and liked to make an impression. Most of all, I think he liked to scare people and was inclined to push things to the brink. He was not interested in being liked.

I suspect I first met P when visiting him to buy pot, which he sold to "friends," as he explained. Clem—the Blondie drummer—introduced us. He had a small, dark, basement flat, not far from the sisters' new place. It reeked of cheap incense and grass. Candles stuck out of empty wine bottles, ashtrays overflowed, the Velvet Underground blared, and the furniture was rickety at best. P was stranger, wilder, more extreme than anyone I had met before. I was eager to break away from my life at home, but also from my friends. Around them, I felt ineffectual. I was not a musician, as most of them were. I wasn't popular and no one took my poetry seriously. Based on the poetry itself, this was perhaps understandable. But I wanted to be taken seriously, in the way that Mr. Daler had taken my interest in philosophy seriously. He had taken me aside, separated me from the rest of the class, and introduced me to ideas that changed my life.

Something similar, but on a different scale, would happen with P. In the same way that I felt a sense of "belonging" with the sisters, I felt I had more in common with him than with my other friends. I hadn't come across the term Outsider yet, and didn't call myself one, but I felt instinctively that P was one, just as I was.

Eventually it would become clear that we had less in common than I thought, and that at bottom P was a manipulative individual. If he was not quite a sociopath, he was not far short of one. His main interest was in dominating others. My hunger for acceptance made me vulnerable to this, and it soon happened that I found myself in the kinds of double binds that had so often made my childhood confusing and miserable. There was nothing sexual in our relations. Although he probably would have appreciated the allusion, there was nothing of Leopold and Loeb about our friendship. If anything, it was closer to Emil Sinclair and Max Demian, although, to be sure, P was no model of individuation.

THE SITUATION WITH MY NEW "FAMILY" could not last very long, and as I recount in *New York Rocker*, things quickly fell apart. It would be tedious to tell the story here. The sisters lost their apartment, and for a time all of us crammed into P's dank basement flat. He wasn't keen on the sisters—they were not *Übermensch* material—nor on the drug addicts they had become acquainted with and who took to hovering around the flat. He took extreme measures to get rid of them.

His father being a policeman had afforded him some immunity in the past. He trusted in this, and called the police to inform them that junkies were on the premises. The police did come to take them away, but P's immunity proved less secure than he'd thought. We were all arrested, and spent a day or two in jail before being released. P gave up his flat after this. I had no choice but to return home. Understandably, I was not particularly welcome, but worse was to come. Not long after I returned, my "girlfriend's" mother discovered that her daughter was pregnant, as well as who was responsible, and called the police. Shortly after, a police sergeant I knew from previous encounters turned up at our door and informed me that I was being arrested for statutory rape. It was not the best homecoming.

In the end, the case was dropped, but only after much pain and misery. The girl refused to have an abortion; although we had grown to like each other, I did not want to marry her. But unless I did, her mother would press charges. I was put on probation and had to attend psychiatric sessions as a "sex offender," a distinction that would turn up later. My paternity was never absolutely determined, but there was little doubt I was the father. At the hearing, the mother didn't show, and so the case never went to court. It came to a sad end anyway. The girl had the baby but it never left the hospital, and died after a year. Long before then, I had stopped seeing her or her sisters.

Life back at home was not very good. Understandably, my parents were disgusted with me. I couldn't blame them. I was disgusted with myself. I had dropped out of college; had been living in squalor; was arrested for drugs, then statutory rape; and now was back in my room, with little but a messy tragedy to show for it. I didn't want to return to college, and took a job at a warehouse to earn my keep. I had no idea what to do. After a while, I heard that P had gotten a new place, this time in New York. R and I visited often. I lost the job at the warehouse and, on the pretext of looking for work, I would head across the Hudson, sign up at some employment agencies, then head to P's in the East Village. Soon enough, I moved in.

Life in the storefront on East 10th Street that P was renting was as squalid as before, but at least now it was in New York. That was worth a great deal, and made up for a lot. Nevertheless, my relocating there required some sacrifices. I wasn't working, and the little money I had saved was soon gone. Until I got more, basic things—like eating—would be problematic, and what I remember most about this period is feeling hungry most of the time. A few years later, when I read Knut Hamsun's *Hunger*, about his days wandering around Kristiania (Oslo), starved half out of his mind, I could say I knew from experience what he was talking about.

I panhandled once or twice, but the return was minimal and whatever self-respect I had left soon made me stop. The one time I shoplifted, I was almost caught, so I decided once was enough. I attended lectures by followers of the Reverend Sun Myung Moon because they offered free coffee and doughnuts, but they soon outed me. I went to some extreme lengths, even cutting my lip on purpose, pretending I had bitten into a piece of glass, so I could skip out on a meal at a diner. All this is in *New York Rocker*. It was all very tiring and stressful.

It was at this point that I sold off my comic collection, bit by bit. I would make my way back home and sneak into the basement, where my collection was kept, and bundle a stack of *Spider-Man* or *The Avengers* or *Fantastic Four* comics into my backpack. There was a shop on First Avenue near Houston Street that bought them. The fellow running it knew I was desperate, and that he was getting them at practically a song. But I had long stopped reading them, and now they would help finance my future. As what? That remained to be seen.

None of the employment agencies I went to panned out, and eventually I got a job with a messenger service in midtown. The pay was minimal, but it was the only job I could land. Most of what I earned went to my share of the rent; this left little for food. P still sold grass, so it was in supply, but cigarettes were often a luxury I couldn't afford, and I took to taking half-smoked butts out of secretaries' ashtrays when I had to go to an office to drop off a parcel.

The messenger work was often hard. The weather had turned cold;

I didn't have a warm coat and was on my feet for several hours a day. I liked walking, and got to know the city and soon discovered a way to make a little food money on the side. If a delivery was far, the dispatcher would give us thirty-five cents or a subway token to take a train. I was a fast walker, and figured that if I kept to a brisk pace, I could make the delivery on foot and keep the money or token. A grocery shop in the neighborhood would accept the tokens in lieu of cash, and I was able to turn a few rides on the subway into some bread and cheese once or twice a week. The fast walking combined with the meager diet led to my losing quite a bit of weight, but being lean and hungry would soon prove to have advantages.

If I managed to save enough, I would treat myself to a book from the twenty-five cent racks that stood outside the Strand Bookshop on 12th Street and Broadway. Not being in college or with the sisters, I had more time for reading, and the Strand proved to be heaven-sent. Later, I learned that people I would meet on the music scene, like Patti Smith, Tom Verlaine, and Richard Hell, had all worked there. From my love of Sherlock Holmes and "gaslight London," I had developed a passion for the *fin de siècle* in Aubrey Beardsley, Oscar Wilde, and poets like Ernest Dowson, of "the days of wine and roses." I read Stanley Weintraub's biography of Beardsley and his account of the notorious Yellow Book over and over, and started writing poems in that style.[2] I became a fan of "decadence," and had already discovered the modern musical version of

---

2. So far, I have resisted including any of the poetry I've mentioned. But, to illustrate youth's eternal fascination with death and other decadent themes, I will offer one example. I don't remember the title—"*Weltschmerz* at Eighteen" might serve—but here are some lines I recall:

Of what use to me, my friend,
The labour, all in vain,
If in the end I am laid to rest?
I shall not rise again.
To hammer every day
On the anvil men call art:
What use to me, my friend,
If in the end we part?

And tell me not of heaven,
And tell me not of hell,
For in my years I've traveled there.
What is there to tell?
Better to lie still upon the ground
And make no move at all
And so be so much closer to the end
If I should chance to fall.

it in glitter. Much later, I would write about what I called the "positive *fin de siècle*," the interest in higher consciousness, creative evolution, and mysticism that informed figures like William James, Ouspensky, and George Bernard Shaw—Weintraub was an expert on Shaw. But then, it was the dark, morbid side of that period that attracted me.

My favorite writer at the time was Henry Miller. As mentioned earlier, it is one of the strange things about my development that today I can't read more than a page of him before putting the book down in boredom (I tried during the course of this writing, but found I couldn't do it). But when I found a cheap copy of *Tropic of Cancer* (in the Grove Black Cat edition, first published in 1961) at the Strand, I took it back to the crash pad and knew it was just what I needed.

I, of course, enjoyed reading about the sex—that was all I could do about it at the time—but Miller's account of starving in Paris as he became a writer was more than encouraging. It gave me the faith in myself to carry on starving, if that was what was necessary for me to find my muse. Miller would beg, steal, or borrow before he would give up his freedom, and I felt the same. *What pains the body is good for the soul*, I thought.

There were other reasons why I felt a connection to Miller. He was a Capricorn, as I was, and his birthday, December twenty-sixth, was close to mine. At some point in *Tropic of Capricorn* (again, a Grove Black Cat edition found at the Strand), relating his life selling the *Encyclopedia Britannica* door-to-door, Miller finds himself in Bayonne, which he calls the "asshole of the world." I had to agree. And, in *Sexus*, the first part of his *Rosy Crucifixion* trilogy, he tells of his time working in New York as a messenger for the "Cosmodemonic Telegraph Company" (actually, Western Union). I wasn't delivering telegrams but I was a messenger, and I could relate to Miller's depiction of the work. Not long after this, looking for a stage name to mark my new life as a musician, I remembered that Miller's middle name was Valentine.

I found other books at the Strand—many in those Black Cat editions—that specialized in avant-garde, "transgressive" literature.

De Sade's *120 Days of Sodom* was one. Having the book itself seemed *de rigueur* for any self-respecting decadent, but I was disappointed in it and felt it wasn't as useful as the soft porn paperbacks I had stolen from my father. (I had better luck with the editions of *The Pearl* and *My Secret Life* I came upon.) I read Burroughs's *Naked Lunch* and his other "cut up" books; as I came to feel about surrealist poetry, their shock appeal works once, but doesn't bear rereading. I tried to get through Samuel Beckett's novels—*Molly, Malone Dies,* and *The Unnameable*—but found them even more unreadable than Burroughs. I did enjoy Jean Genet's *Our Lady of the Flowers* and Frank Harris's *My Life and Loves.* And I have a fond memory of sitting in the dispatch office, reading Camus's *The Rebel* while waiting for a delivery, and talking to one of the other messengers about existentialism.

But it was music more than literature that would have the most impact on me then.

I'VE MENTIONED GLITTER ROCK. While I was living with the sisters, we started a routine of going to New York whenever we could and hanging out at an old drag club in the East Village that had recently opened its doors to rock and roll. Before CBGB on the Bowery became the home of the downtown New York music scene, the place to be was the Mercer Arts Center on Mercer Street. When this literally collapsed, the nascent New York rock scene was without a place to play. Someone must have mentioned to the owners of Club 82—the drag club—that they could fill the vacuum (and the club) by letting local rock bands play. It proved to be a good idea. The club was really put on the hipster's map when it came out that David Bowie and Lou Reed, who both had transvestite "girlfriends" at the time, had taken to frequenting the place. Although he had no musical talent or any creative bent at all, P had vague ideas about starting a band, and when we read in *Rock Scene* magazine that Bowie and Reed could be seen at Club 82, we decided we would start hanging out there too. These were the days when I was wearing makeup: lipstick, eyeliner, earrings, rouge. Our heroes were Bowie, Reed, Iggy Pop, Ian Hunter, from Mott the Hoople, and the New York Dolls.

I saw the Dolls at their notorious drag show at Club 82, when they played in makeup and dresses. Sexual ambiguity and transgression were the rage, and while I had no homosexual inclinations, I did take to dressing up and taking a "walk on the wild side." I relate my adventures in *New York Rocker*. It was exciting, fun, and slightly dangerous; unlike today, going out in one's war paint drew a great deal of attention, and getting to Manhattan from the flat was often like running a gauntlet. We did wind up meeting Bowie and Reed—if hovering around their table while they smoked the joint we gave them constitutes a meeting. (Years later, I would meet Bowie and Reed under different conditions but, understandably, they didn't remember our first encounter.) One of the acts I saw there was a group called The Stilettoes—three girl singers backed up by a band. One of the singers was Debbie Harry, someone I would soon get to know much better, as I would Chris Stein, the guitarist in the band.

Among the other rubbish in the storefront on East 10th Street was a broken-down upright piano. Practically every other key was broken, and it was painfully out of tune, but I had started teaching myself how to play it. I knew a few chords and, with little else to do, I experimented. I had learned a few chords on guitar, and in high school had jammed a bit with some friends who were, like myself, not really musicians—unlike our other friends who were. Without putting too fine a point on it, I was in the same position as many of the musicians who would soon form the ranks of the punk rockers—that is, I was an amateur with a lot of passion and attitude.

But seeing bands like the Dolls, who played very simple but high-energy rock, rather like early Rolling Stones, and listening to the Velvet Underground, whose music was intense but again relatively simple, just a few chords, I came to feel that "I could do that!" As I've said in interviews about this time, by the early '70s, the "progressive rock" of groups like Emerson, Lake & Palmer, Yes, and King Crimson had made it so that you had to have a degree from the Julliard School of Music in order to play rock and roll. Some of my friends *could* play that sort of music. They could learn a complicated guitar lick and play it exactly as it was on the record. But this very meticulous attention to detail and "getting it right" kept them from doing anything of their own. They were too cowed by the talent of Hendrix or Eric Clapton or some other guitar hero to think anything they could come up with could be any good. People like myself weren't interested in getting some difficult bit right but in *getting something out of the guitar*—using it to create something. Soon enough, I stopped writing poetry and concentrated on writing songs. And the idea came that we, P and I, would start a band.

P, however, had recently changed his allegiance from Nietzsche and the *Übermensch* to Jesus—or, at least, to the Bible, and to the Book of Revelations in particular. He had become friends with some Jehovah's Witnesses, and then with some born-again Christians. It took me a while to see what was happening, but it became clear that P was certain the end of the world was coming. The signs, he said, were there.

I imagine they were. I didn't see them, but clearly, he did. He spoke of giving up the storefront and moving to a kibbutz in Israel where, he assured me, we would be safe. I couldn't quite grasp why, if the world was coming to an end, he wanted to start a rock band, but I didn't quibble. I agreed to meet with some of his born-again friends. They seemed nice enough, but I wasn't interested. But P was serious, and told me that if I knew what was good for me, I would be too.

Looking back over what I've written so far, I'm not sure if I ever knew what was good for me. But in this instance, moving to kibbutz in Israel to avoid the apocalypse didn't seem to meet the criteria. I don't know if it was a guardian angel, destiny, or what, but at this point events intervened that had me moving—not to Israel, but first, briefly back home, and then to another part of the city.

Clem had seen an advertisement in the *Village Voice* about a band looking for a drummer. All throughout high school, I had seen him play in bands. A cousin of mine had even played with him when they won a battle of the bands in 1969, and got to perform in Carnegie Hall. The hippie girl who had given me a copy of *Siddhartha* became his girlfriend, and once or twice I helped carry his drums in to a dance. When he answered the ad, he discovered it had been placed by Debbie Harry. The Stilettoes had folded, and her most recent attempt at another band had lost its drummer.

Debbie had gone through several incarnations, none of them quite hitting the bullseye, and time was running out. She was hitting thirty, and she had been at it since 1968, starting with a late hippie effort called The Wind in the Willows. Much water had passed under the bridge since then. Clem answering her ad was the first step on her road to success.

It was also the first step on my road to becoming a bona fide musician. When Clem started playing with Debbie, R, P, and I used to go to their gigs. These were usually in divey bars downtown; Club 82 had stopped letting bands play. The Dolls had broken up; their bid for success hadn't panned out, and the glitter scene was dying. A new place, CBGB, originally a biker bar, had started letting local groups play—one of them, Tom Verlaine's Television, inaugurated the place. The flamboyance—linked in this instance to "flaming"—and sexual ambiguity of glitter was old news. The new look was stripped-down, a reaction to the excess of what had become just another fad. Shag haircuts and lipstick were out, short hair was in. Charity shops provided the clothes. From dazzling technicolor, things went to a rather sober down-market black-and-white. Given my own impecuniousness, this was something to which I could relate.

I had been hanging around the band for a while when Clem turned up at the storefront and asked if I wanted to audition. They had just lost their bass player. Richard Hell, the true creator of "punk rock" (he wore the first ripped T-shirt) had left Television to start a group with

Johnny Thunders, the guitarist from the Dolls. Patti Smith had advised Fred Smith (no relation) that he should leave Blondie—what there was of it—and play bass for Television. At that point, Debbie didn't seem like a good bet. Patti was getting press for her poetry readings, which slowly turned into a musical act incorporating guitar, drums, and keyboards. Television got press too, and were pegged by some as the next big thing. Debbie seemed not in the running. Fred was persuaded to take Patti's advice, and suddenly Blondie lost another band member. That's where I came in.

As I relate in *New York Rocker*, I went to the rehearsal space in midtown. I didn't have a bass guitar, but one was there. I had played a bit in jam sessions, but my technique was primitive at best—more or less one finger roaming up and down the neck. But I was young, thin, and wore dark glasses—the fact that I could barely play was negligible. After jamming on the Stones' "Live With Me" for what seemed forever, they seemed satisfied. Clem then mentioned that I wrote songs. I had played him some of the things I'd come up with on the piano at the storefront, and he thought they were good. There was a piano in the rehearsal space. I sat down and played what I had played for Clem. Chris and Debbie seemed impressed. We talked a bit, and that was it. I was in. I had officially joined a New York underground rock band.

P wasn't happy with this development, nor with my reluctance to join him in Israel. He made one last attempt to convert me, but I was even less interested than before. He then told me I had to leave the storefront. He was giving it up. He had seen the light but I was still fumbling in the darkness. I don't know if he made it to Israel. I didn't see him again until a few years later, after I had left Blondie and started my own group, The Know. We bumped into each other on Sixth Avenue, near Eighth Street. He was still high on religion; it was "better than drugs, better than sex," he told me. I didn't argue with him and didn't mention that the apocalypse seemed to have been postponed. It wasn't until some twenty years later, when I had written an article about this time for *Mojo* magazine, that I learned he was leading a group of born-again Jews for Jesus in the UK. His sister had read the article and recognized him in it, and got in touch to let me know.

Leaving the storefront presented problems. I had already known that it was only a matter of time before I would have to go. I had outgrown P, and found his obsession with the end times disturbing. He felt his influence on me slipping, and his attitude had become increasingly nasty. I would, he assured me, soon be reaping the whirlwind and gnashing my teeth. But where could I go? The little I made as a messenger barely covered my share of the rent; I certainly couldn't afford my own place, and there was little chance of my getting any better-paid work. I knew some people in my situation took to hustling—working as a male prostitute, mostly for older gay men to earn money, but I ruled that out. And I needed time to rehearse with the band. Our practices were going well, and I had already played at a few gigs. There seemed little room to maneuver. In the end, it seemed I had little choice but to return home.

I did, but it lasted only a few weeks. Understandably, my parents didn't care for me coming home at four in the morning after a gig or a night out. I spent most of my time in New York or in my room, listening to music. I received an ultimatum: mend my ways, quit the band, return to college, or leave. I understand how they felt. They were doing what they thought was right. I was young enough to return to school, get a degree, and find a good job. Who knows? Maybe I could have. But destiny was calling. I packed a bag again and left. I would not see my parents again for some time.

For a time, I crashed at the rehearsal space. This was not allowed. I had to sneak in and out of the building, and not be seen in it too often. There was a toilet there, but showering required some initiative. A friend offered his couch, and for a while I crashed in his living room—until his mother got tired of my presence and informed me I was no longer welcome. Eating was again a challenge, and today I honestly don't remember what I did about it. The early-morning ninety-nine-cent breakfast specials greasy spoon coffee shops offered were my most substantial meal then, when I could afford them. I spent a lot of time at the library at Fifth Avenue and 42nd Street.

All this came up at rehearsal. That I didn't have a place to live did not bode well for the band. Debbie felt we had gotten some momentum and didn't want to lose this in looking for yet another bassist. Whatever friction developed between us later on, I have to acknowledge her kindness and generosity. When Chris mentioned that I was homeless, Debbie thought about it, then said that I could live with them. Given that she and Chris lived in a small, one bedroom flat above a grocery shop in Little Italy, this showed commitment. The place was cramped to begin with—Debbie's three cats were living there as well—and now they would have less privacy.

I have quite a few fond memories of that flat on Thompson Street. I write about them in *New York Rocker*. It would be a cliché and not exactly accurate to say that Debbie and Chris became my surrogate parents, but the situation suggests it. Debbie was ten years older than me; Chris was at least five years older. I was still a teenager and had been through some traumatic experiences. I had no money—I left the messenger job when I returned to New Jersey—and didn't even have a bass guitar; for most of my early days with them, I had to borrow a bass and an amplifier. I had few clothes. I was close to living on the street, and by then had spent at least one night in Central Park. If it was destiny that Debbie decided to take me in, I am grateful for it.

But destiny, kindness, and a commitment to your art can go only so far. It was soon clear that the flat was too small for us. Most likely this was clear to Debbie after my first evening there. With the sisters, it had been more or less an ongoing party. People were always around and privacy was not an issue. With P, I was on more even ground—it was his place but I paid my share, and there was a vague sense of working together. But here, I was a homeless waif and they were a couple, and I can imagine it was a bit inhibiting to know I was occupying their living room, which was already crammed with amplifiers, speaker cases, guitars, and other impedimenta of the rock trade. (I guess I could have been seen as just another piece of equipment.)

For the most part we got along and Chris took me under his wing, walking around the East Village with me, telling stories about the Velvet Underground and fallen rockers like Eric Emerson, whose band the Magic Tramps was something of a legend. We'd run into other musicians, like Richard Hell, or Jerry Nolan from the Dolls. Practically the whole New York scene was contained in the few square miles between Houston and Fourteenth Streets.[3]

But other times, Debbie would understandably get stir crazy and had no inhibitions about showing it.

Other problems presented themselves. We were kicked out of the midtown rehearsal space for not paying our rent. We shifted around for a time until Arturo Vega, the Ramones' aide-de-camp, invited us to share the space he was letting the Ramones use to rehearse, until we could find a new one of our own. That was a temporary blessing.

Arturo's space was a block away from CBGB. I had by this time already made my debut there, gracing its rudimentary stage for the first time on July 4, 1975, when we opened for the Ramones—a date that would later have additional significance for me. I had been playing in the band since April, mostly at forgettable bars in the Wall Street area, but this was the first of many performances at the biker bar that was just getting a name for itself. Things were moving, but conditions at Thompson Street were still problematic.

Tensions were relieved one afternoon when Chris told us he had found a new rehearsal space. But, not only that: it was a loft large enough for us to rehearse and live in, too. And it was on the

---

3. Readers may be interested in my map of the milieu I was entering, *Fear City: The New York Underground 1974–1981* (Herb Lester Associates, 2025).

Bowery—as close to CBGB as Arturo's was. And—most important—it was cheap.

THE PLACE CHRIS FOUND, above a restaurant supply shop and a liquor store, was on the south side of Houston Street, the demarcation line between the East Village and the Lower East Side. It was filthy; graffiti covered the door, and winos and other denizens of the lower depths sprawled out on the pavement in front of it. Drunks had pissed so often on the front door, an odor of urine hung around the hallway—a scent to which Debbie's cats soon contributed.

Around the block, on Elizabeth Street, English was not the primary language; the Puerto Rican inhabitants saw to that. And as you headed further south toward Delancey Street, where the Talking Heads had a loft, the neighborhood deteriorated even more, if that could be imagined. Nowadays, the whole area is unrecognizable, transformed by the need for new neighborhoods in which to house the upwardly mobile who can afford the increasingly nosebleed-inducing rents Manhattan's landlords charge. CBGB, a dive even in its heyday, is no longer there, replaced by an upmarket *haute couture* rock boutique, offering attire no one who had been a regular at the club would have been seen dead in, let alone be able to afford. The last time I visited New York, in 2019, just before COVID hit, I took a walk in my old neighborhood and was gratified to see that, while everywhere else looked dauntingly expensive, 266 Bowery, our old digs, was as much a dump as ever—at least, from the exterior. Graffiti still covered the door, and the liquor store and restaurant supply shop, with its stainless-steel sinks and refitted griddles, were still open for business. In a world of rapid change, it was a comfort to see some things remaining the same.

It was in this loft that Blondie—who had by now acquired a keyboardist—would transform itself from a third-on-the-bill support act who would open for practically anyone to a group with its own distinctive sound, and with enough original material to fill an album. By then, we had dropped most of the cover material we had been playing and were concentrating on coming up with our own songs, a few of which were mine. It was an exciting time. A lot happened—including my almost being electrocuted to death.

After living with the sisters, and then with P, I had developed a distaste for squalor. To be sure, there was plenty of it around in our new home, but I decided if I couldn't make a significant cash contribution to our expenses, the least I could do was to keep the place relatively clean, a hygienic habit I maintain today. Perhaps an instinctive need for order, for giving some form to chaos, as Nietzsche advises, was at work. In any case, I was in the process of neatening my part of the loft, which doubled as the rehearsal room, when I picked up a lamp and suddenly had 110 volts running through me. I was frozen. I couldn't let go of the lamp, and felt what seemed like a black cloud moving from the back of my skull to the front—I knew when it reached my forehead, I would be gone. I don't know how long I stayed like that, but I couldn't make a sound, just the sort of raspy whisper we make when we try to call out in a dream.

What drew Chris out of their bedroom, which was far back in the other side of the loft, I'll never know, but he appeared just as I was going under. He saw what was happening and calmly pulled the plug. If he hadn't been there, I don't know what would have happened. If I have Debbie to thank for her generosity, I have Chris to thank for saving my life. My arm ached for days, and I took to falling asleep with my eyes open. Sometime later, I read that many psychics became aware of their powers after an accident of some kind. The Dutch clairvoyant Peter Hurkos, for example, discovered he was psychic after a fall from a ladder. I mention this because, not long after this incident, I not only became very interested in the occult and the paranormal, but I started to have experiences that suggested our normal, everyday way of understanding reality does not cover all the bases, and that we may all possess powers of which we are not aware.

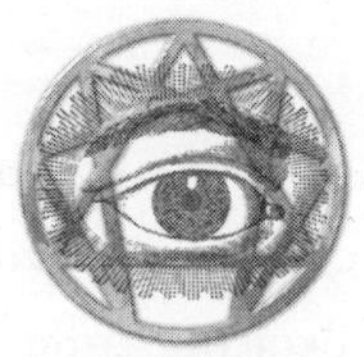

6
Touching the Presence

A hippie girl I had a crush on introduced me to Hesse, and a progressive high school teacher led me to Nietzsche. The individual responsible for opening my way to magic was a flamboyant, gay biker artist with a dangerous fancy for the Hell's Angels and a serious interest in the notorious Aleister Crowley. His name was Benton, and I met him when we moved into the loft. He had the lease on the building—insofar as there was such a thing—and lived on the second floor. We were renting the first—the shops took up the ground floor—and for a time the top floor was vacant. After a while, the fashion designer Stephen Sprouse took that space. What I remember most about him is a fondness for psychedelic drugs.

Chris had a kitschy interest in the occult, which Debbie shared. In the Thompson Street flat, pentagrams, voodoo dolls, vampire fangs, black candles, and other magical bric-a-brac competed with photographs of the Ramones, the Dolls, and other rock iconography for wall space. This décor would soon be repeated in the loft. Among other things, it would sport a statue of a nun with an upside-down cross on her forehead; a series of Tibetan *tankas,* one of which depicted a dead Buddhist monk being eaten by his fellows; and a fireplace decorated with assorted magical insignia. It was all fun, one of Chris's eccentricities, like his penchant for Nazi memorabilia (odd for a Jew) and Japanese Godzilla toys, rather like my love of *Weird Tales* and old horror films.

But Benton was much more serious about magic. He gave impromptu readings of Crowley's then still rare Thoth Tarot deck, and based some of his paintings on some of the trumps—I even sat for one of these. He had read Lovecraft and was a Conan fan. He had read Jung and Nietzsche—at one point he gave me a copy of Walter Kaufmann's translation of *The Birth of Tragedy Out of the Spirit of Music*, with a drawing of a fist bursting through crossed thunderbolts he had made on the title page. We'd smoke grass and he would read from Crowley's *Diary of a Drug Fiend*. He even introduced me to someone who claimed to be Crowley's son—whether he really was or not I never learned. Sitting in Benton's room, listening to music, we would talk about Crowley's ideas, about magic and art and how they were part of the same work of getting in touch with your "true will," which was what magic was all about. This sounded close enough to the efforts of getting in touch with my "true self" I had been making since I'd read *Demian* for me to pay attention.

Benton was gay. I made it clear early on that I wasn't, and he never pressed the point. But, like Debbie and Chris, he was older, and if they were like surrogate parents, I guess he could be seen as a surrogate uncle. Like Chris, he, too, was a Capricorn—they both had birthdays around mine—which may explain why we got along. He was a true individual. Thin as a rail, leather-jacketed, tall, with long blond hair like a lion's mane, a smoky Southern voice that suggested the actress Lauren Bacall, and an unmistakable laugh, his maxim for life, "learn to love it," has proved helpful more than once.[1]

Benton had learned to love much, a great deal of it aspects of life most of us would understandably avoid. His penchant for the Hell's Angels led him to submit to their rigorous and malodorous initiation rituals. He and a boyfriend would go unwashed for days, and then take to wearing clothes they had pissed on. (As mentioned, urine and its odor were a central fact

1. It helped when he, Clem, and I were arrested for smoking marijuana in public by an off-duty policeman, who knocked me unconscious in the process. We wound up spending three nights in three different New York jails, among them The Tombs, in downtown. We were eventually released without charge—the officer had failed to produce his badge and identify himself.

of the place. Not only did Debbie's cats make their contribution, for a while Benton himself collected his in Coke bottles.) His passion unfortunately led to him introducing himself to the Hell's Angels who occupied nearby East Third Street, where their motorcycles lined the block. I'm not sure what he said to them, but he returned from the meeting severely beaten and bruised. That may in fact have been what he was after. If so, they obliged. He passed away a few years ago. I had not seen him for a long time, and was saddened when I heard the news.

THE MID-1970S WERE A GOOD TIME to become interested in the occult, especially if you were in New York. The occult revival of the 1960s—the subject of my first book—had led to a boom in occult publishing that would continue throughout the decade and into the next. Eventually, the occult would establish itself, along with "mind, body, and spirit," as a bankable genre, and diversify into related areas, such as the spiritual and magical gear (crystals, incense, herbs, oils, etc.) that a decade or so later I would be selling at the Bodhi Tree, while earning a degree in philosophy. By then, I would be fairly well versed in the Western occult tradition and have a working familiarity with much of the Eastern traditions. But in the summer of 1975, as a nineteen-year-old college dropout wannabe poet turned proto-punk rocker, it was all a fascinating and seductive *terra incognita* that I was anxious to learn everything about.

In bookshops like Weiser's on Broadway—the largest occult bookshop in town—near Cooper Union, I could do just that. Along with the Strand and Barnes & Noble, it became a frequent haunt of mine. Weiser's published occult titles, too, and in secondhand shops I began to look for their trademark Egyptian ankh on book spines, as I had for Ace Books' "Science Fiction Classic" tag or Lancer's purple-edged pages.[2]

---

2. Another occult bookshop I visited less frequently was Magickal Childe, not far from Barnes & Noble. I found the atmosphere there somewhat darker and less congenial than at Weiser's.

But the occult had become so popular, most bookshops had fairly well-sized sections on everything from flying saucers to witchcraft, and well-stocked "cutout" bins. Publishers had brought out cheap editions of classic works that were out of copyright, so even with the little money I was earning from our shows, I could afford to buy copies of A. E. Waite's *Book of Black Magic and Pacts* or MacGregor Mathers's translation of *The Sacred Magic of Abramelin the Mage*, or Sax Rohmer's (whose Fu Manchu pulp novels I had enjoyed) *The Romance of Sorcery*—all put out by Causeway Books. Causeway's head, Felix Morrow, had already established a reputation in the field with University Books, with whose titles (R. M. Bucke's *Cosmic Consciousness*, Lewis Spence's *Encyclopaedia of Occultism*, Montague Summers's works on witchcraft and Satanism, and many others) I would soon become acquainted. There seemed a whole vast reservoir of hidden, lost, and forgotten knowledge opening up before me, and I was ready to plunge in headfirst. But I wouldn't have learned of any of this, or be willing to take that leap, if it wasn't for that first introduction to Crowley.

It shouldn't be surprising that I came upon Crowley while playing in a rock band. Almost a decade earlier, the most famous people in the world had put him on the cover of their most famous album. This, of course, was The Beatles, who put Crowley—along with C. G. Jung and Aldous Huxley—among "the people we like" on the cover of *Sgt. Pepper's Lonely Hearts Club Band*. I knew the album—I had listened to it religiously at one point—but, until moving to the Bowery, didn't know a thing about Crowley. I soon began to find out.

After listening to Benton read from it a few times, I found a copy of *Diary of a Drug Fiend*—Crowley's idealized portrait of his Abbey of Thelema in Sicily—read it, and enjoyed it. The fact that it was about drugs was enough to make it interesting, but his romanticized picture of his abbey, where one could discover one's true will, was—for my late-teen mind—exciting. Later, I learned that Crowley's abbey was as squalid as some of the places I had lived in. But then, the idea of finding my true will against a backdrop of green hills and sea, with an assortment of drugs available for the taking, seemed appealing. The two lovers who, hooked on drugs, are cured by finding their true will at the abbey (ironically, Crowley wrote the book while under the influence of cocaine) suggested that the pursuit of magic could lead to a happy ending. It didn't for Crowley, or for many of the people who knew him, but again, this was something I would learn only later.

Diary of a Drug Fiend is not a good novel, but it is a good read. The next work of Crowley's that came my way was something different. Crowley considered *Magick in Theory and Practice*, privately published for subscribers in Paris in 1929, his magnum opus. It may be, but it is not as immediately accessible as an earlier work on magick, *Book Four* (1912), which, along with his later *Eight Lectures on Yoga* (1938), is one of the clearest and most concise things Crowley ever wrote. (I should point out that Crowley used the archaic spelling of "magick," with a "k," to differentiate the royal art from common prestidigitation.)

Crowley could be as clear and direct as his older contemporary Bernard Shaw, and often as funny. But he could also be verbose—especially when writing under the influence of any number of drugs—and his lack of a critical sense when it came to his own writing allowed him to indulge himself in ways a good editor would have deleted immediately. This can most easily be seen in his poetry (Crowley was always too aware of himself to be a good poet), but it is also evident in his prose. One of Crowley's worst traits is a taste for mystification and riddles, which is exacerbated by his unfounded belief that his readers are completely familiar with all of his work.

This was my experience when the 1960 Castle Books reprint of the original 1929 Paris edition of *Magick in Theory and Practice* came into my hands. How it got there, I don't remember. What I do remember is a feeling that could be described as one part strange excitement and one part utter bafflement. The "Hymn to Pan" that opens the book is one of the few times when Crowley's poetry rises above its usual highly derivative level—think Swinburne and you have the gist of most of Crowley's verse, both in form and subject matter. But "Hymn to Pan" is powerfully evocative (his taste for alliteration serves him well for a change), and it contains some memorable lines ("With hoofs of steel I race on the rocks / From solstice stubborn to equinox"). It is a truly incantatory work.

And I have to admit that the drawings, based on photographs of a robed magician adopting various Egyptian god forms ranging from that of Set, symbolizing Earth, to the risen Osiris, whom Set had slain but who was resurrected by Isis, reminded me of nothing so much as a caped figure from the comic books I had read. If Crowley is still aware of events on this plane (he died in 1947), the fact that my innocent eye when first looking at these images thought of superheroes may gratify him, for he certainly thought of himself as a superman—although his reputation may suggest he was more of a supervillain.

Then there was the stentorian announcement that "This book is for ALL," followed by the equally bold declaration that "MAGICK is for ALL." A mention of the Beast 666 (Crowley identified with that Biblical character) brought P's obsessions back to mind—but it was clear that Crowley was not born-again, at least not in the Christian sense, although, as I later found out, he was brought up in a radically Christian fundamentalist family. But it was his definition of magick that grabbed me most of all. "Magick," Crowley wrote, "is the Science and Art of causing Change to occur in conformity with Will."

I had read quite a bit about "the will" in Nietzsche. I had read the collection of notes left behind after his death, *The Will to Power*, in the Walter Kaufmann and R. J. Hollingdale translation, and knew that the will was an important theme in *Zarathustra* and in Nietzsche's notion of the overman. For Crowley to link it to magick, and the idea that the will itself—if set in motion properly—can effect change in the world, was stunning and exciting. It suggested that I—and everyone else—may possess powers of which we are normally not aware, but which the practice of magick may waken. Again, the idea of the magician and the superman were not so far apart.

I read through the rest of the twenty-eight postulates about magick that Crowley presents in the introduction. In many ways Crowley had a mathematical mind, and he liked to present his theses logically, step by step. He was a chess master and, as I say in my book about him, he would have made a much better scientist than he did a poet.[3] His argument was convincing, and if I later became critical of "the Beast" it was of his sociopathic personality and adolescent philosophy, not of his belief that we harbor within us abilities that lie dormant simply because we are unaware that we possess them, and so never make the effort to awaken them. This, in fact, became the central belief around which my occult studies, then just beginning, would revolve.

It was not far removed from Nietzsche's notion of a new type of human—one strong enough to say "Yes!" to life, even in its most doubtful forms. And one passage at the end of the introduction seemed to echo what I had already heard from Hesse, Sartre, and Nietzsche—although, to be sure, the magical universe I was just entering was rather different from the absurd, meaningless one of the existentialists. Crowley summed up the core of his magick and of his religion of "Do what thou wilt," which I would get to know better fairly soon, in a simple challenge: "One must find out for oneself, and make sure beyond doubt, *who* one is, *what* one is, *why* one is." If this is done, all else will follow, for, as Crowley optimistically puts it, "A man who is doing his True Will has the inertia of the Universe to assist him."

What young artist, first making his way into the world convinced of his powers and eager to use them, would not find such a notion appealing? But when I turned to the rest of the book, to discover *how* I might go about getting the inertia of the Universe on my side, I met some obstructions. There were, to start, all the references to *The Book of*

3. *Aleister Crowley: Magick, Rock and Roll, and the Wickedest Man in the World* (New York: Tarcher/Penguin, 2014).

the Law—the founding text of Crowley's religion, as well as to a number of other works of Crowley's. I was of course ignorant of these and had no idea what they meant. Then there was a plunge headfirst into Qabalah, which I knew nothing about—even the spelling struck me as odd: shouldn't there be a "u" after the "q"? Later chapters—on ritual; the different "formulas," such as that of the Tetragrammaton, which I later learned is Greek for "four letter word," the word in question being the unpronounceable name of God; and those of the gods Isis, Apophis, and Osiris; of the Lady Babalon and the Beast (again!); and Black Magic—simply left me scratching my head and wondering what trap door I had inadvertently fallen through.

A great deal was in Latin and Greek, and the numerology involved was numbing, my experience with math no help at all. I was heartened a bit when I reached the "Curriculum of the A.·.A.·."—not Alcoholics Anonymous but Crowley's magical society, the Argenteum Astrum, or Silver Star, which I would soon learn more about. In the course on "General Reading," I found some things I had read, like the Upanishads, Tao Te Ching, and Dhammapada, my class in Eastern religion coming in handy after all. But there was much there I didn't know, especially all the references to Crowley's other works. Magick may be for All, but I soon realized that if I was going to learn anything about it, it would take some work.

Luckily, there were other less obscure books I could learn from. One was Francis King's *Ritual Magic in England* (1970). This was an excellent, well-written history of the "modern magical revival," starting in the late nineteenth century. Francis King wrote many books about magic and occultism, and more than one about Crowley. It was in this book that I learned about the Hermetic Order of the Golden Dawn, the magical society Crowley briefly belonged to before his membership led to the society's dissolution. One of the mysterious things Crowley wrote about was what he called the "single main definition of the object of all magical Ritual." This was the "uniting of the Microcosm with the Macrocosm," of the individual inner mind with the outer Universe. I had already come across a version of this in *Demian*, when Sinclair realizes that the entire outer world resides in his soul. But Crowley spoke of it in a particular way, calling it "the knowledge and conversation of one's Holy Guardian Angel."

This was not the kind of guardian angel I learned about in the catechism classes I had to attend when young and still going to church. This was more like some inner voice, that of one's "true self," with which one could commune. I learned that the Golden Dawn system of magic was centered around this, and that the magic involved was much more of a spiritual practice than one of getting demons or spirits to do what you want—which, unfortunately, is what draws many people to magic. I also learned that Crowley wasn't the only poet interested in magic. W. B. Yeats, whom I had read, had been practicing magic long before Crowley joined the Golden Dawn, only to have it disband.

Another important book then was Israel Regardie's *The Tree of Life*. It was originally published in 1932; Weiser brought out a paperback forty years later, in 1972. This was an altogether more accessible introduction to the philosophy and practice of ritual magic than Crowley's magnum opus. Regardie was Crowley's secretary for a time, and later wrote a biography of him, *The Eye in the Triangle* (1970), a copy of which I bought in Portland, Oregon, in 1977, while on tour with Blondie. This was his defensive response to the highly critical but compulsively readable—and often very funny—account of Crowley's life, *The Great Beast* (1951) by John Symonds, which I also came across at the time.

Thelemites understandably hate this book. Symonds was no believer in either magick or Crowley's religion of "Do what thou wilt," and his tactic of giving Crowley enough rope with which to hang himself makes for often hilarious reading. Though I am more sympathetic than Symonds, my own book on Crowley draws on his quite a bit, and is also quite critical. I wonder if attitudes toward Crowley have changed, as it is my best-selling book.

I should mention one other book I read at that time, *The Morning of the Magicians,* Louis Pauwels and Jacques Bergier's very popular if often inaccurate work of fantastic realism, arguing for a revival of magic in the modern age. This breathless survey of magical ideas involving alchemy, extraterrestrials, mutants, and other elements of what would soon be called "alternative thought" was published in France in 1960 and became a surprise sensation, kick-starting the decade's "occult revival." It talked about Crowley, the Golden Dawn, Gurdjieff, and among other things inaugurated the genre of books about "occult Nazism"—the dubious idea that Hitler and other members of the Nazi high command were deeply involved in magic and the occult—which thrives today.

But the book that would have the greatest and longest-lasting influence on me, and would eventually lead to my writing my own books, was Colin Wilson's *The Occult.*

Chris had a flat on First Avenue that he sublet to Tommy Ramone, the original drummer for the Ramones, who later became their producer. Telling this story in my book on Crowley, I mentioned that, of the original Ramones, Tommy was the only one still alive. I'm sad to say that is no longer so. He died of cancer in 2014, shortly after the book was published. I didn't know Tommy well, although we did many shows with the Ramones. I do have to thank him, though, for his part in my discovering Wilson's book.

On one of our walks in the East Village, I went with Chris to Tommy's flat to pick up the rent. Chris had left much of his stuff there—there was no room in the loft to store it—so I don't know if the books I looked at were his or Tommy's, but two caught my attention and I asked if I could borrow them. One was Crowley's other novel, *Moonchild*, a *roman-à-clef* featuring members of the Golden Dawn; Yeats and A. E. Waite come in for particularly nasty portraits. The other was *The Occult*, a paperback that had seen better days.[4] The black

4. Colin Wilson, *The Occult* (New York: Random House, 1974).

cover, featuring a strange psychedelic bird-like image which I thought of as a phoenix, had burn marks and was torn. Tommy—or Chris?—told me it was fine to borrow them. I took them back to the loft. I don't know what happened to those books; I have different editions of both today. I do know that when I started to read Wilson's book, it was clear I had come upon something very important and very exciting.

By now I have read *The Occult* more times than I can remember. I have a copy of it in front of me as I write, and I have to stop myself from reading more than a sentence or two, for fear of not being able to put it down. To call Wilson's prose compulsively readable—as I just did of Symonds's *The Great Beast*—is a reviewer's cliché, but it's one that's apt. A reviewer once remarked of Wilson that he had a narrative style that could make the telephone directory gripping. I have to say this is true, and any readability my own books possess comes from reading and rereading his books obsessively over the years. But it wasn't only Wilson's wonderfully readable style that gripped me. *What* he was saying hit me as much, if not more, as anything I had read before.

Like Sartre, Wilson was obsessed with the question of freedom. But this wasn't freedom in a political or social sense—it was freedom as an *inner experience.* He spoke of a feeling of freedom as "enormous and obvious as sunset," and of our strange habit of losing sight of it through "*the narrowness of consciousness.*" This narrowness leads us to become trapped in "the triviality of everydayness," a phrase he borrowed from Heidegger.

Heidegger? What was a German philosopher I had read about in William Barrett and Walter Kaufmann doing in a book about magic? But I soon saw that Wilson's book was full of references to Hesse, Sartre, Camus, and Nietzsche, as well as other philosophers I had heard of but hadn't read, like Husserl, out of whose "phenomenology" existentialism emerged. It was only later that I learned Wilson had started as an existentialist himself.

The book was also full of references to poets like Blake and Eliot, and psychologists like Jung and William James, whom I had read about in books on altered states of consciousness. Wilson quoted James's much-repeated remark that "our normal waking consciousness . . . is but one special type of consciousness," while all around us lie "potential forms of consciousness entirely different." I had explored some of those potential forms, and had some idea of what James meant.

As I read, I began to grasp what Wilson was saying. Freedom, it seemed, was somehow linked to consciousness, but a *different kind* of consciousness than we normally experience. This was what Wilson called "Faculty X," a way of grasping reality more intensely than what our ordinary, narrow consciousness provides. It enabled us to grasp "the *reality* of other times and places," not merely the *fact* of their existence. This is an important distinction, and throughout these notes I have tried to express it as well as I can. We succumb to the triviality of everydayness because we conflate reality with what our senses tell us, and remain trapped in the present—what is immediately before us—forgetting that whatever it is, reality is always more than the small slice of it that we have right before our eyes.

I felt I had a sense of what Wilson was talking about. We already possess this unknown power, he argued, but don't know that we do—something I was beginning to believe myself. Wilson also spoke of the will. "The will feeds on enormous vistas," he wrote, "deprived of them, it collapses." He also spoke of something I had felt and tried to capture, however clumsily and unsuccessfully, in the poetry I had written: the strange sense of meaning that would come to me out of nowhere while looking at a cloud, a flower, a puddle, or simply sunlight on one of the old tenement buildings in the East Village. This was the "is-ness" I would sometimes see when I tried to sit and meditate. This *meaning*, Wilson said, was the same reality that was involved in magic. He even had a chapter on "the poet as occultist" in which Yeats plays a great part. As I read on, completely gripped, it seemed the dry, austere, meaningless universe of Sartre and Camus was giving way to something altogether more interesting.

The "occult" simply means hidden, or rather, unseen. But the poet and the occultist share a strange ability to see what others do not—something I had come to feel about myself. All of this was part of a vision of human evolution that was breathtaking, and made Nietzsche's ideas about the overman seem humble by comparison. Wilson's grasp of his subject ranged from prehistoric shamans using magic to help hunters capture their prey to modern scientists and cyberneticians peering into the mysteries of the universe. He brought in literature, philosophy, science, history, religion, and art in a narrative that placed the occult at the center of human life.

As I had felt reading Hesse, Sartre, and Nietzsche, I was no longer simply reading a book, which could be any other, simply to pass the time. I was discovering myself and getting a glimpse of the strange reality of which I was a participant, not merely a spectator. The evolution of consciousness: *this* is what the occult is about. If it was true, as Wilson pointed out, that "for all practical purposes our ancestors of two thousand years ago were almost color-blind," what could that suggest about our future? If we can see colors our ancient ancestors could not, what other abilities might we possess? "Magic," Wilson boldly announced, was "the science of the future." "Civilization," he argued, "cannot evolve further until 'the occult' is taken for granted on the same level as atomic energy."

This was all something more than a book of spells, and altogether more understandable than Crowley's mystifying work. The book was an education in itself. I had read a lot, but Wilson seemed to have read *everything*, and to be able to write eloquently and meaningfully about it. Following up on the leads he provided, as I did in the years to come, is the equivalent of getting a liberal arts degree. And, of course, there were all the characters that made up this fascinating history of the unseen. Many of the individuals I met here, I later went on to write about. There was Crowley, of course, but also Madame Blavatsky, P. D. Ouspensky, G. I. Gurdjieff, Swedenborg, and other figures, such as Eliphas Levi, John Dee, and Rasputin—all of whom I would get to know quite well.

I was convinced. Magic was real and it had something to do with consciousness. And although soon enough I would have experiences that would support this belief, it was Wilson's argument, the *ideas* he expressed and his persuasive way of expressing them, that converted me. The power of ideas had won me over. And it would be the power of ideas that became the ruling passion of my life.

WHILE MY INITIATION into the world of consciousness and the occult was taking place, I was all the time playing in a rock band.

I have written about this time in *New York Rocker* and, to be honest, I'm loath to repeat the stories I tell there. The book is still in print, and an interested reader can find them. After hunkering down in the loft over the holidays, the band became tighter and our audiences, initially very small, began to grow. By the end of 1975 another club had opened, and began to rival CBGB for the out of town crowds that were coming to New York to see the "underground" scene.

Max's Kansas City, near Union Square, had been the place to be in the late '60s and early '70s. Celebrities like Mick Jagger, Truman Capote, and Andy Warhol (whose work I never liked) were regulars, but it closed just before the new scene got going. By late '75 it had reopened, and on Christmas that year, it threw a huge party for the local bands. I had just turned twenty, and had spent my birthday, Christmas Eve, alone, freezing in the loft, burning Jimi Hendrix posters in the fireplace to keep warm and reading the copy of *The Birth of Tragedy* that Benton had given me.[5]

We played Max's several times and, like CBGB, its door was always open to any of the local musicians. While I was sitting there one evening, something came to me that would put Blondie on the road to success. Although, at different times, Chris and Debbie would

5. This romantic scenario is corroborated by my bandmates. See Debbie Harry, Chris Stein, and Victor Bockris, *Making Tracks: The Rise of Blondie* (New York: Da Capo Press, 1998), 49.

talk about the band as a kind of art project, I never saw us as that. We were a pop group, and by this time we had more or less settled into a kind of retro-1960s sound and look. Jimmy Destri, our new keyboardist, had a Farfisa organ, the kind many '60s groups had. Patti Smith wore blousy white shirts with black skinny ties. I picked up wearing skinny ties and, while the punk crowd went for leather and ripped T-shirts, did my best with what I could find in charity shops to affect a mod look, having already cut my hair short. One shop in Hoboken, across the Hudson in New Jersey, was thrilled that we wanted the tab-collar paisley shirts and peg legged trousers that had been gathering dust in their storeroom; in a time given to disco, bell-bottoms, and body shirts, no one wanted them.

By the mid-'70s, a nostalgia for the early days of rock had become very popular, with groups like Sha Na Na resurrecting old doo-wop numbers, and veteran rockers like Chuck Berry, Jerry Lee Lewis, and Little Richard all making comebacks. Blondie affected an early-1960s girl group sound, and did a few cover tunes from that time. Bruce Springsteen had made a name for himself with "Born to Run," which featured simple chords and a kind of "Telstar" guitar sound, with a very bright, memorable hook.[6]

Aside from the Dolls and Velvet Underground, my musical influences all came from the '60s, from hearing one great song after the other on AM radio when I was growing up. I had gotten much better on the bass, and also on the guitar (I really was a guitarist, but played bass because that's what was needed), and had also got over my early self-consciousness about being on stage. With my new self-confidence I had taken to pogoing around, a performance style that led to some friction in the band. I thoroughly enjoyed performing, and put everything I had into it. I had by then also written a few songs that we performed, but nothing memorable. Then, one evening at Max's, I heard something over the din of the crowd. It wasn't coming from anywhere in the room.

6. In 1962, "Telstar" was a No. 1 instrumental by the British group The Tornados.

I was hearing it in my head. It was a song, and it sounded like one of the hits I had grown up listening to.

I rushed out of the club and headed back to the loft. I picked up a guitar. By the next day, I had all the music as well as the lyrics to the chorus. When I saw Debbie, I played it for her. She liked it and asked if I had lyrics for the verses. I didn't, so she said she would have a go. The result was "Sex Offender," which—later bowdlerized as "X Offender"—would secure our first record deal.

The song tells the story of a prostitute who falls in love with the policeman who arrests her. But Debbie let it be known that the real inspiration for her lyrics was my own experience of being arrested for statutory rape. Until the case was finally dropped, I had to make periodic journeys to New Jersey to see a probation officer. Technically I was not supposed to cross a state line while under probation, but luckily this never came up.

We worked on the song and, when we debuted the "new and improved" Blondie, it became our signature tune. I insisted on playing guitar on it; understandably, Chris wasn't happy about this. Six months after writing it, we found ourselves in the studio in Rockefeller Center, recording it as our first 45 rpm. Not long after that, we were back in the studio to record our first album. One year after spending a birthday alone, freezing in the loft, on December 24, 1976, I read that in his "Pop Life" column for the *New York Times*, the music critic John Rockwell had given *Blondie*, our eponymous inaugural album, an enthusiastic thumbs-up.

It was not a bad birthday present. Little more than a year earlier, I had been practically homeless, my future prospects looking fairly bleak. Now, a song I'd written had gotten us a record deal, and music critics were paying attention.

WITH THE RELEASE OF THE ALBUM in early 1977, things started to move fairly quickly. We saw the new year in playing live in

Bethesda Fountain in Central Park; it was so cold, I had to play wearing gloves with the finger-tips cut off. But we were on television, so it was worth it. By February, our new manager had taken us to Los Angeles. I never trusted him, and subsequent developments proved my suspicions right, but I was bullied into signing the contract with him by the other band members; later they had to admit my instincts were correct.

We played successful shows at the famous Whisky A Go-Go on the Sunset Strip. Several music luminaries of the previous generation showed up to pay their respects. Among them was the famed "wall of sound" '60s girl group producer Phil Spector, who would later be convicted of murdering his girlfriend Lana Clarkson, and who would die in prison in 2021. Of the others who came to our dressing room, my personal favorite was Roger McGuinn—guitarist, singer, and songwriter with the Byrds, a '60s group I liked a great deal. I had my '60s look down by then, and was gratified when McGuinn told me that back in the day he'd had a suit just like the one I was wearing.

Los Angeles was as different from New York as I could imagine. I hadn't traveled before and the flight there was my first. It took a while to get used to the palm trees and perpetual sunshine, and the fact that one couldn't walk anywhere. Everything was so far apart and public transportation was practically nonexistent—you needed a car to do anything. We did a few shows in San Francisco, in the Mabuhay Gardens, a club in North Beach near Ferlinghetti's City Lights Bookshop; I remember namedropping Clark Ashton Smith in an interview. We also played in Palo Alto, San Diego, and other places. Then we got word that we would be doing a North American tour, opening for Iggy Pop.

I had learned to play guitar listening to Iggy's band the Stooges, who, along with the Velvet Underground, were considered precursors to punk, so this was exciting news. What made it more exciting was learning that David Bowie, who had resurrected Iggy after his career had gone into decline, would be playing keyboards *incognito* with Iggy. Now I would be sharing stages across the country with someone who, not long ago, I had hung out in Club 82 in order to catch a glimpse of.

I've written about that tour in *New York Rocker*. Among the many memories I have of that time, one in particular stands out. After a show in Seattle—where we stayed in the same hotel The Beatles had—some fans invited us to a party at their rehearsal space. Bowie disappeared after every performance, so he was nowhere to be found, and Iggy declined. But Clem, Jimmy, and I went. We ended up jamming with some local musicians and it was soon clear that something special was happening. Word must have got back to Iggy somehow because, at the height of the jam, he appeared, seemingly out of nowhere, and delivered an impromptu performance that I suspect those present remembered for the rest of their lives. The odd thing is, a few years later, I would be playing guitar for Iggy "for real," when on a North American tour with him in 1981.

But something else that stands out from that tour has a direct connection to my growing interest in the occult. Along with the number of books I had brought with me, which weighed my suitcase down considerably, I would also get up early and, whatever city we were in, make my way to any bookshops in the area. By this time, I had been involved with a girl Benton had introduced me to. I had moved out of the loft and into her small flat on Christopher Street in Greenwich Village, in the gay part of town. She knew Benton from the camp off-off Broadway theatre scene, having met working together on a play. She was my age. She was an actress and photographer and had read her poetry at CBGB. Her mother had been a bohemian back in the early '60s and her father worked for *Playboy*. She was intelligent, sophisticated, and sexy. Her name was Lisa Jane Persky, and at the time we met, she was starring in a hilarious camp send up of fifties women's prison films, *Women Behind Bars*, alongside Divine, the transvestite actress of *Pink Flamingos* fame.[7]

---

7. *Pink Flamingos* (1972), directed by John Waters, is notorious for a scene in which Divine eats dogshit. It was one of Iggy Pop's favorite films, and while on tour with him in 1981, he played it often on the coach. Having met Divine through Lisa, I was able to answer a question Iggy asked that always comes up: Was it real dogshit? Divine assured me it was.

Lisa began to read about magic and the paranormal, taking an interest in it because of my own. I can't remember now exactly what she read, but she certainly was aware of my growing obsession with the occult, and indulged me. She was a great reader anyway; among the many books on her overstuffed shelves I remember the complete Dover series of Andrew Lang's *Rainbow Fairy Books*. She also had the Comte de Lautréamont's (really Isidore Ducasse) *Maldoror*, a strange, transgressive series of prose poems that influenced the surrealists, and J. K. Huysmans's *Against Nature*, "the breviary of decadence," as the poet and critic Arthur Symons called it, which I had read. She was also a fan of the photographer William Wegman, and his dog, Man Ray. One book of Lisa's that became a great favorite of mine was a collection of early photographs of Baudelaire, Gautier, De Nerval, and other French Romantics by the photographer Felix Nadar. Another would later play a large part in our lives: Gurdjieff's *Meetings With Remarkable Men*.[8]

She was also a fan of comic art, and on one trip uptown we visited a dealer off Lexington Avenue and bought some prints by Barry Smith, whose work on Marvel's *Conan the Barbarian* series I had loved. Shops on Bleecker Street and MacDougal Street in Greenwich Village, remnants of the hippie days, displayed witchy and Satanic jewelry in their windows. A few pieces caught my attention. I was never much one for jewelry, but thought a magic ring might not be amiss. I bought three, all silver (I've never been one for gold): one of a snake swallowing its own tail, a symbol of the Ouroboros; one of a scarab, the symbol of the Egyptian god Khepri the rising sun; and one of a claw holding an orb.

At one of the stalls on Canal Street we found pins in the form of a Babylonian sphinx and another scarab. These bits of magical dress-up shared space with our other regalia, a *Man From U.N.C.L.E.* badge, 007 cufflinks, a Batman tie, Beatle boots, Ray Bans, and assorted skinny ties. In *New York Rocker*, there are a few photographs of me in which

8. I would later write an introduction to the Penguin Modern Classic edition (London: Penguin Modern Classics, 2015).

some of these items appear. (For those interested, I still have them.) I was never showy about them, and although I didn't hide my magical interests, which were fairly obvious, I didn't put them on display or draw attention to them. I took them seriously but they were also fun.

But at some point during that tour, something odd started to happen that made the fun we were having rather serious. This was well before mobile phones or the internet, so staying in touch required a bit more effort than it does today. It soon turned out that whenever I thought of calling Lisa in New York, from wherever we were on tour, *she* had thought of trying to call me at the same time; she had the list of hotels where we would be staying so knew where I would be. Even more odd, we discovered that we were having the same kinds of dreams. I don't remember exactly when it started, or the details of the dreams, but it seemed that even without the telephone, although we were thousands of mile apart, we were still "in touch" with each other, *through our minds*.

A few years later I would begin to record my experiences with dreams, and some years after that I would write a book about them.[9] But back then, in 1977, I wrote about them in a different way. After the Iggy tour we were slated to return to the studio to record our follow-up album. This meant we needed new material. With the success of "X Offender," I was inspired and started working on several songs at the same time. I kept returning to the odd experiences Lisa and I had with our dreams, and one day at her flat I picked up my guitar and started strumming. A simple hook on an A chord came to me, and then a melody. Then, out of nowhere, I sang:

Was it destiny? I don't know yet.
Was it just by chance? Could this be Kismet?
Something in my consciousness told me you'd appear
And now I'm always touched by your presence, dear.

---

9. Gary Lachman, *Dreaming Ahead of Time* (Edinburgh, UK: Floris Books, 2022).

The rest of the song came fairly quickly. I never was a songsmith, someone who can craft a melody. Either a song came out in one go or it didn't, and I wound up with fragments, a verse without a chorus or vice versa. I guess that is the lyric poet, giving voice to his soul. And I usually needed some inspiration. Lisa supplied that for more than one song, as she had just done for this one. "(I'm Always Touched by Your) Presence, Dear" became one of the songs we would work on for the new album.

It came just in time. As odious as I found him, our manager did get us work. The Iggy tour was a success, and the two weeks we spent in Los Angeles at the end of it were as well. Interest in what was happening in New York had spread across the Atlantic, where the UK punk scene was getting attention. The Ramones had played London and the Brits wanted more. Television's first album, *Marquee Moon*, had become a surprise UK hit, and they were slated to tour. The promoters wanted a "CBGB package," with another New York band as support. In May, 1977, Blondie flew across the pond to open for Tom Verlaine's band in assorted venues in England and Scotland.

I had been excited about going to California, and then about touring the US and Canada, with rock stars that only a couple of years earlier I had been listening to amidst the squalor of that storefront on East 10th Street. But this was even more of a thrill. I had been an Anglophile since first seeing The Beatles on *The Ed Sullivan Show* in 1964, and had grown up reading Sherlock Holmes and watching the Bond films and *The Avengers* on television. A year earlier, I had discovered Crowley, Colin Wilson, and the Golden Dawn. I had occupied a London of the mind for quite some time. But now I was heading for the real thing.

We arrived at Heathrow just at the start of the Queen's Silver Jubilee. The UK economy was in decline, but punk was flourishing; one suspects a causal relation between the two. The Sex Pistols had just released their second single, "God Save the Queen," which was promptly banned by the BBC, thus ensuring its success. We were booked into a hotel in Kensington that had only recently opened under new ownership by an Arab family. Seeing people in turbans was new to me, as were the kebab kiosks I passed in the neighborhood.

We were shown around, taken to clubs, and interviewed in what's generally known as a flurry of activity. The mainstream music press seemed aggressive. Punk had yet to become profitable, and the old-school rockers were on the defensive. Our internecine squabbling didn't help. Although we were a group, the management tended to treat Clem, Jimmy, and me as a backup band, and Chris and Debbie as the stars. Understandably, we resented this, as we did Chris's attempts to answer every question put to us. Some of the reviews of the album and our shows were nastier than anything we had received before. I have to admit, I seemed to draw some of the critics' attention. One writer for *Melody Maker* said I had the "looks of a child rapist." He may have heard the story behind "X Offender," or it may have been a moment of journalistic intuition. Another said my antics on stage reminded him of one of Dr. Who's Daleks. Yet, at the same time, the critic Richard Cromelin called me the group's "token normal."

We had better luck with the punk kids who interviewed us for their fanzines, like *Sniffin' Glue*. I have to say, I was more interested in talking about magic and the occult than about rock and roll. I was reading Bulwer-Lytton's *Vril: The Power of the Coming Race*, an early science fiction novel about a subterranean superior race which subsequently became a central work in the "occult Nazi" genre, and had brought along a few other books. Two young fans, a couple, picked up on this, and one of my fondest memories of that time is of the afternoon they took me on a tour of bookshops in the West End, Soho, and Camden Town.

I can't remember their names or exactly where we went. I don't have the impression that they took me to Watkins or Atlantis, the two main occult bookshops in town, both of which I later got to know very well and which are both still in business. I remember going to a bookshop on Berners Street in Soho, and I'm pretty sure we went to Compendium, near the Camden Market, another shop I later got to know well but which, sadly, no longer exists. I spent a good deal of my per diem—the allowance I was given for food—on paperbacks of Arthur Machen, Algernon Blackwood, Sax Rohmer, and generic occult works whose titles escape me now. Punk rock and the occult may seem like strange bedfellows, but among the new songs we debuted on that tour was "Presence, Dear," and going by the reaction from the audience, the two seemed to go together well.[10]

I had encounters with some of the local punk heroes. I met Siouxsie and the Banshees at the Music Machine (now KoKo's) in Camden Town, where we saw them play. At the same show, I met Billy Idol of Generation X. I tried to tell him that I liked something he had said in an interview, a more positive remark about the future than the moans about "no future" coming from the Sex Pistols. Unfortunately, he exhibited the kind of supercilious cynicism I have come to expect from some Brits. Many don't know how to react to someone who is earnest and sincere; they are generally afraid of appearing to believe in anything, for fear of being taken in and made fun of. (And, now that I think of it, the whole punk attitude seems simply a more aggressive form of this.) I left our meeting thinking he was quite a jerk.

I didn't meet Johnny Rotten per se, but did see him hovering around the crowds outside the club. Clem got into the spirit of the scene, evidently thinking that, when in Rome, etc. Standing around the statue of Richard Cobden near the Mornington Crescent Underground station, he saw Rotten and shouted out, "Rotten! You're a faggot!" Rotten looked around to see who had said it but couldn't be sure. Finally, he twigged that it was us and gave us two fingers. On another vaguely remembered evening, we drank ourselves silly at a pub. In the end, we

10. It is, I believe, the only song with the word "theosophy" in its lyrics to hit the Top Ten.

were reduced to pouring pints of beer over our heads—a punk custom. We were rescued and ferried home by a fellow American, who drove us back to our hotel. My first view of Big Ben was from the floor of the back seat of his car, where I had ended up.

In Glasgow we caught up with the Talking Heads and the Ramones, who were on their own UK tour. With us and Television, it seemed almost all of the CBGB set were in Great Britain at the same time. I have to admit, though, that most of the people who came to our shows were there to see Television, not Blondie. *Marquee Moon* was a surprise hit, and Verlaine—who, sadly, passed away during the time I have been writing this memoir—was seen as a kind of rock god, and the band's performances like religious events.

The praise was justified. Verlaine had a vague, standoffish demeanor, and radiated an attitude that suggested he was above the rest of the rock and roll rank and file. Genius has its privileges, and he may have been right. Whether he was truly arrogant or simply detached, I don't know. But I did come to share the views of the critics who saw him and Television as rock's saviors. He and Richard Lloyd were perfectly paired—Lloyd's melodic, fluid guitar lines floating over Verlaine's more angular, dissonant jabs. They were really atypical of the music coming from the punk scene, much more of a guitar band in the classic rock style. But they were song oriented. Verlaine's lyrics brought pop or rock music just to the edge of poetry, even more than Dylan or Lennon. If they were stretched a bit more, they might break the "pretentious barrier," but he managed to keep them within bounds, and the music complemented them exactly. This was what was exciting about the early CBGB scene, when symbolist poetry and simple rock chords produced something sui generis, unique. It's something I can still get a taste of when I send my mind back to that time. (And yes, that's an example of Faculty X.)

I watched all of Television's performances during that tour. At the end of it, I came away thinking that playing guitar, singing my own songs, and fronting my own band was something I'd like to do.

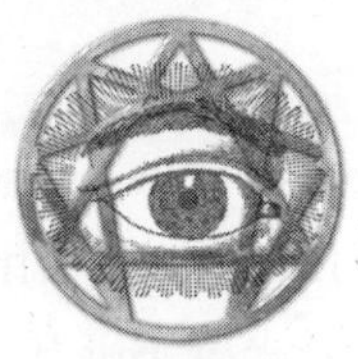

7
Knowledge Is a Funny Thing

The end of that UK tour more or less marked the end of my tenure with Blondie. There had been more than a little turbulence during it, and not only on the flights. My pogoing was not going over well with Debbie and Chris. Jimmy, too, was griping about it, claiming it knocked his Farfisa out of tune. Chris was so disgusted with playing bass on "X Offender" that at one show he threw my new short-scale Rickenbacker bass to the floor. He wasn't the only one who'd had a go at it—Jimmy tossed it across the dressing room at the Whisky A Go-Go one evening; I had to be held back when I went for the fire extinguisher in return. I had gotten the Rickenbacker, a rare guitar, because of their fears that I would inadvertently decapitate Debbie with my old Fender Precision when I was jumping around. It turned out to be a good investment; recently, I discovered that I am one of very few musicians who own one.

The others claimed I was trying to upstage Debbie, but this wasn't true. I was merely more vital and animated than they were. Having gotten over my early self-consciousness, I came to recognize that I had a stage presence. I would be lying if I said I didn't notice that people in the audience looked at me, and that I liked it, especially when they were girls. Clem, who never complained about me, knew that, and secretly told me that I should be the guitarist, not Chris.

I felt this was true when it came to my songs. I had played guitar on another song I'd written, "Scenery," that we recorded for the first album but which got left out at the last minute, something I wasn't happy about and which I made clear to the producer who'd decided to cut it.[1]

I played a twelve-string guitar on that track in honor of the Byrds, as mentioned earlier, the sound was Roger McGuinn's trademark. The producer claimed the track "didn't go with" the rest of the album. I disagreed, and said that the reason it had been cut was because Chris didn't want another song on the album written by me and with me playing guitar. He felt threatened, and I suspect Debbie did too. I was young, full of energy, creative, and not content to play a supporting role. I was writing more songs, music, and lyrics—and they were more in my voice than Debbie's. (As it was, I never wrote a song thinking Debbie would sing it.) They were, as lyric poetry is, an expression of me, my soul. And there seemed to be *more* of me to express than I knew. Had I found my "true self"? Some of it, I think.

Jimmy and Clem weren't absolutely happy with the way things were going either. They, too, felt we were being treated like backup musicians, while Debbie and Chris were the "stars." I suspect that, from the manager's and record company's perspective, they were, although it was true that Jimmy and I produced quite a few songs and that Chris and Debbie wouldn't have been able to come up with enough material to record on their own. For a time, the three of us talked about forming our own band with me as the singer and guitarist, and we rented a rehearsal space and got together with another musician, Rob Duprey of the Mumps—with whom I would work later on—to play some of the songs I had written. It sounded pretty good, and had we continued, who knows what may have come from it. But, after playing together a few times, we didn't carry on. Perhaps doing that was enough for them.

---

1. It later turned up on a compilation, *Blonde and Beyond*, and on their 2022 box set, *Against the Odds*.

It let off some steam and frustration. And I imagine they knew what side their bread was buttered on. But all it did for me was to confirm my belief that I would have to leave the band soon and start my own.

To say my ego was involved in this would be to point out the obvious. Anyone who is creative and wants others to know it has an ego—it's an absolutely indispensable necessity. But there was something else. I felt constrained, held back, and inhibited. I knew I was as good as the people on the scene whose work I admired, like Verlaine, or who were fronting their own band, like Richard Hell, who by this time had split with Johnny Thunders and formed The Voidoids, a name appropriate for the high priest of the Blank Generation. I liked Debbie and Chris, and I enjoyed playing with them. But more and more, I came away feeling it was only a matter of time before I would have to leave.

I decided I would play on the new album and leave after that. I had worked on all the material we would record. We had honed it during the UK tour, and it went over well at our shows on our return. "Presence, Dear" was among this material, as was another song of mine that we played at what turned out to be my last performance with Blondie—at least until 1997, when I wound up playing with them again for a short time. The song was called "The First One," and it would play a large role in what was to come.[2]

My relations with our manager were, as a reader might suspect, never good, and by this time, they had reached rock bottom. I resented his attempts to give us advice about what songs to perform, and I especially resented his attempts to rein me in. I'm sure he didn't care for being told off by me in front of people. But most of all, it was clear to me that he was not to be trusted, and that he knew I was an obstacle. I suspect that, even if Chris and Debbie changed their minds, he would still have been dead set on getting rid of me. If I'd had more

---

2. A recording of this performance, at the Village Gate on Bleecker Street in New York, on July 2, 1977, has turned up online. See "Blondie-The First One-Village Gate(NYC)-July 2, 1977 (live)," YouTube, August 3, 2011.

worldly wisdom, I would have kept quiet, bided my time, and left when it best suited me. But I have never had an adequate supply of this sort of wisdom. Looking back now, I suspect I played into his hands. But I have never been one for strategy, tactics, manipulation, and dissembling. I won't say I'm honest to a fault, but I generally stand with integrity rather than deceit.

In my noble innocence, I visited the manager. He wasn't in, so I left a note spelling out my intentions. I imagine he was waiting for something like this. If I intended to go, why wait? Not long after leaving my note, I got a call from him. My services, he said, were no longer required. It was July 4, 1977, Independence Day. Did he get the irony? I don't know. I certainly did, and took it as a good sign.

When I got his call, I had just come back from JFK, where I had seen Lisa off. She was heading to Los Angeles to follow her acting career. She knew about the trouble in the band and what I intended to do. She advised against it, saying I should draw back, record the album, and then think of what I wanted to do. She had made up her mind that if she wanted to get into the movies—which she did—she had to go to LA. I could stay here, keep the flat, or I could join her later—it was up to me. Again, if I'd had more worldly wisdom, I may have agreed with her. But then, I loved her and wanted to be with her, even if it meant leaving New York for Los Angeles. And I wanted to have my own band.

So, instead of apologizing and begging Debbie to let me stay, as I was advised to do, I said screw it. I now realize that I could have fought it legally; I had a contract with the record company and, technically, I couldn't have been forced out. I didn't know this then, and had no one to advise me—and, in any case, by that time I wanted to get as far away from Blondie as possible. I had faith in myself and my destiny. I had gotten through tough times before. I'd get through them again.

RELOCATING TO LOS ANGELES with the intention of living there and starting over again was a rather different prospect than being there on tour. I wasn't entirely on my own, I was there with Lisa, but this time around there was no record company, no roadies, no fans and—blessedly—no manager. Most of the people I knew thought I was crazy to leave the band and New York. But then others thought I had the talent and drive to make it on my own. I fell into that camp. I never had a second thought about it. Once I decided that, no matter what happened, I *had* to hit out on my own, that was it. I never looked back.

Word of my departure got around fairly quickly. The Saints, a group in Australia, got in touch with me and asked if I was interested in joining them. I was gratified by the offer, and Australia sounded tempting. But I wanted my own band and I wanted to be with Lisa. So I turned them down. I had heard that Richard Lloyd was thinking of leaving Television and that Verlaine was looking for a guitarist to replace him. Friends suggested I audition. But I didn't want to move from one support position to another, even if it would have been with someone I respected. And there were other possibilities in New York. Most likely I could have put a band together there fairly easily. But I wanted a fresh start. LA was still without a scene of its own, and I thought it might be easier to make a splash in virgin territory than in an already-glutted, familiar pond. In fact, soon after we formed, my band, The Know, would play a crucial part in getting a genuine LA "new wave" scene going. Another reason to head west was because that was where most of the record companies were.

It took about a month for me to settle my affairs and to pack everything I intended to ship to LA. Most of this was books. Rob Duprey, mentioned above, gave me a hand packing and lugging the dozen or so boxes to the post office. Thus began a ritual that I would go through several times over the years, of shipping my library across the US—until I eventually shipped it across the Atlantic, as well. Some of the books resting on the shelf across from me as I write this started their tenure in that loft on the Bowery, nearly fifty years ago.

Just before I left, New York suffered a massive blackout. In the Bronx and Harlem there was looting, but in Greenwich Village it was a party, with ice cream vendors giving away their wares before they melted, and people walking through the streets at night carrying candles. Jersey City still had power, so with a friend I took the PATH train under the river and had dinner there, one of the few times when it was better to be on that side of the Hudson. It somehow seemed fitting that I'd soon be leaving a darkened city for the land of perpetual sunshine. Was it an omen? I don't know. After a few goodbyes to friends and a visit to my parents, whom I hadn't seen for quite some time, in early August I took the subway to JFK and started on my journey to the West.

AS YOU MIGHT SUSPECT, my determination to succeed would meet with a buffeting. Being in Los Angeles as a resident took some getting used to and, to be honest, I never did quite get used to it. The constant sunshine wearied me and I soon discovered that my black suits and skinny ties were not made for it. For someone who loved to wander through Manhattan, having to drive everywhere became a bore. I never got my driver's license, and wouldn't until another stint in LA, a few years later. Living in New York, I didn't need it, and for my first tenure in the Golden State, I resorted to the practically non-existent public transportation system. This meant I could get to one or two places a day, with long waits in between. It also meant I often found myself walking for hours along the endless stretches of Wilshire or Santa Monica Boulevard in order to get somewhere. I carried out a kind of guerrilla war against the city, the only casualty of which was me.

Lisa had found a room in a house in the Wilshire district. It was a large place, and a friend she knew from an earlier visit was living there. It wasn't that different from sharing her small studio on Christopher Street, although we had to share the kitchen and bathroom with a few others. Eventually we would take another room as well but for the first year or so, that room was home. The main problem was, as it usually is, money. *Blondie* had earned a gold record in Australia, but I had yet to see any royalties from it—and never would; it was only after bringing a lawsuit against the band many years later that I would see a fraction of what I should have received. The money meant for me had somehow found its way into other pockets, and no one bothered to let me know what I was missing. The manager's and producer's shares were mysteriously supplemented by funds earmarked for someone else. Alas, such is show business.

LISA MANAGED TO BUY a 1966 Ford Mustang, and spent her days barreling from studio to studio. She got work, and went on to appear in many films and much television.[3] But she wasn't earning enough to support both of us, and, in any case, I never expected her to pay my way. We lived frugally, and our diets fluctuated from minimal to the occasional binge courtesy of her father's credit card. But the hard truth was coming home—I had to get a job. Or, more to the point, I needed money.

Word of my destitution must have reached the Blondie inner sanctum. At one point I got a call from the manager's flunkey, asking if I would be interested in selling my rights to "Presence, Dear" for a munificent five hundred dollars. The song had made it to the new album—with no help by me—and he knew, as did others, that it would do well. I was, of course, not pleased by this attempt to steal my future royalties, but I also knew the fact that he was trying to do so meant there would be money down the line. I told the messenger what the manager could do with his offer. There would be money later on, I knew, but, for the moment, it hadn't reached me. There was no way around it—I had to go back to the real world.

The last time I'd had any sort of regular job was when I worked as a messenger in New York. Similar work was out of the question here. At twenty-one, after North American and UK tours, with an album in record shops and my face in magazines, I found myself in pretty much the same position I was in before I'd joined Blondie. Well, not quite,

3. Her film catalogue can be found at lisajanepersky.com and on the IMDb site.

as the place I shared with Lisa wasn't squalid and she was a more welcome roommate than any of the others I'd had. But, financially, I was as broke as I had ever been. I would put a band together soon, but in the meantime I had to bring in some money.

I applied to a 7-11 convenience store, but failed the lie detector test. For a time, I worked the lights at The Roxy, a famous rock club on the Sunset Strip; I lost this job after an ill-timed joint had me slicing off the top of the singer Bill Withers's head during his hit "Ain't No Sunshine When She's Gone." I applied for a job at an adult bookstore, but decided it was too creepy and didn't return. When the holiday season arrived, I got work at a Sav-On drugstore, one of those huge shopping center affairs which sell practically everything. I had to wear a cheery Santa vest and carry Christmas trees to elderly ladies' cars.

I was saved from this fate by Craig Leon, who was the engineer on the *Blondie* album. He was in town producing an album with a singer/songwriter named Moon Martin, and asked if I wanted to play bass. He didn't have to ask twice. The pay was good, it was great to be back in the studio—even if Moon and I didn't quite get on—and I worked with Phil Seymour, the drummer with the Dwight Twilly Band, whose hit "I'm On Fire" I had liked. Craig even arranged for a jam session with Dwight, Phil, and myself, but nothing came of it. Cheap Trick was recording in the studio next door, and we all wasted time and brain cells winning free games on the rigged pinball machine.

It wasn't long after recording with Moon Martin that I would put my band, The Know, together. But amidst the frustration and annoyance of having to find work—and the painful blows to my self-esteem that being demoted from pop star to indigent ex-member of an increasingly popular band entailed—fate threw across my path another book that would change my life.

AFTER MY FIRST READING of *The Occult*, my fascination with magic and its most flamboyant modern practitioner, Aleister Crowley, kept my attention focused fairly tightly on magick, Crowley-style. And while I devoured books about this with an indiscriminate appetite, I hadn't yet found Colin Wilson's earlier existential work. That changed in the autumn of 1977.

Loving books so much, and having a fairly wide acquaintanceship with literature, I thought working at a book shop would be a relatively pleasant way to bring in some income. At least it was something I felt I had some qualifications for. I discovered this was true when, a decade later, I found myself working at the Bodhi Tree Bookstore, which at that time I'd visited only as a customer. I've mentioned applying for work at an adult bookshop; on another excursion looking for work, I applied at a mainstream bookshop in Westwood, an upmarket part of town on the way to the Pacific, near the University of California, Los Angeles, where nearly twenty years later, I would briefly work as a science writer. After I explained how much I loved books and how much I would enjoy working at a bookshop, the manager said, "Look, kid, the stuff on the shelves here could be apples or oranges, or anything. I'm not interested in books and I don't care how much they mean to you. I sell them, I don't read them. If I could make a profit selling something else, I would."

I left the shop thinking that even if the manager called me, I wouldn't go back (he didn't, by the way). His deflating assessment of his stock suggested that, while I might enjoy working at a bookshop, I wouldn't enjoy working at his. This depressed me and left me unfit to look for any other work that day. I did go to another bookshop, not to apply for a job—but to find a book that might cheer me up. This didn't mean I was looking for a comedy or some light reading—I've never been one for that—but a book that would grip me, a book of ideas that would make me think. Such books have always been a tonic, reminding me that the world is much larger than the small section of it immediately before us, which we call "the present."

I had enough money for some lunch and for the bus ride home, but in the mood I was in, I forgot such practicalities. I browsed the philosophy section and almost at the very end, somewhere between Whitehead and Wittgenstein, I saw a book by Colin Wilson. It was called *The Outsider*.

It was the Dell paperback edition, published in 1967, with a black cover and the title and author's name in bold, white lettering. In the upper right-hand corner, in a slightly green-tinted font, a blurb let me know what I would find inside. It was, it told me, "The Seminal Book on the Alienation of Modern Man." In the mood I was in, that sounded right. I bought it and, with the money I had left, got a sandwich somewhere for lunch. That emptied my pockets and meant I was faced with the long walk home from Westwood to Western Avenue, where we lived, along the seemingly endless stretch of Wilshire Boulevard, a distance of nearly ten miles. By the time I got home and started reading the book, I knew the long hike had been worth it.

In a letter, Nietzsche relates the effect reading Schopenhauer for the first time had on him. After finding Schopenhauer's *The World as Will and Representation* in a secondhand bookshop—a work that presents one of the grimmest, most pessimistic visions of human existence ever conceived—Nietzsche took the book home and let its "forceful, gloomy genius" work on him.[4] And, although he would later reject his philosophy, at that juncture in his life, in Schopenhauer Nietzsche found a "mirror" which reflected "the world, life" and his "own soul in frightful grandeur."[5] Wilson himself has related in several of his books the effect of hearing a radio broadcast of Shaw's *Man and Superman* as a teenager, and being stunned by the discovery that *someone else* had been obsessed with the same questions about human purpose and meaning that had troubled him. He'd thought he was the only one filled with the necessity of knowing why he existed, and was amazed to find that *he was not alone*.

---

4. Quoted in Colin Wilson, *The Outsider* (Boston: Houghton Mifflin Company, 1956), 125.
5. Wilson, *The Outsider*, 125.

Sitting in our room, with *The Outsider* in hand, I had a similar experience. It was the same as when I'd first read Hesse or Nietzsche, the feeling that the person writing this was speaking *to me*. If *The Occult* had introduced me to the world of magic and mysticism and to the hidden powers of consciousness I would spend the rest of my life exploring and trying to understand, *The Outsider*, I can say, introduced me to myself. It did not take long for me to recognize myself in it.

As is the case with *The Occult*, I have read *The Outsider* more times than I can remember. I have a copy of it in front of me as I write, and, once again, it is difficult for me to read a sentence or two without getting drawn in and finding myself rereading it yet again. Many years after that first reading, and following his death in 2013, I wrote a book about Wilson; if asked of which of my books I feel most proud, I would have to say *Beyond the Robot*, my study of his life and work. Yet an even greater source of honor, one with which I was able to repay in some small way a debt of gratitude, was the foreword I contributed to a new edition of *The Outsider* that my publisher released at the same time as *Beyond the Robot*.[6] I had so convinced my editor of the importance of Wilson's work that he decided to republish *The Outsider* in a new edition, thinking that it and *Beyond the Robot* might spark a Wilson revival.

Whether such a revival took place or is taking place, I can't say. I can say that I have received many emails from Wilson readers who enjoyed my book and who were grateful to be reminded of how important *The Outsider* and Wilson's other books were to them at different times in their lives. That I was invited to introduce new readers to a book that had changed my life—while reminding seasoned readers of what an important book it is—is something that, as they say here in the UK, I was quite chuffed about (for US readers, this means delighted).

---

6. Colin Wilson, *The Outsider* (New York: Tarcher/Penguin 2016). Some years earlier Wilson had performed a similar service for me by writing a foreword to my book *A Secret History of Consciousness* (Greast Barrington, MA: Lindisfarne Books, 2003).

own problems, as it made them unfit for the dreary business of life. Coming down to Earth after their ecstatic flights, the Romantics were faced with the same world they had tried to escape. The world-rejection this produced only made their lives even more difficult.

Many Outsiders succumbed to drugs or alcohol or depression. I had already seen many people on the scene destroy themselves with drugs; it was, in fact, in many ways *de rigueur*, with heroin the preferred expedient. I was determined not to be one of these. Only the strongest Outsiders were able to reach the source of "power, meaning, and purpose" within them and not crack up. I felt instinctively that I was one of them. I had a cheerfulness and optimism that made me reject the pop nihilism of the Sex Pistols and other punk bands, and I lacked the anger that seemed to inform many of my contemporaries, whose names—Richard Hell, Johnny Thunders, or Alan Suicide—suggested resentment and frustration as sources of their bad-boy scowls. I was too intelligent to be pessimistic, and my sense of humor would not let me take the negative view of things seriously.

I really had nothing to be angry about, but I had set myself a hefty challenge. If leaving a band just as its star was beginning to rise seemed a dubious career move, deciding to move in the opposite direction to the reigning zeitgeist was only making an already uphill struggle even more difficult. But I've always preferred taking the path of greatest achievement to that of least resistance. I suspect my being a Capricorn has something to do with this, a point I will return to later. The Outsider's task is *not* to remain "outside" as one of society's rejects or misfits, grumbling on the sidelines, but to learn how to develop the visionary faculty that will enable him to impose his values and insights on society. Outsiders are, as Shelley had said of poets, "the unacknowledged legislators of the world." They reject the everyday world, not in order to destroy it (the nihilistic "no future" of the punks) but it order to transform it.

It may seem quite a leap from these portentous observations to the world of rock and roll, but for the time being, that was the milieu in which I worked. It's a poor workman who blames his tools, but eventually I would come to see that what I wanted to express and my means of expression were not quite suited for each other. Intelligence is not necessarily an advantage in the rock world. In many ways, it can be the opposite. In the end it eroded my ability to write songs. But before it got to that point, I did my best with the means available.

IN EARLY 1978, I RELEASED my first and only solo 45. Beat Records, a small label run by Steve Zepeda, a local pop entrepreneur who put out a fanzine and booked acts for a club, approached me with the idea. I was ready for it. I had yet to form The Know, but The Mumps, a band I knew from New York, were in town and I borrowed some of them to record it. The A-side was "The First One," a tune slated for *Plastic Letters*, Blondie's second album, and which we had played at my farewell performance. As was "Presence, Dear," it was a love song to Lisa.[7] (If there is ever any doubt about my being a romantic, the fact that I used to write love songs should dispell it.)

But the B-side was something different. It had a message. "Tomorrow Belongs to You" was my response to the dreary, predictable nihilism that had become fashionable on the scene. It had started in the UK and had spread across the States. Even New York, citadel of cool, had succumbed—the arty, beatnik character of the early CBGB days drowned out by the abrasive ruckus coming from Britain, accompanied by safety pins and torn T-shirts. It had an upbeat message—rather than whining about "no future," I asked: "What will you do? / Tomorrow belongs to you" and suggested that there was quite a bit we could do.[8]

It was the start of my trying to bring some of the ideas I had been

---

7. It is something of a collector's item now.

8. Another rarity is the CD collection of tracks by myself and The Know released in 2003 by Overground Records, *Tomorrow Belongs to You.*

devouring for the past few years into my music. It is always easy to write songs that complain about something or that tell everyone how miserable you are. Earnestness rarely goes over, and a more positive theme generally has more resistance to overcome. But I was never one for the blues.

Although it didn't make a dime, "The First One" did well on the "new wave" charts, smaller, more niche versions of the mainstream hit parade that, in a nod to the rising popularity of the new music, several pop magazines had started to feature. I was, of course, happy that it topped heavy hitters like Patti Smith's "Because the Night" and Plastic Bertrand's "Ça Plane Pour Moi," a French version of punk's "nothing matters" (it means "It's all the same to me.") But, although I was rightly proud of producing a "power pop" classic, as the track has come to be called, that another song of mine was meeting with even greater success was even more cause for celebration.

"Presence, Dear" had been released in the UK as a single, and in a short time had hit the UK and European top ten. It didn't do as well in the US, but the Brits and Europeans had taken to Debbie, and the producer knew a hit song when he heard one. When we discovered the song was in the charts, Lisa and I headed to the newsstand at Cahuenga and Hollywood Boulevard (a remnant of old Raymond Chandleresque Hollywood that, sadly, no longer exists) and paged through the pop magazines looking for it and laughing with glee. My street cred went up considerably. Not only had I written the song that landed Blondie their record deal, and not only had I put out a solo effort that was garnering acclaim, now I had a song on the top ten charts. I thanked the self-belief and self-esteem that had me tell the manager what to do with his "generous" offer of five hundred dollars for the rights to "Presence, Dear" when Lisa and I were broke and starving. Soon, the royalties would come in. There was no longer any danger of having to look for work.

Word had gotten out that I was looking to put a band together. Hopefuls came—many of them—but it took a while to find the right people. I had met a drummer, Joel Turissi, while working at the Roxy, and he expressed interest. Then Steve Zepeda introduced me to a bass player, Richard D'Andrea. He had worked with an LA band, The Motels, and came highly recommended. The three of us got together a few times with another guitarist. He was good, but, for some reason, I wanted to keep the band members down to a minimum. It was, I suspect, a sign of my penchant for working alone, at least creatively. I had a clear idea of how I wanted the group to sound, and having the bare necessities—guitar, bass, and drums—seemed the best way to go about it. I'm not a believer in the democratic style of creative work. Whether it makes for good relations or not, I'm usually pretty clear about what I want and do not collaborate well. Creation is a solitary affair. The performance may require more than one individual, but the actual work is the product of one person's attempt to express something, and he or she is best placed to know what that is and how to do it.

For a while I wasn't sure what to call the band. "The Few" was a possibility. Numerically it certainly fit. But then it came to me. I had been reading quite a bit about Gnosticism, an early, mystical variant of Christianity that was eventually wiped out by the official church. They were called Gnostics because, rather than accept dogma and belief, they sought experience and knowledge, something that understandably put them on the wrong side of church authorities. As mentioned, Jung was very interested in the Gnostics, and saw his psychology as a form of modern Gnosticism.

Gnosis is a Greek word for knowledge, but this is not the kind of knowledge we are used to, the sort we acquire through study or learning; that, as I later came to know, was called *episteme* by the Greeks, and epistemology is the philosophical study of how we know what we know. Gnosis is something different. It is an immediate experience which is also a knowledge. It was the kind of experience I was learning about through my study of the occult. It *hits* one in the same way that a cold drink does on a hot day, or a sudden insight lights up in your mind—the "Aha!" experience I had been reading about in a book by Arthur

Koestler, another writer whose work has influenced my own, and whose clarity of style, like Wilson's, I have tried to approximate.[9]

I'd had experiences like this and wanted to have more. I wanted such knowledge and sought it in different ways. One could say that I wanted to "be in the know." And soon, I was, because that is what I called the band. A song I wrote, "In the Know," said as much.

Knowledge is a funny thing, and sometimes I laugh.
Of its gifts to thee I sing.
I would give up everything to be in the know.

For many people, it seemed that I had.

THE KNOW DEBUTED AT A SURPRISE special performance in March 1978, opening for The Mumps at the Whisky A Go-Go. Soon, we would be headlining there, as well as at other famous clubs, like the Starwood and Troubadour. I have to say, I was gratified to see my name on the Whisky's marquee, the same that had advertised The Byrds, The Doors, Buffalo Springfield, and other top groups from the heyday of the Sunset Strip. It was a long way from starving in a storefront or freezing on the Bowery.

The Know played all over Los Angeles. We traveled up and down the coast, playing in San Diego and other cities south of LA. In San Francisco, we played at the Mabuhay Gardens, sharing a bill with my friend Jonathan Postal's group, The Readymades. I had last been there with Blondie, and was glad to return with my own group and to find an appreciative audience. Soon we became one of the few bicoastal bands

---

9. I came across Koestler's book *Janus: A Summing Up* (New York: Random House, 1978), his follow-up to his classic *The Ghost in the Machine* (New York: Random House, 1967), at an outdoor bookstall at the old Pickwick Bookshop on Hollywood Boulevard. As with Wilson and a few other authors, I subsequently read all of Koestler's work, and periodically reread it.

on the scene, shuttling back and forth between LA and New York on the Red-Eye Express, cheap flights that left at midnight and which more often than not ferried several squalling babies.

We became regulars at Max's Kansas City and at a new club, Hurrah's, which was uptown on West 62nd Street. It was a discotheque that had opened its doors to rock and roll. By this time, CBGB had lost pride of place among the underground, having been overrun by out-of-town bands wanting to garner some of the prestige of having played there. On one New York trip, I had lunch with Timothy Leary. A mutual acquaintance knew of my interest in consciousness; Leary was making a comeback after spending time in prison, and thought sharing a bill with a new wave act might bring him a new audience. Nothing came of it, and I don't remember much of what we said, but he seemed an upbeat, intelligent character, only a slight sparkle in his eye suggesting the madcap LSD messiah of the '60s.

We did mini-tours of the East Coast, playing in Boston, Washington, Philadelphia, and venturing further afield to Salt Lake City and Minneapolis. And whenever I could, I hunted down second-hand bookshops. In Cambridge, Massachusetts, I found a US first edition of *Religion and the Rebel*, Wilson's sequel to *The Outsider*, for a few dollars. But I didn't skimp when it came to his books. I remember scandalizing a friend when I spent fifteen dollars on *Mysteries*, Wilson's follow up to *The Occult*, which had just come out; a quick calculation tells me that is about seventy dollars in today's economy. Both books are on the shelf behind me as I write.

Historically, probably our most important performance was at Madame Wong's, a restaurant in LA's Chinatown that, in late 1978, decided to open its doors to local pop bands, rather as Club 82 had done a few years earlier in New York. On October third that year, The Know headlined at Madame Wong's, with The Furies as the support act. We were the first bands to play there. It was the official start of LA's own "power pop" scene, and we had inaugurated it.

The show was a success—nearly four hundred people in skinny

ties, narrow lapels, and Converse sneakers crammed into a room built to hold half that number. Many had to be turned away. The weekend before, I went on a local radio show and told the listeners that if they wanted to have their own scene, they had better get down to Chinatown. They did.

The place was so packed, Lisa barely got in. I remember pulling her up the stairs through a thicket of tab-collared, polka-dotted shirts. After our sets—we each did two—a crowd of us were invited to a free dinner at the Atomic Café, a Japanese eatery in Little Tokyo not far from Chinatown that was popular with the downtown arty set. After that, it was a power pop hangout too. A single night had given birth to two watering holes for the new pop demimonde. As I mention in *New Rock Rocker*, in New York, a week after our debut at Madame Wong's, Sid Vicious, bass player with the Sex Pistols, was arrested for the murder of Nancy Spungen, whom I knew. She had been found stabbed to death in their room at the Chelsea Hotel. Vicious himself would, a few months later, be found dead from a heroin overdose. It seemed that when they said there was "no future," the punks were more accurate than they knew.

It was at this time that my interest in Aleister Crowley took on a problematic character. More than anything else, it probably was the reason for Lisa and I drifting apart.

One afternoon, I saw an advertisement at Gilbert's Bookshop on Hollywood Boulevard. This was, of course, long before the internet, and Gilbert's had a bulletin board, allowing its customers to put up notices. Back then, Hollywood Boulevard was as much a book lover's haven as it was a tourist magnet. There were several secondhand shops, and more than one catered to besotted occultists like me. Gilbert's was one of these; Jimmy Page, Kenneth Anger, and David Bowie were among its clientele. I made the trek there from our room at least once a week and usually came back with a stack of books.[10] This time I returned with something different.

The advertisement was for an Aleister Crowley group. I didn't expect much from it, but I answered it and asked about the group. A few days later there was a knock at the door. When I opened it, an unprepossessing character in his twenties asked who I was. When I told him, he asked if I was ready to take the oath of the probationer for the A∴A∴, the magical society Crowley started after the breakup of the Golden Dawn. To fell two magical birds with one stone, he also asked if I was prepared to be initiated in the O.T.O. (Ordo Templi Orientis), the quasi-Masonic society that had "sacred sex" at its center, which Crowley had also headed.

I have to admit, I was a bit taken aback by such an abrupt request, rather as if a Jehovah's Witness had handed me a copy of *The Watchtower* and then asked if I wanted to join the club. I thought about it for a minute. I had been reading about magick and my true will and Holy Guardian Angel for a few years now. Was I ready to turn theory into practice? Never the armchair magician, I said I was.

Not long after this, after some study and preparation, I was initiated into Crowley's religion. The ceremony took place somewhere outside LA. I can't remember much of it, other than the Oriental-style tent in which I sat, and that it must have taken place somewhere near canals or a harbor, and it must have been Christmastime, because I can recall small boats going by spelling out *Feliz Navidad* in bright festive lights on their sides. Something else I recall is that a kitten belonging to someone officiating at the ceremony seemed to have died during it, and that someone remarked that as one life ended, a new one began. Again, I can't say for certain, but I believe Grady McMurtry, a US military officer who

10. Another favorite bookshop was Papa Bach in Santa Monica. They imported paperbacks from the UK, among them books by Colin Wilson, Lyall Watson, and Stan Gooch, with whom I would correspond many years later. I much preferred the literature about consciousness and the paranormal coming from across the pond to what was being produced in the US, which tended to have an Eastern flavor, and even then, to be informed with what came to be called New Age spirituality.

knew Crowley in his last days and took on the mantle of head of the O.T.O. after his death, performed the ceremony. Odd to think that I had some contact, however slight, with someone who knew the old Beast.

Alas, today I wish I hadn't answered that advertisement at Gilbert's. I tell the story in *New York Rocker*, and am loath to repeat it here. Suffice it to say that my open-mindedness and willingness to give people the benefit of the doubt, admirable and helpful traits as they are, sometimes work against me—as on this occasion. Whatever magical qualifications the character who knocked at our door may have possessed, they were overshadowed by his also possessing all of the bad traits of Crowley himself. Crowleyites like to say that "do what thou wilt" doesn't mean "do what you like." If so, I can only say that most of the Crowley devotees I have encountered seem not to have gotten this message. I am not saying there are no serious practitioners of his belief, only that I have not met many of them. The fellow who I let across our threshold proved to be one of the worst. It soon became apparent that he was, like Crowley, an occult freeloader. For several months, until I tired of him and Crowley, he found a cozy spot in our life.

Eventually, I broke with my erstwhile magical tutor. I had by then already become disenchanted with Crowley; later, when I sold my collection of Crowley's works, it fetched a tidy sum. A kind of psychic claustrophobia had seemed to gather round me, a suffocating atmosphere in which everything echoed "Crowley." As I read and studied more, my sensibilities became more critical. I didn't doubt magic, and I learned much from following the exercises for a variety of occult faculties that were part of my magical practice. But it became clear to me that however larger-than-life Crowley may have been in some ways—not everyone climbs the Himalayas, starts a religion, and has an abbey in Sicily—in many ways he was really much smaller. He had the potential for greatness and more than a touch of genius. But Crowley never outgrew his insatiable ego and his insensitivity to the people around him. He may have been a "hell of a holy guru," as he called himself. But in the end, he was a small, often petty human being. And the fellow who turned up at our door was smaller still.

My plunge into Crowley's universe did not go down well with Lisa. She pegged my meretricious mentor as a sponge the minute she saw him, and asked if I had gone insane. It must have seemed so. The clincher was a Gnostic Mass I attended at which the participants ingested communion wafers spiked with menstrual blood. Whose, I didn't know, nor did I ask. Sex magic was part of the curriculum, but the prospect of somehow using the ecstasy of our lovemaking for magical ends did nothing but dampen Lisa's libido. As you can imagine, this led to some disharmony between us. And when, during a two-month sojourn in New York with the band, I found myself the subject of more than one punkette's interest, the hairline fractures widened into precipitous rifts. We were no longer quite in touch with each other's presences. When I returned, she knew something had changed. So did I, and New York began to look more promising.

My decision to return to New York precipitated the last days of The Know, although, when I made up my mind to relocate yet again, I had no notion of this. One reason I decided to move is that I felt we had done as much as we could in Los Angeles. We'd played several showcases for record executives and made a few demo recordings, but nothing came of it. We got close, but . . . According to one critic whose tastes I respected, we were "too spare and brainy." Unfortunately, a band with a similar name, The Knack, had a huge hit with their first single. I didn't begrudge them their success, but I felt that now no one in LA would be interested in The Know.

I had to admit, too, that I was tired of LA and missed New York. One reason I missed it was a girl I had met there, a successful model, during one of our trips. She was sexy, funny, and had made her interest in me unmistakably clear. My tenure among the Thelemites had soured my relationship with Lisa. I was frustrated, hungry, susceptible, and Lulu, the model, knew it. On our first date we took *Psilocybe mexicana* at a café on the Upper East Side. After a circuitous cab ride that had us changing directions and destinations half a dozen times, we ended up at her room at the Gramercy Park Hotel (she was, as I said, successful). Our six-month affair had started, and I decided once again that sex, drugs, and rock and roll were fun.

For the first few weeks, I lived with Lulu at the Gramercy Park. I can't say that I didn't enjoy it—room service was a delight—but, not wanting to be a kept lover, I found a flat on Thompson Street in Greenwich Village, not far from Debbie's old place in Little Italy. It was around this time that I read J. W. Dunne's book, *An Experiment with Time*, about his experiences with precognitive dreams. By chance, Dunne discovered that bits and pieces of his own future—what he would read in the newspaper or hear from someone—would turn up in his dreams "in advance" of when he should have known about them. Dunne suggested that we all would notice such temporal anomalies if we bothered to pay attention to our dreams and to write them down. I took his advice and soon discovered that he was right. I did dream the future, and, off and on, have been doing so ever since. It was also around this time that I had an experience of Faculty X in which, for some moments "out of time," I found myself hovering above India, witness to a panorama of the subcontinent's history that would have taken years of study to acquire in the usual way, a story I tell, along with those of my precognitive dreams, in *Dreaming Ahead of Time*.

I WON'T SAY THAT NOW, more than forty years later, I don't look back on this time with some nostalgia. We were a rock and roll couple and we did it well. I was twenty-three, collecting royalties and, on a good weekend at Hurrah, pulling in two or three thousand dollars for our shows.[11] Lulu worked for the top fashion magazines and was often away

---

11. A video of one of our performances at Hurrah is available on YouTube, "Gary Valentine and The Know Roadrunner."

in France, Italy, or Japan. We went to the Oyster Bar at Grand Central Terminal, drove around in a limousine in between my sets, and made love often. For one shoot in France, I met her in Paris, my first time there. Today, when I catch a whiff of a particular cologne, our two weeks there come back to me, as the madeleine returned Proust to his childhood. I was gratified when, at a café in Les Halle, we heard "The First One" on the sound system.

Again, who knows what direction things may have taken, but something Lulu brought back from one of her sessions in Tokyo was a factor in loosening my rock and roll moorings. When she returned from one shoot there, she handed me a gadget that hadn't hit the States yet. It was a Walkman.

This was well before iPhones and all the other personal technology that dominates our lives today. I suspect that Lulu was not the only person in Manhattan to have brought a Walkman back from Japan. But I can say that I didn't see anyone else with one then. When she let me borrow it, I can honestly say that I was one of the first people in New York to have one.

I had by then started listening to classical music. Once again, Colin Wilson was responsible. In his novel, *The Philosopher's Stone*, two scientists discover a way of inducing more intense, ecstatic states of consciousness through a brain operation. One of the practices they engaged in, in order to strengthen their powers of concentration, was listening to long, sprawling symphonies by Mahler, Bruckner, and other late Romantics; he even mentions a colossal work by the conductor Wilhelm Furtwängler. My exposure to classical music at that time was mostly through films—think Kubrick—but after reading *The Philosopher's Stone*, I started buying classical cassettes from the cutout bin at Barnes & Noble, and playing them on a cheap cassette player.[12]

---

12. Vox Classical and Sine Qua Non were two very good budget labels then. A performance of Bruckner's Seventh Symphony by William Steinberg and the Pittsburgh Symphony Orchestra, released by Sine Qua Non, was a particular favorite.

I got to know quite a few pieces and became familiar with several composers that way. But the Walkman was something entirely different.

I imagine it is difficult for people today, having music, podcasts, and much else piped into their consciousness practically twenty-four hours a day, to put themselves in the position of someone for whom this was not the case. It is difficult for me to capture the feeling of first walking around New York with Bruckner, or Mahler, or Sibelius (who became a favorite) as a film score. Suddenly, *everything* took on a dramatic character. What I liked best was to head to the Hudson and sit at one of the old piers, watching what few ships there were go by, listening to whomever I had put in the Walkman that day. Lulu and I had seen Visconti's film of Thomas Mann's *Death in Venice*, which features music by Mahler, Mussorgsky, and Beethoven. The most well-known piece from the film is the *adagietto* from Mahler's Fifth Symphony, a slow, languid, liquid tugging at the listener's heartstrings. It has, of course, become something of a cliché, but at the time I hadn't heard anything more beautiful, and I would play it over and over as some oil tanker headed out to New York Bay.

When people saw me with it, they were curious—both about the Walkman and what I was listening to (the headphones were a giveaway). When friends saw that I had Bartok or Prokofiev rather than the Ramones or Modern Lovers in the machine, they seemed worried. And it's true that from then on, my interest in rock and pop dwindled and I more or less stopped listening to it—not the best strategy for someone looking for a record deal. Lulu, too, wasn't that keen on my sudden change in musical taste. She had bought a small flat near Gramercy Park, and one afternoon, while I was varnishing her hardwood floor, I had put Mahler's Ninth Symphony on her stereo, with Bruno Walter conducting. She came in and, hearing what I had on, in her forthright way asked, "What's this shit?" This gave me a hint that our erotic holiday was drawing to a close.

Something else that suggested this was the fact that I had stopped writing songs. Lisa had been the inspiration for many, and the ideas I was laboring to understand had informed others. I had by this time written "Amor Fati," and it had become the band's signature tune. But something had changed in me and, although I would have been happy to, I just wasn't able to write for Lulu as I had for Lisa, and she knew it. And without new songs, there was little reason to keep playing the old ones.

LULU AND I LINGERED in our relationship for a time. We both felt the sex was too good to give up and we still enjoyed each other's company, but it was clear that things were temporary. My increasing lack of interest in the pop world and obsession with ideas and now classical music suggested that my position on the scene would soon change. The band continued to perform, but I was really only going through the motions. There seemed little else to do.

Lulu and I continued to go to the clubs. A new one, the Mudd Club, an ultra-outré hipster hangout below Canal Street, had recently opened, and we went a few times. On one occasion, we were invited into the afterhours inner sanctum, the holy of hipster holies. Among the others who had made the grade that night was David Bowie. It's doubtful that he remembered me from the Iggy Pop tour a few years back, but we somehow got into a conversation. I soon twigged that his interest was more in Lulu than in me. We waxed portentous for a few minutes, David going on about an upcoming WWIII, me nodding approvingly. Then he suggested to Lulu that he would very much like to continue the conversation—monologue, rather—somewhere private, just the two of them, *sans* me. I was gratified that Lulu, as gently as possible, turned him down.

But that was more or less the end. And not long after, I decided that I'd had enough of trying to get a record deal. New York turned out to be just as much a dead end as LA had been. We had made demos, had met with the suits, had even released a 45 with

Planet Records.[13] But we did not get a deal. We played a few more gigs but my heart wasn't in it. By the end of 1980, The Know were no more.

At some point during this time, Lisa and I tried to get back together. But it was soon clear that we were friends now—very close friends, but nothing more. She had come out to New York, and in December we decided to go to London for a holiday. We stayed in an old-style B&B in Bloomsbury. We were there for Christmas and New Year's Eve, which we spent in Trafalgar Square; I laughed when I saw girls kissing policemen—"bobbies"—at midnight, a quaint custom no doubt abandoned in our hypersensitive age.

It was sort of a business trip. I brought along our demo recordings and had appointments to see a few people, contacts in the music business I had made over the years. People politely listened, made some comments, and let me know in a very nice way that they weren't interested. I didn't mind. I really wasn't interested either. I was more excited about going to bookshops and the British Museum and wandering around London, thinking I'd like to live there one day.[14]

It was on one of our wanders that Lisa discovered the Village Bookshop on Regent Street, which, like much else, sadly no longer exists. They had a fantastic collection, and I spent a hefty sum on books of Wilson's, but also on those of an author I had discovered through reading *The Occult*, the novelist and mystic John Cowper

13. "I Like Girls" was a parody pop song, written while living on Christopher Street, Greenwich Village's gay main drag, if I can be excused an atrocious pun. It was backed with "Out of Reach," a song we composed and performed with our new drummer, John McGarvey, for a television film called *A Cry for Love* (1980) in which we appeared. The 45 sank soon after its release.

14. Oddly enough, while going over my dream journals for material for *Dreaming Ahead of Time*, I came across several dreams from the early 1990s, in which I am in London and am asked directions, as well as others in which the differences between British and American English are an important theme. These suggest to me that before relocating to London, some part of my psyche was, as it were, already there.

Powys, with whose work I would later become obsessed for a time.

When the owner saw how many of Wilson's books I was buying, he let us know that Wilson himself would be giving a talk there in a week or so. Our return flights were for sooner than then. Lisa couldn't change hers; she had an audition coming up. *The Great Santini*, a film she was in, had done well and she was being offered more parts . But she insisted I stay. She had wanted me to meet Colin Wilson on this trip, and lo, here he was.[15] I changed my return flight and attended the talk. It was about Wilson's book *Frankenstein's Castle*, about the left and right brain. I had just bought a copy at the shop, and had read it. I recorded his talk on my Walkman (I had bought my own by this time) and for years listened to it, although now I no longer know where it might be. Some years later, a fellow Wilsonian, his bibliographer Colin Stanley, told me someone had videoed that talk, and at the very end of it you can see me coming up to Wilson, asking him to autograph my copy of the book. He did, and it is on my shelf with the others.

When I got back to the States after that trip, my life took another strange turn. My tenure in music was coming to an end, but was not quite completely over.

---

15. Lisa had also predicted that the Yorkshire Ripper would be caught while we were there. He was, on January 2, 1981.

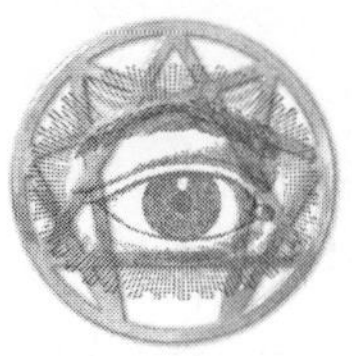

8 Do the Work

The first few months after my return to New York from London, at the beginning of 1981, seem a blur to me now. I know that I gave up the flat on Thompson Street and for a brief time returned to Los Angeles. I had turned twenty-five and had a vague idea of trying once again to get back together with Lisa, even after our recent failure to do so. (I possess a persistent streak that is sometimes a problem.) I had shipped my books across the country again, and I can remember sitting with them, lined up against the walls, in the flat I had taken near hers, which remained empty except for myself and the books for the duration of my stay there.

Looking back now, I don't think winning Lisa back was my real motivation. She was the closest thing to family that I had. My "real" family, of course, were across the river in New Jersey, but my relations with them had never healed and, although I visited now and then, our get-togethers were never pleasant. I really had no idea what to do with myself. I was tired of the milieu I had inhabited for several years, but had no idea of how to find another. I did know that I wanted to write—or, more accurately, to be a writer.

The old idea of being a poet had transformed into being a singer/songwriter. Now, after so much reading, it had resurfaced. But this time I fancied myself a writer of ideas. As I had modeled myself on Verlaine and Hell after seeing them—the finished product differing considerably from either—I now modeled myself after Colin Wilson. The trouble was, while songs had bubbled up in me and emerged practically fully formed—that is, when I could write them—writing prose was another story. I remember writing some long essay about consciousness, more or less rewriting but in a much less readable form, ideas I had absorbed from Wilson's books. I gave it to a friend who had published a novel and whom I respected for getting into print.[1] I now wince at his having to struggle through the many pages I gave him and which he let me know in no uncertain terms were absolutely unreadable.

Song lyrics express a feeling or mood. What I wanted to do now was argue a point and articulate ideas, which is a very different matter. It would take a good decade before I learned the trick, insofar as I have. And it was something I did have to learn how to do, unlike writing songs. All throughout that time, I felt a profound dissatisfaction with myself, an unhappiness, a sense of not fulfilling my potential. My novelist friend could not understand why I put so much importance on writing; I had, after all, a hit song to my credit and was successful as a performer, accomplishments that would suffice to secure most people's self-esteem. But my self-image had changed. I had set my goal posts higher. I no longer wanted to be a pop star, but a philosopher. More than forty years later, I can say the first part of that formula has been achieved. I am not a pop star. The second is still a work in progress.

I had been back in LA only a short time when a friend mentioned that he needed to find someone to sublet his apartment in the East Village. I told him I'd be happy to do that. He agreed, so I packed my books once again, and once again shipped them across the country. What the postal service thought of my moves I can only imagine. I had wasted time in LA, burdened Lisa with my presence—she was, in a way, babysitting me—and realized that sitting in an empty flat, wondering what to do was not a healthy pastime. At least in New York I didn't need a car to get around.

---

1. John Browner, *Death of a Punk* (New York: Pocket Books, 1980).

The move precipitated two things: a brief return to rock and roll, and an introduction to an esoteric society.

OF THE MANY WRITERS AND THINKERS I was introduced to through reading *The Occult*, one of the most important for me was Ouspensky. *The Occult* in fact starts off with a quotation from Ouspensky's book *A New Model of the Universe*. The passage relates Ouspensky's boredom at having to write an article about the Hague Conference, an international gathering in 1907, aimed at preventing the outbreak of war. At the time, Ouspensky was working as a journalist in Moscow and St. Petersburg, and the prospect of writing an article about European politics did not excite him. What did excite him were the books about occultism he had crammed into his desk drawer. All the articles he had read about the conference were, he wrote, full of lies, clichés, and automatic phrases. But here, in these books, he found "a strange flavor of truth." Wilson had written that this passage "never failed to move and excite" him, and I discovered that it had the same effect on me.

I started reading Ouspensky in 1977, when Lisa and I were living in the Wilshire District in Los Angeles, near Western Avenue. A local bookshop stocked his books in the Vintage paperback editions, which had brightly colored covers with images of human faces illuminated by some mystic light. I don't remember the order in which I read them, but I know I often did while doing our laundry at the local laundromat. There was his early work, *Tertium Organum*, his "third organ of thought," after Aristotle's and Francis Bacon's—Ouspensky was, it seemed, not afraid of comparing his work to theirs. Although rather dated by now—the physics referred to is pre-quantum—*Tertium Organum* is still a thrilling metaphysical excursion into the realms of higher space and cosmic consciousness. Its central argument is that the "positivism" of the nineteenth century was sorely inadequate to deal with phenomena of a higher nature, much as the "scientism" of today still is. One such example for Ouspensky was the fourth dimension.

This was thought of as time, as H. G. Wells had considered it in *The Time Machine.* But, for Ouspensky, who in his early days was something of a poet, the fourth dimension, while related to time—about which Ouspensky had some remarkable ideas—was really a metaphor or symbol for what he called "the miraculous," something he had been in search of for years. It was this combination of a poetic sensibility, an urgent desire for knowledge, and a clear, vigorous prose style that made Ouspensky an archetype, as Jung would say, of the artist-philosopher for me. He was someone who united a romantic outlook with a finely-honed intellect—a combination I wanted to achieve myself.

But if *Tertium Organum* had got me thinking about higher dimensions and states of consciousness in which they could be entered, *A New Model of the Universe* introduced me to an idea that would have an even greater immediate impact on my life. Ouspensky had written much of the book before he went on the "search for the miraculous," that had him in Egypt, Turkey, India, and the Far East, and which ended with him meeting the enigmatic teacher Gurdjieff in a backstreet café in Moscow. He went back to the book after his tenure as Gurdjieff's student and rewrote some of it from the point of view of Gurdjieff's teaching.

It is a curious collection of chapters on a variety of mystical and occult ideas. There's the fourth dimension again, chapters on the tarot (which I had studied during my time with Crowley), the "superman" (Ouspensky knew his Nietzsche), The New Testament, dreams, yoga, "experimental mysticism" (facilitated by inhaling nitrous oxide), modern physics, sex, the "eternal recurrence" (Nietzsche again), and accounts of his travels in "search of the miraculous."[2] But a central theme loosely linked these disparate subjects, and it was one that had sent Ouspensky out on his search in the first place. What was that? The idea of esotericism, the notion that alongside the outer, exoteric surface of our

2. Eternal recurrence was practically an obsession of Ouspensky's. The gloomy side of the idea is spelled out in his novel *Strange Life of Ivan Osokin.*

knowledge—the episteme I mentioned earlier in talking about gnosis—there runs a hidden, *inner* tradition of knowledge totally unlike what we usually understand by that term.

"The idea of a knowledge," Ouspensky wrote, "which surpasses all ordinary human knowledge, and is inaccessible to ordinary people, but which exists somewhere and belongs to somebody, permeates the whole history of the thought of mankind from the most remote periods." This knowledge can be detected, Ouspensky said, in ancient monuments, myths, fairy tales, legends, in the tarot, and in the counter-tradition of mystical philosophies and teachings—Hermeticism, Gnosticism, and such. He also believed that there existed schools, somewhere in the East, in which esoteric knowledge and the way to achieve it were still taught. These schools were hidden, and entry into them was difficult if possible at all. He had gone on his search precisely in order to make contact with such schools, but had, he admitted, come back empty handed. The irony is that in the end he found what he had been searching for in exotic lands practically right in his own backyard.

The idea of some secret or lost knowledge thrilled me. It seemed to combine the notion of a romantic quest with deep metaphysical speculation—rather like the Indiana Jones films which had yet to appear—which was a stock theme of much of the pulp adventure fiction I loved (think Talbot Mundy's *Om: The Secret of Ahbor Valley*). My critical instinct balked at the idea of some actual inner circle sequestered in some Himalayan or Central Asian fastness, helping mankind in its evolution—a notion Madame Blavatsky had popularized. (What did they do in between meetings?) And I thought Ouspensky made too strict a distinction between this esoteric knowledge and what we can achieve through our own efforts. After all, Nietzsche and others I had read were no slouches. But then, there *was* a difference between gnosis and episteme. And weren't there traces of *something* the ancients had known, left in the fantastic structures they had erected, like the pyramids, the Sphinx, and Stonehenge . . . ?

But the next book by Ouspensky that I read really brought the point home. This was *In Search of the Miraculous*, his account of his years with Gurdjieff in Russia during the First World War, the Bolshevik Revolution, and the Russian Civil War. As mentioned, Ouspensky met Gurdjieff in Moscow after his search for schools proved fruitless. Gurdjieff had sought him out, and sent some of his students to attend Ouspensky's lectures on his travels, with the idea of bringing him into his fold. It worked. When they met, Ouspensky was immediately impressed by Gurdjieff as a man who *knows*. Ouspensky wanted such knowledge, and so for a time he became Gurdjieff's student. Eventually he would break with Gurdjieff but, strangely, he would teach his system, known as "the Fourth Way" or, more colloquially, "the Work," for decades, until shortly before his death in England in 1947.

The early '80s saw a kind of Gurdjieff revival, with many books about him, Ouspensky, and their teachings. Peter Brook's rather solemn film of Gurdjieff's *Meetings with Remarkable Men* had come out in 1979, and it seemed to have gotten his name across to a wider public. Wilson had written a short biography of Gurdjieff, *The War Against Sleep*, that I read and reread as much for the story as for the ideas. Another book that impressed me was James Webb's more substantial study, *The Harmonious Circle*.

What was interesting about Webb's book, aside from its intrinsic value as a brilliant work of history and biography, is that although he had a rather critical, skeptical view of much of what Gurdjieff was about, and was not interested in higher consciousness, I nevertheless found myself enjoying the book, even if I disagreed with much of what it said. This struck me as important. It suggested that I had reached a level of some objectivity which meant I wouldn't dismiss what an author was saying simply because it didn't agree with my opinions or feelings. I could appreciate his work for its own sake. This may sound obvious and elementary, but it is not as easy a position to achieve as we might think. What I enjoyed about the book was the intellectual and imaginative stimulation it afforded, not that it confirmed what I already believed. This suggests some level of maturity, at least in the area of ideas, had been achieved.

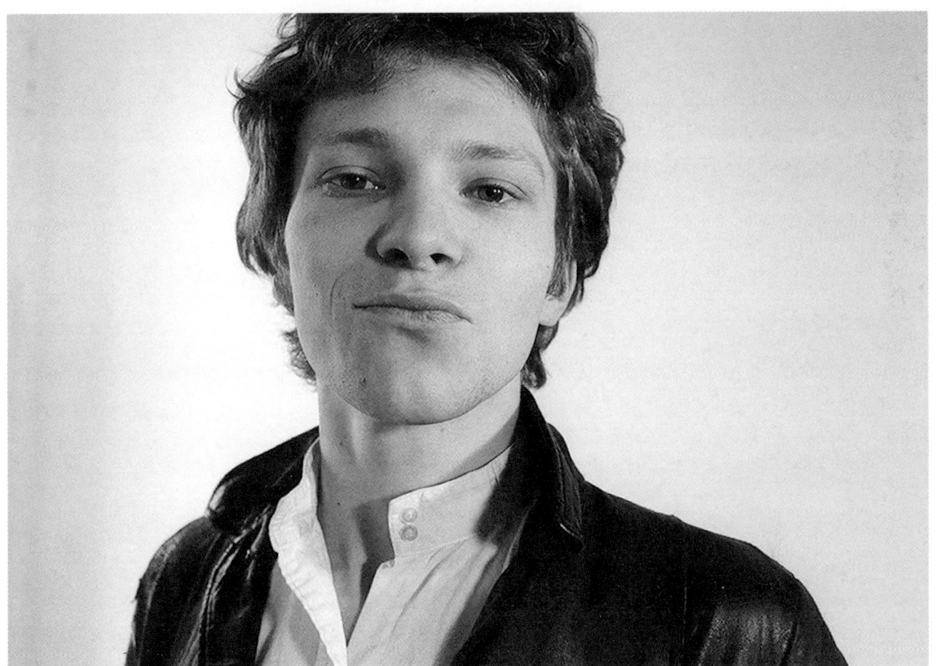

Plate 1. The ex-offender. The Blondie loft, 1975. Photo © Lisa Jane Persky

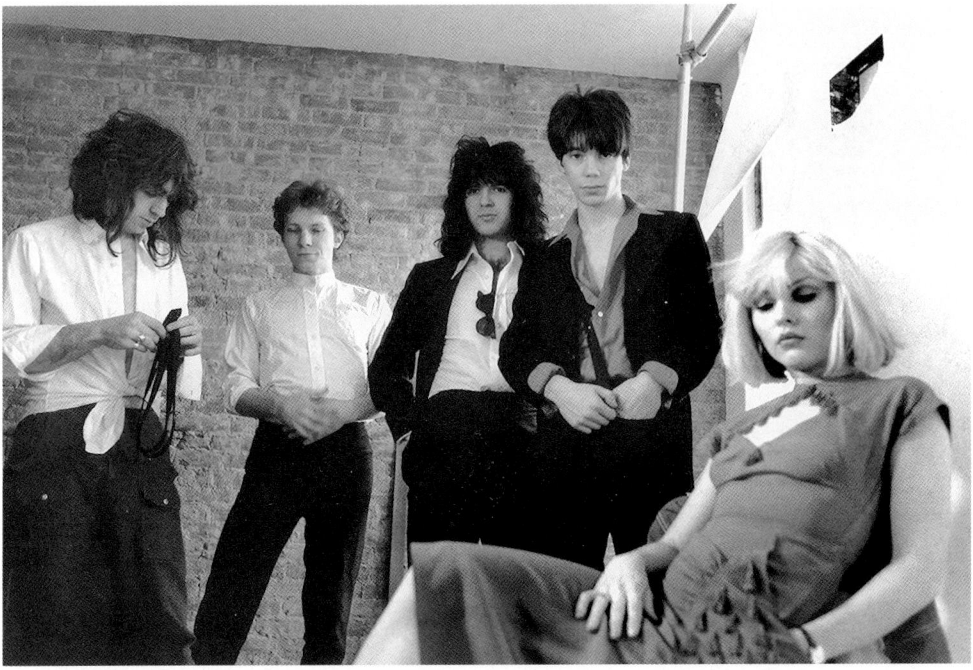

Plate 2. The band, the loft, 1975. Note that Jimmy and I have short hair; Clem and Chris hung on to theirs for a while. Photo © Lisa Jane Persky

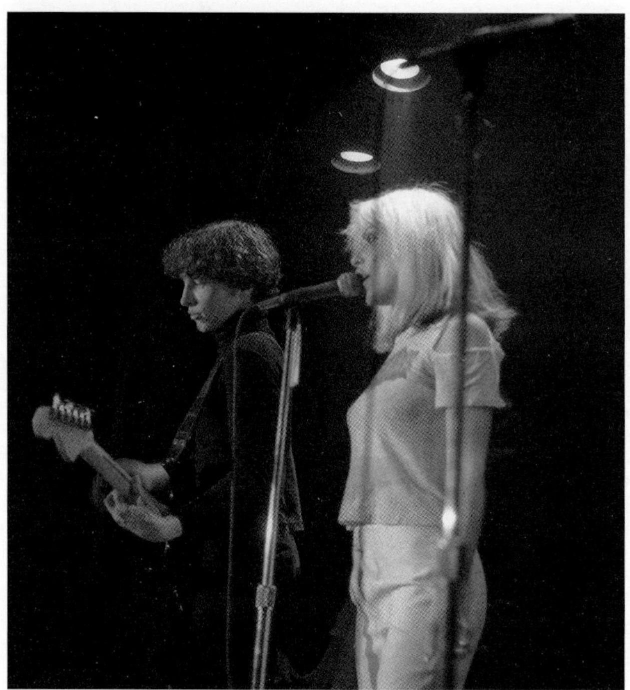

Plate 3. Debbie and me, with my old Fender Precision bass, Max's Kansas City, 1976. Note Debbie's Batman T-shirt. Photo © Lisa Jane Persky

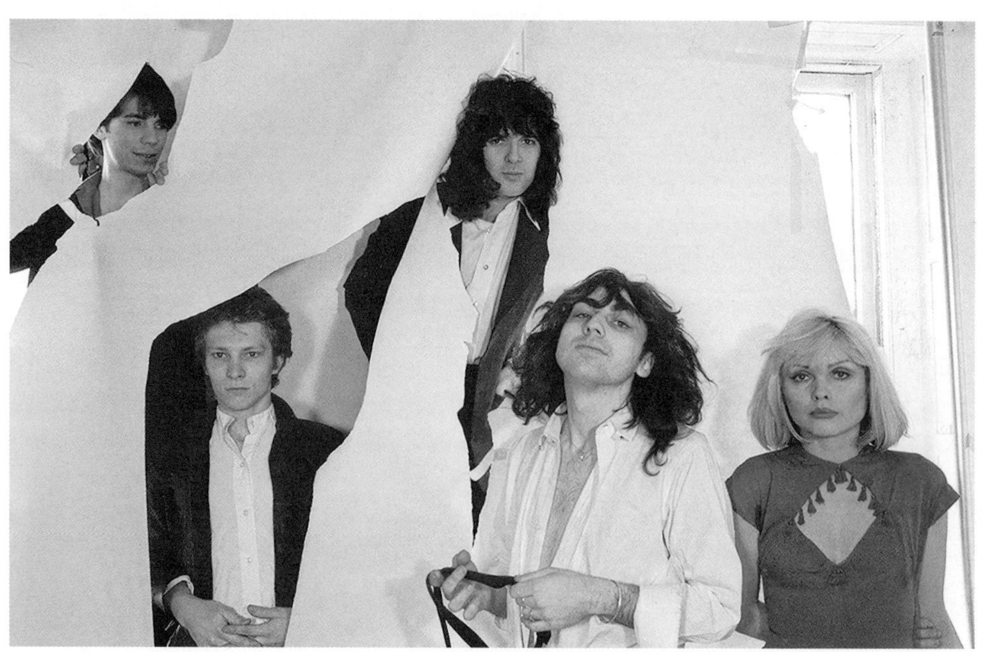

Plate 4. Ripping it to shreds, with apologies to Cecil Beaton. The loft, 1975. Photo © Lisa Jane Persky

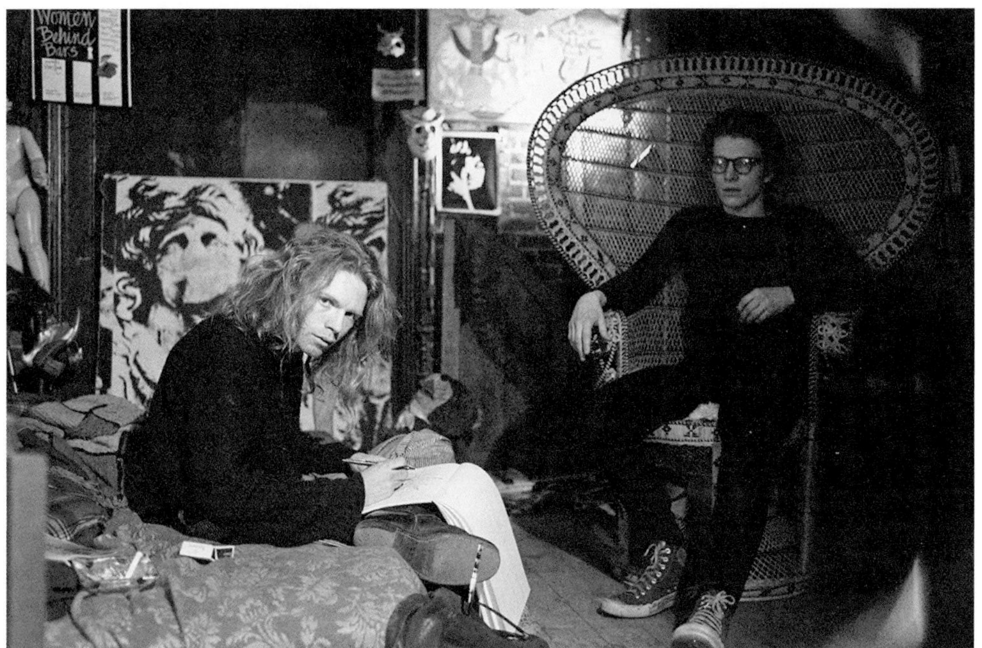

Plate 5. The inimitable Benton in his lair, with a poster for *Women Behind Bars* and an early selfie by Chris in the background. The loft, 1975. Photo © Lisa Jane Persky

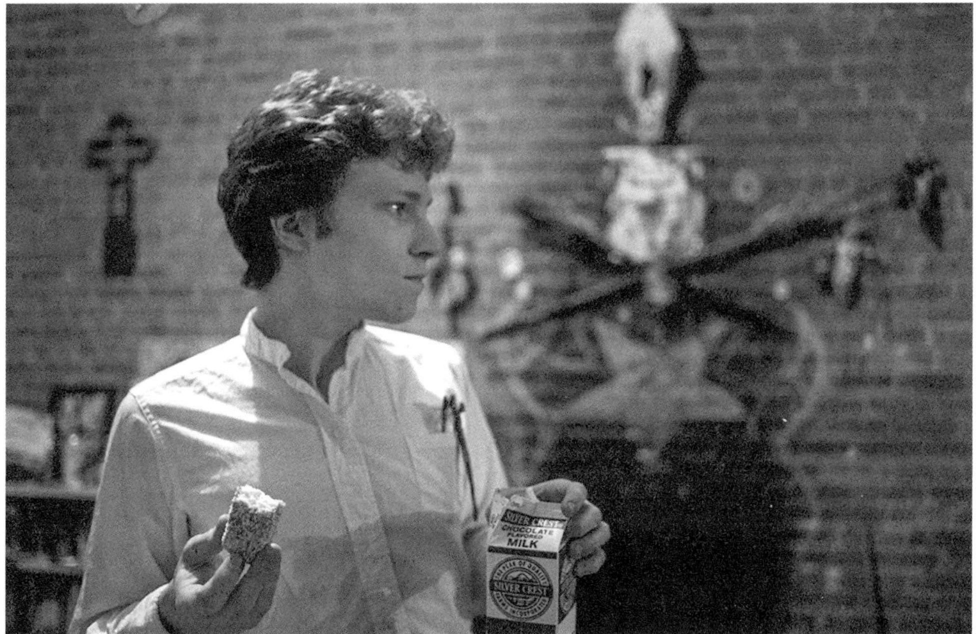

Plate 6. Proust had his madeleine. I made do with Twinkies. Note assorted magical bric-a-brac on the wall. The loft, 1975. Photo © Lisa Jane Persky

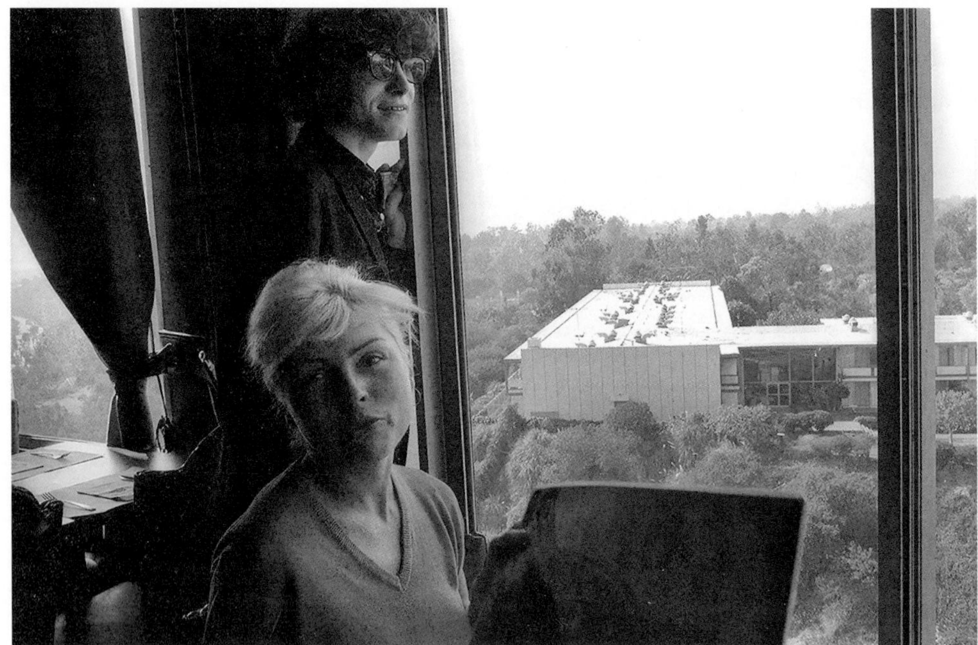

Plate 7. LA, just like I pictured it. Breakfast at the Holiday Inn, the junction of Sunset Boulevard and the 405 freeway, 1977. Photo © Lisa Jane Persky

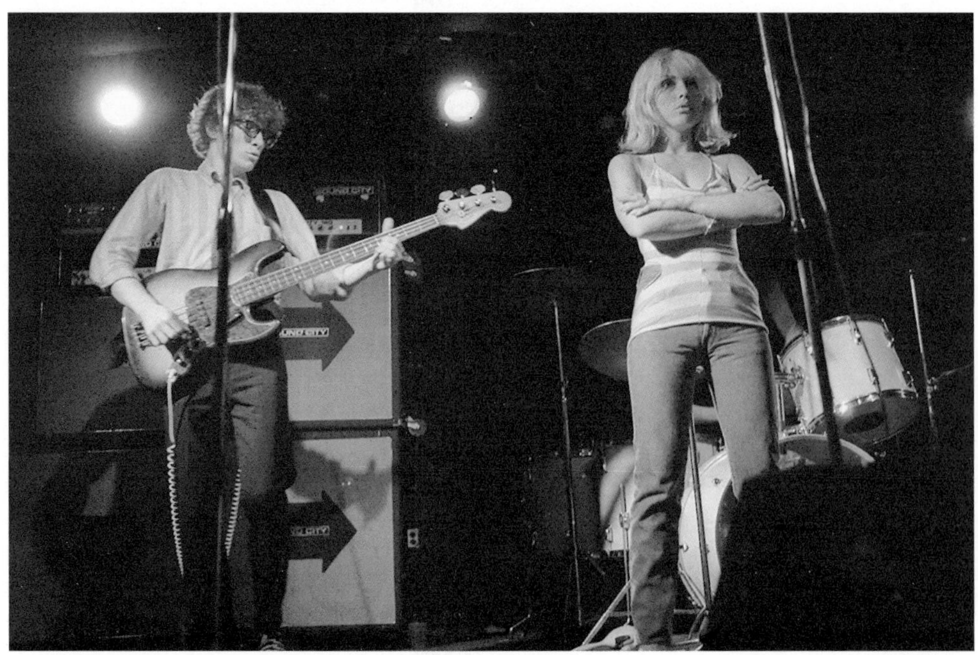

Plate 8. My Father's Place, Rosslyn, Long Island, opening for John Cale of the Velvet Underground, 1976. Photo © Lisa Jane Persky

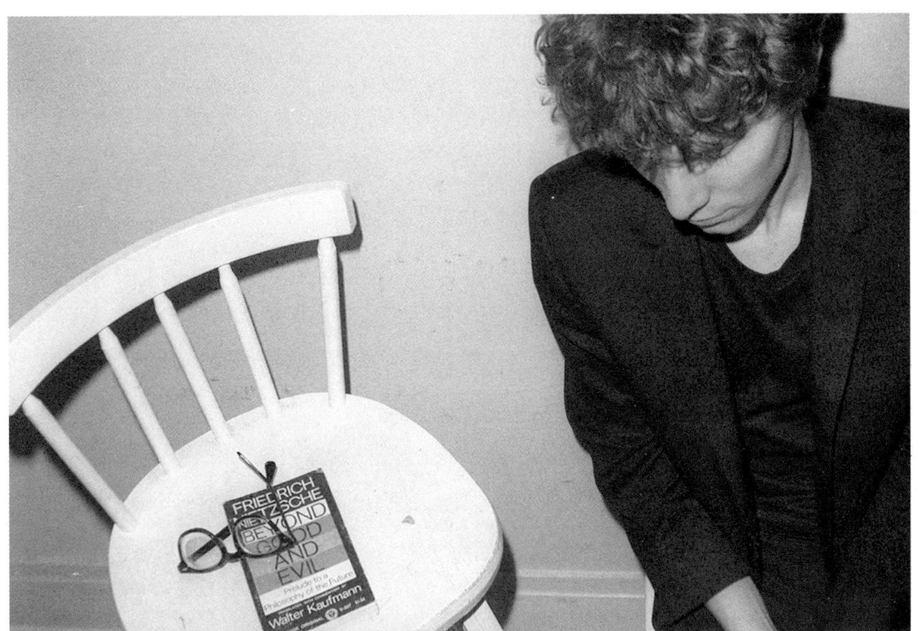

Plate 9. "That which is done out of love is beyond good and evil"—Nietzsche. The cover shot for "The First One/Tomorrow Belongs to You." LA, 1978. Photo © Lisa Jane Persky

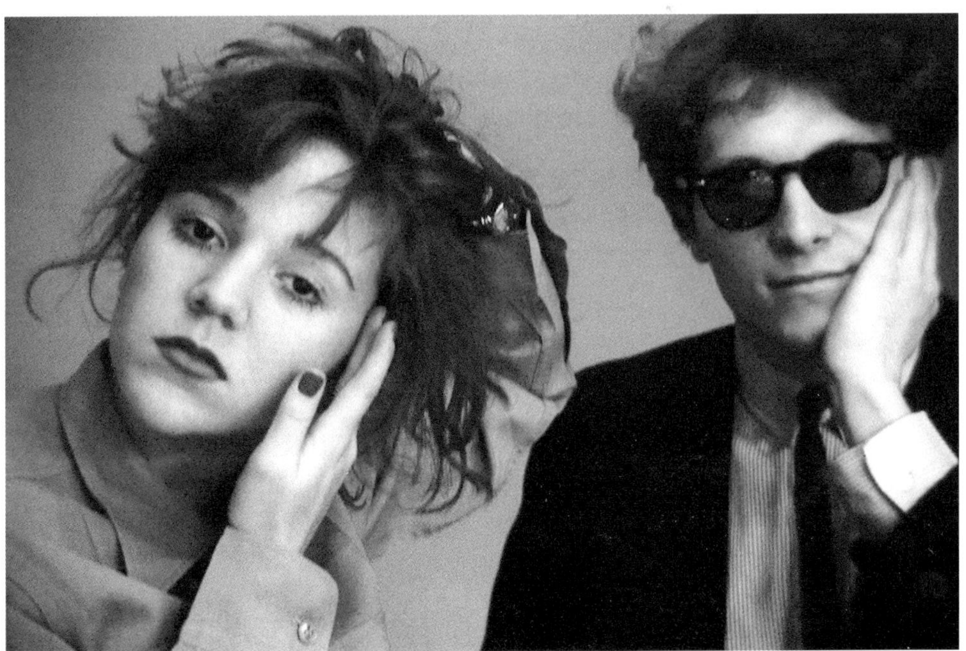

Plate 10. Touched by our presence. Photo by Jack Baran, LA, 1978. Photo © Lisa Jane Persky

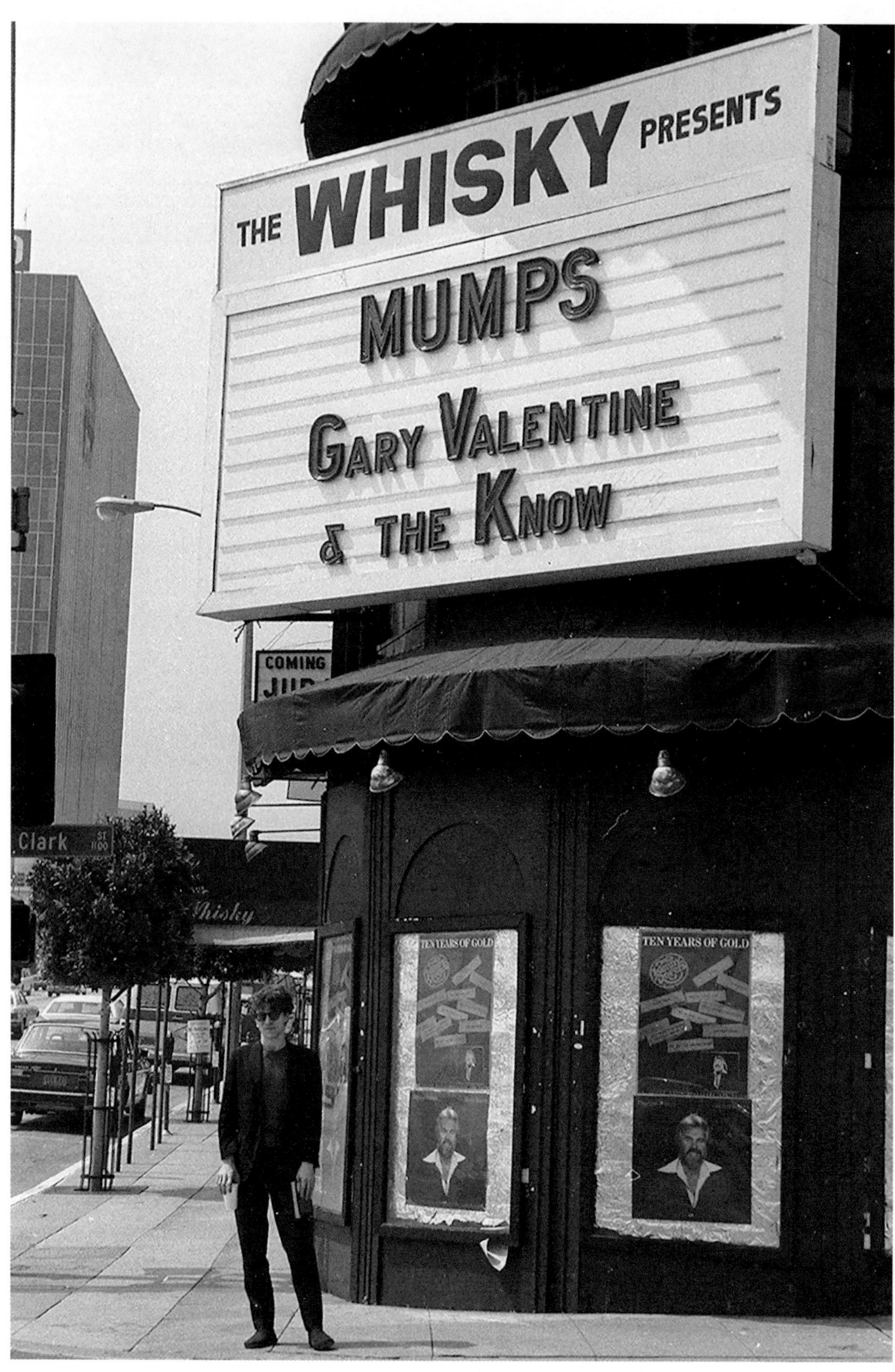

Plate 11. The Whisky A Go-Go, the Sunset Strip, LA, 1978.
Photo © Lisa Jane Persky

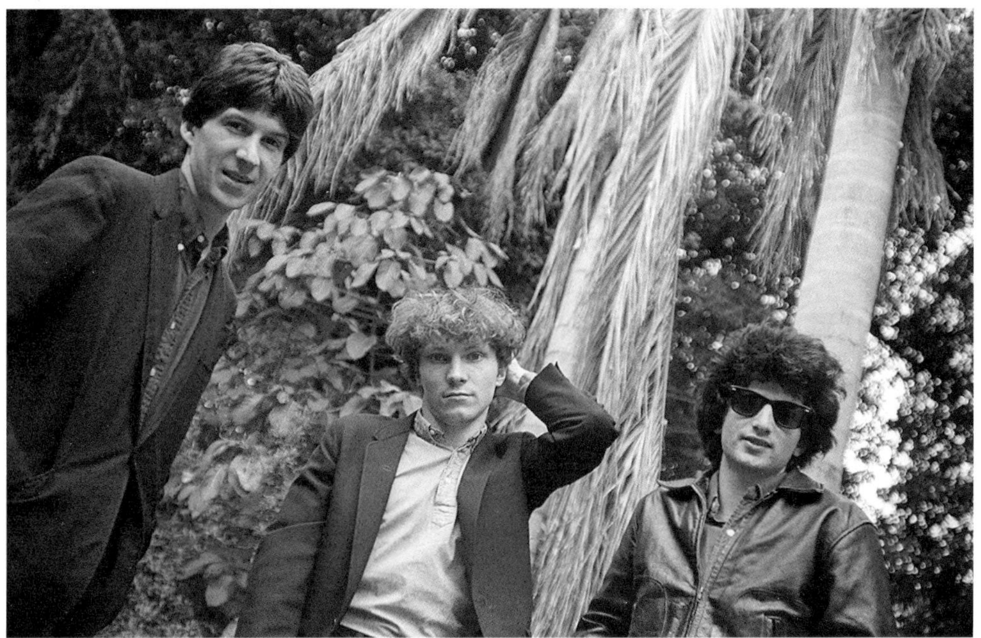

Plate 12. Richard D'Andrea, Joel Turrisi, and me, the back garden at Wilton Place, where Lisa and I lived. LA, 1978. Photo © Lisa Jane Persky

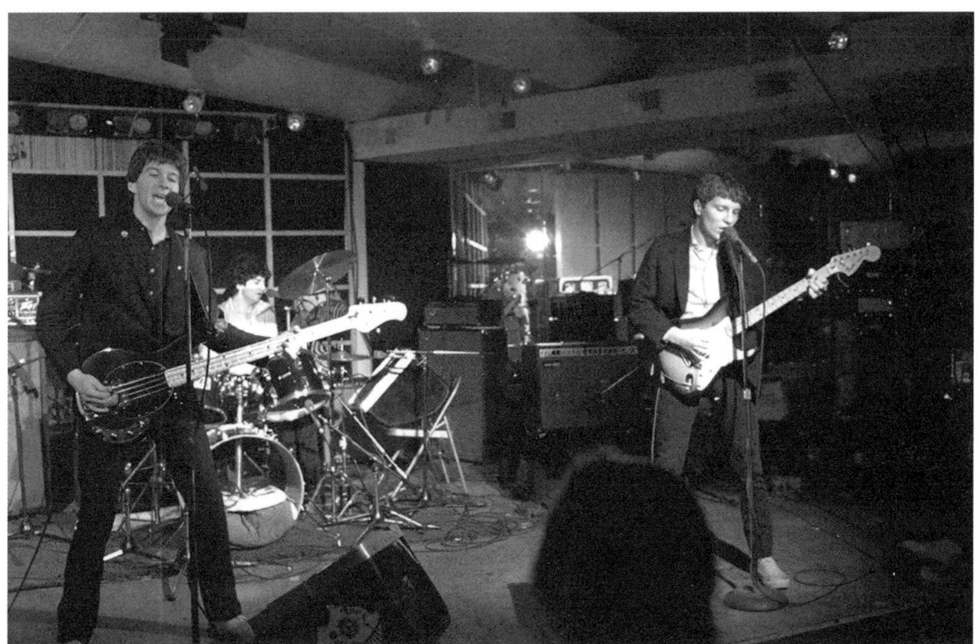

Plate 13. The Know at Madame Wong's, 1978. My beautiful Fender Stratocaster was later stolen when I toured with Iggy Pop. Photo © Lisa Jane Persky

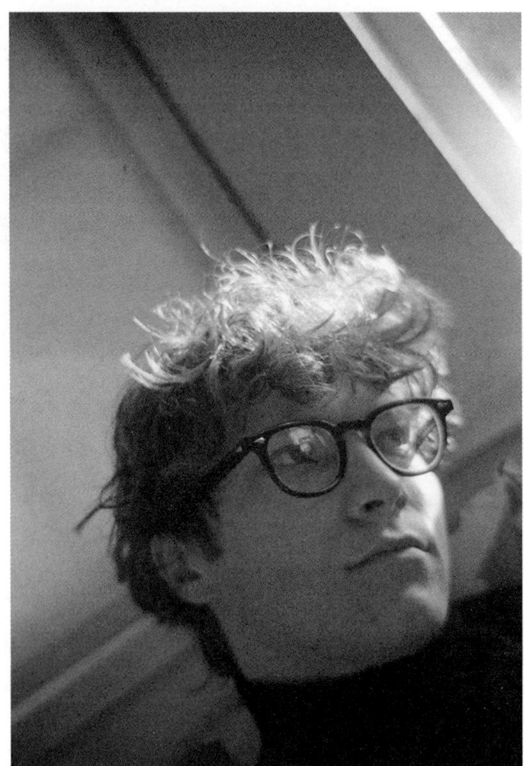

Plate 14. "The author's photo." Our room at 549 S. Wilton Place, LA, 1977. Photo © Lisa Jane Persky

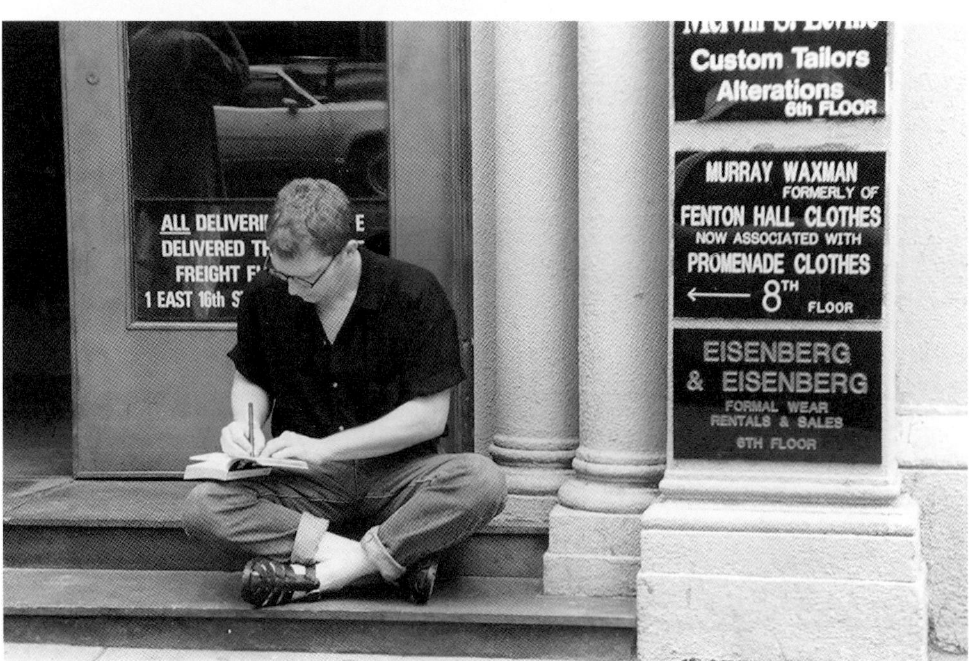

Plate 15. Studious as ever. Between lives, somewhere on Fifth Avenue, NYC, circa 1994. Photo © Lisa Jane Persky

What was Gurdjieff's teaching? When he and Ouspensky first met, Gurdjieff shocked—an important Work term—Ouspensky by telling him that he, and everyone he knew and *would ever know*, were asleep. He didn't mean they were really home in bed—although, from his perspective they may just as well have been. He meant that the state of consciousness we take to be "awake" is really just another form of sleep. Or, to put it another way, human beings are machines moved entirely by external stimuli. We think we are free and can make decisions, but in truth we aren't. We are trapped in a kind of psychological prison we call our personality, which is made up of habits we have adopted from others around us. Hidden within this shell is our true self—that elusive entity again—what Gurdjieff called our "essence." The austere array of psychological, physical, and emotional exercises and challenges making up Gurdjieff's system are aimed at cracking open this shell and freeing our essence from its prison.

Key to this was an odd state of consciousness we experience intermittently when in danger or unfamiliar surroundings, but of which we are usually ignorant. This is what Gurdjieff called "self-remembering," a vivid awareness and sensation of one's own being.

"Being"—I was familiar with that term from my reading in existentialism. And Wilson had talked about how narrow and limited our everyday state of consciousness is, compared to what it really should be. For him, this was because of a labor-saving device we have developed which he called "the robot," whom we have inadvertently allowed to live our life for us. And "self-remembering" rung a bell too. I could recall moments when I suddenly felt more alive, more active, more *present*, and when everything around me looked as if it had just been freshly scrubbed and polished.

A moment like this had happened while on the UK Blondie tour. We had driven to Bournemouth, along the English Channel, in the evening, and would be performing the next day. On the drive I hadn't taken in exactly where we were. I can't remember where we stayed, but that morning, having gotten up early, I went for a walk to explore the area. I remember strolling down a lane, looking at the houses and gardens, and then turning a corner. Suddenly, there was the sea and cliffs and wide blue sky and brilliant clouds. I hadn't expected this, and was taken by surprise. Everything seemed extraordinarily *real*, and it came to me that I was in England and that across the water was France and the rest of Europe . . . I already knew that, of course. But now I *really* knew it, not just as a fact, but as a *reality*.

Ouspensky had said that the sensation of self-remembering often comes when we are somewhere we haven't been before, and suddenly think, "What? *Me, here?*" We are aware of being in new surroundings but we are also aware *that it is ourselves* who are in them. That was exactly how I felt. Nearly fifty years later, the delight I felt then still comes back to me. I decided that this, and other moments like them, were experiences of self-remembering.

I would also rank them as what the psychologist Abraham Maslow, whom I had learned about from reading Wilson, called "peak experiences," sudden moments of inexplicable delight.[3] I know Gurdjieff purists will say they are nothing of the sort, but then they are prone to want to maintain a peculiar uniqueness about his ideas. This is unimportant. What I have come to understand is that moments of self-remembering and peak experiences are both moments when our consciousness is *working as it should*, and not at the minimal energy-saving level it is usually stuck at, courtesy of our robot.

More and more, I was impressed with Gurdjieff's ideas. Yet, at the same time, I found it difficult to accept some of them. Were Nietzsche, Hesse, Sartre, Wilson, and others I had read and learned much from *really* asleep? I could see that I was not as awake as I might be, that my consciousness was working at a lower level than it could. But if I could feel moments of "wakefulness," surely they did too. And must I really

---

3. As an example of a "peak experience," Abraham Maslow tells the story of a jazz drummer who spoke of performances when it was as if the music was playing *him*, and he couldn't miss a beat. I can confirm that this sort of experience was not foreign to me in my years as a musician.

work in a group to make any progress, as Gurdjieff insisted? A man alone could do nothing, he said. But then, Wilson seemed to be making important headway—and I've never been much of a joiner, being an Outsider and all. I hemmed and hawed about this, arguing with myself and others, and decided I would have to find out.

At Weiser's, I came across a notice for a lecture about the Fourth Way being presented by something called the Gurdjieff-Ouspensky Center. This organization would later become infamous as the "People of the Bookmark," because of their habit of going to bookshops and inserting bookmarks with information about how to contact them into Ouspensky's and other Fourth Way writers' books. I subsequently learned they were bogus, with no link to Gurdjieff's original groups, but at the time I didn't know this.

The lecture was at the Barbizon Hotel on 63rd Street, and I was surprised at the number of people it drew. Apparently, I wasn't the only person in Manhattan who wanted to "wake up." One speaker made a point of emphasizing the difference between "I" and "it." He repeated a phrase several times throughout his talk: "Like what 'it' does not like." "It" was our mechanical, habit-ridden self, which we mistakenly believe is awake. "I" was our true self, submerged beneath layers of sleep and automatism. At present, "it" dominates us, and a brief period of self-observation shows how little free will we really possess. The aim of the Work was to study "it," to learn its habits and character, while at the same time gradually making "I" stronger. I returned to my apartment excited by what I had heard, wondering if I should call the telephone number on the flyer handed out at the lecture.

The irony was that my entry into the Work was much closer than I knew. A friend who was interested in spiritual ideas knew I was reading a lot about Gurdjieff. We had talked about a variety of things—Jung, Kabbalah, Hinduism, Buddhism—and when I mentioned the lecture to him, he showed great interest. A few days later, he asked if I was really interested in getting involved in the Work. I said yes. "In that case," he said, "call this number," and handed me a piece of paper. On it was a telephone number, but not the one on the flyer. "It's my teacher. I mentioned you to him," he said. "He's expecting you to call. I've been working with him for about a year, but I wanted to see how serious you were before telling you about it. If you are serious, I'd call soon."

I did. The man's voice on the other end was steady, deep, and to the point. Would I like to come next week and have a chat? Then he gave me the address.

I found the building on the Upper East Side, rang the bell, and was let in. A woman ushered me into a small room and asked me to wait. Around me I could see Persian carpets and other decorations and bric-a-brac in an Oriental, Eastern fashion. Several paintings adorned the walls, and I learned that these were the work of the man I had come to see. Then my host appeared and introduced himself. His name was Paul Reynard, and I later learned that he was one of the principal teachers of the Gurdjieff "movements," the extremely difficult "sacred dances" that Gurdjieff claimed he had learned at the mysterious monastery of the Sarmoung Brotherhood.

I didn't know it then, but I had seen Paul perform them in Brook's *Meetings with Remarkable Men*; the dances are one of the few times when the film shows any vitality (the others are when Terence Stamp, a professional actor—unlike the amateurs Brook tended to use—was on the screen). Some years ago I learned that Paul had died in 2005, at the age of seventy-eight, which means he was around fifty-four when we met. Whether Gurdjieff learned his "movements" during his time with the Sarmoung Brotherhood or devised them himself remains an open question, but sometime later, when I began practicing them, where they came from seemed irrelevant. What was clear was their ability to evoke unusual states of consciousness.

I was impressed by Paul's composure; he seemed the most relaxed, yet alert person I had come across. After introducing himself, we sat in silence for a few moments. He seemed untroubled by the nervousness we often feel in awkward moments and which we hope to dispel with talk. Then he asked about me. What did I do and why was I interested in his group? I had quite a bit under my belt by then, but after rattling off Blondie, my hit record, my own group, and much else, Paul just nodded. Then he again asked why I wanted to join his group. Why was I interested in the Work? It turned out to be a more difficult question than I thought. How serious was I? I had already spent time in the Crowley group and found that it wasn't for me. Was I simply curious? I hesitated and finally said that I "wanted to wake up," or something equally lame. "That will take time," he replied, "and effort." Was I ready to take on that kind of commitment? I said I was. He then told me where and when the next meeting would be, and said he would see me there.

Paul's group met in a basement room in a building in the lower Sixties, between Lexington and Park Avenues. The meetings were very much like the Fourth Way gatherings I had read about in the accounts of their time in the Work by Kenneth Walker and J. G. Bennett. We met in a bare room and sat on hard wooden chairs, with little to distract our attention but a wooden table on which stood a vase with flowers, a pitcher of water, and some glasses. Two chairs flanked the table—Paul occupied one, the other was used by a fellow teacher on occasion. Paul didn't lecture. We sat in silence until someone asked a question. General queries were rejected but practical questions about the exercises the group was given were encouraged. It usually took several minutes before someone got up the nerve to speak.

We were given exercises in "sensing ourselves." We were to sit in a chair with our legs slightly apart and our hands on our knees. Then we were to sense our right arm, from the shoulder down to the hand. Then sense the right leg, then the left, then the left arm, and so on, in a kind of canon. After a while, we were told to end by standing up and taking a few steps while maintaining the sensation. It took a while, but after a time I started to feel a kind of tingling, as if a gentle rain or mist were passing over me. I did this every day, and also made and kept what Paul called "appointments" with myself, moments during the day when

I would stop whatever I was doing and try to remember myself. It was not easy.

I HAD BEEN ATTENDING Paul's group and practicing the exercises he gave for some months, as well as going to what were called "ideas meetings," where the various ideas and concepts involved in Gurdjieff's system—the Ray of Creation, our various different centers, our lack of a stable "I," and others—were discussed. I also attended readings from Gurdjieff's difficult work, *Beelzebub's Tales to His Grandson*, an extremely obscure text that makes *Finnegan's Wake* or Hegel's *Logic* exemplars of clarity by comparison. But I was really doing little else. I had stopped playing, and hadn't touched my guitar since returning from London. I tried to write, but if a nonwriter can have writer's block, I had it. This was well before word processors, let alone computers, and I sat in front of a typewriter, banging out some paragraphs, then filling the waste basket with them. I listened to music and became familiar with the standard repertoire. I can recall one afternoon in late winter, listening to Sibelius's string quartet *Voces Intimae* (Intimate Voices) while watching snowflakes fall into the courtyard my window opened to, and feeling an unusual contentment.

But most of my time was spent in bookshops or the library, or on occasion a museum. Royalties had come in, and for a time I didn't need to worry about money. I had few close friends and frequent one-night stands. I continued to go to clubs out of habit, keeping late hours and seeing the dawn more mornings than I should have. These night owl excursions were facilitated by a ridiculously expensive pharmaceutical powder that was very popular at the time and which provided the illusion that you were enjoying yourself so much you didn't want the party to stop. It was during one such anesthetically fueled evening that I had another encounter with David Bowie.

I was invited to attend a session at Bowie's court, which at the time was held in a midtown loft, somewhere on the West Side. For a time, a friend supplemented his income with the small earnings he garnered by delivering supplies of the sought-after magic powder. He was making such a delivery and suggested I come along. When we got there, David was happy to see us—or, at least, to see my friend—and quickly availed himself of our parcel. Soon he became voluble, waxing rhetorically about a number of subjects, and as he walked about the place, his guests hovered attentively, hoping for a dropped pearl or numbed nostril.

Somehow, the conversation got onto the occult, about which Bowie was very enthusiastic. He had gone through an "occult Nazi" phase and had devoured books like *The Morning of the Magicians* and Trevor Ravenscroft's *The Spear of Destiny*. I had read these myself, and shared his interest. When Bowie paused and no one seemed ready to break the silence, my friend interjected that I knew all about the occult because I read Colin Wilson.

Bowie may have remembered me from our encounter at the Mudd Club, but I doubt it. It made no difference. At the mention of Colin Wilson, he seemed to grow excited.

"Colin Wilson!" he exclaimed. "He runs a coven of witches in Cornwall, and traces pentagrams on the doors of people who have crossed his path!"

I had been reading Wilson for several years by then, and was sure this wasn't true. I said so.

"Oh, yes!" Bowie continued. "He evokes the spirits of ectoplasmic Nazis and calls down their astral forms to do his bidding!"

"I don't think that's true, David."

"I tell you, Wilson is a witch and practices black magic!" the Thin White Duke insisted.

Our volley went back a few more times and much magic powder was ingested. I had been a devotee of Bowie years back, when living with the sisters, and had nothing but respect for his music. But I knew that, in this case, he didn't know what he was talking about. Mine, however, was the minority opinion, and I soon realized that I was making a scene. The better part of valor—or, at least, of ingratiating yourself with hepped-up pop stars—seemed to be to defer to their greater, if inaccurate, knowledge and drop the subject. But I had never learned how to kiss ass: the only ones I ever did were those of the women I was sleeping with, and then it was a pleasure. Bowie soon wearied of my obstinacy and made that clear. The message was received by his two female bodyguards, who made their way to me. They were big girls, like the centerfold assassins, Thumper and Bambi, in *Diamonds Are Forever*, Sean Connery's penultimate appearance as James Bond. They quietly got me away from Major Tom, and in no uncertain terms let me know the party was over. "David's tired," they informed me. "We think you better leave." Funny, I thought the same, and did.

The odd thing is that, years later, when writing about this in *New York Rocker*, I realized where Bowie had gone wrong. In *Mysteries*, Wilson writes about the paranormal investigator T. C. Lethbridge, and relates his account of meeting a witch in Devon who did "trace pentagrams" on her neighbors' door, as a way of protection. Bowie had jumbled the story up until he had Wilson leading a coven of witches. Remarkable what that magic powder can do.

I WAS SAVED from what was quickly turning into a life of purposeless and increasingly pointless activity by my friend Rob Duprey. The Mumps had disbanded—like The Know, they had failed to get a deal—and he had been playing with Iggy Pop for a while. They were ready to go on tour, the first of two North American jaunts. But at the last minute, Ivan Kral, who had played with Debbie in the early days, jumped ship and the band needed another guitarist. Was I interested?

I had listened to Iggy and the Stooges almost as religiously as I had Bowie, and we had, of course, opened for him back in 1977. I knew most of the material, and would be able to pick up the new numbers fairly easily. The pay was good and I could save a great deal of it, with food and drink provided at most of the gigs. I hadn't touched my guitar in months, but the idea of being a kind of hired gun touched my fancy.

I wouldn't be leading the band and I wouldn't be singing my songs, just playing guitar. And with Iggy, after all.

Iggy's record company, Arista, had just put out the third and last album of his deal with them, *Party*, and had told him if it wasn't a hit, they would not be renewing their contract. This was, in fact, what happened. Iggy had garnered much critical praise and was seen, along with Lou Reed, as a kind of grandfather of punk. But his albums hadn't sold as much as Arista had expected. A lot was on the line, and I liked the idea of being on a sort of "Wild Bunch" tour, taking part in possibly the last roundup of some seasoned rockers. I knew some of the other musicians, like Rob. (On the second tour, my ex-bandmate Clem was the drummer, and Carlos Alomar, David Bowie's guitarist, joined us as well.) So, I said yes. After one brief rehearsal, we hit the road—I learned some of the material on the tour bus—and from August to December of 1981, I was back in the music business again.

Iggy knew I had written a hit song, and suggested that at some point we get together so I could do the same for him. I must have been a disappointment. Writing songs was the last thing on my mind. I also decided that on this tour I would try to be "one of the boys." This meant I wouldn't bring along my usual supply of books. For my inaugural outing, I brought only one, Stuart Holroyd's *Briefing for a Landing on Planet Earth*, about a group of extraterrestrials who make contact with several Earthlings in order to save the world and, more or less, bring about the millennium. (Holroyd had been a friend of Wilson's in the Angry Young Men days.) Iggy asked what it was about and I told him. He said, "Ok, you're our expert on extraterrestrials." That made sense. As I say in *New York Rocker*, playing with him was like being out of this world.

My abstention from books, however, was not sustainable. In Detroit, I broke down and found a copy of Nikos Kazantzakis's autobiography, *Report to Greco*. And I have an odd memory of reading Alfred North Whitehead's *Science and the Modern World* while sitting at an outdoor café in New Orleans's French Quarter.

Again, I tell all the stories in *New York Rocker*, and don't want to repeat them here. The five months I spent working with Iggy on those two North American tours were truly an experience. To say they were filled with the obligatory sex, drugs, and rock and roll would be to confirm what anyone familiar with Iggy's history would expect. Rereading my account of that time in order to refresh my memory, I surprised even myself with what I'd gotten up to. My life certainly has changed.

To say that Iggy was a unique personality would be an understatement. He was labile, and could shift from being charming and warm to coldly cruel without missing a beat. This was a psychological quick-change tactic that most of the "stars" I met engaged in—it was a way of maintaining dominance and keeping people around you insecure. I hated all that pop star pecking order business and generally treated everyone the same—it was also good sense to not alienate the road crew or the soundman by being overbearing. The flip side of this was that I was not easily impressed, and grew to dislike and distrust people who tried to impress or to get a reaction from me. I could say that I began to sense that much of the dominance establishing going on stemmed from some deep insecurity. I am not suggesting that I wasn't insecure; I suspect I'm as fragile as the next person. But I didn't try to overcome this by bullying someone else, as happens more often than not.

Iggy's real name was Jim, and it wouldn't be too much of an exaggeration to say he was a dual personality. Jim wore glasses, and when he had them on he was more or less a normal individual. When they were off, anything might happen. During one of the tours, he took to wearing women's clothing. He said it was more comfortable. One night it was a skirt, another a dress. Sometimes he wore stockings, on others panties. Some audiences loved it, with others it didn't work. Somewhere along the line, a cap on one of his front teeth came loose, and in certain moments of inspiration, Iggy would pull the cap off and grin. He then lost the cap entirely and until it could be replaced he did without it. Added to his sartorial statement, the black gap in his smile had a peculiar effect.

Probably the highlight of the tours were the two shows at the Silverdome, in Pontiac, Michigan, where we opened for the Rolling Stones. Keith Richards was a friend of Iggy's and wanted him to do the shows. The other act was Santana, who had made their name at Woodstock. If I hadn't yet, at this point I had certainly hit the big time.

The Silverdome is a massive indoor football stadium, with a ninety-thousand-plus capacity. I don't think Iggy had played in such a space before, and I certainly hadn't. One could say it was rather like playing to the Grand Canyon. Backstage, I met Carlos Santana, whose music I had listened to in my teens, and watched Bill Wyman and Charlie Watts play Ping-Pong. After their game, I met them briefly. Jagger, Richards, and Ron Wood milled about. I didn't meet them, but Iggy and Keith hung out.

It was a prestigious, important show, and we were geared up for it. Unfortunately, the crowd was not there to see us. They would appreciate Santana, but they were, of course, there to see the Stones. They made this clear soon into our set. The booing started early on. Understandably, Iggy didn't care for this, and cut the set short. If they didn't like our act, I suspect the audience appreciated our ending early.

That night, Iggy hadn't cross-dressed. The second night was different. Logically, the audience at the second show was not there the night before, and so couldn't be held responsible for their behavior. Such clarity escaped Iggy. He demanded revenge. On the second night, he wore a brown leather miniskirt and coffee-colored stockings. Whether it was intentional or an oversight, he neglected to put on underwear. As another performer named Jim had once exposed the family jewels onstage, so, too, did Iggy.[4]

One wonders if the crowd would have reacted differently had he not wanted to show them—which he did, in more ways than one. As it was, we got through a few numbers before I noticed anything. Then

---

4. This, of course, refers to the famous Doors concert when Jim Morrison was arrested for indecent exposure.

it started. From out of the darkness, projectiles were hitting the stage. Everything you could think of came hurtling at us, and continued to pelt us for the rest of our set. When Iggy twigged to what was happening, he fired back, lifting his miniskirt, spreading his legs, fondling his crotch. It was as if some primitive rite was being performed by a tribal mass and the sacrificial victim. In his memoirs, Bill Graham, the great rock impresario, wrote that, "Never in the history of rock and roll have more material objects been thrown at *any* artist." I have not checked the figures but I well believe him.[5]

There were a few other memorable moments. For one show, we traveled up and down the Mississippi on a riverboat for hours. At another, in San Francisco, Allen Ginsberg came backstage and he, Iggy, Clem, and I shared a joint.[6] Years later I would meet William Burroughs, when I was briefly reunited with my old bandmates at a tribute to him in Lawrence, Kansas, shortly before his death in 1997.[7] Kerouac had died in 1969, the result of slowly drinking himself to death, but I had, at least, met two of the Three Beat Musketeers.

Opening for the Rolling Stones was one of the last shows on the second tour. Not long after that, toward the end of December, I found myself back in New York. I had made a decent amount from the tour, had been around the country twice and up to Canada, and had an inordinate number of adventures. I had run the sex, drugs, and rock and roll gauntlet and gave a good showing. But I didn't want to do it again. And now the problem of figuring out what to do with my life, given I no longer wanted to get a record deal or to play music at all, returned. I would have to think of something.

---

5. Lisa, who was at the concert—it was such a big affair that some of the band members invited their family—remembers it differently, with Iggy cross-dressing on the first night. It was a long time ago, and I include her version for completeness' sake.

6. A video of this gig, complete with a cross-dressing Iggy, is available on YouTube: "Iggy Pop Live in San Francisco 1981."

7. A video of my performance with Debbie, Chris, and Chris's then girlfriend Iyla at the Nova Convention in 1996 can be found on YouTube. Unfortunately, it is inaccurately titled "Laurie Anderson Performing at The Nova Convention (1996)."

I had put my Fourth Way pursuits on hold for the tours. I did try to "remember myself" when I remembered to do this, but to be honest it did not come to me that often. I indulged, and I would be dishonest to say I didn't enjoy it. But it had been enough. I let Paul know that I was back in town and asked about coming back to the group.

Devotees of the Work celebrate Gurdjieff's birthday on January 13. When I received the invitation to attend the celebration that year, 1982, I was surprised. I had only been involved a short while, and even then had broken off to travel around the country, playing rock and roll. But the friend who had introduced me came to pick me up, and we and some others drove to a location outside of the city. I was impressed by the house—it was more a mansion—and by the number of people.

It was an odd gathering. Although there were many people, the atmosphere wasn't festive. Neither was it solemn, although there was certainly an air of seriousness. After someone took our coats, we were invited to move into a large room and take a seat. Then I was introduced to Gurdjieff's ritual of toasts, accomplished with powerful vodka. We were each given a tumbler and, after an appropriate toast, were obliged to empty it. This happened several times. I hadn't eaten yet, and the effect came on quickly. This added to the oddness of what happened next.

Someone announced that, in honor of the occasion, we would be treated to a special performance of the Babylonian epic *Gilgamesh*. That in itself was unusual, but no preparation for what followed. I looked to the center of the room where a small stage had been erected, and recognized the actor Bill Murray, from *Saturday Night Live*. I'd had no idea that he was interested in Gurdjieff's ideas, nor that he was involved in the same organization I was. I enjoyed the performance, but it was difficult after my toasts to keep a straight face whenever I heard him say "Enkidu."

This was the last time I participated in any gatherings given by the New York branch of the Gurdjieff Foundation. Not long after this, the friend whose flat I was subletting told me he was coming back and that

I would have to find a new place. It seemed that change was in the air. I looked at a few other places in New York. I had gotten used to the reasonable rent I was paying and the condition of the flat, which was in very good repair, and the good neighborhood, the East Village again.[8] Most of the places I saw were in less good shape, worse neighborhoods, and at rents guaranteed to induce a nosebleed. I had some money, but at the rate I would have to spend it, it wouldn't last long. I was hemming and hawing again when I heard from Lisa. She knew I had gotten involved in the Work and mentioned that she had met some people who were interested in it, too, and whom she thought I would like. I mentioned that I had to find a new home and she said, "Why not come here?"

I thought about it. Suddenly the warm California sun seemed appealing. New York's a lonely town when you haven't close friends and are going through a substantial life change, especially in winter. I had last seen Lisa at the Rolling Stones concert. Did I want to go to LA again, and this time take root?

"Why not?" I said.

So once again I packed up my library, took it to the post office, and headed west. I was leaving New York for the last time, and would remain in Los Angeles for the next fourteen years, until events swept me once again across the country, then carried me further: to London.

---

8. The flat, again on East 10th Street, off Second Avenue, was in a Ukrainian neighborhood. It was during my time there that I went through my "Russian phase," reading through Dostoevsky and eating borscht at the Kiev, an all-night coffee shop on East 6th Street, or blini at Veselka, just at the corner of Second Avenue and 9th Street. I remember this time fondly, and say so in my book *The Return of Holy Russia* (Inner Traditions, 2020).

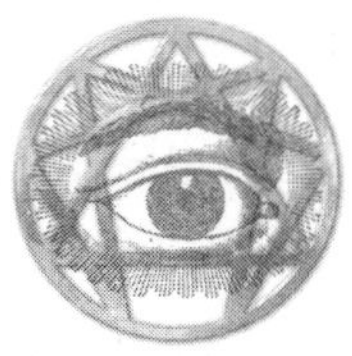

9
Looking for the Miraculous

I arrived in Los Angeles sometime in the early spring of 1982. I had met the friends Lisa had made, the people she mentioned who were interested in the Work and with whom she thought I would get on. One was an actor who went on to have a very successful career playing character roles, much as Lisa would. They had, in fact, met on the set of a television show. X, as I shall call him, was not an intellectual; he was much more a physical type and, as I came to understand, it was the performance and role-playing aspects of Gurdjieff's teaching that attracted many actors to the Work. This was, however, an aspect of it that had never interested me and which, truth to tell, I found tiresome. The difference in our temperaments would later cause some friction between X and myself, a positive state of affairs from a Work point of view. But that was further on.

The other character Lisa introduced me to was a friend of X's, whom he had known since they were teenagers. They had both come out from the East Coast, which was true of practically everyone I met during my tenure in Los Angeles. D, the friend, was something of a poet and an artist—at least, that was his temperament. He had talent, but unfortunately lacked the discipline to produce anything more than the occasional late-night, feverish scribbling and sketching. He was younger than X and myself (we were both the same age) and was something of a lovable rogue, what Jung would have called a *puer*, a Peter Pan type, refusing to grow up. This could be a charming personality trait, but sadly it often prevents its possessor from becoming an adult. It didn't take long for me to catch on that D's charm had infected Lisa and that they were more than friends.

As I soon learned, X's parents had been students of Ouspensky during his last years in America, when he lived on a huge estate called Franklin Farms, in Mendham, New Jersey, sitting out WWII. X had grown up in Mendham, and was more or less brought up in the Work, as one might be brought up a Methodist or Mormon. A few years later, while we were all in New York over the Christmas holidays to see Lisa perform on Broadway, X invited us to his parents' house, and they arranged for us to have a tour of the farm, which had by then reverted to less esoteric use.

It was an odd sensation to find myself walking over grounds that forty years earlier, Ouspensky had occupied. As I relate in my book about Ouspensky, his time at Franklin Farms was not happy. By then, he was experiencing much doubt about the decision he had made to suppress his own creativity in order to teach Gurdjieff's system, and spent his evenings reminiscing about the old days in Russia, while getting through a bottle or two of Montrachet. But if I reflected on any of this during that stroll around the farm, I kept it to myself. At the time, my own doubts about the Work had grown, and I would leave it soon after.

Although I had committed myself to following the discipline offered by the Work, I was never a true believer. My engagement with it was always as an experiment, to test it and see what would happen, which is exactly what Ouspensky suggested one do. It was with this same "scientific" approach that I studied Crowley's magical system, until I outgrew it. I was not in search of a teaching or a belief—I've never been a religious sort, although I accept the general religious notion that the universe is meaningful and our appearance in it especially so. (What that may mean is spelled out in my book *The Caretakers of the Cosmos* [Floris Books, 2013].) Consciousness was my central interest—my own in particular and humanity's in general, and I was willing to devote time and energy to learning the "system," in the same way that I would devote time and energy to learning how to play a musical instrument or speak a foreign language, or follow any serious pursuit, for that matter.

Unfortunately, X did not share this detached, objective approach, and my tentativeness often rubbed him the wrong way, his more histrionic nature requiring a more passionate involvement. I was drawn to the Work because of the ideas, and ideas are only as good as the intelligence you devote to understanding them—and that requires asking questions, a practice of which X did not approve. Adopting a set of ideas unreflectingly means embracing an ideology, which aims precisely at taking away from a person *the responsibility of thought.* It doesn't matter what the ideology is—whether Marxist, Freudian, Jehovah's Witness, or Gurdjieff—the result is the same: dogma and "chapter and verse" which the thoughtless but passionate true believer wields against the apostate.

The gadfly in me often stung X with some importunate observation that would lead to esoteric sparks and, not infrequently, some fur flying. Nevertheless, Lisa proved right. For a time, the four of us were something of a coterie, trying, though rarely successfully, to keep each other from backsliding into sleep, but more often injecting a bit of levity and camaraderie into what is too often a very grave pastime.

AROUND THE TIME OF MY ARRIVAL, X was breaking up with his girlfriend and moving out of their flat, and suggested that the two of us share a place. We looked at a few, but while the financial aspect of being flatmates was attractive, my solitary nature felt otherwise. I saw a sign advertising a studio flat above a garage and had a look. It was tucked away in a courtyard off the street in leafy West Hollywood, about as central a neighborhood in Los Angeles as one could get, and which was just then beginning to take on the gay character associated with it today. The studio was larger than the one Lisa had on Christopher Street and had an octagonal shape; a girlfriend who often visited called it a "teapot." The garage below was used for storage. Some steps led up to a balcony walkway shared by the studio next door. A ceiling fan hung from a point where the white crossbeams holding up the roof came together, giving the impression of a barn. The wood floor was shiny, the kitchenette and bathroom small but sufficient.

The bungalows below, fronting the street, had been built in the 1940s, following the mass migration of G.I.s returning from the war who headed west to invest in orange groves. They made me think of Philip Marlowe in one of Chandler's novels. But what definitely sold me on the place was the bookshelves. One wall sported a mock fireplace and mantle, and above this stretched several shelves. "Good," I thought, "they will come in handy." When, some weeks later, my books arrived at the post office, this proved true. Like myself, they had found a home for the next several years.

They would also, as I had, make new friends. Los Angeles in the 1980s was still a book lover's dream. Secondhand, collector's, and what we would call "niche" bookshops could be found all over LA, from downtown to the Pacific, and out in the no-man's-land known as the Valley, beyond the Hollywood Hills. The flat I had found, in fact, was very near one bookshop that I would become quite familiar with and, a few years later, work at. This was the Bodhi Tree.

One could spend an entire day getting to just a few of these bookshops, and I often did. Only, this time I would not be dependent on public transport. My previous times in the city impressed on me the need to get a car. That first required a driver's license, which I secured. Throughout the rest of my stay, I owned in succession four Volvos, all the 1966 122S model. The dry air of Southern California prevented rust and so old cars had a much longer lifespan there. Why did I own four of the same model car? I liked its shape and the fact that it was

European, and when one broke down beyond repair or—as did happen once—was totaled by another car, I simply got another.

As I write this now, a faint trace of the smell of that car, the leather upholstery, the warmth of the seat when, in winter, the automatic heating went on (the car was Swedish, after all, and winter nights can be chilly in LA), the glow from the light of the AM radio, and other vagrant memories well up from their inner, inexhaustible source. Living in London is rather like living in New York; the public transportation is good and owning a car is more often a burden than an advantage, so I have not owned one for the past twenty-seven years. I get around as much as I can on my bicycle or simply walk. But during my time in LA, as everyone else did, I drove practically everywhere.

One reason for this is that in LA everything is spread out; there is no "center of town." A bookshop I wanted to visit and a café whose coffee I liked could be a half-hour's drive from each other. When tourists come seeking "Hollywood," they are dismayed when natives tell them that it's just a name. As Gertrude Stein said of her hometown of Oakland, California, "There is no there there."

What is there? The ocean, the mountains, and the desert. The cliché about Los Angeles is that you can swim in the Pacific in the morning, hike in the mountains in the afternoon, and watch the sunset in the desert all in the same day, if you don't mind driving. I didn't mind, and my old Volvos took me out to all three locations on many occasions. I also made the journey from Los Angeles to San Francisco—a much more walkable city—along the Pacific Coast Highway and the cliffs of Big Sur, where Henry Miller once lived, as often as I could. More locally, one of my favorite spots was the Griffith Observatory, a beautiful Greek-style Beaux Arts building high in the hills of Griffith Park, overlooking the vast, flat expanse of the city. Nearby, in Los Feliz, still stands Manly P. Hall's Philosophical Research Society, with its Egyptian statue symbolizing the wisdom of the ancients, where I often would hear Hall himself lecture on a variety of esoteric subjects.

One reason I was able to enjoy these excursions was that, once again, I was not in immediate need of finding work, although soon enough that problem would present itself. For the moment, though, it wasn't a concern. I arrived in LA with a robust bank balance. Royalties for "Presence, Dear" continued to come in and would do so for a while. (They continue to today, as well as for my other songs, although over the years there have been more than a few fallow periods.) I had no contact with any of my ex-bandmates, but some portion of their success made its way to me and, every six months, I received a healthy check. That continued for the first few years of my stay. Soon enough, I would be faced with the usual problem of having to earn a living, but in the meantime I was graced with money and the freedom to do what I liked. No greater blessing could be desired. What I wanted was to read and, eventually, to write. That would take time and some not inconsiderable pain. But in the meantime, there were books.

One book that made a powerful impression on me at that time was Rilke's *Duino Elegies*, the poetic outpouring that came to him while he was a guest at the Duino Castle, on the shore of the Adriatic Sea. Rilke spent most of his life as a guest among the rich and aristocratic, and on this occasion, while walking along the cliffs, he heard a voice in the wind saying, "Who, if I cried, would hear me among the angelic hierarchy?" Rather than chubby seraphs gently plucking heavenly harps, Rilke's angels are beings of overwhelming power. "Every angel is terrible," he tells us, for they present us with a "beauty which is nothing more than the beginning of a terror we are just able to bear." This is the sublime I spoke of earlier, when I mentioned the peculiar frisson one gets from the best weird fiction. Rilke first heard his angelic voice in 1912; it took him a decade to finish the elegies, which he did while staying at a chateau in Switzerland. He died of leukemia in 1926, at the age of fifty-one.

For a while Rilke's elegies shared space with *Thus Spake Zarathustra* as a kind of bible for me, a kind of scripture. What impressed me about both was their philosophy of yea-saying, what Rilke in his *Sonnets to Orpheus* called *dennoch preisen* (praise in spite of), which is a form of

Nietzsche's *amor fati* (love of fate). The poet's job was to praise, not denounce life and everything in it. What I also found in Rilke was that sense of the precariousness of being I had become aware of from reading Nietzsche.

I had felt, in some inarticulate but nevertheless insistent way, that our task—here, now—was to somehow save the world from dissolving into insignificance and nonbeing. We were here to "save the world," not in the way many people today think of this, in the sense of protecting endangered species or stopping climate change or other environmental threats. These concerns are of course important. Yet it does strike me that many people who have very little else going on in their lives derive some sense of personal meaning by becoming "activists" for this cause or that, and are drawn to it for that reason, just as they are drawn to a political party or to one of the ever-growing "special interest groups" that crowd contemporary social life. In them they achieve a sense of identity—a very desirous thing these days. This strikes me as a form of what Sartre called "bad faith"—adopting some belief for the sake of personal advantage and to avoid one's own emptiness.

My sense of saving the world was something different, and I tried to spell it out as best as I could in *The Caretakers of the Cosmos*, a book I wrote many years later in which Rilke is a central figure. In the Ninth Elegy, Rilke writes, "*Truly* being here is so much; because everything here apparently needs us, this fleeting world, which in some strange way keeps calling to us." We can save the fleeting world from nonexistence, Rilke tells us, by drawing it into ourselves, into our consciousness. In a famous passage, Rilke enumerates the articles of existence in need of our help. "Perhaps we are here," he writes, "in order to say: house, bridge, fountain, gate, pitcher, fruit-tree, window . . . But to *say* them more intensely than the Things themselves ever dreamed of existing." Our task, Rilke tells us, is to "interiorize" the world, to bring it within ourselves and to make it "invisible." "Earth," he asks, "isn't this what you want: to arise within us *invisible*?"

This act of inwardness is what Rilke called *Herzwerk* (heart work), and those who participate in it are "the bees of the invisible." As he wrote to his Polish translator, Witold von Hulewicz, "Our task is to stamp this provisional, perishing Earth into ourselves so deeply, so painfully and passionately, that its being may arise again, 'invisibly' in us."

We may think it the height of arrogance to suggest that the universe—which has existed, so astrophysicists tell us, for some fifteen billion years, and is of a mind-numbing size—has any need of us insignificant creatures occupying a tiny speck of cosmic matter. But Jung made the same point when, in *Memories, Dreams, Reflections*, he tells us that until the advent of consciousness, and the peculiar form of it that we possess (our consciousness of being conscious), existence was mute, unknown, and unwitnessed. Millenia passed, great herds of living creatures swarmed over the face of the Earth. But until the first consciousness to regard itself and the world and know it existed arose, all was as if it did not happen, for there was no one to know that it did. We are not chance creatures of no importance in a purposeless universe; such a belief is merely a way of avoiding our task. The universe, the cosmos, needs us, and we would not be here if it didn't.

One thing that happened during that first year in that flat in LA was that my interest in classical music became an outright passion. I had upgraded from my cassette player, and the central space on my bookshelves was reserved for an odd turntable I had come across—a vertical one, with an amplifier and receiver—which fit perfectly, with its speakers at either end of the shelves. This was, of course, well before CDs appeared (not to mention downloads), and one of my favorite things to do then was to visit secondhand record shops, flip through the stacks of classical LPs, and come home with a handful of recordings of pieces I was unfamiliar with.

One of the best places to do this was Aaron's Records, on Melrose Avenue, which I knew from my musician days when I haunted it in search of old '60s albums. Now, instead of The Seeds or Thirteenth Floor Elevators, I was seeking out Bruckner and Mahler with performances by Wilhelm Furtwängler and Otto Klemperer. Most secondhand bookshops had a record section, and soon I had acquired a sizable collection. I would often spend whole mornings or afternoons listening to one performance after another, comparing composers and conductors, or experimenting with works I didn't know, pieces by Varèse, Ligotti, Messian, Cage, and other difficult composers. I had yet to get a television, and wouldn't for some time, and I spent evenings working my way through Bartok, Prokofiev, Shostakovich, Stravinsky, Debussy, and the rest. I had become such a devotee that Lisa, recognizing this, gave me a baton as a gift. I would often work myself up into a frenzy Nietzsche would have envied, slicing into the air in front of the speakers, convulsing to a symphony by Mozart or Martinu.

One of the most poignant memories from this time is of an evening spent listening to Beethoven's late string quartets, works that in his day were considered unplayable. I had a set of performances by the Budapest String Quartet. I can't now remember which quartet it was, but as I listened and looked out my window, I saw a star. Some combination of the music and the tiny white light flickering in the darkness triggered something in me, and I became aware of the distance between myself and the star, and of the sheer size of the universe. This brought on feelings I didn't know I possessed, and a sense that, even in the face of that immensity, Beethoven's music was eternal and spoke of a reality greater than space and time. I think at that moment I became aware of eternity. But it was more than this: it was a certainty that there is something in us that partakes of it, that is eternal. Whatever happens, there is something in us that endures, that is outside the flux of change, and occupies some realm of absolute value. All true art is aimed at reminding us of this reality, but music—and, perhaps to a lesser degree, poetry—seems to possess a power to awaken it most vividly. At least, this has been my experience.

It was also at this time that I became a regular listener of KUSC, the classical music station broadcast from the University of Southern California, which, some years later, I would attend. Listeners from this time will remember the programs hosted by Jim Svejda, which I listened to practically religiously. Svejda was intelligent and outspoken, and possessed a remarkable wealth of musical knowledge. He had a sense of humor and was not concerned about ruffling sponsors' feathers by his forthright, often controversial remarks and challenging playlist. I can remember making sure I was home in order to record his broadcast of Karel Jusa's "Music for Prague," a powerful work composed after the Soviet suppression of the "Prague Spring" of 1968; Svejda himself was Czech, and he opened his show with the third movement of Bohuslav Martinu, a Czech composer's, First Piano Quartet. I made a habit of looking at upcoming playlists, and this was only one of the many recordings I made of works that would otherwise be difficult to find (those recordings, alas, have been lost in the wreckage).

On recent visits to Los Angeles I was saddened to find that KUSC was no longer so adventurous, and had become something of an "easy listening" station, it's choices never veering far from the familiar tones of the Baroque and early classical periods. (I must confess that I find Bach something of a bore and that my own tastes stretch from Haydn's *Sturm und Drang* to mid-twentieth century, with a weakness for the late Romantics.) The effect was rather of listening to classical muzak, as if its audience were made up of people waiting at a dentist's office. Something of this development was presaged, I believe, in the early 1990s, when political correctness began to rear its head and broadcasters began to make a point of informing the listener of the nationality of the composers, as if anyone needed to know that Chopin was Polish. It was the beginning of the move to make everything "safe," and I would encounter it in more immediate ways when, a few years later, I returned to university.

But before I did that, I started class at a school of a different sort.

Before I left New York, I had asked my group leader, Paul, if he could put me in touch with a Fourth Way group in LA. I was determined to continue with the Work if I could, and intended for my involvement with it in my new life to be more sustained. There was no danger of my going on tour and no other obstacle to this, as far as I could see. Paul was under no obligation to vet me, and the people in Los Angeles were equally not obliged to accept me. But I must have made a good impression. He gave me a telephone number and a name and said—as the friend who had introduced me to him had a year earlier—that if I was truly interested I should call the person soon.

When I mentioned this to X, he nodded in approval as if my membership to a very exclusive club had been accepted. In a way, it had.

The name of the person I would get in touch with was Mrs. Langmuir. I later learned that she had been involved in the Work for some time. She first became involved in the 1950s, not long after Gurdjieff's death, and was one of the people responsible for establishing the Gurdjieff Foundation in Los Angeles.

Marianna—who was known as Nancy, but whom I always knew only as Mrs. Langmuir—was the wife of David Langmuir, a prestigious physicist with many honors. Years later, when writing *Dark Star Rising: Magic and Power in the Age of Trump*, I discovered that David Langmuir and the philosopher Jacob Needleman—whom I met some time later in London, at a tribute to Ouspensky at Colet House, where he had taught in the 1930s—had translated *Le Biosphere*, by the Russian geophysicist Vladimir I. Vernadsky, from a manuscript belonging to a student of Maurice Nicoll, another teacher of the Work.

Vernadsky was a Russian geochemist who belonged to a school of thought in the early twentieth century known as the Cosmists, about whom I write in *The Return of Holy Russia*. Among other ideas, the Cosmists believed that life on Earth was profoundly affected by influences coming from outer space, the planets and the Sun, notions that played a large part in Gurdjieff's teachings and which are very influential in contemporary Russian thought. Vernadsky's ideas were crucial to

Biosphere 2, the experiment in establishing a self-sustaining ecological environment capable of supporting human life on another planet, that began in Arizona in the early '90s.[1]

As I point out in *Dark Star Rising*, one of the people involved in the running of Biosphere 2 was Steve Bannon—for a time Donald Trump's political advisor. Bannon's interest in a project linked to Gurdjieff's ideas was only one of the odd esoteric connections associated with Trump; more directly significant was Bannon's interest in twentieth-century Italian esoteric thinker, Julius Evola, an outspoken devotee of far-right politics and a favorite of the alt-right, whom Bannon celebrated on his Breitbart website.

All of this, however, was far in the future. When I called the number Paul had given me, I was received politely and invited to introduce myself at the Langmuirs' home in Santa Monica, a suburb of Los Angeles along the Pacific coast. I got the address and, one afternoon, drove out to it. If my memory serves me well, it proved to be a spacious, well-appointed house on a quiet backstreet, with a neat, well-tended garden and general air of middle-class success if not affluence—at least, that is the impression I retain some forty-plus years on. Although Gurdjieff and Ouspensky were picked up by the counterculture of the 1960s—for a time, the LSD guru Timothy Leary sang their praises—most of their serious students came from fairly well-off backgrounds. Gurdjieff himself said that only people who were successful in life could be so in the Work, which demanded the sort of responsibility and conscientiousness associated with the bourgeoise. It was not an escape from life's demands but an acceptance of even greater burdens; the bohemians and artistic types drawn to the Work under the impression that it will aid them in "doing their own thing" generally drop out fairly soon. Throughout the few years I was involved in the Work, my general impression was that

---

1. The polymath John Allen, whom I once met in London at the October Gallery, an establishment associated with his coterie, was the systems ecologist at work on Biosphere 2. He incorporated many ideas of J. G. Bennett, a student of Gurdjieff and Ouspensky, in his plans for the experiment.

most of the people I met were serious, well-adjusted, and more or less successful in their lives. Their interest in the Work was not as a substitute for life, but as a means of living more.

Mrs. Langmuir proved to be a soft-spoken, self-possessed woman of mature years. She died in 2006, at the age of ninety, so she would have been around sixty-six when we met; oddly enough, around the age I am now. I was twenty-six then, young enough for her to serve as a mother figure for me, although our relationship was never close enough for that association to take hold. If I recall correctly, she had a slight stutter, something I could sympathize with—if sympathy were needed—given that I possessed one myself; it generally makes its appearance when I am excited or speechless at some outrage. Given my sensitive nature, such outrages are not as infrequent as one might hope. She interviewed me much as Paul had, but where his presence had been somewhat intimidating, Mrs. Langmuir's invited confidence and the lowering of defenses. She would later tell me that the best way to deal with people is to ask them about themselves—a topic about which they generally have a lot to say.

How much this had to do with Paul or Mrs. Langmuir's own character and style of interviewing, and how much my own projection, is difficult to say. She asked some general questions, and some more specific ones about how far I had got in the group in New York. No doubt more was exchanged, but what it may have been has vanished from memory. At the end I was invited to join a group that had only recently started, given the address where to go and the time I should be there.

Mrs. Langmuir wasn't leading my group, though I would have contact with her regularly over the next few years. I have to admit that I don't recall the name of the gentleman who did lead it. Whether this speaks of memory loss or the lack of impression he made on me is debatable. As I sit here, raking through this past, I can't say that I remember many names from this time, although isolated impressions and strong memories of different events do stand out.

The group I joined met in a house in the Valley. As I write this I can remember driving through Laurel Canyon, where many of Hollywood's well-heeled lived, in order to reach it. This in itself was a different affair than getting to the meetings in New York, which required only a short ride on the subway. I'm sure I am romanticizing it—of what else should I be romantic?—but having to drive at night through the Hollywood Hills, along the sharp curves of Laurel Canyon Boulevard, made me think of Gurdjieff's remark to Ouspensky that it was salutary to make attending meetings somewhat difficult, to weed out the irresolute and merely curious. The conditions Gurdjieff created in St. Petersburg and Moscow were, of course, more stringent than anything I encountered in New York or LA, but even so, it did cost an effort to get into the car and make the journey.

As in New York, I attended weekly meetings in which questions about the exercises we had been given were addressed. As in New York, the ambience was rather dry and austere. We sat in a similar room, likewise bare except for rows of hard, wooden chairs and a table on which rested a vase of flowers, a water pitcher, and some glasses, the table itself flanked by two chairs. Were there portraits of Gurdjieff and Ouspensky on the wall? There may have been—I seem to remember it but I could be wrong. I do remember some books and pamphlets available for purchase on display in the hallway, and the book in which we registered our attendance at the meeting.

Along with these weekly gatherings, I also attended readings of *In Search of the Miraculous* and *Beelzebub's Tales to His Grandson*, as well as "ideas meetings," which were more of an open discussion group where the kinds of questions usually avoided at the regular meetings could get an airing. By then, I had been reading widely in the Fourth Way literature available at the time. Along with Gurdjieff and Ouspensky's books, I absorbed J. G. Bennett, Rodney Collin, Maurice Nicoll, Kenneth Walker, C. S. Nott, Fritz Peters, and Thomas and Olga de Hartmann, but also A. R. Orage, whose links to Shaw, Wells, and the *fin de siècle* by way of his magazine, *The New Age*, opened up a whole other area of the history of ideas.

Although I did not know it at the time, this would become more or less the center of my interest. It may seem an odd path by which to have reached a fascination with intellectual history, but it was my obsession with knowing the history of the Work—which most of the Fourth Way people I knew were unaware of, or positively ignored—that led to a wider, more comprehensive desire to understand the *ideas* that have informed Western thought for the past few centuries.

One difference between my involvement in the Work in New York and that in Los Angeles was that here there were more hands-on activities. Perhaps, had I stayed in New York, I may have been invited to something along these lines in the mansion I visited for Gurdjieff's birthday celebration. As it was, I was soon invited to attend "Work weekends" at the house in the Valley. At these, people from different groups, perhaps thirty or forty of us, got together and spent a Saturday and Sunday performing physical activities—cooking, gardening, cleaning, painting, carpentry, handcrafts—all while trying to "remember ourselves," or to not express "negative emotions," something the leaders of the groups purposely set out to create, by putting together people they believed would have difficulty getting along. I soon discovered how this kind of magnetic repulsion worked.

Early on, with two other men, I was assigned the task of beating some rugs. My attitude was "Well, let's get this done," figuring it was better to put myself into it rather than step back and hesitate. As I rolled up my sleeves—literally and metaphorically—one of the others made some remark about my gung ho approach that made me stop. They were sitting there, in no rush to do anything, finishing their cigarettes—for some reason, smoking was very popular among people in the Work. They made me think. Was I being naïve? Or trying to make a good impression? How should I respond? What was the right way? Was there one? Suddenly, something seemingly simple and ordinary became rather ambiguous.

It was in uncomfortable situations like this that one could observe one's usual reactions, to recognize the mechanical behavior it was the aim of the Work to undo. It was not always pleasant, but the idea was to experience what Gurdjieff called "intentional suffering." Mostly, we suffer unconsciously—that is, to no end—and we often enjoy it, no matter how much we grumble. Intentional suffering is an unpleasantness we consciously endure in order to learn something about ourselves.

These Work weekends generally began fairly early. There would be coffee on arrival, and later a simple lunch and dinner prepared and served by people assigned to that task. Others would be assigned the washing-up. There would be a morning talk, a kind of Fourth Way sermon, setting out some ideas of the Work, like self-observation, self-remembering, use of the different centers (intellectual, emotional, moving), or Gurdjieff's strange "food diagram," and the creation of higher energies needed to "work on oneself." An exercise centered on the talk would be given, and we would be assigned to different groups and given certain tasks to perform throughout the day. Later, we would meet and discuss our efforts at trying to do the exercise, and specific questions about them could be asked.

We were instructed to perform our tasks with "conscious labor," that is, to attempt to remain aware of ourselves while doing it, rather than go through it mechanically. (Today, this goes by the name of "mindfulness.") How successful we were at this is debatable, but I know that on at least a few occasions I felt my efforts at working consciously paid off.

Conscious or not, at times the labor, if not hard, could be intensive. It was a less demanding version of what went on at the Institute for the Harmonious Development of Man that Gurdjieff had established in his Prieuré in Fontainebleau, outside of Paris, in the 1920s. By this time, I had read several accounts of what is was like to have been there (and by now, have written two books about central figures in the Work) and knew most of the stories.

One well-known anecdote involved A. R. Orage, the portly, chain-smoking "desperado of genius" (in George Bernard Shaw's words) who was one of the first to arrive at the institute after hearing Gurdjieff speak in London. If Orage expected to be met with words of wisdom from the mystic master, he was in for a surprise. Almost upon arrival,

Orage was given a shovel and told to dig. He was also forbidden to smoke. Orage dug until his back ached and his clothes were covered in sweat. He was then told to fill in the hole. The next day, he did the same. The editor, who could hold his own with Shaw and H. G. Wells, very literally cried himself to sleep each night, only to be woken up after a few hours and faced with another day of hard, pointless labor. (Going through nicotine withdrawal at the same time could not have helped.) He had, it seemed, dug a very deep hole for himself indeed. Then, one morning, as he returned to his back-breaking work, he suddenly found himself flooded with new energy and positively enjoying the labor, feeling he could carry on for hours. What had happened?

Orage had broken through his mechanical, habitual response, and gained access to the hidden reservoirs of energy Gurdjieff believed lay dormant within us. There are several accounts by different people who were subject to Gurdjieff's teaching that attest to this; perhaps the most impressive is the one J. G. Bennett recounts in his autobiography, *Witness*.[2] I later came to see that Gurdjieff's method of pushing his pupils beyond their usual limits was his version of what William James, in an essay called "The Energies of Men," called the "bullying treatment." James speaks of neurasthenic patients who have fallen into such a state of low vitality that any effort—even simply getting out of bed—is too much for them. James discovered that if such a patient is *forced* to make an effort, his vitality is quickly restored and what had seemed impossible is now child's play. The phenomenon is linked to what athletes know as a "second wind;" when, at the point of collapse, if one last effort is made, suddenly they are fresh as a daisy, as if they had discovered a secret reserve of fuel.

Gurdjieff had certainly not read James's essay, but he had hit on the same insight: that we live "subject to degrees of fatigue which we have come only from habit to obey."[3] If pushed past our habitual limits, we

---

2. J. G. Bennett, *Witness* (London: Turnstone Books, 1975), 114–118.

3. William James, "The Energies of Men," Internet Archive.

discover that we have enormous reserves of energy of which we were unaware. Gurdjieff's method of what we can call "induced inconvenience" and "artificial crisis" is designed to do just that. It isn't foolproof, and there have been casualties along the way, but on the whole it has proved beneficial to the recipients of his instruction.

I experienced something of the "Orage treatment" one weekend when I was given the task of painting a fence. I worked at it all morning and was ready to give it a second coat when my group leader came by, gave it a once over, then told me it was the wrong color and that I would have to paint it again. I was indignant at first, then remembered Orage and laughed, and cheerfully went about repainting it. On another occasion, I was given the task of raking leaves and collecting them in bin bags. Nothing unusual happened until, one moment, I found myself transfixed. I had scooped up a handful of leaves and was about to put them into the bag when I found myself staring at them in amazement. It was as if I had never seen a leaf before—a cliché, of course, but nonetheless true. For a moment it was as if I was seeing them as I had as a child, fresh and clean and crisp, as if some inner light, until then muted, had been turned up. I was seeing the leaves from "essence," rather than from "personality," from, that is, my true self and not the persona with which I usually face the world. It was, I believe, an unalloyed moment of wakefulness. I knew then that being "asleep" was something more than a metaphor.

But the most powerful experience I had during my tenure in the Work came from my attempt to perform the difficult Gurdjieff "movements." I've mentioned that Paul Reynard was one of the principal teachers of these movements, which are not quite ballet, although Gurdjieff spoke of them as sacred dances. They are rather like very complicated versions of the old trick of trying to pat your head and rub your stomach at the same time. After I had attended a few Work weekends, I was invited to observe a group who were teaching the movements to newcomers. Mrs. Langmuir accompanied them on piano, but she needed to find another accompanist for classes she couldn't make. When it came out that I had been a musician, she asked if I could fill in for her, but was disappointed when I told her I had played guitar.

The house in the Valley included quite a bit of property, and the movements took place in a hall set apart for that purpose. The music that accompanied them was by Thomas de Hartmann. He and his wife Olga had been Gurdjieff's pupils in the early days in Russia and at the Prieuré—she had been Gurdjieff's secretary—and they had written a book about their experience with him.

Photographs I had seen of performances of the movements at the Prieuré showed men and women in flowing white robes, scarves, and headbands—dress not dissimilar to other artistic dances of the time, such as we find with Isadora Duncan, Rudolph Laban, Emile Jaques-Dalcroze, or even Rudolf Steiner's Eurythmy. Here in LA in the 1980s, home of the leisure suit, sweat suits sufficed. But if the costumes were not as striking as they had been in Fontainebleau, the performance was nonetheless gripping. I wouldn't call it beautiful or even aesthetically pleasing. Some have suggested that Gurdjieff learned these dances from a Sufi order during his travels in Central Asia. That may be so. Years later I attended a performance of the whirling dervishes of the Mevlevi Sufi order. Their ecstatic spinning was mesmerizing, truly hypnotic. But it was nothing like the movements. And as I remember it now, there was something slightly disturbing about the performance of the movements I observed that evening.

It is difficult to put my finger on exactly what was troubling about it, except to say that the precision and unity displayed suggested something *mechanical*, which is ironic, given that the aim of the Work was to eliminate mechanical behavior. Think of the pistons moving in a well-oiled engine, or a troop of crack soldiers on parade. I suspect that what was slightly unsettling was the inhuman character of the movements, with several different body parts—hands, feet, head—turning in unusual ways simultaneously. Others have remarked similarly. In the audience for Gurdjieff's students' performance of the movements in New York in the 1920s was the writer William Seabrook. He noted the "brilliant, automaton-like, inhuman, almost incredible docility and robot-like obedience of the disciples," who struck him as a group of "perfectly trained zombies."[4] I wouldn't go as far as this, but one could say the impression the movements made on me was that of a group of perfectly balanced marionettes, whose limbs were pulled by invisible strings controlled by slightly eccentric puppeteers.

I had my own chance to join the marionettes soon enough. At one of the Work weekends, I was invited to join a group who were just starting on the movements. With the weekends and other meetings, my involvement with the Work was beginning to take up quite a bit of time. This, as I came to see, was part of the process, and my detached attitude resisted it. It struck me that, for many people I met who had been involved for some time, the Work had become a way of life, much as religion becomes for the very devout. Everything centers around it. In my case, this wouldn't happen, but over time I began to feel a certain pressure in that direction, an encouragement to get even more involved. It was one of the factors that would eventually have me leave.

As usually happens with beginners, my first attempts at the movements were not successful. Although I'd pogoed on stage and was fairly athletic in my teens, I was never a dancer, and was always slightly awkward and self-conscious when it came to physical coordination. I have no hesitation speaking before an audience; I enjoy it and have been told I do it well, that I am lively and spontaneous. But at heart I am an introverted, cerebral type who likes to step back and observe rather than plunge in headfirst. So, it required an effort to even begin my instruction. Once I did, efforts became more and more necessary. Gurdjieff spoke of what he called "super-efforts," doing more than you actually had to in performing some task. So, if you've walked ten miles and are exhausted, walk another two before resting. Clearly, super-efforts are part of the bullying treatment, and are what athletes make before they

---

4. William Seabrook, *Witchcraft: Its Power in the World Today* (New York: Harcourt, Brace and Co., 1940), 166.

hit their second wind. One evening, I had a chance to make one of my own.

I had mastered—if I can say as much—some of the simpler steps, and the time came to move on to something more difficult. The new, more complex steps were demonstrated, and we were walked through them. Then it was time to do them on our own. The music started up and so did we. If the simpler steps had been difficult enough, the new ones seemed downright impossible. I kept losing my place, forgetting the order in which I was supposed to move *this* hand then *that* foot, and then my head, while turning in *that* direction. Others were having the same trouble. The repetitive music kept going, insisting we keep up with it.

I had been at it for several minutes—or it could have been much longer, it was difficult to tell. I was growing more and more frustrated and annoyed, both at myself for making such a bad show and at the music for pushing me on. I said to myself that I'd had enough. I was simply bad at this and there was no point in trying to do it. I would stop. But then I made one more attempt to get it right—and suddenly, I did. I was moving in time and in what seemed perfect rhythm. I carried on, filled with renewed energy, utterly surprised. I felt I could have kept going for hours. The feeling of vitality remained the rest of the evening. I felt so awake, I wanted to drive to San Francisco and back just for the fun of it. My super-effort had paid off. I had broken through to energies I didn't know I possessed.

I don't know if Gurdjieff devised his movements himself, put them together from bits and pieces he had learned during his travels—I'm sure by now there must be academic treatises about their origin—or was actually taught them, as he says, by the Sarmoung Brotherhood. What I do know is that they worked.

In the summer of 1983, X and I decided to have a European adventure. I had already been to London twice, and Paris. X hadn't, and to these cities we added a third, Amsterdam. Such was the itinerary for what I later called my "mini search for the miraculous." It qualified as such because during it we visited sacred sites such as Stonehenge and Avebury in England, and the cathedrals of Notre-Dame de Paris and Chartres in France. (The sacred sites in Amsterdam were the coffee shops, where one could purchase hashish.) Our schedule included two other destinations. One was 6 rue des Colonels Renard, in Paris, where Gurdjieff lived and held meetings during the German occupation. The other was the Prieuré in Fontainebleau, home of his short-lived Institute for the Harmonious Development of Man.

There was one additional stop for me. After X and I separated, I made a pilgrimage of my own. This was to Cornwall, in the far west of England, in order to meet Colin Wilson.

Forty years on, much of the trip is a blur. I know that at the time I was very interested in ley lines, standing stones, and other megalithic sites, and that, along with Stonehenge and Avebury, I intended to visit some lesser-known stone circles and see if there was anything to the idea of "earth energies," powerful underground forces that supposedly stretched web-like across the planet. I had read about them in Wilson's *Mysteries*—especially his chapters on T. C. Lethbridge—and had brought a copy along with me. I had also read Francis Hitching's very popular *Earth Magic* and John Michell's *The View Over Atlantis* and *City of Revelation*; years later, I would interview John Michell for my book *Turn Off Your Mind*.

I had also read an odd book, *The Mysteries of Chartres Cathedral*, by Louis Charpentier, which spoke of Chartres's architecture as a "book" written in the "green language" of alchemy. Although my math was execrable and much of it was over my head, I was interested in sacred geometry and the idea that, in their masonry, Gothic cathedrals like Notre-Dame de Paris and Chartres housed esoteric and alchemical secrets. Ouspensky had written as much in *A New Model of the Universe*, in an evocative passage in which he speaks of Notre-Dame's towers as witnesses to the tragic events making up what he called "the history of crime."

I had sat and looked at Notre-Dame's remarkable façade on my first visit to Paris, and by now have visited it several times, each time struck by its mysterious beauty. I was saddened in 2019 when a fire destroyed its spire and roof, and posted about it on Twitter. I have visited Chartres only once, during my search, but the impression it made, of there being more space *inside* the cathedral than without, remains to this day. I remember slowly tracing the labyrinth, a site of pilgrimage and penance for centuries. One need not be Catholic or Christian or even religious to feel that something mysteriously transformative takes place, if one can be open to it, below those vaulted ceilings and within the light beaming through those extraordinary stained-glass windows, especially the rose windows of the transepts.

Of Stonehenge and Avebury on that journey, my impressions are sadly vague. Since living in London, I have visited both more than once, and what I can conjure now is a general feeling of what it is like to be there. I do remember that on my first visit, X and I walked some way down the road from the entrance to Stonehenge. We climbed over a fence and huddled beside a small hillock or mound in order to get a view of the stones without all the tourists. I imagine we wanted to see them as the people who erected them may have. The stones themselves were partitioned off, so one couldn't touch them, but this wasn't the case in Avebury, a much larger site. There, we walked freely among them, stopping now and then to sit with our backs against a stone, hoping for a tingle of telluric energy to spurt up from a magnetic ley line or two.

We traveled before the Eurostar made it easier to get from London to Paris than it is to get to other parts of England. We had bought Eurail passes but our passage across the English Channel was by ferry. I hadn't traveled by sea before and was surprised at how long the journey took and how cold it was, lying out on deck in the middle of summer. When we arrived at Dunkirk it was the middle of the night and we had to wait some hours for our train to Paris. I can remember the sheet lightning over the Channel suddenly illuminating the darkness as we smoked cigarettes and walked along the tracks. Along the way, in the early morning, we passed farmhouses and haystacks. My first impression of Paris that trip was of the empty streets we passed on the way to Gare du Nord.

Through some mutual acquaintance, X had arranged a place for us to stay. I was open for adventure, but when we arrived at the address, it turned out to be in Belleville, a down-market district in the north of the city. Fashionable today, back then Belleville was edgy and far off the beaten track. If it wasn't a slum, it was not far removed from one. To say the place itself—a single room, several flights up a filthy stairway—was squalid would be an understatement. The toilet does not bear mentioning. I guess free lodgings in Paris should not be looked askance, but I have to admit it was something of a surprise. X, though, was perfectly happy. He had been reading Orwell's *Down and Out in Paris and London*, and it had made an impression. He had grown up in upper-middle-class comfort, and now could indulge his romantic ideas about bohemian poverty to no end. I had already lived in squalor for real, and knew there was nothing romantic about it.

After an uncomfortable night, I decamped and found a room in a cheap but clean hotel near the Boulevard Saint-Michel. The copy of *Frommer's Europe on $20.00 A Day* I had with me was proving helpful. There was a bath in the hall, and coffee and a croissant for breakfast. X stuck it out with Orwell, but was happy to sneak in a bath when the hotel concierge wasn't looking.

Rue des Colonels-Renard, near the Arc de Triomphe in the 17th arrondissement, is situated in a well-heeled part of Paris featuring fashionable apartments at vertigo-inducing rents. In the late 1930s and throughout the Nazi occupation, it was not so affluent a neighborhood. Rents were low and the occupants of nearby buildings led modest lives. When Gurdjieff finally had to let go of the Prieuré, which had fallen into disuse after the collapse of his institute little more than a year after its opening, it was here that his followers found him a new home.

He would live at number 6 from 1937 until his death in

October 1949. It was here that he held his legendary lunches and dinners during which up to fifty people crammed into his small flat and were treated to lavish dishes prepared by the master himself (like Aleister Crowley and C. G. Jung, Gurdjieff was a good cook). Kenneth Walker and others have left accounts of what these dinners were like, and what the effect of the notorious "toasts to the idiots," carried out with vodka, could be on the unprepared. They have also described the flat's décor, with amateurish paintings by indigent locals adorning the walls (bought by Gurdjieff so they would have money to eat), Oriental bric-a-brac filling the shelves, and the aroma of exotic spices from Gurdjieff's pantry saturating the place.

When X and I arrived, walking up from the Etoile, there was little to do but stand outside the building, smoke a *Gauloises*, and think of the people—like Walker, J. G. Bennett, Fritz Peters, and others—who had visited Gurdjieff and written about their experiences there. We did find the café Gurdjieff used to frequent, and had a café noir in his memory.

The train from Gare de Lyon to Fontainebleau took about an hour. Someone in Los Angeles who had been there had given us directions from the train station to the Château Le Prieuré where, some sixty years earlier, the first wave of Gurdjieff's English students—people like Orage, Maurice Nicoll, and J. G. Bennett—had submitted themselves to the master's tutelage.[5] Although Gurdjieff had lived and taught in France for more than twenty years, the French had never taken to him. The strong Catholic and Traditionalist elements in French esotericism saw him as a positive danger, and the rationalist streak in the French psyche rejected any form of mysticism *tout court*.

In Paris, writers and philosophers are honored with street names; even the alchemist Nicolas Flamel has a rue named after him. Gurdjieff gets no mention, but *en route* to the château, we saw a plaque

---

5. An account of what that was like can be found in my book *Maurice Nicoll: Forgotten Teacher of the Fourth Way* (Rochester, VT: Inner Traditions, 2024).

commemorating "The Forest Philosophers," a tag given to the people attending Gurdjieff's institute by the journalists of the day. Mention is made, though, of Katharine Mansfield, the young New Zealand writer who, dying of tuberculosis and desperate to try any means of staving off the disease, asked her friend Orage for an introduction to Gurdjieff. Mansfield arrived at the Prieuré in late October, 1922, and died there in early January the next year. A rue leading from the train station to the cemetery where she is buried is named after her as well.

Again, forty years on, details of our visit are vague, but some strong impressions remain. I can remember walking in the forest, thinking of the account J. G. Bennett left of his experience when, as they had in myself, his attempt to master a difficult series of movements led to the opening of what Gurdjieff called his "accumulator," an internal storage device housing our energies. Bennett's experience was, however, altogether more powerful than mine. He writes not only of how his dysentery miraculously vanished, but of his going into the forest and digging at a rate even the galvanized Orage would have found daunting, and of Gurdjieff's speaking to him of the Great Accumulator, a source of power and force that only few individuals could access.

I remember seeing the goldfish pond that I had read about in different accounts of life at the institute. But what stands out the most is what I saw when I looked through one of the windows into the château itself. It was closed, and apparently had been unoccupied for some time. Yet, what I saw when I peeked inside made me laugh. What was there? Rows of washing machines, lined up, as if in a laundromat. What they were doing there I had no idea, nor was there anyone to ask. But, given that Gurdjieff's mission was to fight our mechanicalness, the fact that his old institute was still home to machines seemed superbly appropriate.[6]

---

6. While in London, before crossing the Channel, X and I attended a lecture by P. L. Travers, author of the Mary Poppins books and a devotee of the Work, at the College of Psychic Sciences. Her topic was the symbology of the bee.

When X and I decided to go our separate ways, I returned to England from Amsterdam, once again on the ferry, and made my way to London. I intended to travel west, to Cornwall, to visit some of the megalithic sites I had read about. At a map shop near St Paul's cathedral—the name escapes me now—I bought an ordnance survey map of the area; I had already been finding my way around London, Paris, and Amsterdam with the excellent old Falk Plan maps. Another stop was the Village Bookshop on Regent Street. I remembered from my past visit, in 1981, that the owner knew Colin Wilson. My ultimate aim was to find Wilson's home, Tetherdown, in Gorran Haven, and I thought he might be able to help in this.

He was. And he made my quest significantly easier by giving me Wilson's telephone number. "He likes visitors," he said. I found this very helpful and encouraging at the time, but I subsequently wondered if this was a bit of a friendly dig at Wilson. In any case, I had the number and would call it.

My exact itinerary is hazy. I intended to get to Penzance, and from there walk the coastal path toward Land's End. Two of the megalithic sites I wanted to see—the Merry Maidens and the Pipers—were in that area. And, according to my ordnance survey map, there were other, smaller sites that I should be able to find. I had read Alfred Watkins's *The Old Straight Track*, and was looking forward to following any ley lines I could discover. But there was one sacred site that I wanted to visit before Cornwall. This was Glastonbury, in Somerset.

I had read about Glastonbury in John Michel's books and in other books about "Earth magic." I had also read Geoffrey Ashe's books *King Arthur's Avalon: The Story of Glastonbury*, *The Quest for Arthur's Britain*, *Camelot and the Vision of Albion*, and also his interesting mystical novel, *The Finger and the Moon*. I knew he lived in Glastonbury in the house that the magician Dion Fortune, one of the Golden Dawn, had lived in. It was a site that no self-respecting seeker of the miraculous could pass up.

I have never attended the Glastonbury Festival, but since that first visit forty years ago, I have been to Glastonbury at least twice more, once to speak at a Dion Fortune symposium. But my first impressions of it remain strong. To get there, I hitchhiked part of the way and also took a coach; I remember reading Ian Wilson's *The Turin Shroud* for part of the journey. At a bulletin board in the town center—it was already a New Age crossroads, with metaphysical bookshops offering crystals and tarot readings lining the street—I saw a notice for a room. It was in the vicarage and proved to be comfortable and cheap.

I spent three days in Glastonbury. I visited the remains of a prehistoric lake village not far out of town. In ancient times, the area was flooded and the people then built dwellings on mounds rising out of the water; all that remains now are the mounds. I walked to Wearyall Hill, where legend has it that Joseph of Arimathea—said to have brought the Holy Grail to Glastonbury—rested, and where his staff miraculously blossomed into the Glastonbury Thorn. I lingered in the gardens of Chalice Well, where Geoffrey Ashe lived, and drank from its healing waters. And I wandered through the ruins of Glastonbury Abbey, which was destroyed during the dissolution of the monasteries during the reign of Henry VIII. Legend has it that the abbey was founded by Joseph of Arimathea and that the grave of King Arthur can be found on its grounds (according to Geoffrey Ashe, Glastonbury was Avalon).

I can remember sitting in a café across from the abbey, reading, when a woman who was sitting with a group at a table nearby came up to me and smiled. She then looked at me and asked, "Are you a seeker, too?" I guess I gave that impression. Perhaps whatever I was reading suggested it. She was travelling with a religious society, and, like myself, visiting different sacred sites. Was I a seeker? I guess I was.

Like everyone else who comes to Glastonbury, I walked the spiral path to the top of the Tor, where stands the ruins of St. Michael's Church, erected in the fourteenth century on the grounds of an earlier church from the eleventh century. St. Michael's, like Glastonbury Abbey, was destroyed during the dissolution of the monasteries, but its roofless tower remains and is a site of pilgrimage. I made mine on a very hot afternoon, passing the ancient oaks Gog and Magog, who rival the sequoias in age, on the way. (I was saddened to learn recently that Gog has since died and that Magog is also ailing.) I reached the top and took in the view, then sat within the tower and meditated—which basically meant keeping quiet—for some time. It is difficult to put myself back into the psyche of my younger self. The forty years between us is quite a stretch, but I know I was hopeful that *something*, some kind of magic, would happen. That is why we go on these sorts of journeys, with the "adventurous expectancy"—as H. P. Lovecraft calls it—that something out of the ordinary will be revealed to us. What that may be is unknown, but we travel with the faith that we will stumble across it, whatever it is.

What I stumbled upon when I left the tower was a woman of mature years, slowly tracing the top of the Tor with a forked branch in her hands. She was dowsing. Wilson had written about this strange ability we possess to detect subterranean water, as well as other substances, and I had carried out my own experiments with a pendulum after reading Lethbridge. I watched her for a while, and when she noticed me she asked if I would like to give it a try. I did. I took the branch, one end in each hand, and slowly took a few steps. For a few minutes nothing happened. Then, I felt it. The branch jerked up, then down. I did nothing—it moved on its own. The woman was not surprised. "It always happens," she said, as I handed the branch back to her.

I HAD BEEN IN PENZANCE a few days before I rang the telephone number the owner of the Village Bookshop had given me. There was a heat wave that summer, and in my book *Dreaming Ahead of Time*, I recount how, while walking the coastal path in the blistering sun, I fell into a kind of trance, gazing at the colored stones in a shallow tidepool. There was no one else on the path, and I can't say how long I sat there, absolutely content, looking through the transparent water. On another hike, my ordnance survey map informed me that, just at the top of the cliff above me, I should find some standing stones. I scrambled my way up, feeling myself a genuine ley hunter, only to find no stones but many standing cows.

Yet other outings were more successful. I did reach the Pipers and the Merry Maidens. I spent some time sitting with my back against one of the Maidens, who legend says were young girls turned to stone as punishment for dancing on the Sabbath. Although I very much wanted to, I can't say that I felt anything unusual, any telluric tingle, certainly nothing like my experience of dowsing on Glastonbury Tor. Yet, the long walk back under the stars, to my room at the remarkably cheap bed and breakfast, was magical enough.

When I finally called the telephone number, the voice on the other end was polite and friendly. It seemed the owner of the Village Bookshop was right—Wilson did like visitors, or, at least, he gave the impression he did. The easiest thing, he said, was to get the train to St. Austell, where he could pick me up. It was, in fact, Joy Wilson, Colin's wife, who met me. I imagine she had greeted Colin's visitors this way more than once.

When we arrived at Tetherdown, set back off the road by a long driveway and with the English Channel not far in the distance, Colin greeted me warmly. I met his young sons, Damon and Rowan—I would meet his daughter, Sally, on another visit—and was surprised to see that his mother was there. The heat wave was still on and, after some lunch, Colin invited me to join him and the others for a swim at the beach. Before this, he had handed me a typescript of his book on Jung, which he said he had just finished. I decided to stay behind and read the typescript, which I did while sitting in the living room with his mother. I remember her remarking on the many books Colin had written. "But I haven't read any of them," she added.

As I've mentioned elsewhere, I was impressed with the number of books lining the walls. They were everywhere—bookshelves were in every room, including the kitchen—as were stacks of VHS tapes, cassettes, and LPs. Aside from at a well-stocked secondhand bookshop or public library, I hadn't seen that many books in one place before. Estimates today of the number of books in Colin's library are between sixty and one hundred thousand. In addition to the books in the house, he had built two sheds to accommodate the overflow. And the chalet where I stayed, set back from the main house, was also filled with books—old paperbacks and complete sets of Sir Walter Scott, Havelock Ellis, and others—that filled the air with that peculiar odor of slowly disintegrating paper. Damp was unavoidable, being so near the sea. Over my many subsequent visits, I would get to know that musty scent very well.

That evening, after dinner, Colin spoke with me about his ideas about consciousness and what Husserl meant by "intentionality." I remember him saying that if he performed a certain mental exercise, he could create in himself a mild version of what Huxley felt under the effects of mescaline. As the wine flowed and Colin spoke in that full, warm voice he had worked hard to develop—long ago jettisoning his broad Leicester accent—I felt I could understand what he meant, and decided this was something I'd like to do myself. My experiences of "seeing" were already something like it. I would, it seemed, have to get a better grasp of phenomenology.

We drank a lot of wine that evening. Colin must have made an exception to the rule that I subsequently came to understand: he usually went to bed relatively early, around nine o'clock, because his day usually started at six a.m. I know we were at it late because, at around midnight, Muz Murray, an old friend whom Colin hadn't seen in years, turned up with an attractive younger woman.[7] Colin very graciously put them up as well. By that time, I was feeling the effects of travel, wine, and sitting across from one of the most important writers of the twentieth century. I had argued with David Bowie, gotten drunk with Iggy

7. In the late 1960s, Muz Murray published *Gandalf's Garden*, an early New Age magazine that combined psychedelia with an attraction to Tolkien's hobbits. I write about him in *Turn Off Your Mind*.

Pop, and Debbie Harry had ironed my skinny ties, but if I was ever starstruck it was then, getting through a bottle or two with the man whose work had changed my life.

Yet one exact quote from that evening I can recount. I had talked about my interest in Wilson's ideas with some of my workmates in Los Angeles, and the general feeling was that, after *The Outsider*, Wilson had taken too intellectual a route and that his work suffered from that. I disagreed with this, and when I mentioned the "Gurdjieffian" attitude toward his ideas, Wilson stopped. "Well," he said, "I can tell you the Wilsonian response to that: fuck off." I would not put it in quite those terms myself, but I could see what he meant.

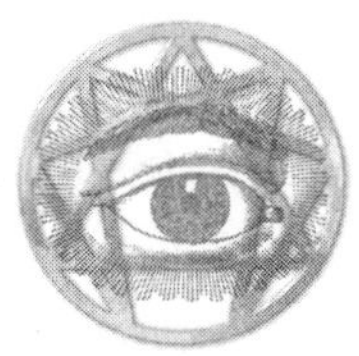

10
The Love of Wisdom

After my pilgrimage to Gorran Haven, I left Cornwall and headed back to London, a hangover and heady intellectual excitement vying for my attention on the train. In London, I spent the last week of my European adventure staying in a youth hostel in Paddington. My funds had run very low and by this time I could not afford a separate room, so I took a bed in a room shared with several other travelers. The breakfast included with the bed—egg, bacon, tea, and toast—was welcome. I had enough money for one meal a day—usually one of the cheap "early dinner" specials some cafés offered—and a pint of beer at a pub in the evening. After my pint, I wandered around the city, slowly making my way back to the hostel, where I read the copy of *The Essential Hemingway* some other traveler had left behind.

I spent my days at the old Reading Room at the British Museum, where I knew Colin Wilson had written much of his first novel, *Ritual in the Dark*; this was during the time he slept in a waterproof sleeping bag on Hampstead Heath. At the Reading Room I found a copy of one of Wilson's books that had so far eluded me, *Eagle and Earwig*, a collection of literary essays setting forth his notion of an "existential criticism," to complement more straightforward literary criticism. Some years later, in 2018, I had the pleasure of contributing a preface to a new edition of the book. By that time, I had written introductions to new editions of two of Wilson's novels—*The Mind Parasites* and *The God of the Labyrinth*—and contributed an introduction to a new edition of his second book, *Religion and the Rebel.*[1]

On my last day in London, I had just enough money to pay for the coach from Victoria Station to Gatwick Airport. There, for some reason, I attracted the attention of some security guards. I can't imagine why. Perhaps I looked suspicious. I arrived early and had to wait a few hours for my flight. Maybe the guards were bored or had a quota, but they approached me, asked some questions, then asked me to follow them. I did. They brought me to a room, deposited me in it, locked the door, and left. To this day, I have no idea why. I was there for some time, wondering what was going on and worrying that I'd miss my flight. They released me just in time to catch it, and I remember asking them if they treated all their foreign visitors this way. I don't remember their reply.

WHAT I REMEMBER NOW of my return to California at the end of summer, 1983, is reading through the Penguin edition of *The Complete Poems of William Blake*, cover to cover—aided by S. Foster Damon's *A Blake Dictionary*—and discovering the work of the artist and writer Wyndham Lewis at the Central Library, a remarkable pyramid-topped art deco structure in downtown Los Angeles. I don't remember what led me to Lewis, but I came upon a copy of his quirky and combative *Time and Western Man*, which was first published in 1927. The title alone would have attracted me. I was interested—obsessed would be more accurate—with time and its mysteries, and assumed the book would cover ground I had already explored with Ouspensky. What I found was quite different.

Lewis was critical of Ouspensky, whom he dismissed with a single

---

1. *Eagles and Earwigs: Essays on Books and Writers* (London: Eyewear Publishing Ltd, 2018); *The Mind Parasites* (Rhinebeck, NY: Monkfish Book Publishing Company, 2005); *The God of the Labyrinth* (Kansas City, MO: Valancourt Books, 2013); *Religion and the Rebel* (London: Aristeia Press, 2017).

mention, as well as others he called "fancy time thinkers" (he referred to Gurdjieff as a "Levantine psychic-shark"). His main targets were philosophers like Alfred North Whitehead and Henri Bergson, whom I had read and with whose vision of things I more or less agreed. For both Bergson and Whitehead, reality is more of a process than a fixed state, and both were critical of the reductionist view of materialist science, which relegated human values and meaning to subjective status, meaning, that is, that they had no "real" objective existence—as material things did—but only a subjective one, within our heads. (Whitehead famously said that if this view were correct, then the poets have been wrong to sing of the beauty of nature; their praise should instead go to their own subjectivities.)

What Lewis objected to was the idea that if all reality is in flux, then there are no stable, "eternal" values; everything is a creation of time. It is an argument going back to the beginning of Western thought, with Heraclitus stating that there is nothing but change, and Parmenides answering that change is an illusion, as the Absolute is perfect. In more recent time, Heraclitus's view has reappeared in the idea that all values are social constructs, a product of the society in which they appear—a view that is rooted in Marx's notion that culture is only a façade decorating what is really real, i.e., the economy and the means of production. Whether the purveyors of the social construct philosophy see their own ideas as social constructs is rarely every mentioned. If they do, then they have no more claim on truth than any other "social construct." And if they don't, one wonders how they avoid a status shared by every other idea—not to mention that by claiming this unique grasp on truth, the idea undermines itself.

Lewis was one of the few avant-garde painters to emerge from England, and as such he was a kind of Platonist, defending eternal aesthetic values against the dissolving flux of change. (We could say he had an Apollonian, not a Dionysian, temperament.) I didn't accept his arguments against Bergson, Whitehead, William James, and the others he placed in the "flux" camp, but I appreciated the vigor and pugilistic tone of his writing, and went on to read much of his other work. (I never enjoyed his fiction, though; its static character isn't suited for a narrative flow.)

Being able to enjoy reading Lewis while disagreeing with him was another example of my increasing maturity as a reader. It meant that I could appreciate an argument and its presentation without having to agree with it. Lewis's sharp, critical clarity and punchy tone was bracing in itself, and following his criticisms of thinkers I felt sympathetic to helped me articulate my own view, insofar as I had one. It was a repeat of my experience of reading James Webb's book on Gurdjieff: I could appreciate what was being said as well as the way it was communicated without having to agree with it.

But intellectual stimulation wasn't the only thing to greet me on my return. Royalties for "Presence, Dear" had begun to diminish; the track had been out for five years and by this time Blondie had disbanded, and sales of their records, including the ones with my songs, had gone down. Money still came in, but the time when I did not have to worry about an income was ending. Whether I wanted to or not, I would soon have to find a way to earn a living.

I HAD NOT HAD A REGULAR JOB since hauling Christmas trees out to elderly ladies' cars six years earlier, and at first the idea of looking for one paralyzed me. I have never enjoyed the experience—I can't imagine anyone does—and avoided the inevitable as long as possible. But as the royalty checks steadily increased my bank balance by smaller and smaller amounts, I knew I could not put it off much longer.

I was so apprehensive about having to once again enter the "real world" that I allowed fantasy to overtake my grip on reality. I first thought that, with my background in music, I might find a place with a record company. That I had no interest in pop music, no experience working on the other side of the business, and absolutely no capacity to schmooze—a *sine qua non* in the industry—did not deter me, at least at first. I still knew a few people in the business, and decided I had nothing to lose. I made one telephone call and met with someone for what turned out to be a rather awkward lunch.

After circling around the question of whether he might find some place for me in—well, exactly what I had no idea—my acquaintance came to the point.

"Wait," he said. "Let me get this straight. You're asking me for a job?"

I nodded.

"You're kidding? Do you really think you can turn up and I can just hire you?" He seemed insulted. It was true that I hadn't been in touch with him for quite some time, and no sooner had he said this than the ridiculousness of what I had in mind became embarrassingly clear. I made some excuse and got away as quickly as I could and never thought to look in that direction again.

A friend of a friend ran a telephone marketing service. I tried selling their product to voices on the other end of the line, but after a week of failure I was politely shown the door. For a time, I found work at a gourmet market not far from my flat. I was first put in the meat department, but when I showed inordinate delicacy trying to dismember a chicken, as well as a clear revulsion to blood, they took pity on me, the chickens, and their customers, and moved me on to fish. Butterflying a trout was less of a challenge, as was descaling a salmon or shelling shrimp. I thought of my tenure there as doing my Larry Darrell routine, mimicking Tyrone Power in the 1946 film version of Somerset Maugham's *The Razor's Edge* when, for a time, the hero, in search of life's meaning, worked on a fishing vessel. I did not last there long and soon enough had to look for work again. One casualty from my time among the fruits of the sea were my clothes, which absorbed a fishy smell I was unable to dispel, no matter how many times I washed them. I guess, nodding to Melville, you could have called me Fishsmell.

I picked up a little cash working as an extra in some films. During my time with The Know, I'd become friends with the director

Jim McBride and screenwriter Jack Baran, and every now and then I turned up at a shoot, did my bit, got lunch, and was paid.[2] But these were few and far between, and my attempts to work as a script reader, wading through the slush pile on some producer's desk, also came to nothing. But when I did finally find congenial work, it was within the film industry—sort of.

By the mid-1980s, VCRs and video tapes had hit, and video rental shops were opening all over the place. One did not far from my neighborhood, and I went there one afternoon and asked the owner if he was looking for any help. He was, and soon I was opening or closing the place, depending on my shift that day. With the constant access to films streaming provides, people today may find it difficult to conceive of a time when, in order to watch a film at home that wasn't on television, one either had to buy a VCR player or rent one, as well as the film.[3] We provided both.

It is remarkable how expensive the tapes were at first and how limited the selection was. My knowledge of classic, horror, sci-fi, and foreign films came in handy, and I often picked what we should stock from the catalogues of new releases. Most customers wanted whatever the latest release was, and we did a brisk trade in the adult entertainment department. The people renting the pornography went about it in different ways. Some tried to get through the process as quickly and quietly as possible, hoping no one would notice; others would be bold and brazen, almost daring me or anyone who saw their selections to make some

2. An attentive viewer can catch a glimpse of me in McBride's remake of Jean-Luc Godard's *Breathless* (1983), in which Lisa has a part as well. In a scene shot at the old World Book and News newsstand at Cahuenga and Hollywood Boulevards, I'm standing reading a paperback of Colin Wilson's *The Philosopher's Stone*.

3. The unlimited access to films and other media that we now enjoy—our ability to watch whatever we want wherever and whenever we want—is, I suggest, evidence of Jean Gebser's insight that our age would feel an increasing "irruption" of time, a permeation of it into our everyday lives. When I was young, if I wanted to watch something on television, I had to be at a certain place at a certain time. Today, these constraints no longer apply.

remark about it. The owner himself, a young fellow—it was, I think, his first business venture—wasn't immune, and would take home a few double features to, as he said, "familiarize himself with the stock."

It was relatively painless, decently paid work, and much of my time on the day shift was spent neatening the shelves and enduring the MTV videos the teenager the owner hired to help me constantly played. But I did have a good amount of time to myself, and spent most of it reading.

I had started a habit of reading very long novels. At that time, I worked my way through Thomas Mann's *The Magic Mountain*, Robert Musil's *The Man Without Qualities*, Jacob Wassermann's *The Maurizius Case*, the novels of Hermann Broch, and those of John Cowper Powys—like his gargantuan *A Glastonbury Romance*—whom I mentioned earlier. I also enjoyed the middlebrow novels of Lion Feuchtwanger, a German writer who immigrated to California to escape the Nazis. PBS broadcast a BBC production of Feuchtwanger's *The Oppermans* around that time, about a powerful Jewish family who fall to the Nazis, and I was enthralled by it.

For a time, I became fascinated with the experience of European intellectuals who came to Hollywood in the 1930s.[4] There was Aldous Huxley and Christopher Isherwood, of course; I actually met Isherwood and Huxley's second wife, Laura.[5] But quite a few German-speaking *émigrés* showed up as well, anxious to escape Hitler's Third Reich. Mann was one of them, as was the composer Arnold Schoenberg, Bertolt Brecht, and a philosopher whose work I would soon become acquainted with—the neo-Marxist Theodore Adorno. The plight of the intellectual under fascism—of culture confronted with barbarism—fascinated me, and for some reason I began to identify with it.

---

4. An excellent and very readable book about this is *Strangers in Paradise* (1983) by John Russell Taylor.

5. I write about meeting Christopher Isherwood in the acknowledgements to *Turn Off Your Mind*. Laura Huxley was a regular customer at the Bodhi Tree Bookshop. My adventures there are related in the next chapter.

Not long after I took the job at the video rental shop, I made what I considered a serious career decision. I knew that, ultimately, I wanted to write. But, as yet, I hadn't written anything that anyone would want to read—not even myself—and my failure to do so was a cause of much anxiety. I was in a perpetual state of dissatisfaction with myself, and spent much time keeping thoughts of ultimate failure at bay. Perhaps I *wasn't* the genius I believed I was? What then . . . ? The question of what I was going to do with my life preoccupied me, and I often brought it up with friends. During one conversation about my future prospects, one made a suggestion which in hindsight seems obvious.

"You read all these books," she said. "Why not go back to university?"

The idea of going back to school and earning a degree hadn't occurred to me. But as soon as my friend mentioned it, I thought, why not? What did I have to lose? I had read a great deal. Perhaps there was something I could do with that? The question of where to do this did not occupy me for long. I have never been very good at planning. Almost at random, I picked a school and looked into the prospects of getting a student loan. Soon after, I found myself enrolled at California State University, Los Angeles. I was twenty-eight, what in the UK is called a "mature student," though my level of maturity was debatable. Nevertheless, my destiny had taken another turn. Soon, the way would be clear and I would be embarking on a new life.

What would that be? Teaching philosophy.

Going from being a pop musician to wanting to seriously study philosophy—which meant not only reading it haphazardly, as I had been—with the idea of eventually teaching it may seem counterintuitive. But then, I had dedicated my first 45 to Nietzsche's overman. After I settled on philosophy as my major and my professors learned that I had been a professional rock and roll musician, their response to my intention to join their ranks was disbelief. Why would I want to devote myself to something as boring as that, especially after having written hit songs, earned gold records, and worked with famous pop stars? There was very little one could do with a degree in philosophy *except* teach it. Its practical value was nil. To go from jumping around on stage and having one's pick of groupies to studying Plato and Wittgenstein—which I did—seemed to them aberrant. What was wrong with me?

From the ordinary point of view, their incredulity isn't surprising. Playing in a famous rock band has an almost sacred status in our culture, even more so than having been in films. It is a kind of ultimate, unsurpassable achievement in comparison with which every other accomplishment pales in significance. I was used to this reaction, as I had already encountered it with friends and acquaintances. They couldn't accept that I had turned my back on all of that, and more than once I had to firmly refuse to play my old songs on someone's guitar, which gave me a reputation for being stuck up and "superior."

To them it may have simply been a case of sour grapes. I didn't "make it"—meaning my band didn't get a record deal—so I rationalized my failure by professing a loss of interest in anything to do with pop music. I was "above" all that.

There may have been some element of this, but the real reason—as I see it now but only unconsciously felt at the time—was that I was going through the same world rejection and withdrawal that many of Wilson's Outsiders had. Aside from the fact that I had been bitten by the philosophy bug years ago, when my high school teacher gave me Sartre and Nietzsche to read, my decision to return to university in order to study philosophy was a kind of act of asceticism, a withdrawal from the common, all-too-human world to a kind of internal wilderness. It was a decision to abandon ordinary life in order to devote myself to something far more demanding, prompted by a hunger for *reality*, stripped of all illusion. Many of Wilson's Outsiders gave up comfortable lives and put themselves into, if not necessarily dangerous conditions—as some did—certainly into less comfortable and convenient ones.

Wittgenstein, for example, gave away a fortune and hid himself away teaching schoolchildren in some Austrian backwater. Disgusted by the celebrity his adventures in Arabia had achieved, T. E. Lawrence rejected it, and tried to lose himself by enlisting as a private in the Royal Air Force. Until he achieved success with *The Outsider*, Wilson himself had lived a rootless, vagabond existence, giving up jobs as soon as boredom set in. Even after the success of *The Outsider*, Wilson gave up the frenetic London literary life and sequestered himself in faraway Cornwall, writing books that he knew were practically guaranteed to be attacked, if not ignored.

Wilson had written that the "comfortable life causes spiritual decay in the same way that sweet, soft food causes tooth decay." His Outsiders knew this intuitively, and many went to great, often eccentric lengths in order to prevent their spirits from rotting. In some obscure way, I embraced this idea, and, although on a much less intense scale—but a no less genuine one—my rejection of my previous life and embracing of a kind of intellectual asceticism followed the usual Outsider pattern.

As it turned out, I enjoyed my undergraduate work and did well in it. At one point I even won an award for "most promising student." My interest remained in existential, "continental philosophy," but although I was less keen on some classes than others, my desire to learn was genuine. But some classes simply failed to stir my interest. I've mentioned my mediocre showing in symbolic logic. That, I think, was the only class in which I did not get a top grade. Although they did not grip me, I dutifully worked my way through Leibniz, Spinoza, and Descartes, and even got a good grasp on Logical Positivism. I was determined to put aside my preferences in order to get a good working overview of the history of philosophy. I wanted the knowledge, and some of that desire was motivated by ego—I wanted to be able to hold my own against any critics in any future metaphysical debates. When a professor asked the class if they would rather read contemporary "philosophy is fun" material or classics like David Hume, I always chose Hume, or whomever it may have been. I wanted the classics, not the easy stuff.

I worked with most of the professors in the department, but three were especially important to me. These were Henry, an Aristotelian with whom I became fairly close and for whom I worked as a teaching assistant, grading papers on Plato and Descartes; Joseph, who taught Kant, Hegel, and Marx, and through whom I came into contact with people who would play a part in my later career as a writer; and Daniel, a new professor, starting just around the time that I did, who was my age and with whom I studied Nietzsche, Wittgenstein, and Heidegger.[6]

Although I became friends with Henry—I think he got a kick out of having an ex–punk rocker as a TA—I had little interest in Aristotle. When I was first taking his class, getting a good grounding in Plato, I was reading a great deal of Russian philosophy, works by Nikolai Berdyaev, Lev Shestov, and Vladimir Solovyov, thinkers that, years later, I would return to when writing *The Return of Holy Russia*. When I mentioned this to him, he rolled his eyes and said, "That isn't philosophy!" I liked him, so didn't care to argue. I soon saw that practically everything I was interested in would receive a similar assessment. Nevertheless, I enjoyed working with him, even if grading papers on the *Euthyphro* and Descartes's *Meditations on First Philosophy* became something of a chore.

Under Joseph's tutelage, I became something of a Hegelian—at least to the extent that I could understand him, Hegel that is. The work we focused on was *The Phenomenology of Spirit* (or *Mind*, depending on the translation), and I was stunned by this "Odyssey of the mind" in which Hegel lays out a remarkable and exhilarating spiraling evolution of consciousness, from the simplest bare perception to the all-encompassing Absolute. Joseph impressed on me that "everything" came out of it—Marx, Sartre, Heidegger, and much else. One of the books that helped in my understanding of Hegel's vision

6. Some time after writing this book, I was saddened to learn that Joseph had passed away.

of a Spirit that, in order to "become itself"—as indeed I had been struggling to do for some time—must alienate itself from itself so that it could return to itself at a higher stage was M. H. Abram's study of Romanticism, *Natural Supernaturalism*, which looked at this process of "withdrawal and return" in the context of poetry. I was gratified when an essay I had written about the famous preface to *The Phenomenology*, in which Hegel makes clear that philosophy is not merely the conclusions at which it may arrive but the *process of arriving at them*—that is, the "becoming what it is," the making explicit what was only known implicitly—was singled out and made available for the rest of the class to study.

Daniel taught a class in aesthetics. I remember that we read Nietzsche's *Birth of Tragedy*, which I hadn't looked at for some years, and Heidegger's essay "The Origin of the Work of Art," and also some writing by the contemporary philosopher Arthur Danto. We also read Thomas Mann's *Doctor Faustus*, whose protagonist, the composer Leverkuhn, was based on Nietzsche, and whose music was modeled on the twelve-tone system of Arnold Schoenberg. We often listened to music—I remember a class on Wagner's "Tristan chord" and another on Beethoven's Piano Sonata No. 32, Op 111, which Mann had said was a "farewell to the sonata form." It was an overall course in modern Western culture, specifically that of *Mitteleuropa*, and I thoroughly enjoyed it. I was becoming increasingly fascinated with Central Europe, and began to identify with the sort of intellectual it produced.

This fascination continued in the class Daniel taught on Wittgenstein's *Philosophical Investigations*. Although Wittgenstein's work gave birth to philosophical schools or movements with which he really had little in common—logical positivism and linguistic analysis—at heart, he was one of Wilson's tortured Outsiders. Daniel taught Wittgenstein's work in the context of other cultural developments happening in Austria in the early twentieth century. I learned that Wittgenstein's aphoristic style, the gnomic sayings making up the *Tractatus* and its follow-up, the *Philosophical Investigations*, came out of a tradition in Vienna, most eloquently exemplified in the writings of the satirist Karl Kraus.[7]

Early twentieth-century central Europe was obsessed with the *Sprachefrage*, the question of language. There was Wittgenstein himself, whose obsession with what language *cannot* say—at least explicitly—led him to "end" philosophy, twice. There was Kraus, who believed a society that had a loose grasp of grammar would have an even looser one on morality and ethics; he famously asked, "How can half a man write a whole sentence?"[8] There was Hugo von Hofmannsthal, the librettist for some of Richard Strauss's operas, whose "The Lord Chandos Letter" portrays a writer who had become so sensitive to the inadequacy of language that he could no longer communicate. Hermann Broch's *The Death of Virgil*, depicting the last hours of the Roman poet, brought language to its absolute limit in the face of eternity. The limits of expression were explored in music, too, with Mahler bringing the tradition of symphonic music to a close and Schoenberg inaugurating the era of the atonal, with Berg and Webern making their own contributions.[9]

All of this fascinated me, and for a time I became quite obsessed with Viennese modernism, so much so that I came to dress very severely, cut my hair very short, and annoyed friends by insisting on playing Schoenberg whenever they visited. Looking back now I can see that this was a form of compensation for my ongoing writer's block, the few aphorisms I squeezed out over coffee at the Farmers Market notwithstanding.[10] At the time, I must have been insufferable. My

---

7. The book to read on this subject is *Wittgenstein's Vienna* (1983) by Allan Janik and Stephen Toulmin.

8. My favorite of Kraus's one-liners is, "A journalist is someone with no ideas and the ability to express them."

9. Mention of Mahler reminds me that an essay I wrote on the links between Mahler's Third Symphony, the philosophy of Arthur Schopenhauer—of which Mahler was a devotee—and Wittgenstein's *Tractatus* was, like the one on Hegel's *Phenomenology of Spirit*, made available for other students in the class to read.

10. Located near CBS's Television City in Hollywood, the Farmers Market started in the 1930s, its open-air food stalls and cafés a popular haven for indigent film and television actors as well as costive would-be writers.

intolerant attitude to what I considered "sloppy thinking" (what Ludwig hath wrought!) led to me being asked to leave more than one social occasion. If I was not yet an Outsider, I was surely becoming one.[11]

ALONG WITH THE PHILOSOPHERS I STUDIED in class, I became aware of other intellectual currents and fashions that, until then, I'd known nothing about but which were apparently very popular. The two most prevalent were deconstructionism—with which I saddle postmodernism—and the critical theory of the Frankfurt School. This was also the time when Foucault was all the rage. I quickly came to reject all three, but for a time became obsessed with understanding what they were about.[12] In fact, one can only reject a school of thought *if* one understands it. Otherwise, you are simply dismissing it out of ignorance.

Deconstructionism, most widely associated with the work of Jacques Derrida, emerged from Heidegger's project of "deconstructing" Western philosophy, at least since Plato. Western consciousness had lost touch with *being* and, according to Heidegger, this was a result of a wrong turn taken by Plato. All of Western metaphysics—which for Heidegger included Nietzsche, his "will to power" being its last manifestation—was little more than a dead end, and its applied form, technology, was rapidly transforming the Earth into a desert.[13] We needed to return to

11. Looking back now, I imagine that in trying to develop a "left brain," Apollonian sensibility, devoted to philosophy and ideas, rather than the more "right brain," Dionysian one interested in poetry and music, I overcompensated.

12. Another popular work at the time was Richard Rorty's *Philosophy in the Mirror of Nature* (1979).

13. In fact, a prominent Heideggerian, Hubert Dreyfus, came to our campus once and lectured on this theme. I don't remember any details of his talk, but I do remember it being altogether more comprehensible than the lecture I attended by Saul Kripke, a philosopher of logic who, I was assured, was a bona fide genius. I can't judge on that, but I can say I found his talk absolutely impenetrable, although Henry assured me it was brilliant.

the pre-Socratic philosophers, like Heraclitus, in order to regain our contact with primordial *being*, which in his later work Heidegger came to call "presence."

I would not call myself a Heideggerian, but I appreciated this view and did feel that my moments of seeing were brief glimpses of being or presence. (I had, of course, been in touch with presence in other ways, too.) I forget his name, but in one class, the instructor pointed out that the French philosopher Derrida took this one step further and denied there was even any "presence," that is, no primal reality or being which we could get at by removing the layers of language covering it. In fact, there was *nothing but language*, nothing but "the text," as I came to understand, and the notion of reality itself was a kind of fiction (something Nietzsche had already suggested).[14]

Words had no intrinsic meaning, no direct relationship to the things they named. The relationship between the signified (thing) and the signifier (word) was arbitrary, and any meaning words possessed was a product of their relations with each other. What I understood Derrida's position to be was that it was the philosopher's job to find the loose thread, as it were, of some philosophical text, what he called its "aporia," a kind of knot or linguistic paradox of which the author—who naïvely believed he *knew* what he was saying (that, of course, was only truly known to the deconstructionist)—was unaware, and which, when pulled, revealed the hidden ambiguities in the work. This strikes me

---

14. Derrida, and deconstructionism in general, made much of Nietzsche's thought, and by the time I was taking classes, the Nietzsche I knew—the Nietzsche of Walter Kaufmann—had long been superseded by a new, Frenchified Nietzsche. One of the books making this clear to me was *The New Nietzsche* (1985), edited by David B. Allison, which included essays by Derrida, Gilles Deleuze, Pierre Klossowski, Maurice Blanchot, and others. The main thrust of the essays was to present Nietzsche as a much more radical critic of the Western philosophical tradition than he had been interpreted to be. At the time I found it an exciting read, but subsequently came to see that, as had happened to Nietzsche before, the deconstructionists had appropriated him for their own purposes.

as more of an unraveling than a deconstruction, but let's not quibble.[15]

I already knew that the relationship between language and reality was complex and often insecure. But the thinkers pointing this out knew something important was at stake. True, Wittgenstein spoke of playing "language games," and the linguistic analysts who ran with this idea tended to emphasize the trivial aspects of it. But Wittgenstein himself *knew* the reality language wanted to capture was tremendous, that language could not do it justice, *not* because there was nothing to say, as linguistic analysis and logical positivism insisted on, but because there was *too much to say.* (Among other recipients of Wittgenstein's shunned fortune was the poet Rilke.) He wanted to keep clever philosophers like Bertrand Russell from summing up everything in a neat package and claiming to have understood the universe. (It should be seen that existentialism is fundamentally a rejection of the Russell approach to philosophy.)

I didn't agree with Wittgenstein's conclusions (which meant that I did not give up philosophy, as he suggested) but I could appreciate why he came to them. Yet, although I felt no connection to Russell and indeed had criticized his approach when in class we read his *Problems of Philosophy*, finding it too shallow, I did believe in a reality "out there" to which our minds have access. There were certainly difficulties in the way of this, but if I had to declare one way or another, I'd say that at bottom—in essence—I am a Platonist or Realist of sorts, with certain qualifications. Reality is not all flux nor is it mere brute fact. Behind, beneath, within lies an order, a meaning, what used to be called the *logos.* Indeed, I would even say that yes, it *is* a text, but one that does contain a meaning, not one open to infinite and equally arbitrary inter-

---

15. One point that seemed never to come up in discussions of deconstructionism was whether the person deconstructing a text had any valid reason to believe that his reading of the text was true, accurate, correct, or whatever term denoting a clearer grasp of the matter at hand than the original author had. What was to stop his reading from being deconstructed itself, and so on, ad infinitum. But then it strikes me that this is precisely the point: there is no "true" reading. At first perhaps liberating, the semantic vacuum thus created soon produces a sense of indifference and cognitive apathy.

pretations. And it is a text that requires very deep reading, the kind of reading I have discussed in some of my books.[16]

The text of the world may be written, as Arthur Koestler said, in invisible ink. But every now and then, something remarkable happens to our vision—like a kind of X-ray, it can reveal what is otherwise hidden. What was invisible stares us in the face. I had this happen too many times to ignore or deny it, and my hunger for reality was too great to be put off by either Russell's unsatisfying fare or by the critical pyrotechnics of the deconstructionists.

As Wittgenstein had, the deconstructionists played games. But that was *all* they did. If there was no reality to get to, no message provided by the text—that is, its meaning—but only "the text," then they were free to play around with language as much as they liked. And they did. Truth was a game. Reality was a game. (As Roland Barthes, a deconstructionist fellow traveler, believed, there was no meaning in literature or life, only pleasure and *jouissance*, which carries sexual connotations.)

Their view of the text we called "the world" was rather like Heraclitus's—it was all a flux, and any truths or values or notions of reality that a society held were merely a part of the "text," and did not point to anything stable or real outside it. (And so, the roots of reality as a social construct.) It was after reading a few of Derrida's books that I came to see the political aspect of his philosophy, or anti-philosophy. To put it briefly, Western philosophy—Western culture in general—was oppressive, its "logocentricism" (its orientation toward rational meaning) a form of imperialism. Although not explicitly Marxist, Derrida did accept the general criticism of the West then in vogue, and believed it had promoted and maintained a form of tyranny.

Having spent years studying esotericism, mysticism, the occult, and the paranormal, I could easily agree that strict rationalism, which relegated these pursuits to the realm of nonsense and superstition, was an inadequate means of apprehending reality in all its complexity. But to

16. See, for example, *Lost Knowledge of the Imagination* (Edinburgh: Floris Books, 2017).

move from a rigid rationalism to the kind of philosophical free-for-all Derrida seemed to promote struck me as little more than leaving the frying pan for the fire. Reason needed to be expanded, not rejected—logic needed to become more accommodating to reality, not abandoned. This was something Ouspensky had attempted in *Tertium Organum*, with much more positive results than what the deconstructionists could claim. Wilson's "new existentialism" had made important inroads to this challenge as well, as had other thinkers, not on the syllabus, that I had been reading over the years. But they were not included in the debate.

All this came out in a conversation I had with Joseph during which he asked what it was about deconstructionism that put me off.

"Is it the nihilism?" he asked.

I said, "Yes."

I FOUND SIMILAR PROBLEMS with the other hot thinkers on campus. Foucault, for example. My familiarity with modern French philosophy had stopped at Sartre and Camus. I hadn't heard of Foucault until I saw copies of his books occupying a few shelves in the campus bookshop. He, like Derrida, was one of the French intellectual celebrities to emerge from the radical days of the 1960s, May '68 and all that. I soon discovered that Foucault had made it his aim to topple Sartre from his position as the leading French intellectual; it seemed that a great deal of his motivation was winning a kind of philosophical popularity contest. (The French adore their intellectuals in the same way that Americans do their film stars—when Foucault "made it," his face was seen on the cover of national magazines.) Although I had ploughed through *Being and Nothingness*, I didn't follow Sartre after the early existentialist days.[17] I knew he had become obsessed with far-left politics, champi-

17. Sartre died in 1980. I lived in New York at the time, and I remember, the week of his death, on *Saturday Night Live*, Bill Murray made a joke about him "passing from being to nothingness."

oning Mao and calling for the overthrow of Western capitalism, and had labored over an impossible marriage between existentialism and Marxism in his *Critique of Dialectical Reason*. None of that interested me, so I wasn't concerned that he had lost his place in the French philosophical pantheon. But who was this Foucault, and what had he done to push Sartre out of the limelight?

When trying to out-Heidegger Heidegger—as he does in *Being and Nothingness*—Sartre can be a wearingly obscure writer, unlike the clear, hard outlines of his fiction or drama. (One of the long novels I read at the time was his *Roads to Freedom* trilogy.) But, although I may not always have had a clear idea of what he was saying, I at least knew he was trying to get somewhere, that he was writing to some definite purpose, and that I shared his central obsession: freedom. That is, although I rejected Sartre's ultimate assessment of human existence—it is, he tells us, a useless passion—I appreciated the seriousness with which he approached thought and life. Something important was at stake in both. An element of risk was involved, an urgency. It was this lack of seriousness that put me off deconstructionism. Its nihilistic leg-pulling, though amusing at first, became very thin fare after a while.

When I finally sat down and tried to read Foucault to get an idea of what the fuss was about, I quickly ran into trouble, a difficulty of a different sort than that presented by Derrida. I got a copy of *The Order of Things*, the book that made his name in France. If this was what knocked Sartre out of the running, well, I thought it must be something.

I very soon saw that it was a work of immense erudition, great learning, and that Foucault was certainly an impressive scholar. But as I read on, I had to admit that I really had no idea where he was going or the point he was trying to make. Facts, figures, obscure references, literary allusions, and other scholarly impedimenta became a dense forest, and it did not take long for me to accept that I had become lost in it—or to suspect that the path on which the author was leading me through this thicket may indeed not head anywhere in particular. Foucault certainly had much knowledge at his fingertips, but it was never quite clear what he was saying with it. I struggled on for a while, but eventually had to admit defeat—or, at least, that I required a pause in my attempts to digest this material. I tried again not long after with another work, *The Archaeology of Knowledge* (1969). But, although the title was evocative, I got no further with it.

It was only after reading some interviews with Foucault (collected in *Power/Knowledge* [1980]) that I began to get an idea of what he was saying—or, actually, avoiding saying in simple, straightforward language. Ironically, for all its reputation for clarity and logic—its Cartesian heritage—France has produced an inordinate number of purposefully obscure philosophers, thus creating much work for philosophy professors in explaining what they are trying to say. (If you wish to have as little impact as possible in the academic world, write as clearly and directly as you can.) Hegel and Heidegger are notoriously difficult, but the difficulty is a feature of the terrain they are trying to cover. Foucault, Derrida, and the postmodernists all seem to aim at obscurity for its own sake. But in the interviews, Foucault was a bit more straightforward.

I gathered that Foucault was writing a kind of history of ideas, but it wasn't a history in the way we usually think of it, as, say, Russell's *History of Western Philosophy* presents it, as a consecutive, sequential narrative. It struck me that Foucault's view was rather like that of Oswald Spengler, the early twentieth-century German historian whose *The Decline of the West* was a bestseller in the aftermath of WWI. Spengler argued against the idea of a single, continuous history, starting with the Egyptians and leading up to ourselves. We can see this as the general view of progress, from prehistory to our modern technological age. This Enlightenment view, Spengler argued, was incorrect. Civilizations are like organic beings: they are born, reach maturity, and die, like flowers in a field. There is no linear progress in our modern sense, but a great variety of different civilizations, each with their own culture, their own science, mathematics, philosophy, politics, religion, and so on. Spengler argued that our civilization, which he called the

Faustian, was on its way out, and that a new, very different civilization was set to emerge.

Foucault did not share Spengler's organic view of history, but he did share with him the idea of there being no single, linear history. Instead of Spengler's morphology of organic historical forms, Foucault posits what he calls *épistémè*—what we might call different zeitgeists or "spirits of the age"—that provide the uniformly accepted, unquestioned, unconscious background to a culture and its beliefs.

We may think we have free will and can choose what to think and to believe. Sartre certainly did. But Foucault insists this is an illusion—we cannot escape the *épistémè* in which we "live and move and have our being," just as a fish cannot escape from the water in which it lives. And, like the fish, we do not *see* the water—that is, we are not aware of the limitations on our thought imposed on us by the *épistémè* in which we are embedded. Sartre, for all his pessimism, at least believed that we are free and can make decisions about how to live, and that we should use this freedom to try to improve the world. He chose to do this through radical politics, but that is not a necessary choice. What is important is that the *burden* of our freedom lies on us. We are faced with the question of what we *do* with our freedom.

What Foucault was saying was that this was all hot air—it was, in fact, a form of what Sartre called *mauvaise foi*, "bad faith." We are not free and our actions can do little to improve the world. Derrida argued that our freedom was severely curtailed by language and its inherent ambiguities, its tendency to a serious semantic slippage. For Foucault, what imprisons us is the *épistémè* in which we live, which compels us to see things in certain ways and to act in certain ways too. In the face of this, Sartre's insistence on our moral and ethical obligation to use our freedom to improve the plight of the "oppressed" is childishly naïve. Whether we like it or not, we are trapped—although it must be said that Foucault nowhere explains how *he* has managed to escape his own *épistémè*, which he must have in order to show, as he believes he does, that thinkers prior to him have not escaped theirs.

And behind our *épistémè*, keeping it afloat, are the institutions that derive power from and maintain it. This is the same tyrannical spirit of Enlightenment reason that Derrida and his colleagues wanted to take apart. So, in a series of books, Foucault argued—in as obscure a way as possible—that a variety of modern institutions (medical, political, criminal, social) that are ostensibly humanitarian, progressive, and enlightened are really centers of power aimed at maintaining the status quo. (I only discovered later that R. D. Laing's ideas about mental health and society, which I had absorbed in my teens, were influenced by Foucault.)

Just as the deconstructionists were proclaiming the "death of the author," in the sense of he or she being someone who knows what they want to say and who does their best to say it in their work (it is the deconstructionist, remember, who is privy to this), Foucault announced the "death of man," meaning the death of the Enlightenment vision of rational man. And in its place, Foucault seemed to see a variety of possible alternatives.

Why would Foucault want to demolish any idea of human freedom and the responsibility that comes with it? Why would he want to undermine the kind of seriousness that Sartre and Heidegger took as a given for anyone wanting to live authentically? Why would he want to be free of that burden? In a sense, like the deconstructionists, he wanted to play games, but of a rather more radical, transgressive sort. Like the deconstructionists, Foucault was influenced by Nietzsche. But where Derrida found support in Nietzsche's reflections on language—it was, Nietzsche said, little more than a play of metaphors—Foucault was a devotee of the Dionysian Nietzsche, the philosopher of eruptive ecstasy and explosive power. And it was not until many years later, after reading James Miller's remarkable biography, *The Passion of Michel Foucault*, that I came to see just how Foucault expressed his Dionysian frenzy.

Foucault was homosexual and a devotee of sadomasochism. And I was surprised to discover, through Miller's book, that at the time I was living with Lisa on Christopher Street, in the gay part of Greenwich

Village, circa 1976–77, Foucault was being initiated into the S and M scene in San Francisco's equivalent, Folsom Street. I did not partake, but I knew of places in our neighborhood that, at the time, catered to the kinds of tastes Foucault was developing, for dark pleasures such as "sex with the stranger" and "fist-fucking." It was through inflicting and receiving pain that Foucault practiced his Nietzschean frenzy and achieved a kind of transcendence of the self, or so he claimed, through the experience of being sodomized in the dark by an unknown masked ravisher, usually while under the influence of hallucinogenic drugs. (I cannot but wonder what Crowley would have thought of this.) I can't say for sure, but from what I heard about the goings-on in our neighborhood, he was not alone in this—although I don't know if any other participants were led to similar philosophical reflections.

What Nietzsche may have thought of this is unknown. The philosopher with a hammer, who was not a man but "dynamite," was of a rather gentle, frail disposition—hence his compensatory celebration of brutes like Cesare Borgia—and his erotic exploits were severely limited. The syphilis that eventually drove him insane and killed him may have been contracted during a single visit to a brothel in his student years. As mentioned, he was too timid to propose to Lou Andreas Salome and had to ask his friend, Paul Rée, to do it; naturally, she declined. It may not be an exaggeration to suspect that what Nietzsche knew of sex came from masturbation. That he was aware of its power is clear from his writing. But one wonders if he would have considered the lengths to which Foucault and his fellow devotees went in order to feel the kind of ecstasy they desired somewhat extreme, and if they were an example of the kind of decadence against which he warned? (The need for strong stimulants is a sign of a weakened vitality . . .)

It is, of course, irrelevant, but the image of Foucault dressed in the sort of leather outfits I saw regularly when living on Christopher Street—our flat was near The Leatherman shop—does raise an eyebrow, and makes it difficult to take his analysis of Enlightenment tyranny seriously. It seems a kind of special pleading. Rather than openly admit to enjoying sadomasochism and other forms of "dark sex" (as one of his heroes, the Marquis de Sade, did) or writing outright pornographic works (as his "transgressive" countryman, Georges Bataille, an influence on Foucault and Derrida, did), Foucault instead worked to undermine notions of "normality" and "perversion," and other expressions of the oppressive *épistémè* that considers his predilections somewhat *de trop*.

One question that arises from Miller's biography is whether Foucault practiced Nietzsche's advice to "live dangerously" in a way that endangered others as well. Foucault enjoyed "living on the edge," and pursued a kind of dual life—one half that of a respected, typical French academic on a traditional career track, the other the radical sexual mystic seeking out transgressive encounters. There is some suspicion that Foucault, who would die from AIDS in 1984—around the same time that I returned to university—continued to frequent the S/M clubs that catered to his tastes, knowing he was infected with the disease. We cannot say for certain, but one can ask if an individual who believed human beings were trapped within their *épistémè*, with no possibility of escape, would be prone to a kind of fatalism, a dangerous form of *amor fati*?

With the Frankfurt School and Critical Theory, of which I first became aware at this time, there was no hint of transgression or of the kind of looniness deconstructionism reveled in—although the Freudian-Marxist mélange of Herbert Marcuse and its advocacy of polymorphous perversity, very popular in the 1960s, came close. Indeed, for the most part a kind of dour abstemiousness, a sober puritanism characterized them. Like deconstructionism and Foucault, Adorno and the other thinkers associated with the Frankfurt School believed that Western man had imprisoned himself in the "iron cage" of modernity (Weber) which had been built by the excessive rationalism of the Enlightenment. This is the message of the school's central work, *Dialectic of Enlightenment*, written by Adorno and Max Horkheimer.

But it was not language or all-encompassing *épistémès* that eclipse our freedom, but the economic system of late capitalism. We were just as trapped and helpless, completely under the spell of consumerism and what Adorno called "the culture industry." But there was the slimmest chance of release from our imprisonment through the kind of neo-Marxism that Adorno, Horkheimer, Ernst Bloch, and others in their camp championed.

This was not, I was informed by my professor Daniel, the "crude Marxism" of Bertold Brecht and his "lumpen proletariat." It was a more sophisticated form of Marxism, that wanted, so Daniel told me, to bring culture—initially believed to be a kind of camouflage obscuring the economic reality—back into the dialectic. But not just any culture. Adorno embraced the kind of fastidiousness and intolerance I had been infected with in my fascination with Wittgenstein and Viennese modernism. He had been a student of Schoenberg, whom he championed against the "reactionary" Stravinsky.[18] Aesthetics were very much a part of this neo-Marxism. And in order to understand it, I worked my way through Adorno's posthumous *Aesthetic Theory*, a difficult slog, given that Adorno had high praise for Samuel Beckett, whom I found unreadable and whose work Colin Wilson considered a kind of cultural poison. He was also fond of Kafka, whom I had long outgrown. I also worked my way through what struck me then, and continues to do so now, as one of the most sterile works of philosophy ever written, Adorno's *Negative Dialectics*.

In *Minima Moralia*, a collection of aphorisms written while in exile in America during WWII, Adorno had, as Marx had before him, turned Hegel on his head, although in a more succinct way. For Hegel, "the whole is the true." For Adorno, "the whole is the false."[19] With

---

18. Theodore Adorno, *The Philosophy of Modern Music* (1973).

19. Years later I would see similarities between Adorno's vision of an inescapable "false" world of late capitalism and commodification—in which even the protest against it turns a profit—and the metaphysical prison in which the Gnostics believed we were all inmates, subject to the tyranny of a false God. Only the initiated few—the esoteric elite of neo-Marxism—can find a way out of this trap.

his more well-known pronouncement that "after Auschwitz, no poetry," this testifies to Adorno's belief that we live in a time of unspeakable evil, and that if we are not actively trying to eliminate it—through introducing a Marxist form of society—we are complicit with it. For him, existentialists fretting about living authentically were navel-gazing, fiddling with their precious selves while Rome and everything else burned, an argument he put forth in *The Jargon of Authenticity*. (What he thought of the occult is summed up in his assessment of astrology as "metaphysics for dunces.") I am not sure, but is this intolerance of anyone not hitting the barricades with him the source of the '60s tag that "if you aren't part of the solution, you're part of the problem," a dangerous simplification that still has currency today?

It was not, however, Adorno who first caught my attention. I had little interest in politics and none in Marxism—sophisticated or crude—and I would not have found myself struggling with ideas with which I fundamentally disagreed if I hadn't come across references to the German-Jewish critic Walter Benjamin.

Benjamin was one of those brilliant, romantic, self-destructive personalities whose fate seems as determined as those portrayed in ancient Greek tragedy, and whose seemingly inescapable end compels our interest. In 1940, while trying to escape from Vichy, France, into Spain—after already abandoning Berlin and Paris to the Nazis—Benjamin committed suicide, taking an overdose of morphine. Ironically, his death so shocked the border guards that they allowed others they had detained with him to pass. This was, as Hannah Arendt pointed out, a final example of Benjamin's proverbial bad luck. He was practically unknown during his lifetime and published little; his magnum opus, the "Arcades Project"—a sociological study of nineteenth-century Parisian arcades (an equivalent today would be the shopping mall)—remained unfinished. A manuscript in his possession at the time of his suicide disappeared. It was Benjamin's bad luck to have waited until the last moment to make a bid to escape. He'd had offers to come to New York, where fellow Jewish intellectuals had found a haven. But he put off accepting these until it was too late. Procrastination was one of his character traits; apparently, he took forever to make a move in chess.

It was only some years after his death that Benjamin's now-worldwide posthumous fame began. He had been rediscovered in the 1960s—an inspiration for May '68—and had become an icon of the New Left.[20] When I came upon him in the mid-1980s, Benjaminmania was in full swing—I even saw graffiti about him in the toilet of a hip, arty café. By now, practically everything he ever wrote has been published and thoroughly scrutinized by experts in the Benjamin industry. Years later, I would write about him in *Dead Letters*, my book about writers and suicide.[21] Benjamin's life seemed a kind of archetype of the intellectual on the run from barbarism—although Benjamin himself would not care for the term "archetype," believing that Jung was a closet Nazi and, as his fellow Marxist Ernst Bloch called him, a "frothing Fascist."

I had not come across this accusation of Jung's "fellow traveling" with national socialism before, and was surprised. But then, Jung was an ardent critic of the Soviets and of any form of collectivization, and I soon got used to the kind of name-calling and downright nasty invective many Marxist and "progressive" thinkers employ against those with whom they disagree.

Benjamin's work was in truth unclassifiable. He was a Marxist, but his Marxism was leavened with hefty helpings of Kabbalah, and his version of the coming classless society was as much a vision of the millennium as anything his friend Brecht had in mind. (His other good friend was the Kabbalah scholar Gershom Scholem, who tried to convince Benjamin to move to Palestine, as Scholem had.) Benjamin did, in fact,

---

20. In 2002, during a stay in the Pyrenees, I visited the site of Benjamin's grave in the Spanish border town of Port Bou, and also the remarkable monument to him by the artist Dani Karavans. "Passages" is an eerie flight of steps leading nowhere, cut into the stone of the cliff overlooking the Mediterranean near the cemetery where Benjamin is buried.

21. *The Dedalus Book of Literary Suicides: Dead Letters* (Sawtry, Cambs, UK: Dedalus Books, 2008).

have visions of some kind of "divine violence" wiping the slate clean, returning us to a prelapsarian state from which we could start all over.

He was a kind of mystic, but his mysticism was of a peculiarly secular, urban sort. Our contemporary interest in urban pursuits like psychogeography (mapping out the psychic impact of cityscapes) owes much to Benjamin's fascination with the figure of the flaneur, the nineteenth-century Parisian stroller of the boulevards, whose aimless sauntering, free of the capitalist demands of work, allows for a "profane illumination," at least if you are the poet Baudelaire, whose work obsessed Benjamin. With the Viennese modernists, Benjamin was fascinated with the *Sprachfrage*, and his philosophy of language reached back to the notion of some primal, *Ur*, Adamic speech, when the relationship between signified and signifier (a nod to the deconstructionists) was not arbitrary but necessary, an idea he explored in his essay on translation. He had also experimented with drugs, writing about his experiences with hashish.

Benjamin's most well-known work—and one Daniel had us read for the aesthetics class—was his essay "The Work of Art in the Age of Mechanical Reproduction." This looked at the impact that modern methods of reproduction would have on our appreciation of works of art. The original work has an aura, a glow, we might say, of authenticity. But what happens to this "glow" when the original possessing it can be copied almost exactly, so that the difference between it and the copy is negligible and the copy can be mass produced? Today, when images of artworks across the centuries can be easily had on the internet—and with AI threatening the whole idea of an "original"—it is difficult for us to share Benjamin's concern. But in his time, the reproduction of famous paintings was in its infancy, and the postwar boom in investment in social art—making it available to the masses—was unknown. Art still seemed like some precious commodity that only the rich could afford.

Benjamin believed that the new developments in media technology (radio, film) would undermine the class-based divide between those who can experience art and those who cannot. The new technologies would "liberate" art while at the same time they would do away with the bourgeois, romantic notion of some magic possessed by the inaccessible original. In true Marxist fashion, Benjamin thought of artists, poets, writers, and other creative individuals as workers, as much proletarians as the street sweeper or factory hand. They held no special place in the revolution, although Benjamin himself, the pampered son of a bourgeois family, grew up with servants and, aside from writing, never worked a day in his life. As Hannah Arendt, who did much to initiate renewed interest in Benjamin, described him, he was incapable of opening a window or making coffee for himself, displaying the kind of cultured neurasthenia we associate with another of his heroes, Proust, whom he translated.

Today, when images of everything from Michelangelo to Banksy adorn T-shirts and shopping bags, it is easy to agree with Benjamin's prediction about the loss of prestige of the original, but difficult to find the revolutionary potential he expected from this. Accessible art has hardly liberated the masses, and by many accounts, the sort of hands-on, interactive installations and "disposable" art that fills museums today seems to operate on a lowest common denominator approach, rather than one aimed at raising its audience's standards.

In another well-known essay, Benjamin outlined his view of history, which, with James Joyce, he saw as a nightmare; had he known of it, he would have agreed with Ouspensky's coinage of a "history of crime." With Adorno, he saw nothing but disaster. In "Theses on the Philosophy of History," Benjamin presented his vision of the past, not as "a chain of events" but as "a single catastrophe which keeps piling wreckage upon wreckage," rather as a highway accident can produce a pileup of autos, one smashed into another. He writes of an angel, the model for which he found in a painting by Paul Klee.

This is not the kind of angel Rilke encountered when the terrible vision of the *Duino Elegies* came to him, and who entrusted him with the task of saving the world from oblivion. Benjamin's angel can do nothing. The storm of history blows him backward; his wings are of no avail. He is forever pushed beyond reach of the disaster which, were he able to embrace it, would end. But there is nothing he can do except look on, helplessly, as the pileup increases. It was this paralysis that led the Marxist critic Georg Lukacs—whom I also read at this time—to say that Adorno, Benjamin, and others associated with the Frankfurt School had taken up residence in the "Grand Hotel Abyss." The one hope we have—or the one Benjamin allowed himself—was the possibility of the "violence of divine intervention" and a "sudden eschatological change." It was this hunger for some eruptive, redeeming act that informed both Benjamin's vision of the world and his suicide.

I could appreciate Benjamin's vision of a world in which everything has gone wrong, but I didn't share it. It is, indeed, the vision of Lurianic Kabbalah, which posits a means, *tikkun*, of repairing creation, and which I write about in *The Caretakers of the Cosmos*. Benjamin's vision lacked this means of reparation. Only an idiot could be blind to the suffering in life, or its inequities. But, at bottom, I was too optimistic to accept his pessimism or Adorno's vision of a totally unredeemable society. I also rejected deconstructionism's nihilism and the sort of epistemological bondage served up by Foucault. Any vital mind instinctively rejects philosophies of helplessness, however brilliantly they are presented. The only hope any of them offered was contingent upon the eradication of Western civilization. It had to go. This was the *épistémè* in which I found myself—at least, insofar as I considered the philosophical climate of the academy. Western civilization was rotten to the core and the sooner it was shut down, the better.

Forty years ago, this indictment was limited to extreme voices in academia. Now, people argue about it on Twitter.

IT WAS AROUND THIS TIME that the first signs of a nascent "political correctness" appeared, or at least when I first caught sight of them. One of the hot topics of debate was "the Western canon," the works of literature that constituted the essence of Western culture. These were under attack from a variety of critics: feminists, post-colonialists, racist theory, as well as from the deconstructionists and the postmodernists. It seemed to go without saying that anyone with any serious intention of having an academic career—at least in the humanities—would accept that the era of Western intellectual imperialism was over, or, at least, that it should be. All the most progressive thinkers thought so.

My own relation to the Western canon was ambivalent. There was much in it that I felt no attraction to (remember my missing out on Shakespeare?), and I also felt that figures like Samuel Beckett—whom Adorno celebrated and who had won the Nobel Prize for Literature in 1969—and others, like James Joyce, were vastly overrated. Writers I found much more significant were barely read or mentioned. So, I had my own disagreements with the canon. But the sort of all-out rejection of the "great books" that I encountered struck me as no answer. It was an emotional rejection, and it was driven, I felt, by an unquestioned assumption that Western civilization *must* be "bad." There was no debate about this. All "right thinking" people *must* feel this way. And if you didn't? Well, then you were, as Adorno and his readers insisted on, part of the problem. Which meant, I guess, that you would have to go, too.

I simply didn't share this animus against Western civilization that seemed *de rigueur* in the academic world. Nor did I agree with Marcuse that the overthrow of capitalism and the establishment of society based on polymorphous perversity was the answer. Must I here repeat the banal truism that, yes, of course there was much wrong with the world and which needed to be changed? Gurdjieff, whose work continued to occupy me throughout this time, was a much more stringent critic of the modern world than any critical theorist; *Beelzebub's Tales*—as impenetrable as anything the deconstructionists or Foucault produced—is in essence a twelve-hundred-page indictment of it.

But his criticism was in the context of a teaching that saw the possibility of real change, not merely a transfer of power from one source to another, from the "haves" to the "have nots." By all means, let us read more underrepresented writers and thinkers; I, myself, had been reading many for several years, although the writers and thinkers I had in mind—like Colin Wilson—were not those celebrated by those wanting to throw out the great books. The people they did have in mind did not impress me. They certainly didn't seem of equal stature with Plato, Milton, Dostoevsky, and other writers who were now held up as examples of Western chauvinism or some other discreditable characteristic. They and others like them were corralled under the heading of "Dead White European Males"—DWEMs, for short—and it was not unusual to hear calls for their "oppressive," "imperialistic," "intolerant" works to be cast out of the academy.[22]

Perhaps I have an inherent tendency to go against the flow. Perhaps, like salmon, I have to swim against the current. Perhaps I identify with the underdog and enjoy being contentious. I had, after all, given up playing with a band that went on to be enormously successful in order to pursue my own creativity. And even then, I went against the tide of punk and its sophomoric pop nihilism when it was all the rage. And I had also given up pop music to study the "melancholy science," as Adorno called philosophy. I may simply enjoy banging my head against a wall. But all this unquestioned rancor against Western civilization irked me. Books had changed my life. More than this: they had shown me how *I* could change, how I could *be* more. They had raised me out of the morass of ignorance and limited horizons that I had been born into and shown me a much more interesting and meaningful way of life. They seemed to me a treasure to be protected, an absolute necessity to be defended from attack.

More than anything else, I was repelled by the presumptuous, self-righteous self-importance of the defamers of the West, and their ignorant insistence that it had to go. They seemed shallow, self-satisfied, and their critique little more than a rationalizing of their emotional

---

22. One has to say, though, that Dead White European Males is a good name for a band.

rejection of their own history and culture. I later came to see that much of this animus against the West was rooted in a sense of guilt combined with a naïve idealism. This tends to create a rejection of one's own society for not being perfect, and a romanticizing and idealization of other societies who seem to be doing a better job but which actually are worse than your own. Who doesn't like a lost cause? I took up my cudgel on the side of the great books, and when asked what my area of work was, replied "DWEM studies."

A book that became very important for me in this context was *The Closing of the American Mind*, by Allan Bloom. Bloom was a Platonist and a political philosopher. He had translated *The Republic* and Rousseau, and had edited the lectures making up Alexandre Kojève's *Introduction to the Reading of Hegel*, which I read while working my way through the *Phenomenology of Spirit*. Bloom was in Cornell during the student riots of the 1960s, and was disgusted by the way the faculty capitulated to the demands of the student rioters. There and elsewhere, they had caved without putting up a fight, and allowed the student radicals to take possession of some of the campus, much of which they vandalized. This pusillanimity repelled Bloom. He tells the story of how some students broke into his class on *The Republic* and demanded that he stop teaching such "irrelevant" stuff and address the issues of the day—civil rights, Vietnam, and other more immediately urgent concerns. Bloom replied that he could think of nothing more relevant than teaching Plato. He believed it was his task as a teacher to infect his students with the germ of a philosophical life, in the way that I had been infected in my last year of high school.

Twenty years later, in his book Bloom argued that the student radicals of the 1960s had become the tenured radicals of the 1980s, and that American students were suffering from this. Rather than receive a grounding in the literature and thought that could help them come to know themselves and their potentials—via the "classics" then under fire—they were receiving instruction in the radical anti-Western ideology that their instructors had received from Adorno, Benjamin,

Marcuse, and other critics of the West. This was served up in a mélange of Marxified, vulgarized Nietzsche and Heidegger. This was a remarkable dialectical feat indeed, a deconstructive reading of two "men of the right" as actual presages of the even newer New Left. The radical rewriting of history (a practice sadly continuing today) deprived students of any true idea of the past, or infected them with a debilitating sense of guilt. The dogma of cultural relativity informed the diffidence that neutralized any positive belief and inhibited any expression of it.

Bloom also believed that pop music and other forms of popular culture infantilized the youth addicted to them, and made them incapable of envisioning any future other than that of finding some well-paying place for themselves in the system. By then I had so rejected my rock and roll past that I agreed with him. A few years later, when looking into possible places in graduate school, I wrote to Bloom at the Committee on Social Thought, at the University of Chicago, expressing my appreciation of his work and letting him know that I was an ex–rock and roller who agreed with his assessment of it and the state of academia. I never heard from him. He died in 1992, and, as with Foucault, his death is thought to have been AIDS related.

Bloom seemed to me to be much more serious about thought, philosophy, ideas, and their necessity in order to be a fully actualized individual, a mature human being, than anything I had been reading. He seemed to offer the genuine article and turned the question back on oneself, rather than fixing one's critical gaze on society, "the system," or some other abstraction which one could conveniently blame for all one's shortcomings. In one of his books, he quotes Goethe as saying—I'm paraphrasing—"Do something good without having to change the world." It seems the easier task to complain ad nauseum about how much the world needs to change.

Bloom struck me as fulfilling the task of the true philosopher. So I was surprised when, on seeing me carrying a copy of *The Closing of the American Mind*, Henry—who knew his Plato—pulled me aside and in a hushed voice told me I should be careful not to let anyone know I was reading it.

"It's a dangerous book," he told me. Foucault, Derrida, Adorno—all condemners of Western civilization—were perfectly fine, harmless. But a book that argued against their vision of futility and helplessness, and upheld the value of the great work of Western culture—that was dangerous.

Of course, I carried it openly and did nothing to obscure the fact that I was reading it.

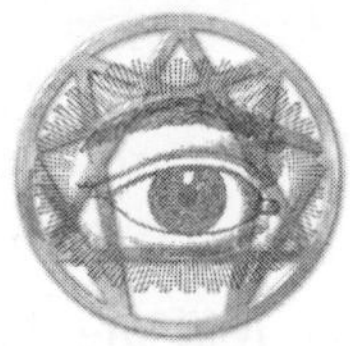

11
Into the New Age

While taking classes and reading up on current trends in philosophy, I was still involved with my work with the Gurdjieff group.[1] This did continue for a time, but soon I would decide to leave the Work. It was not philosophy or anything I read in Derrida or Adorno that led me away. Hardly. But I have always been very eclectic in my interests—the fact that I was going out of my way to familiarize myself with schools of thought I fundamentally disagreed with might suggest as much—and within the Work there was an understandable intention to keep it pure. It had a particular approach to the aims it pursued, and the general idea was not to mix the system with outside sources.[2]

I could understand this. If you looked at it in the sense of learning a language, say French, you don't want to start bringing in examples from other languages. But I was more interested in consciousness and its questions than in the teaching, per se, and could not stop myself from seeing similarities between Work ideas and others I was coming across in my reading. Initially I would mention this, but the response

1. At one of the Work weekends I attended while taking classes, I was surprised to discover that a professor whose class I had taken was there as well. I can't remember her name, but I do remember that she had been a student of Heidegger and that I asked her many questions about her time with him.

2. In the Work jargon, this would mean keeping "C influences," coming from the Inner Circle of Humanity, free from "B influences," those of culture.

was always the same. "Interesting, but that is only a book," or "Perhaps, but that is just an idea," give a sense of the usual reply. The unspoken assessment was that all this was just another form of sleep. A very interesting sleep, perhaps, but sleep all the same. Even the few friends I had in the Work would make similar remarks, and jokingly suggest that I was "backsliding." It was almost as if I was a kind of Trotskyite, veering dangerously close to revisionism.

After a time, I stopped mentioning anything and kept my insights to myself. This contributed to an increasing sense that the system emphasized the negative aspects of the problem, focusing on what was wrong with one's current state of being rather than the potential positive possibilities. There was, in a word, more stick than carrot, at least from my perspective.

I remember one conversation with Mrs. Langmuir, a kind of regular update she asked for on a student's progress. I mentioned that I felt I had been at the same spot for some time—I was doing the exercises, keeping my "appointments" with myself (when I would "remember to remember myself"), attending the Work weekends and the readings and "ideas" meetings. I believed I was making efforts—not necessarily super ones, but I was fairly disciplined and applied myself. There were times when I did not want to go to a meeting, but I forced myself. But it seemed to have become routine. I was not getting much return back on my investment. It all seemed rather dull. Even the physical work on the weekends failed to dispel the feeling that things had become quite flat.

This loss of interest and motivation in pursuing a spiritual practice is well known. The medieval monks called it *acedia*, a kind of "dryness" and emptiness. Anyone seriously practicing meditation encounters it. It bores you and you just want to quit. It becomes the last thing you want to do. Mrs. Langmuir nodded and merely suggested that I carry on, saying the feeling would pass. I said I would, but the truth was that I was losing interest in the system.

Earlier I mentioned that I didn't remember many names or people from my time in the Work in Los Angeles. I do remember meeting, very briefly though, one very important senior figure in the Work. If the reader will allow some leeway with my chronology, this must have been during my first years in the LA group.

Lord Pentland (Henry John Sinclair) had been Ouspensky's student in London and America in the 1930s and '40s. After Ouspensky's death in 1947, Pentland traveled to India, then spent some months with Gurdjieff in Paris before Gurdjieff's death in 1949. The story was that, before his death, Gurdjieff had appointed Lord Pentland as the leader of the Work in North America. He founded the Gurdjieff Society in 1953 and was its president until his death in February 1984.

It must have been sometime in 1983 that he paid a visit to the house in the Valley. I can remember a certain tension in the air that weekend, as if we were in the military and our camp was about to be inspected by the top brass. This was understandable—Lord Pentland had known Ouspensky and Gurdjieff, both of whom were quasi-mythical figures for many people there that weekend. He had, as it were, kept company with the gods. I also remember X telling me that Lord Pentland was "big in the Work," at the same time that he expressed some skepticism about Gurdjieff's anointing him with the directorship of the American branch. His qualification for this distinction seemed, at least according to X, doubtful. But then, X had grown up in the Work, and most likely had heard gossip about many of the elders.

The idea of anyone being "big in the Work," struck me as odd. This made it sound as if it were something you could make a career of, "working" your way up the ladder to some prominent, authoritative position. Years later, a close friend, now departed, who had been involved in the Work for many years in London, made a similar remark about another important figure in it.

It struck me as typical of most alternative schools or teachings, that they eventually form a hierarchy, a power structure, that people—usually dominant types—learn how to use to their advantage, just as in everyday life. But even earlier, back then in Los Angeles, it struck me as somehow antithetical to what the Work was supposed to be about. Even

Gurdjieff said that the Work was not something one should pursue as an end in itself, but as a means to an end, toward an aim outside of it. I don't know what Lord Pentland would have thought of this line of thinking, but I did get the impression that X would not mind becoming "big in the Work" himself.

That morning, Lord Pentland gave a talk. It was a larger group than usual, with pretty much everyone showing up for the special occasion. I remember him being a thin, frail, well-dressed, distinguished gentleman with an English accent, who spoke in a rather soft, dry voice that was at times difficult to hear. That may have been a Work tactic, forcing his audience to make an extra (super?) effort to make out what he was saying. Or he might just have spoken that way. I don't remember much of what he said, other than a refrain he returned to several times. There was in our lives, he said, "something missing." We may not be sure exactly what it is, but we feel its lack nonetheless.

I am of course paraphrasing from dim memory, but the drift of the talk was something along these lines: We may find ourselves occupied with our daily routine and getting on with life when, out of nowhere and for no reason, we have this sense of something being missing. What was it? What was missing? Ourselves. We are missing, because we are not conscious, but asleep. We are not at home.

We were to do our Work that weekend, keeping this in mind and keeping an eye out for our missing selves.

I don't remember much else from that meeting. But it is curious, I think, that this memory came to me as I was writing about my decision to leave the Work. I appreciate the reader's patience with the lapse in chronology, but the workings of the unconscious—or whatever the source of memory is—stick to no timetable. Why did I now remember this talk and its refrain of "something missing"? Could it be because that was what I felt during my last days in the Work? That something was missing, not in me—although, to be sure, there certainly was—but in it? Was something missing from the Work, and was its absence, whatever it was, the source of my dissatisfaction with it?

In any event, after much soul-searching and painful indecision, I decided that it would be dishonest for me to continue. I asked Mrs. Langmuir if I could meet with her. I explained my reasons for deciding to stop, thanked her for allowing me into the group and for what I had gotten from it, which in truth was quite a lot. But I wouldn't be carrying on.

She didn't try to dissuade me. She did ask what I wanted to do with my life. I said that I wanted to write. "Why do you want to do that?" she replied, rather as my philosophy professors had expressed their astonishment at my intention to teach philosophy. I don't remember what I said, but with that the interview was over and so was my time in the Work.

Sometime after leaving the Work, I left work of another kind—my job at the video rental shop. The owner complained that I was spending too much time reading instead of dusting or neatening the shelves. Truth was, there really wasn't much to do during my day shifts except tend to the occasional customer. So, I took advantage of the quiet times and worked my way through Hegel. The owner was not, he let me know, paying me to grasp the dialectic. After a few awkward exchanges, he gave me my pink slip, some token severance pay, and let me go.

It was inconvenient to have to find work again. The shop was a tolerable perch. It paid the bills, I got to watch a lot of films, and a girl I met who worked nearby joined me in a brief affair. Nevertheless, there were more than a few times when my native intelligence overrode my talent for customer service, a problem I would encounter at my next place of employment.

The Bodhi Tree Bookshop, on Melrose Avenue, was just around the corner from my studio in West Hollywood. It was started in the early '70s by Stan and Fran Madson, and Phil and Elsa Thompson. They story was that they were Buddhists working in aerodynamics who wanted to do something more meaningful with their lives. So, they opened a metaphysical bookshop, one of many sprouting up in different cities across the country following the "occult revival" of the 1960s. The shop was named after the tree—a *Ficus religiosa*—that Gautama Buddha sat under when he gained enlightenment. I'd first visited the bookstore in 1977, during my first tenure in LA. There were two branches, one for new books, and a smaller secondhand shop that also sold various herbs, spices, and teas.

On my visits then, I'd spent most of my time at the secondhand shop. Their prices were very good and the shop itself was very cozy and inviting, with free herbal tea and Eastern music playing in the background. Statues of the Buddha, charts marking the positions of the chakras, and other spiritual bric-a-brac decorated the place. Both branches were very well stocked, with large sections on astrology, meditation, tarot, Buddhism, parapsychology, mysticism, the Fourth Way, Jung, and everything else you'd expect to see in a metaphysical bookshop. My interest then was in Crowley and the Golden Dawn, and although they had a decent section on magic and the occult in the new book shop as well as in the secondhand branch, I tended to visit the new shop less.

One reason for this was the strong smell of incense that filled the place. I later discovered that the powerful scent wasn't from any incense they were burning—it was the smell coming from their stock: they had so much of it, they didn't need to burn any, and a book bought from the new shop invariably reeked of it. Another reason I tended to avoid the new shop was that, along with the incense, there was a certain air about the people working there. They all seemed rather mild and gentle, but there was something a bit too nice about it. It was all a little too tranquil, a little too "Zen," as we'd say today. In my Crowley phase, I preferred something more lively. After all, I was still a rock and roller.

Ten years later, I wasn't, and I found myself working there.[3]

WHEN I STARTED WORKING AT THE BODHI TREE, it had become very popular. It had always had a steady, loyal clientele, but in 1983, it was put on the mainstream popular culture map. In her book, *Out on a Limb*, the actress Shirley MacLaine talked about her interest in reincarnation, meditation, UFOs, and other aspects of what was becoming known as New Age spirituality. The book charts her journey in search of her "true self," a quest that took her from Southern California to what she describes as a life-changing experience in the Andes. One spot on her spiritual itinerary was the Bodhi Tree, and she describes deciding to go there on a whim as one of the most important decisions of her life.

It certainly was an important decision for the shop. And what made an even greater impact was the television miniseries made of the book, starring MacLaine, which aired in early 1987, the year I started working there. The clientele, already large, doubled practically overnight, and now included not only the usual mystical eccentrics that had been part of California for decades, but a good many of MacLaine's fellow Hollywood stars.

Exactly when the New Age began is debatable. Some people put

---

3. One thing I remember from this time was attending the famous "The Spiritual in Art" exhibition put on at the Los Angeles County Museum of Art (LACMA) in 1986, the first major exhibition to acknowledge the influence of mystical, magical, and esoteric ideas on modern art. The exhibition featured artists well known for their spiritual pursuits, people like Kandinsky and Mondrian, who were both Theosophists. But there were others less known. One of the surprises of the exhibition was the then little-known Hilma af Klint, a Swedish woman whose remarkable paintings, based on Theosophical, anthroposophical, and Spiritualist ideas, have in recent years been the focus of many major exhibitions around the world, several of which I have spoken at. She is thought to have predated Kandinsky and produced "abstract" painting before him. Today this is a popular debate, but then it was virgin territory. Oddly enough, it was at around the same time as the exhibition that an academic interest in esotericism started up. Today, both the arts and academia display a lively interest in the esoteric; back then it was a radical, even dangerous area of study, and most artists and academics steered clear of it.

Marilyn Ferguson's book, *The Aquarian Conspiracy* (1980), which I read and enjoyed, at the start. (I remember a girl I dated at the time asking if I was an "Aquarian conspirator.") Others see the "channeled" teachings—a new form of spirit communication—of David Spangler, a central figure at the Findhorn community in Scotland, as the beginning. I talk about it in *The Secret Teachings of the Western World*. Whatever may have gotten the New Age ball rolling, by the summer of 1987, it had certainly picked up speed and was heading toward what seemed a particularly propitious, if not apocalyptic, moment.

Soon after starting work at the Bodhi Tree, I became aware of an event of global, even cosmic importance that was on its way, and would in fact arrive very soon—at least, according to the people who told me about it. This sudden shift in the "collective planetary karma"—as one person described the coming occasion—was known as the Harmonic Convergence. What was that? It was, I discovered, an idea that emerged from an interpretation of the ancient Mayan calendar by the New Age philosopher José Argüelles in his book *The Mayan Factor: Path Beyond Technology* (1987). This was augmented by the "timewave" theory of the then head psychedelic guru, Terence McKenna, as presented in his book *The Invisible Landscape* (1975).[4]

According to Argüelles, 1987 would mark the end of a long 1144-year cycle charted by the Mayans, which is itself divided into different "heavenly" and "hellish" sub-cycles. The current "hell" cycle would close that year, and mark the start of a new "heaven" cycle, which, again according to Argüelles, would reach its climax twenty-five years later, in 2012. That year would see the "return of Quetzalcoatl," the ancient Aztec creator god, and would mark the end of what Argüelles called "the Long Count," and thus initiate the end of history. McKenna's timewave theory posited an unprecedented explosion of "novelty"—a term

4. There was around this time the beginning of a renewed interest in psychedelics, a kind of return to the acid philosophy of the 1960s. Although I knew people involved in the '80s rave scene in LA, I didn't partake. I did see Terence McKenna speak once. I wasn't convinced by his arguments, but he had certainly kissed the Blarney Stone.

borrowed from Alfred North Whitehead—in 2012 as well, leading to what he called the "singularity," an event that would change not only human life, but the very fabric of being, initiating a new ontology. As the singularities we think we know of include the Big Bang and what happens inside a black hole—if, indeed, black holes have insides—this is certainly something to look forward to.

Alas, as anyone who was around at the time knows, 2012 didn't quite meet the expectations of those who were around for the Harmonic Convergence. There was a great deal of millenarian hoopla about it, much of it coming from the then head doyen of the new psychedelic cult, Daniel Pinchbeck, whom I met in 2003 after reviewing his first book for *The Guardian*. Pinchbeck believed he had spoken with Quetzalcoatl himself, in the Brazilian rainforest in 2004, facilitated, he admits, by a dose of the powerful hallucinogen ayahuasca. Quetzalcoatl might not have showed in person in 2012—unless you had some ayahuasca—but he certainly turned up in the avalanche of books, seminars, workshops, DVDs, and other essential items his proponents assured the expectant many were needed to prepare for his arrival.

Yet, this was in the future, and for the people crowding into the shop in the days leading up to the main event that summer, there was little doubt that something of fundamental significance was approaching. They took it very seriously. Wanting to ensure a safe and harmonious conversion to the new times, on August 15 and 16, the crucial days, many people gathered in various "power spots" around the planet, and engaged in group meditation. Two very popular places in the States were Sedona, Arizona, which had already become a site of pilgrimage for the many people convinced of the beneficent powers of crystals—in which the shop did a brisk trade—and Mount Shasta in California, which had been a location of interest to UFO devotees for decades. In the UK, as one might expect, Stonehenge and Glastonbury drew crowds, and there were similar gatherings in other places. If nothing else, the gatherings marked the start of what we can call "esotourism," sacred travel, and the metaphysical holiday industry.

When I asked a Harmonic Converger, who was planning on spending the crisis point meditating on the beach, why people needed to help the event along, given it was predicted long ago and had the cosmos behind it, she informed me that these sorts of transitions are very delicate, sensitive periods, and that if we weren't careful, the energies released might go "in the wrong direction." "It is a dangerous time," she said. When I expressed concern, she hastened to assure me that I had nothing to worry about. Here, at the shop, I was in one of the safest places on the planet. It was protected—its aura would repel any negative vibrations. As I lived practically around the corner, I wondered just how far the protection reached.

I ENJOYED WORKING AT THE BODHI TREE. It took a while to get used to the incense—as well as to some of the clientele and, I must admit, some of my colleagues—but, soon enough, I felt at home there. The clientele could be broken up into different categories. There was a small number of serious students of, say, the Bhagavad Gita, or Sufism, Buddhism, or other traditional teachings, who could find literature on their subject here that would be difficult to locate anywhere else. This was well before the online economy made it so practically anything could be had whenever you needed it. But there were not enough of these serious seekers to keep the place going on their own, and the owners had to cater to a wide range of tastes. Whatever one might have thought about the quality of the more popular items we stocked, it was clear that only by providing these could the more serious material also be available. If the shop depended on the number of Sanskrit dictionaries it sold, it would never have seen the Harmonic Convergence.[5]

---

5. Not to mention 2012, which it didn't. The shop closed on New Year's Eve, 2011, although it continued an online presence.

Another group were the curious ones who, having seen Shirley MacLaine's miniseries or read her book, wanted to see what it was all about. They may have bought a crystal or two, perhaps some incense and a book about past lives or the aura. These might come back once or twice more before their interest waned and they stopped trying to meditate or find their true selves.

Then there were the very earnest New Agers, people who embraced its beliefs wholeheartedly and organized their lives around it. These made up the bulk of the customers, and there were many of them. Exactly what constitutes New Age spirituality is debatable, and much has been written about it, but it certainly included ideas about past lives, reincarnation, the aura, meditation, "being positive," chakras—energetic power points within the body—yoga, health food (forerunners of today's vegans), out-of-body experiences, dreams, ideas about Atlantis and ancient prehistoric civilizations, and about Egypt and the pyramids, UFOs, nature worship, and an assortment of other notions and practices that were not necessarily related to each other but which found a space under the generic New Age umbrella.

Much of it was no doubt dubious, little more than spiritual consumerism. But many people embracing these ideas did so from a genuine desire to understand their lives and have some experience of their inner worlds. For these folk, the New Age was a lifestyle choice, as we say today. Fashions and fads came and went. This week rose quartz or hematite was the rage; next it would be burning sage or having your mercury fillings removed (one co-worker spent a considerable sum doing this). Tibetan bells and singing bowls, Reiki therapy (a kind of Japanese "laying on of hands"), a new form of breathwork (perhaps Stanislav Grof's "holotropic" therapy), or Neuro-Linguistic Programming would follow past-life regression, Jungian "shadow work," or guided meditations in quick succession as the latest thing. One outgrowth of esotourism were the "vision quests" that had many people heading to the rain forests—or, more locally, the desert—to partake of native entheogens (the new term for psychedelics) in hopes of having a transformative experience. And many did.

One of the most popular fashions at the time was "channeling," which I mentioned earlier. This was a late-'80s refit of nineteenth-century Spiritualism. In channeling, though, it wasn't the spirits of the dead that were speaking through mediums but entities from other dimensions, other times, other planets, other worlds. Ramtha, channeled through J. Z. Knight, was from Lemuria, an ancient continent like Atlantis that sank some thirty-five thousand years ago. Seth, an "energy personality essence no longer focused in physical matter," spoke through the novelist and poet Jane Roberts. Sanaya Roman was the channel for Orin, a "spirit guide" and "timeless being of love and light."

Other similar entities communicated various vague but generally positive cosmic messages about love, spirituality, evolution, and consciousness not that different in tone and character from the spirit messages of a century before. (It is interesting that, as in Spiritualism, women seemed to predominate channeling.) And, like Spiritualism, channeling became a kind of pastime, with people trying it for themselves. They did this by making themselves available to entities that were known as "walk-ins," meaning that they "walk in" and take up residency in a person when his or her own soul is temporarily absent. Predictably, this led to jokes about the best channelers being people who were mindless to begin with.

For a time, one of the people working at the shop held gatherings during which he made space for a "walk-in" and allowed it to communicate through him. He had quite a following among the employees and some customers, although I never attended a session.

Another popular trend was goddess worship, and the variety of books on women's spirituality it produced. Part of this included the revival of the idea, promoted in the nineteenth century by the Swiss historian Johann Bachofen, that a matriarchal form of society preceded that of the patriarchy, a theme then advanced by Marija

Gimbutas. Marion Woodman, Starhawk, Riane Eisler, and Margot Adler were some of the most popular authors in the "goddess movement." Predictably, this led to a counter "men's movement," headed by Robert Bly, whose book, *Iron John*, led to quite a bit of male bonding at sweat lodges. Another popular author then was James Hillman, whose revisioning of Jungian psychology as a form of "soul making," led to a score of books on the subject, like Thomas Moore's bestseller, *Care of the Soul* (1992).[6] And around the same time, Joseph Campbell told us about the power of myth and, as mentioned earlier, advised us to "follow our bliss."

Some of the individuals coming to the shop could be fairly demanding, and just as fussy and tiresome as any customer at any shop. I came to encounter more than one impatient Buddhist. On one occasion, a regular who always came accompanied by his parrot, which perched on his shoulder and cared nothing for hygiene, wasn't happy with my service. In the middle of my trying to help him, he stopped, shook his head, and told me he didn't like my aura. It was a blow, but I kept my aplomb and asked to be excused while I found a colleague whose aura he might like.

On another occasion, I had to help a woman who was just learning about crystals. She wanted one that would "dispel all negativity," but was unhappy because she had been told it had to be green (clearly, she didn't realize that if it worked, she wouldn't have minded what color it

---

6. I have to say that I read quite a bit of Hillman at the time, and knew people who attended the Pacifica Graduate Institute along the coast, where his archetypal psychology was taught. I never came away having a clear idea exactly what he was saying. He mentioned many interesting people and seemed to be getting to something but, at the end, I really couldn't say exactly what that was. I remember having a conversation with one colleague who was studying Hillman, and being told that my dissatisfaction with him not being clearer was a sign that I was too rational—one of the few times I have been accused of that. I also believe Hillman misunderstood Maslow, whom he accused of ignoring life's "vales" in his search for its "peaks" (the peak experience). Maslow never saw peak experiences as something one pursued. They came of themselves and often involve rather everyday things. With his obsession with depression and melancholia, Hillman simply couldn't see this.

was). Some exchanges were charming. I remember showing a woman of mature years how to consult the I Ching using the three-coin method (I had, myself, been consulting it since 1978). On another occasion, one individual asked me if he had a soul. I replied honestly that I didn't know.[7]

Some regulars made their appearance only in the evening. As the new branch was open until eleven p.m., it attracted a good share of lonely people looking for company. The free herbal tea we provided helped. I was made a manager fairly soon into my time there, and worked both day and evening shifts, so I got to see the full range of customers. One type of customer—I use the term loosely, as they rarely bought anything—were the men who haunted the astrology section, targeting likely women and chatting them up. "I knew you were a Pisces the minute I saw you" or "You have Aries written all over you" were some of the lines thrown out. Often, the bait worked. Sometimes it didn't, and on more than one occasion I had to tactfully ask the offender to leave.

Other evening regulars were harmless enough. One fellow, a Jamaican, very polite and quiet, was making his way through the work of Alice Bailey, convinced that it held the clue to exactly what, I'm not sure, but it was of great importance, certainly to him. He never bought a thing and carried a sheaf of notes with him all the time, which he added to as he sat and read each evening until closing.

The secondhand branch had its own regulars. I worked there on

---

7. Occasionally a celebrity would show up. One evening, William Shatner of *Star Trek* came to the shop. On another, Barbara Steele, who had been in many of the horror films I watched growing up, was there. I don't remember what they purchased. Other celebrity visitors were closer to home. Some time in 1989, Chris Stein and Debbie Harry turned up. Debbie was recording her solo album *Def, Dumb & Blonde* and invited me to the studio to sing backup on the track "Bike Boy." On another occasion, Tom Verlaine walked into the used branch on an afternoon while I was there. I was surprised to see him and, although we didn't know each other well, walked up to him and said hello. As I say in *New York Rocker*, he "looked at me as if I had uncovered the fact that he had three arms and walked away."

weekends, usually with the same people, and we became a good team.[8] I have fond memories of that time, and have written about some of my odd experiences there in *Dreaming Ahead of Time*.[9] What I enjoyed most was pricing the books that people brought in to sell. A good deal of my library here in London came from my time as a buyer back then. Professional book scouts would bring in several boxes, and I'd hole up in the office and spend a few hours pricing the new arrivals. We had first pick of anything that came in, plus a staff discount, and I made very good use of this.

Occasionally a rare item would arrive. Once it was an original edition of Crowley's occult magazine, *The Equinox*. I myself found a 1910 first edition of J. B. Baillie's translation of Hegel's *Phenomenology of Mind*. Some books we couldn't buy. I felt sorry for the ex-Scientologists who would bring in boxes of books by L. Ron Hubbard—we had to turn them away. One of the rules of Scientology was that members could buy only new editions of the literature—secondhand copies were outlawed. Since only Scientologists would be interested in the

8. I became close friends for a time with one of my workmates, N, a Jew who had converted to Russian Orthodox Christianity and who was a reader of Kierkegaard, Schopenhauer, C. S. Lewis, and the Traditionalist philosopher Frithjof Schuon. We spent many evenings in philosophical discussion. We also attended the lectures that Stephan A. Hoeller, a Gnostic thinker with a Jungian background and author of many books, presented at the Gnostic Church on Hollywood Boulevard. Now in his nineties, Hoeller, Bishop of the Gnostic Church, still performs a Gnostic Mass regularly at the Annie Besant Lodge of the Theosophical Society in Los Angeles.

9. In that book, I also tell the story of a precognitive dream involving one of my workmates. Several of the people working there were followers of Tibetan Buddhism. One night, I had a dream in which I was with a group of Tibetan Buddhists. We stood in a circle and were tossing a ball of yarn back and forth to each other. The ball opened up into the kind of net that used to be used to catch someone jumping from a burning building. We held on to it and began to dance around in a circle; as we did, it opened further into a beautiful mandala. That morning, when I got to the shop, one of my colleagues, a devotee of Tibetan Buddhism, told me that he had found a picture of me in my past life. Remembering the dream, I asked if it was in Tibet. He said yes, it was, and produced a photo from Alexandra David-Néel's book *Initiates and Initiation in Tibet*, showing herself and a round-faced, bespectacled Tibetan monk, who my colleague said looked rather like me.

books, and they wouldn't be able to buy them, they were of no use to us.

I BECAME QUITE CLOSE with the shop's owners and, on one occasion, when I was house-sitting for Stan and his wife Fran at their Zen castle, as I called it, in Laurel Canyon—a fantastic three-story, tower-like structure with a terraced garden and jacuzzi in the Hollywood Hills—I invited Colin Wilson and his wife Joy to stay there with me. Since meeting him in 1983, I had kept up a correspondence, and we'd met again when Colin had come to California on an earlier lecture tour. He was in town again, giving a series of talks, and had been booked into a small motel. When I saw where he was staying, I suggested he stay with me in the castle in the hills. There certainly was space, and it would be much more pleasant than where they were. He and Joy were delighted at my offer, and for a week or so he was my—and Stan and Fran's—guest.

One afternoon, he came into the secondhand branch and bought five hundred dollars' worth of books to be shipped back to England. We had more than one gathering at the Zen castle with some people from the shop and friends who knew his work. Sadly, after one memorable evening, I was too hungover the next day to join Colin, who was meeting Robert Anton Wilson, whose *Cosmic Trigger* I had read years earlier, for lunch—a missed opportunity I sincerely regret.

ALL THE TIME I WAS WORKING at the shop, I was continuing my studies in philosophy. At times, the contrast between the two made it seem as if I were leading two radically different lives, a split I had already experienced during my musician days. One was spent correcting papers on Plato's *Meno* or *Apology*, working my way through Wittgenstein's *Philosophical Investigations*, and filling my notebooks with existential ponderings; the other was spent telling customers who

Madame Blavatsky was, fetching the latest Louise Hay book for them, or locating a CD—just then getting popular—of the latest New Age music (think Kitaro and *Silk Road*).

In a sense, this polarity later appeared in my writing, in that I try to bring a philosophically critical but open mind to ideas of a mystical, esoteric character that often repel critical thought. (How successful I am at this is another question.) Even then, I found myself trying to balance the two opposites, if unconsciously. That is, when at the shop, I kept up a rigorous critical outlook toward much of what went on, taking the skeptic's position toward what others accepted without batting an eye. I was the resident rationalist. But at class, I argued against the reigning scientific reductionist paradigm and in favor of a much more spiritual—for lack of a better word—view of reality.

In a sense you could say that, like the comic book heroes of my childhood, I had two identities: one a sharp-minded philosopher critic, the other, if not a New Ager, certainly someone who took mysticism, the occult, and the esoteric seriously. It would be some time before the two learned how to live together. In the meantime, the polarity produced not a little tension.

My professors had different reactions to my new job. When I told Henry, the Aristotelian, where I was working, he laughed in the peculiarly uninhibited way he had and reminded me again that all that sort of thing was rubbish. Joseph, who was deeply religious and interested in some aspects of the "new spirituality," as some New Age beliefs were beginning to be called, took advantage of my position at the second-hand shop and asked if I could purchase some items for him using my discount. Daniel's response was something different. I've mentioned that he was my age and that, if this wasn't his first teaching position, it was certainly one of his first. I was one of his best students, and we had already discussed universities I could possibly apply to when it came time to move on to graduate work. He had mentioned one of his own professors to me, and thought he might be of some help. As in other aspects of life, in the academic world who you know is very important.

I'm not sure how it came about, but one afternoon Daniel and the professor he had spoken with me about turned up at the shop. I was surprised to see him. It was not the sort of place I imagined he would visit. He was there to see me, and he'd brought his professor along to introduce me to him.

My memory of the visit is vague; what I can recall is walking them around, showing them the different sections—astrology there, alchemy here—I even took them to our modest section on Western philosophy. I can't recall a particular remark, but as we went along Daniel and his professor would comment about what they saw. The tone was one of gentle dismissal—with raised eyebrows, shaking heads, and muffled chuckles—and I came to see that it was assumed I would share it. I don't recall any specific disagreement, and one might think, given that I was in my "philosopher in the New Age bookshop" mode, that I would join their mood. But I found myself being oddly noncommittal, not wanting to agree with them but not wanting to openly disagree either. It wasn't the time or place for me to explain exactly what I did think about the things the shop was selling—but I also didn't want to just go along with their remarks.

I can't say anything particular happened after this, only that I got the impression that I somehow hadn't made the grade with his professor, and that Daniel somehow felt he had made a mistake in suggesting I meet him. Suggesting a covert New Age fellow traveler as good graduate material may not have reflected well on him. My two worlds had briefly come together, and the difference between them was made fairly clear.

It was philosophy, though, that led to my becoming interested in someone who had a whole section to himself in the shop. This was Rudolf Steiner. I had, of course, come across Steiner in my reading, but had relegated him, with Madame Blavatsky and Theosophy, to the less credible and less interesting areas of the occult world. (Neither Gurdjieff nor Crowley had anything good to say about either of them, and at the time I took my cues from them.) It would take my writing a book about Blavatsky to see how much I thought I knew about her was merely myth or hearsay, and what an important figure she actually was.[10] I would also write a book about Steiner, and the impetus for doing that began with my coming across a photograph of the original Goetheanum—a fantastic work of "anthroposophical architecture"—in a book about expressionist architecture.[11]

I had become very interested in German expressionism, an important art and literary movement of the early twentieth century, and took a particular interest in the work of architects like Bruno Taut and Erich Mendelsohn, whose strange Einstein Tower I would visit in Potsdam, Germany, in 1996. With its fascination with curves, spirals, and flowing organic forms, expressionist architecture had much in common with Art Nouveau, which also interested me.[12]

Although anthroposophists will disagree, Steiner's first Goetheanum shared much with both expressionism and Art Nouveau, and I was struck by its strange, dreamlike contours and absence of straight lines. Sadly, the building, which was made of the same wood used to make violins and which Steiner and his students, coming from all the warring nations, labored to erect during the dark days of WWI, burned down on New Year's Eve, 1922, possibly the target of arson. Today, a rather different second Goetheanum, this one made of concrete, stands as the center of the anthroposophical movement, in Dornach, Switzerland.

When I learned that Steiner was the architect behind the Goetheanum—which at first I had trouble pronouncing—I was

---

10. *Madame Blavatsky: The Mother of Modern Spirituality* (New York: Tarcher/Penguin, 2012).

11. *Rudolf Steiner: An Introduction to His Life and Ideas* (New York: Tarcher/Penguin, 2007).

12. At the time, I often visited the Robert Gore Rifkind Center for Expressionist Studies located at the Los Angeles County Museum of Art. I remember one season devoted to expressionist cinema, and watching rare films such as Frank Wisbar's 1936 occult classic *Fährmann Maria*, one of the last films to be made before the industry was Nazified.

impressed and wanted to know more about him. Finding myself at the Bodhi Tree was a good way to do this. He had practically a whole wall to himself, with several shelves given over to works by his followers. At first this put me off. Steiner was a polymath. Not only had he designed the two Goetheanums (named after the great German poet and scientist, Johann Wolfgang von Goethe), Steiner had also developed a whole system of education, as well as methods of organic farming, well in advance of our interest in such things. His ideas also informed a range of "health and well-being" products, as herbal and other natural remedies were beginning to be called. Steiner was also a seer, a visionary who claimed to be able to read the Akashic records, the occult history of the universe inscribed on some kind of intangible cosmic ether.

With all these accomplishments, I wondered why he wasn't published by mainstream publishers; everything seemed to come from one anthroposophical press or other. That suggested he was a crank of sorts. But then, he had designed and built that remarkable structure . . .

Looking at the Steiner section in the shop one day, I saw he had written a book about Nietzsche.[13] That was interesting. He had also written a book about philosophy.[14] Not being busy at the moment and curious about what he had to say, I took it down from the shelf and paged through it. I can't remember now exactly what I read, but it had to do with Kant and his theory of knowledge.

Briefly put and grossly simplified, Kant believed that we never know the world in itself, that is, when we are not observing it; we only know the world through what he called "categories," the necessary conditions for any knowledge whatsoever. Kant's categories include time, space, cause and effect, and others. They are like a pair of glasses we must wear in order to see the world. But we never see what the world is like *without* the glasses. So, we can never know if it really is in any way

---

13. Rudolf Steiner, *Friedrich Nietzsche: A Fighter Against His Time* (1895).
14. Rudolf Steiner, *The Riddles of Philosophy* (1914).

like the way we see it. It is rather like the old conundrum about whether a tree falling in the forest when no one is there makes a sound or not. We can never know, because in order to do so, we—or a tape recorder, which is the same thing—would need to be there, which would invalidate the experiment.

Such puzzles may suggest that philosophers have a lot of time on their hands. But Kant's ideas had a tremendous impact on Western thought. And some sensitive individuals, like the German poet Heinrich von Kleist, were so dismayed by the idea that we can never know reality as it "really" is, they were driven to suicide by it (I tell Kleist's story in *Dead Letters*). Others, like Steiner, had a more robust response. Steiner refused to accept that there were any barriers to our knowledge of the world, a belief he shared with his hero, Goethe (Steiner got his start editing Goethe's scientific writing). His own experiences of perceiving the spiritual world—what he called "supersensible perception"—told him as much. So, instead of blowing his brains out as Kleist did, he argued that Kant was wrong, and went on to develop an epistemology and methodology to prove it.

This fascinated me. Like Steiner, I could not accept the kind of fractured view of human consciousness that Kant, for all his importance, bequeathed the Western mind. That was one reason why I became interested in Hegel, who also rejected this view and developed his sometimes-baffling philosophy in reaction to it. Ouspensky, too, in *Tertium Organum*, argued that we can have experience not only of the world of effects (the everyday world of the senses), but also of the world of causes (the noumenal world behind that of the senses)—this was the location of the fourth dimension and the miraculous. So, I had some idea of what Steiner was getting at.

But then I would look at another of his books or transcripts of his lectures, and a kind of "tilt" sign would go off in my head. Steiner certainly had some outlandish ideas. He spoke about the Buddha on Mars, or about ancient Atlantis—descriptions of which he would relate from the Akashic records—or about the "life between death and rebirth" and our experiences there. Like Madame Blavatsky, he spoke of conditions on Earth long before it was a solid planet. Or he gave instructions on how to read to the dead.

Some ideas were less fantastic but strange nonetheless. Steiner believed children shouldn't be taught to read until they were at least seven years old. I had certainly jumped the gun on that. He was also not keen on the cinema, believing that watching films would interfere with our capacity for "supersensible perception." Television wasn't around in Steiner's day, but he no doubt would have seen it as an even worse distraction. Given that I had grown up with my eyes practically glued to the screen—when they weren't to a comic or a book—I imagined I was most likely doomed.

Yet, his remarks about epistemology were cogent, even if I found his writing very "tough sledding," as a colleague at the bookshop used to say. It's not that Steiner's prose was difficult—after all, I was making my way through Hegel and Heidegger, and neither of them were page-turners. Steiner was simply dull. Nevertheless, I persevered, and starting reading from his lectures at random. And after a while I developed a taste for them. Steiner had taken the structure of Theosophy—with its "root races" and ancient civilizations and previous Earth "incarnations"—and added to it a good helping of German Idealism, which I had been studying, as well as an overarching Christian theme. I wasn't taken with his Christocentric view, as we would say today, but his emphasis on thinking as a spiritual activity—one that offered proof of free will and the irreducibleness of the "I," as he argued in *The Philosophy of Freedom* (1894)—made an impression on me. As did his ideas about the evolution of consciousness.

I was intrigued. I wanted to know how on one page Steiner could offer a powerful, original, and, as far as I was concerned, philosophically supported critique of Kant—a rejection of his belief that there are limits to knowledge—and on another could make unverifiable statements about life in Atlantis or what happens when we die. Gurdjieff made more than a few preposterous assertions—such as that the moon is alive and growing into a planet like the Earth, and that human souls feed it—so strange ideas weren't new to me. What I wanted to know was, how could Steiner possibly *know* what he claimed to know?

Did I ever find an answer to that question? I believe I do go some way toward arriving at one in my book about Steiner, written many years later. But well before writing that, I had an experience that, if it did not answer my question, gave me an idea of the form that answer might take. I mention it in my book about Steiner, but it bears repeating here.

I had been reading Steiner's book, *Knowledge of the Higher Worlds and Its Attainment* (1904), a kind of how-to guide to supersensible perception, and practicing some of the exercises Steiner gives in it. On a walk, I found myself in a garden and looked at a rose, and thought of Rilke's line about a peculiar meditative state that had come over him which he said was like "the interior of a rose." As I thought this, I remembered Steiner's suggestion to meditate on the processes of growth in a plant, and how this can help make our own thoughts, too often static and dead, more supple and mobile. As I did this an odd thing happened. I felt that my perception of the rose had changed. I was no longer simply looking at it; I felt as if my thoughts, my consciousness, was cradling it, holding it gently, as one might a small, living thing. The experience was fleeting but nonetheless definite, as if a picture I was looking at had come to life for a brief moment.

Since Descartes, we have looked at consciousness as a kind of mirror, simply reflecting the world. Steiner argued that this was incorrect—our minds *reach out* and take hold of the world in the same way that our hands can take hold of a table, or my hand could the rose. This was essentially the same idea Wilson had, of the intentionality of consciousness, its active character. The experience was not unlike the moments of "seeing" I've mentioned, except that it was somehow more tactile, as if my consciousness was somehow touching the rose. And the converse was also true—I could "feel" my consciousness, as if it exerted a kind of very subtle pressure on what it was looking at.[15]

If practicing some of the exercises in Steiner's book brought this on—aided, perhaps, by a relaxed state and the thought of Rilke—then it suggested that his ideas about the relationship between consciousness and the world being much more participatory than we believed deserved attention. Our inner world is not as separate from our outer one as we have been led to believe. The barrier between the two is permeable, and is breached in mystic, aesthetic, and poetic moments. Did this mean that Steiner's claims about previous conditions of existence and earlier civilizations were true? Hardly. But it did suggest, to me, at least, that with his notion of supersensible perception, Steiner may have been on to something.

Others had the same idea. And a development at the store brought me into contact with some of them.

IN 1991, THE BODHI TREE DECIDED to bring out a catalogue. In advance of the online economy, still some years away, and hearkening back to the catalogues for Golden Age comics that I coveted in my youth, that winter it launched itself as "The Quarterly Bookstore by Mail," with what became known as the Bodhi Tree Review. Rather like a New Age Sears & Roebuck, the catalogue listed everything in stock. With sections ranging from New Age Philosophy, Jung, and Spiritual Quests to Eating Disorders, Recovery, and Astrology, it was like having the bookshop in

15. I should mention that at the time I was also reading quite a few of the novelist John Cowper Powys's self-help books, written in the 1930s and '40s—titles like *The Meaning of Culture* (1929), *In Defence of Sensuality* (1930), and *The Art of Happiness* (1935). These and other of Powys's philosophical works promote a view of consciousness that is very much along the lines of Steiner's and Wilson's, although presented in his own highly personal way. Its essence is the belief that one can train one's consciousness to extract a kind of pleasure or value from the simplest objects. This is done by recognizing the active nature of consciousness, its ability to reach out and take hold of its objects. Readers of Powys's novels, such as *A Glastonbury Romance* (already mentioned) and *Wolf Solent* (1929), will be familiar with the essentially *erotic* character of their protagonists' relationship to nature and the physical world.

print (and without the incense) delivered to your door. Along with what was for sale, it carried interviews, news items (such as the Dalai Lama announcing that 1991 was "the year of Tibet"), and book reviews.

For the first issue, I was asked if I would like to write some reviews. I had by then many months—years, really—of a protracted not-yet-a-writer writer's block behind me. I can still remember agonizing afternoons when I had the time and freedom to write, yet when I sat in front of the proverbial blank page I felt a cramp in my consciousness from which nothing emerged except an immediately discarded sentence or paragraph. After a few hours of this frustration, I would get up and take a long walk through the nondescript backstreets, working off the energy I should have put into writing but somehow could not. Because of these times, I am atypical of most writers, who usually work either in the morning or the night. I have to fill up the afternoon. If I am not working, say, between noon and five or six, an anxiousness, a kind of panic, comes over me, when I feel that I am not justifying my existence. (Whether the work I do produce during those hours justifies it or not is another story.) We might say that what finally drove me into writing was existential dread.

I agreed to write the reviews, provided I chose the books. The two I chose were not about crystals, channeling, past lives, or yoga. One was a history of the Western intellectual tradition from its inception with the Greeks to its apparent breakdown in postmodernism. The other was a bleak epitaph to the New Age, which its author had helped bring to life.

The philosopher Richard Tarnas had for many years been associated with the Esalen Institute, the alternative spiritual center and retreat that had started in the early 1960s in Big Sur, California, and which I passed whenever I took the Pacific Coast Highway on my Los Angeles–San Francisco jaunts.[16] At the time the catalogue came out, along with

---

16. Although I passed the Esalen Institute several times during my years in California, I never visited. In 2019, I finally did when I was invited to take part in a symposium there on the "perennial philosophy" that took place just before the advent of COVID-19.

Stanislav Grof, a pioneer of psychedelic research, Tarnas was one of the central figures at the California Institute of Integral Studies, a more academic venture that grew out of the earlier American Academy of Asian studies, which began in San Francisco in the 1950s. Tarnas worked on *The Passion of the Western Mind* (1991), one of the books I chose to review, from 1980 to 1990. That decade's worth of effort showed.

The book is a magisterial overview of the history of Western thought, from the earliest hints of rational inquiry emerging during what the philosopher Karl Jaspers called the "Axial Age"—circa 500 BC—to its contemporary eclipse in the hands of Derrida, Foucault, and the other postmodern thinkers I had been reading for the past few years. But, where the deconstructionists and postmodernists eagerly anticipated our intellectual breakdown and looked forward to a gleeful plunge into philosophical anarchy, Tarnas saw the current fashion for nihilism as a symptom of a larger issue. It was, in fact, a sign of recovery, or at least of the last stages of the disease that had led the rational mind into a cul-de-sac.

Tarnas argued that the Western intellect's *auto-da-fé*, in a rigid scientific materialism that sequestered consciousness solely within our individual skulls, and a self-destructive postmodern anti-philosophy that pulled the rug out from any rational thought, were the end product of a necessary but now-debilitating separation of mind and world—the kind I had balked at in Kant and which we had been saddled with since Descartes. This split was needed in order for the human mind to free itself from its embeddedness in the cosmos, so it could develop its powers. But now it had left us high and dry, master of a disenchanted nature but lost in a meaningless universe. But this alienation from our roots, Tarnas believed, was the preliminary to a return to them, yet at a higher turn of the evolutionary spiral—an idea that had attracted me to Hegel.

Taking a cue from Jung's notion of the archetypes—collective psychic blueprints that evolve over time—Tarnas argued for the kind of participatory epistemology I had found in Steiner, and which he revealed in many other thinkers. The book traces the history of this counter-tradition to the mainstream Western intellectual heritage, finding it in the Neoplatonists, the Romantics, and others. The widespread grassroots movement of popular spirituality emerging in the last decade of the century was also a sign that the need to overcome the isolation of the Western ego was not an abstract idea but something felt by many people. We were, as the title of my review had it, taking "the long way home," and the crisis in Western consciousness was a sign that we were nearing our destination.

The book did what very few books were doing at the time—it offered hope and ended on a note of optimism. It was a thrilling, inspiring work, and I said so in my review, calling it a work of "high adventure and intellectual daring." When the paperback edition came out, I was gratified to see that I was among the many writers and thinkers singing its praises who were quoted on the opening pages. The book went on to be a bestseller—a remarkable feat for a work of intellectual history—and continues to attract new readers more than thirty years after its publication.

Someone had sent Tarnas or his agent a copy of the review and one day they came to the shop, wanting to see me. I believe it was his agent who said that my review should have been in the *New York Times.* I agreed. Not long after this, Tarnas invited me to contribute to *ReVision*, a journal he was editing. He said they were planning a series of "life work reviews" of important contemporary thinkers. Could I think of anyone I'd like to write about? Yes, I could: Colin Wilson.

Soon enough, my essay "From Outsider to Post-Tragic Man: The Work of Colin Wilson" appeared in *ReVision*, as well as some further book reviews. The essay would later make up one of the *Two Essays on Colin Wilson* (1994) that Colin Stanley, Wilson's bibliographer and friend, would publish a few years later in his Pauper's Press Colin Wilson Studies series.[17] Although not much more than a pamphlet, it

---

17. I would also contribute to another Pauper's Press release, sharing covers with the philosopher John Shand. *Colin Wilson as Philosopher & Faculty X, Consciousness and the Transcendence of Time* (1996) includes a lecture I gave on Faculty X at the Philosophical Research Society in 1995.

would be my first published book. Another surprise was that the philosopher Robert McDermott, whose *The Essential Steiner* (1984) had helped me get a grip on some of Steiner's more challenging ideas, was one of Tarnas's colleagues at the CIIS.

The other book I had chosen to review also had our intellectual and spiritual history in view. But where *The Passion of the Western Mind* saw the New Age, however dubious, as a sign of a positive hunger for a new world view, William Irwin Thompson's *The American Replacement of Nature* (1991) was a discouraging if vigorous jeremiad about the failure of the New Age to bring about any change. Thompson's insights into this, however despairing, were worth considering, as he was one of the few academics who took the New Age seriously and, in his writings, helped it along.

Thompson had gotten his PhD at Cornell and had taught at MIT. But in the 70s he dropped out of academia and started the Lindisfarne Association, a loose group of intellectuals dedicated to the advance of what they called a "planetary culture." Thompson had written several books promoting this idea, and I had read them; one I remember making a strong impression on me at the time was *The Time Falling Bodies Take to Light* (1981), which looked at the rise of civilization out of the mists of prehistory. Thompson had high hopes for his new "planetary culture," but by the late '80s, his faith in a positive change coming over humanity had curdled. What remained was a shrill, near-hysterical tirade against what he called the "Disneyization" of the world.

When I look at the review now, as well as the one of Tarnas's book, I am half-dismayed, half-impressed that many, if not all, of their concerns are still with us: artificial life and intelligence, bio-engineering, virtual reality taking over from the "real thing," and other sources of technological angst. I'm dismayed that we are still confronting them, and impressed that thirty-plus years ago, minds were prescient enough to see the writing on the wall. Thompson did, and it drove him into a rage.

In many ways, the closest neighbor to the book in my own reading is the last work of H. G. Wells, *Mind at the End of Its Tether* (1945), a dark, depressing admission that his vision of a rational, scientifically ordered world was a pipe dream. We might say that Thompson's work, although radically different, shares with Wells's the pain of a bankrupt dream mixed with the self-inflicted bruises of a repentant idealist.

I don't know if Thompson ever read the review. I didn't meet him, but years later, shortly before he died in 2020, he came across my book *The Secret Teachers of the Western World*—modeled, to some extent, on Tarnas's masterpiece—and provided an endorsement for it on Amazon. We corresponded for a time, and I was glad to have the opportunity to let him know how much I had appreciated his work over the years.

For the second issue of the catalogue, which came out in spring of 1992, I was asked to review some books again. My choice this time was Leonard Shlain's fascinating work *Art and Physics* (1992). Shlain was a San Francisco heart specialist with an interest in consciousness. In *Art And Physics*, he argues that, throughout history, advances in physics have been anticipated by changes in art. Artists somehow know in advance the kind of breakthroughs physicists will be making, but, rather than express them in rational, logical thought, they instead create pictures or tell a story. To make his argument, Shlain drew on research into the division of labor of our cerebral hemispheres, which has the left cutting the truly seamless fabric of reality into manageable pieces (one-thing-at-a-time), while the right gives us the total, global picture (everythingallatonce).

This holistic view, which Shlain relates to Einstein's ideas about the illusory character of time, is what enables the artist to, as it were, dream in advance of reality and so see what is on its way before it arrives.

Again, looking at this review to refresh my memory, I see that I am still writing about the differences in how our two brains experience the world, something I had first come across in the work of Colin Wilson a decade earlier, and which today I add to, drawing on the work of Iain McGilchrist. In his second book, *The Alphabet Versus the Goddess* (1998), Shlain argues that the rise of literacy in the second millennium BC promoted left-brain dominance and ensured the "superior" status of men—which led to the downgrading of the more feminine, image-based right brain and the women who possessed them. Along with McGilchrist's *The Master and His Emissary* (2009), *The Alphabet and the Goddess* was one of the books I drew on in writing *The Secret Teachers of the Western World*.[18] I never met Shlain, but we corresponded for time, and in 2003 he kindly provided an endorsement for my book *A Secret History of Consciousness*. He died in 2009.

I DIDN'T CONTRIBUTE to later issues of the review. In 1993, I left the Bodhi Tree and began the series of misadventures that would lead to my leaving Los Angeles for London. Why writing the reviews for the catalogue broke my writing deadlock I can't say. But it did, and soon I began to contribute articles to magazines like *Gnosis: A Journal of the Western Inner Tradition* and *Quest*, published by the Theosophical Society, as well as many others. The long years of wanting to write—a good decade of them—were over. Now, new challenges would present themselves. And soon enough, they did.

18. Another was *The Ever-Present Origin*, the *magnum opus* of Jean Gebser which I came across one day in the used book branch. I write at length about Gebser's work in *A Secret History of Consciousness*, and his notion of evolving "structures of consciousness" informs much of my book *The Secret Teachers of the Western World*.

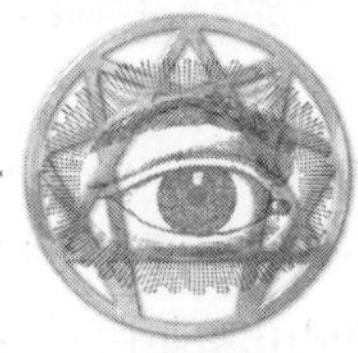

12
Living in the Real World

Before I left the Bodhi Tree, a few other things of importance happened. One was that I finished my degree at university, earning my BA in 1990. I intended to carry on with school, but with my interest and background in continental philosophy, my choices were fairly limited. At the time, most American universities were dominated by the "Anglo-American" school, coming out of logical positivism and linguistics analysis. Heidegger, Nietzsche, Sartre—the philosophers I was most familiar with—were not on their menus. I had neither interest in nor talent for that approach. Deconstructionism and postmodernism had found a home in comparative literature departments, but the followers of Ayer, Russell, Frege, and their epigone would have none of it. I was not keen on deconstructing anything myself, but I accepted that, if I wanted to continue studying philosophy in order to teach it, I would most likely have to put up with those who were at whatever perch I found.

For a time I thought of studying in Germany, although most likely this would have meant tutelage with the Frankfurt School, which was then represented by the philosopher Jürgen Habermas. I had taken courses in German at the Goethe Institute in Los Angeles—it was, in fact, during one class that we heard of the Berlin Wall coming down. As you can imagine, there was much celebration. But my German wasn't good enough and still remains fairly rough (*Ich verstehe mere Deutsch als Ich sprechen kann*). Another possibility was Stony Brook University in New York, which had one of the best departments in continental philosophy in the States. They published a great deal in phenomenology and existentialism, much of which I had read, and I had heard good things about them. Another possibility was Northwestern University in Illinois, where the German scholar Erich Heller had taught for many years. His books *The Disinherited Mind*, *In the Age of Prose*, *The Artist's Journey Into the Interior*, and others had made a powerful impression on me, and I continue to go back to them. But by this time, he had long been retired; he died in 1990.

All of these possibilities, however, came to naught. The reason was that I had become involved with one of my colleagues at the shop. We started as friends, became lovers, and not long after married. It didn't last, and, as I mention at the start of this memoir, it was the collapse of our marriage that sent me first across America, and then the Atlantic. But I am getting ahead of myself. There is still quite a bit to tell before I made my way to the UK.

Once I began to write articles and book reviews, I took any opportunity I could to see print, in a way making up for lost time. I pitched ideas and accepted any invitations to review. I was happy to do this, and nothing pleased me better than to see my name as the author of some article or book review. It was gratifying to be able to show my colleagues at the shop that I was published in *Gnosis* that month, or in *Quest*, or in some other magazine. I even helped a customer, a Deepak Chopra wannabe, edit a manuscript he was sending to a publisher. Nothing came of it, but the practice was useful. But as pleasing as it was to see my name in print, or to have others see that I could turn a phrase, it was not enough to satisfy my desire to become a writer. I was closing in on forty. A few articles were nice, but I needed to write a book. I hadn't, and I hadn't any ideas for one, and began to wonder if I ever would.

I began to identify with characters I called "late bloomers"—writers who didn't start their careers until relatively late in life. Henry Miller, whom I hadn't read in years, was one. He starved and struggled for years in New York and Paris, and didn't publish his first work until his forties. Another writer, a more important one than Miller, was the Scot David Lindsay, who didn't produce his first book, the unclassifiable work of genius *A Voyage to Arcturus*, until he was in his forties as well. Owen Barfield, a close friend of C. S. Lewis and a follower of Steiner, whom I learned about through Robert McDermott's *The Essential Steiner*, started out writing in his twenties, but couldn't make a living at it and had to take a place in the family's law firm. He came back to writing in his sixties, producing a number of important philosophical works on language and consciousness.

There were others, and I came to see that there was a precedent for late starters. I began to identify with my astrological sign, Capricorn, and read up quite a bit about them. They tended to be serious, determined hard workers for whom accomplishment is all-important. They have a strong sense of long-term purpose, and are willing to put up with a lot in order to fulfil it. They may take some time achieving their goals, but they invariably get there in the end. It helped to remember that the late bloomer Henry Miller was one. The challenge, though, was to produce something that made up for the long gestation period. Could I do that?

I started writing what I hoped would be a novel. It was an occult thriller, and I borrowed the title from Gurdjieff. *The Struggle of the Magicians* pitted a character based on Rudolf Steiner, the good magician, against one based on Aleister Crowley, the bad magician. They came to psychic blows over the destiny of a female clairvoyant whom the Crowley character wanted to use to create a break in the dimensional barriers that would allow a Lovecraftian entity of some sort entry into our plane. It was set in London in the 1920s and, although it was nothing more than apprentice work, I enjoyed creating the atmosphere and writing the dialogue. I never finished it—it took on the character of pastiche after a while—but on more than one occasion, I experienced that wonderful corroboration of one's creativity: when one's characters take on a life of their own. Once or twice this happened, and it made me realize that, once set in motion, the creative imagination has its own rules and necessities, and one can only follow them or give up.

For a time, I gave readings from some chapters at a few coffee houses in Hollywood. The early '90s saw a revival of coffee house culture in LA, with yuppie entrepreneurs filling empty spaces with second-hand furniture in which fashionable clientele sat and perused Proust or Kerouac while sipping overpriced cappuccinos. I enjoyed giving the readings and found that I was very good at it. My time as a musician meant that I was comfortable in front of people and that I knew how to work a crowd. I was relaxed and casual, and the experience helped later when I came to London, where, over the years, I have given many talks.

What I read was rather different than most of the fare, which tended to be stream-of-consciousness poetry or a social rant of some sort. I told a story and, however primitive and amateurish my technique, I could see that people were interested and wanted to know what happened next. Although I have not gone back and tried to write fiction again, something nonfiction writers often turn to in their "sunset years," I do try my best to give my books, whether biographical, historical, or philosophical, a sense of narrative, a direction, and to instill in the reader a need to turn the page. If I am able to do this, it is because I keep in mind that the reader is under no obligation to devote his or her free time to me, no matter how brilliant what I am saying may be. My first obligation is to keep him entertained, which simply means being readable.[1] If I can do that, then I am halfway to having aroused his interest in whatever ideas I am trying to get across.

F, WHOM I REFER TO as my "future ex-wife" in *Dreaming Ahead of Time*, worked upstairs at the Bodhi Tree, where the offices and storerooms were located. I didn't see much of her, but, somehow, we got to

---

1. Another reason that I delayed applying to any schools after receiving my degree is that the papers I submitted as examples of my work were, according to my professor Joseph, "too readable," too essayistic and personal. "They aren't looking for Wittgensteins," he told me.

know each other. I liked her, and although she wasn't classically pretty, she was cute and had a charming smile. She was half-Japanese and it showed—combined with her Eastern European other half, it made for a certain exotic look. It turned out we had some things in common. She spoke German and had studied in Germany for a time. She was interested in classical music and had studied the violin. She read quite a bit and was interested in Jung. But what made the most impression on me at first was the fact that she'd had some clairvoyant dreams about me before we knew each other. She mentioned a few things, and I was struck by their accuracy. As mentioned above, I write about some of the dream experiences we had while married and afterward in *Dreaming Ahead of Time*, and an interested reader can find them there.

Not long after our getting together, F left the Bodhi Tree. She had found a good, well-paying position at Sony Studios. By then we were living together and, for a time, in love—or in something approximating it. I hadn't decided on what to do about my future. I had grown attached to F and didn't want to leave her. I was also unsure about continuing with philosophy. Daniel had suggested that my real talent was for the history of ideas; some of the books I went on to write may suggest he was right. I continued to write articles and book reviews but I was beginning to feel that I should be doing something better than working at a bookshop. Call it ego, but I felt I had powers and talents that were not being put to their best use. I wanted something more.

The Bodhi Tree was a very good place to work, but its coziness could also be something of a trap. Some of my colleagues had worked there for many years, and would stay until the place closed down. It paid the bills, wasn't demanding, and was often more like an extended family than a workplace. But it could be too comfortable. I didn't like envisioning myself still there, a few years down the line. At one point I got in touch with the "mind-body-spirit" publisher Jeremy Tarcher, who was based in Los Angeles, about finding some sort of position there. He said there wasn't anything available and that, frankly, they usually took on younger people when there was. Ironically, some years later,

Tarcher, having been acquired by Penguin, became one of my publishers.

I went through several months of indecision. The idea of finding some place in academia still lingered. The thought of becoming a Waldorf teacher—the name of Steiner's system of alternative education—briefly flitted through my head, but I couldn't swallow anthroposophy and quickly rejected it. For a time, my love of German literature led me to think I should pursue that, but a sense of wanting to do something that would have some kind of positive effect on the world—to help in some way the struggle for greater consciousness—suggested this was not the way. I imagine I was an idealist in search of a cause.

I had continued to read Whitehead over the years, at one point working through *Process and Reality*, as difficult and obscure a work as any Heidegger produced. One contemporary philosopher whose work on Whitehead I had read and enjoyed was David Ray Griffin, who was to become one of the chief proponents of a 9/11 conspiracy theory. At the time, this was far in the future, and Griffin's books, like *The Reenchantment of Science* (1988), *Spirituality and Society* (1988), *Archetypal Process* (1990), written in collaboration with James Hillman, and others appealed to me in their attempt to envision a positive postmodernism, using Whitehead's "process philosophy" as a foundation, in response to the nihilistic brand exported by the French. I remember one week when, taking some time off from work, I rented a cabin in Idyllwild in the San Jacinto Mountains, not far from Palm Springs, and brought some of his books along with me. I can recall sitting in the sun on a rock outcropping and trying to "prehend" the scene around me.

Griffin taught at Claremont University, not far from LA, and I decided to get in touch with him. We arranged a visit, and one day I drove out there and spent the afternoon on the campus. My enthusiasm for studying with Griffin, though, was quickly dampened. In the first place, if I wanted to study Whitehead, it would mean earning a degree in theology. This would have been even more useless than the one I already had in philosophy. I believed Whitehead was one of the most important and most ignored philosophers of the last century—and still do—but I had no interest in theology.

But even more than this, Griffin's demeanor during my interview was far from encouraging. I was still an idealist and enthusiast for the life of the mind. He had lived it for a time, and the sense I got from him was that it was not as fulfilling as he may once have believed it would be. I had gotten the same feeling from some of my professors, but at the time was still hopeful that such a life could be possible. I remember him remarking something along the lines of, "You think you will have interesting and stimulating conversations with your colleagues, but you don't. You think people will be interested in your insights and ideas, but they aren't. Not even people in your family." He did suggest, though, that we had something in common—he, too, had been a musician in his early years; if I recall correctly, he had played the trumpet.

I left our meeting much less interested in studying Whitehead than when I'd arrived. But I did sit in on a class on Whitehead, and got into an exchange with the professor.

"Where did you read so much Whitehead?" she asked.

"At home," I said.

For a time, I thought I might find a place at the CIIS. I had kept in touch with Richard Tarnas, and one weekend drove to San Francisco to meet with him. I took in a few classes. One was with Stanislav Grof, who lectured on his theory that the collective mind was experiencing something like Otto Rank's "birth trauma" but on a cosmic scale, and which Tarnas had used as a paradigm in *The Passion of the Western Mind*. I also sat in on a class by Charlene Spretnak, a feminist philosopher whose *States of Grace* (1991) I had reviewed for *ReVision*, but I can't say that I remember much of it. Oddly enough, one class I enjoyed a great deal was on Marx. I can't remember the instructor's name but he certainly made dialectical materialism more understandable for me, although not any more convincing.

To study there would mean moving to San Francisco and starting over again. When I asked Tarnas if there were any grants or scholarships I could apply for, he shook his head and said no. I was surprised at this, and left a bit crestfallen. Years later, while on holiday in Ascona, in the Italian-speaking part of Switzerland, I was working on my book on Jung. Tarnas was there as well, and he invited me on a tour of Casa Gabriella on the shores of Lago Maggiore, where the fabled Eranos gatherings over which Jung presided were held. A few years after that, I would teach several online courses based on my books for the CIIS.

Sometime after my visit to the CIIS, Colin Wilson was in the States on a lecture tour and F and I went to San Francisco to hear his talk for the local anthroposophical society. It was at this talk that I met Robert McDermott. I had by this time published my long "life review" of Wilson in *ReVision*, and Colin had read and enjoyed it. At dinner at McDermott's home, we sat around the table with him and his wife, Tarnas and his wife, and Colin and Joy. What I remember most of that evening is Tarnas and McDermott being impressed that, while playing with Iggy Pop, I had opened for the Rolling Stones.

Later that trip, I attended a workshop Colin gave on inducing "peak experiences." His method was to combine the kind of deep breathing relaxation exercises that Wilhelm Reich had taught his patients—which we did lying down—with a curious mental exercise Colin called the "pen trick."

This consisted of taking a pen—or any handy small object—and holding it in front of you. The idea is to focus one's consciousness solely on the pen, concentrating on it as though your life depended on it. Then, when you are completely focused on the pen, relaxing your concentration and letting whatever is in the background in. So, intense concentration and then total relaxation. After one does this a few times, a kind of strain begins to appear in the space between the eyes. It becomes painful and one wants to stop. But if you continue, something odd happens. Suddenly the pain goes and you slip into a kind of peak experience. Or, at least, that was the idea.

The "pen trick" was based on an account the poet Wordsworth gave to Thomas De Quincey when De Quincey asked Wordsworth how he wrote his poetry. Colin used it to illustrate the differences between the right and left brain. Wordsworth told De Quincey that he had no idea how his poetry came to him. Then, Wordsworth put his ear to the ground in order to hear the approach of the mail coach from Keswick—they were in the Lake District at the time. When he was done, he looked up and saw a star, which appeared incredibly beautiful. "Now I know!" he told De Quincey. "Whenever I concentrate on something having nothing to do with poetry, and then relax, the first thing I see strikes me as remarkably beautiful." So, left-brain concentration followed by right-brain relaxation equals the peak experience.

I don't know what anyone else there felt, but after doing the "pen trick" several times, I began to feel an odd giddiness and couldn't stop myself from laughing. Colin heard me, and I remember him saying that "strange things sometimes happen when practicing this." He was right.

I CAN'T SAY WHERE THE IDEA of applying to earn a MA in English Literature at the University of Southern California, in downtown Los Angeles, came from. Probably the fact that I could get there easily on the freeway had something to do with it. Looking back with the clarity of hindsight, the notion now seems like a complete nonstarter. But at the time, I was profoundly uncertain about what to do with my life and deeply troubled by a sense of frustration. I felt I had energies that were not being put to their proper use and I walked around in a constant state of tension. I continued to write articles and book reviews and worked on outlines for possible books—the articles and reviews were published but nothing came of the outlines. For a time, I tried to carry on a philosophical discussion group with people from the bookstore, but after a few evenings it was clear that people came to socialize, not to think. After one session, when one workmate, a follower of Eckankar—a spiritual teaching of questionable descent—held court all evening, I gave it up. There is no tactful way to tell someone that a belief they have devoted their life to is rubbish. It was clear the kind of exchange I hungered for would not be forthcoming, and its failure to appear left me only more unsatisfied.

F, of course, was aware of my plight—I'm sure I was not fun to be around, and I here offer a belated apology and also some gratitude for her patience. She had shown a friend, a retired academic, my life review of Wilson for *ReVision*. His response was that it was clear I could write and that I didn't need to earn another degree. But I was getting tired of the shop. Other people, too, were moving on, and I felt that I was wasting time. The fact that F was earning a considerable salary—much more than what I brought home—no doubt had something to do with my unease. But what comes back to me now is an exchange I had with the partner of one of her workmates.

We had lunch together, and the topic of my musical past came up. As a young boy, the workmate's partner had appeared in a few films and television shows, and so he, too, had a past as a performer. I can't recall his exact words, but at one point he made a remark, something along the lines of, "Yeah, I know what it's like to have 'been somebody' for a while, and then you're in the real world. Well, you get used to it."

What was it about this that troubled me? Was it simply that I resented his equating my past life as composer and performer with his as a child actor? That is, was my ego offended at his putting us on a par? No doubt. But what struck me was the idea that it was altogether possible he was right—that I used to be "somebody" but now wasn't, and would have to get used to the idea. Yet, more to the point, was the realization that my disquiet wasn't about who or what I used to be but what I wanted to become and wasn't yet. Would I ever? The clock was ticking and I was anxious to get somewhere, but no matter what I did, I seemed to stay in the same place.

At the time, my ego's immune system quickly rejected the thought, and psychological antibodies packed with high self-regard attacked it and drove it away. But not all of the infection had been cleansed. It would take a bit of time, but the dreaded possibility that sooner or later

I would have to join the former child star in the "real world" would return and I would feel its effects.

I DECIDED ON ENGLISH because that had always been my best subject. In any case, the philosophy department at USC had no time for Heidegger or Whitehead, and was adamantly in the Anglo-American tradition. I would find no home there. I thought I could bring philosophy in because I decided that I would write a thesis on "the metaphysical novel." The works I would choose were John Cowper Powys's *A Glastonbury Romance* (1932), David Lindsay's *A Voyage to Arcturus* (1920), and L. H. Myers's *The Root and the Flower* (1935), all of which I had read and knew well.

I had become familiar with them all from reading Colin Wilson, and I intended to apply Wilson's ideas about an existential criticism to their work. Myers, the son of F. W. H. Myers, one of the founders of the Society for Psychical Research, was another late bloomer, publishing his first novel—a strange work, *The Orissers* (1922)—in his forties. (He was also the most depressed of the lot, and committed suicide in his early sixties, during WWII.) Sometime into my first months in the department, I mentioned my idea to one of my professors. He looked at me and shook his head.

"This sounds interesting," he said. "But I'm afraid it won't do. In the first place, no one knows who these people are, so no one will want to read it. Why not try to focus on something more contemporary and popular?" This meant deconstructionism, postmodernism, postcolonialism, feminist theory, Marxist theory, and a few other fashionable schools that held absolutely no interest for me and which I very strongly felt to be the sort of thing I profoundly rejected.

In an earlier conversation, I had mentioned my interest in Colin Wilson. I hadn't thought to write on Wilson himself, assuming quite rightly that no one would take it seriously. That assessment was confirmed when my professor, hearing me say how highly I rated Wilson's work, replied, "Wilson is a good example of what can go wrong with autodidacts." I didn't bother to argue.

In order to apply for a position in the department, I had to take an aptitude test. I forget now exactly which one it was, but it was national and focused on verbal ability and knowledge of English Literature. I scored in the ninety-sixth percentile. This meant that, across the nation, among all the applicants for all university English departments that year, I scored in the top four percent. So, I knew my stuff. The English department at USC was glad to have me. My tuition was covered and I received a stipend—less than what I was earning at the bookshop, but enough to cover my share of our expenses. To earn it, I had to teach one class a day.

Technically, I hadn't yet taught a class, although I had helped several of Henry's students get through Plato and Descartes. The instructor who was my advisor was a large, friendly fellow—I forget his name—who had written a book about Henry Miller. When I told him that Miller had been one of my favorite writers, he said I had good taste. He was less happy when I mentioned that I had lost interest in Miller and now found him something of a windbag.[2] An essay by Orwell, "Inside the Whale," about Miller's essential nihilism had helped to change my mind. That I knew Orwell's essay impressed him; that I agreed with it did not.

Again, it was quite some time ago and I can't recall many names. But there was a feeling from early on that I really didn't fit in. Most of the other MA students in the department were women, and most of them were rather adamant feminists. But the real chasm between myself and my fellow students was that they were postmodern through and through. Radically so. The nascent political correctness I'd observed in

2. Although I was no longer reading Miller, I did get much out of a short book about Miller's time in Paris, *Henry Miller: Down and Out in Paris* (1974) by George Wickes and published by the Village Press. Wickes's account of Miller's writing routine was inspiring. Whatever we might think of his work, when it came to writing, Miller was one disciplined Capricorn.

my undergraduate days had by now become even more *de rigueur*. In the time between then and finding myself at USC, a sensibility that had once hovered on the fringe had now taken center stage. USC was a much bigger campus, with more students, so the anti-DWEM sentiment seemed stronger and more firmly in place. In conversation and in exchanges in class, it became more and more clear that I was very much out of step with the campus zeitgeist.

The worst thing one could be called at that time was an essentialist. This meant you believed there was an "essence" to human existence, some central, fundamental reality that remained at the core of one's being, as Plato and the classic philosophers had maintained. This was precisely the *bête noire* of the postmodernists, who, as mentioned, believed that everything was a social construct. It was created and produced by "culture" and was, in essence (!), historical. Truth, reality, and many other things were up for grabs—and my fellow students were out to grab them. This is why I would later write that the kind of "post-truth" and "alternative facts" Donald Trump introduced us to had their roots in the academy.

We have heard this argument before. It didn't take long for me to be outed as a kind of Platonist. I can remember one class on the Romantics when we analyzed Wordsworth's poem "I Wandered Lonely as a Cloud." The instructor was, not surprisingly, one of the "new historicists," and took a materialist view of literature. People did their deconstructive best to pull the loose thread of Wordsworth's sweet lyric, to get to its "real" meaning, unknown to the poet. I remember one of the very ardent feminists suggesting that the poem was "really" about Wordsworth's incestuous desire for his sister. For all I know, she may have been right. But that wasn't how I read it.

Earlier, I had asked if we would be looking at the work of the great Blake scholar Kathleen Raine, who wrote much about the Romantics. Years later, I would interview Raine not long before her death in 2003, and my book *Lost Knowledge of the Imagination* is dedicated to her. I was told we wouldn't be, so what followed should have been no surprise. When it came time for me to offer something, I suggested that, whatever it "really" meant, Wordsworth's poem was nevertheless beautiful, and shared in the Platonic essence of beauty. The lines then were clearly drawn, and postmodern equivalents of "Get thee behind me, Satan" were uttered. Later, at a department gathering, the same student who had suggested that Wordsworth wanted to sleep with his sister approached me and asked outright why I was taking the course. "What are you doing here?" she asked. That was all anyone said to me that evening. I don't remember what I said. It was, however, a good question—and I began to ask it myself.

A reader can get an idea of the atmosphere I had entered from an odd encounter I had with one of the female professors in the department—I don't remember her name, but she was known as a very strong critic of the "patriarchy." Our encounter took place outside the academy. At the time, F and I lived in an upmarket apartment complex in the Wilshire District, and one day I saw this professor in the laundry room in our basement. Apparently, we lived in the same building. I had met her only recently on campus, and so, recognizing her, I said hello.

This was a mistake. She looked at me as if I had pulled a knife on her or had made an indecent proposal. Or both. I explained who I was and where we had just met, but it made little difference. She didn't say a word, just stared at me like a deer caught in someone's headlights. I let it go at that, collected my laundry from the dryer, and left. Later, one of my male professors told me he had heard that I had accosted the ardent anti-patriarch when she was alone, cornering her in a basement. This, he told me, was simply not done. If saying a friendly hello is accosting someone, then yes, I did.

I can't say now that I truly enjoyed any of my studies at USC, but at the time I did try to make them interesting. The professor who cautioned me about chatting up feminist professors in dark laundry rooms taught a class in James Joyce. I had already read *Dubliners* (1914) and *Portrait of the Artist as a Young Man* (1916) years earlier, and did not much care for Joyce. But the other choices must have been even less appealing, so I settled for the lesser evil. At least I made my way through *Ulysses* (1922), which the professor scrutinized for evidence of Joyce's radical progressive politics. When it came time for a paper, I decided to avoid any political approach or any postmodern method, and instead focused on what other writers thought of the work. I based my account on Wyndham Lewis's devastating criticism of Joyce's prickly temperament in *Time and Western Man*, and followed up with J. B. Priestley's reading of the work in *Literature and Western Man* (1960). At the time, I did not pick two references with the phrase "Western man" in their titles on purpose, but no doubt some unconscious motivation was at work.

In a conversation with this professor later, he tried to let me know as gently as possible that if I intended to go on to teach, I was not going about it the right way. I remember him saying something along these lines: "We all remember when we first felt the magic of books, of literature, and the hope and idealism they produce. We'd all like literature to be about ideals and high values, and for it to be able to change our lives. Then we grow up and we see that it isn't really like that."

What it was really like, I don't remember him saying—if he did. But the point was that I was naïve to see literature in this romantic way. (I was in my thirties at the time, but he spoke to me as if I were fresh out of high school.) He tried to impress on me that teaching literature was a profession like any other. He might as well have said that it was no different than learning how to be a plumber or an electrician. (When I think of it now, he must have been a Marxist, one of the "tenured radicals" Allan Bloom had warned about.) I thought about this for a moment, then asked him if he didn't think I had the potential to do well. "Oh, there's no question that you have the goods," he said. Then, after a pause, "But do you *really* want to do this?"

Again, it was a good question. When I mentioned to my advisor that I hoped to be able to write and teach, he was surprised. "You think you'll have time to write?" he asked, incredulous. I wondered: had he thought this himself, then discovered it was unrealistic?

Some professors prompted more spontaneous responses. The one class in which anything like continental philosophy raised its head was one in comparative literature. Again, I can't remember the professor's name, but she was German and that alone suggested the class might be good, at least to me. I remember that writers I had read, like Robert Musil and Hermann Broch and some others, were on the agenda. I very much looked forward to this course, but was soon disenchanted with it. The professor took a very offhand and supercilious tone when speaking of Musil, and was outright dismissive when it came to Broch. I remember her saying that at one time his novels were very fashionable but that he was now considered overrated.

I was outraged. Broch's *The Sleepwalkers* (1930) and *The Death of Virgil* (1945) are two of the most important novels of the twentieth century. Who was she to say he was overrated? My disappointment soon turned to indignation. I didn't come here to listen to some academic pooh-pooh works of genius or make sarcastic remarks about their authors. I sat through it for several classes until I could no longer hold my temper, and finally let her know what I thought of her teaching style. I did well on my paper but my outburst did not help my final grade.

A more profitable exchange emerged from a class I took in film and literature with a professor whose name I do recall, Leo Braudy. Although I didn't know it at the time, Braudy had a prestigious career and had written several books exploring how changes in history affect the expression of human emotion in film, literature, and popular culture. I imagine his work falls under the all-purpose umbrella term "cultural studies," which at the time—and still today—could mean just about anything. His most well-known work is *The Frenzy of Renown: Fame and its History* (1986). During my time at USC, I didn't mention my pop star past to my professors; had I, Braudy might have asked me about it and gathered some insights for later editions of the book. My reason for not mentioning it was simple—by that time, I was simply tired of it and thought it better to keep it to myself. As it was, there were classes in Madonna and other pop celebrities offered on the curriculum, as part of "cultural studies," so, had I mentioned my background it might have done me some good.

Braudy's class focused on the 1950s. Among the films we watched was one of my favorites, the sci-fi classic *The Day The Earth Stood Still* (1951). I remember a text we read for class—its title escapes me—that interpreted the film as a kind of fascist propaganda, with the "elite," superior being from a more advanced race come to save us and solve our problems. I wrote a response to this, ignoring the political interpretation—which, as you might suspect, was all the rage in this class—and argued for sci-fi and fantasy as vehicles for exploring possibilities of human experience and development, a form of what I called "evolutionary fiction." The instructor's response was that it was obvious I could write but that I had clearly misunderstood the text. I can't remember the other films we watched, although one starred Marilyn Monroe, whom Braudy had coupled with Sylvia Plath, his reason being that both of them had committed suicide. (Years later, I would write about Plath in *Dead Letters*.)

Of the novels we read, I remember three in particular: Norman Mailer's *The Naked and the Dead* (1948), which I enjoyed; *The Naked Lunch* (1959) by William S. Burroughs, which I had already read along with Burroughs's other "cut up" works, years earlier; and Kerouac's *On the Road* (1957), which I had also already read. Along with *The Naked and The Dead*, Braudy had assigned Mailer's controversial essay, "The White Negro" (1957), in which Mailer celebrated violence and crime as acceptable means of achieving "authenticity" in our repressive modern society. It is also here that he presents his unequivocal existential challenge: "One is Hip or One is Square." Mailer, of course, is Hip.

One criterion for hipness, at least according to Mailer, was the ability to recognize that when "two strong, eighteen-year-old hoodlums beat in the brains of a candy store keeper," what is really taking place is not the murder of a "weak, fifty-year-old man, but an institution," by which, one assumes, he means "the system." Such behavior is not criminal but merely the redemptive acquiescence in the existential imperative to give free reign to the unrepressed self.[3]

Similarly, Burroughs's premeditated apprenticeship in criminality produced the seminal insight that society suffers "a considerable semantic confusion about the meaning of crime." Such a revelation propels the adolescent logic behind the argument that, since a company is "guided by no other principle than profit" and "never trusts anybody with anything," it is fair game to be defrauded or otherwise robbed.

Such sentiments may have appealed to me when I was living in the storefront on East 10th Street in 1974. If so, by the time I wrote my paper that appeal had long since evaporated.

Mailer's essay and Burroughs's and Kerouac's books were examples of the kind of anti-society, anti-civilization attitude that had first emerged in the late nineteenth-century aesthetes and decadents when it became *de rigueur* for artists to want to *épater la bourgeoisie*, to "shock the middle classes." By the '50s it had blended with existentialism and the Beat attitude to form an attractive, seductive philosophy of revolt. (It is still around today, as a visit to most modern art museums will show.)

As a teenager I had swallowed this whole and sought it out, and for a time in my late teens, I lived it. But by the time I was taking the course, my assessment of it had changed. I was much more inclined to regard it as Albert Camus had in a book I had read while working as a messenger in New York years earlier, *The Rebel* (1951). In

---

3. Some years earlier, in 1981, Mailer's romantic fascination with the criminal led to gruesome results. While writing about the convicted killer Gary Gilmore (*The Executioner's Song* [1979], Mailer started a correspondence with Jack Henry Abbott, a convict serving time for a number of offenses, including manslaughter. Abbott convinced Mailer that he had literary talent, and Mailer helped Abbott's book about his life behind bars, *In the Belly of the Beast* (1981) get published. The book was a success, and received positive reviews. Through Mailer's help, Abbott was released. Six weeks after his parole, Abbott stabbed to death a waiter at the Binibon café on Second Avenue in New York's East Village. I was living there at the time, and went to the café often. Abbott was arrested; through the advocacy of the novelist Jerzy Kosiński, the murder charge was changed to manslaughter. Abbott committed suicide in prison in 2002.

The Rebel, Camus argued that rebellion of the kind Mailer and the Beats advocate, is, in essence, "adolescent," because it wants to throw over all constraints on its behavior, exactly as an unruly child does. It wants to get rid of what it finds repressive without offering anything in its place.

Camus had in mind the sort of radical political extremism that a postwar Sartre found himself inextricably drawn toward; the book actually cost him Sartre's friendship. But his analysis applies to the kind of aimless revolt against "society" that in my late teens I found attractive, and which the Beats and Mailer took as a matter of course. What these and others of like mind want is what the historian Jacques Barzun, whom I learned about at this time and began to read avidly, called an "unconditioned life," a life without restraints or controls.[4] That is, essentially, a child's life, or at least its dream of one.

I had by this time also become very familiar with Colin Wilson's many writings on the links between creativity and criminality, spelled out in books like *Encyclopedia of Murder* (1962), *Order of Assassins* (1972), and others. In them, Wilson writes about a particular kind of criminal that has emerged only in recent times, what he calls the self-esteem murderer. These are often highly intelligent, creative individuals who for some reason or other are frustrated in their creativity. They are too intelligent and dominant to accept the mediocre position in which they find themselves in life, but not intelligent or determined enough to do better by acceptable means. So, they turn to crime as a means of getting back on "life" or "society" or some other abstraction which they hold responsible for their failure. Crime becomes a twisted form of creativity for them. If it is life or society that is holding them back, then any blow against them is deemed justified and practically anything becomes a target.

There is, of course, a whole history of the creator as criminal, or

---

4. I have to thank F for introducing me to Barzun's work, which I continue to read and which I refer to frequently in my own work.

at least as a rebel, starting with Prometheus. Lord Byron was the original Romantic wild boy, "mad, bad, and dangerous to know," and many have followed him (Crowley immediately comes to mind). The desire to avoid anything like bourgeois respectability has driven many creative individuals to the depths. But having lived for a time in those depths, I was immune to the romanticizing of them.

For my paper on the course, I engaged in some existential criticism. I took Wilson's idea, of crime being a form of creativity for some individuals who are unable to create legitimately, and turned it around. I looked at Mailer, Kerouac, Burroughs, and others—throwing in Jean Genet, the thief, pimp, and homosexual hustler who Sartre held up as a paragon of authenticity—as creators who looked to crime as a form of rebellion against society. I did not, however, celebrate this. Rather, as Camus had, I showed this tactic to be, at bottom, little more than a childish insistence on having one's own way, and a way of thumbing one's nose at the "repressive" society that prevents one from having it. The same sensibility that led me to see little more than anarchy in the transgressive ideas of postmodernism and deconstructionism now saw little more than childish tantrums in the "transgressions" that writers like Mailer and Burroughs—and so many others—held up as symbols of freedom.

I also included the idea that much of contemporary art, basing itself on the unquestioned notion of the artist as critic of society, was itself criminal in the sense that it was fraudulent and the artist a confidence trickster. I had in mind such outstanding works as Andres Serrano's *Piss Christ* (1987), a photograph of a plastic crucifix immersed in the artist's urine, which at the time made quite a fuss. There was a lively art scene in LA then, and I remember suggesting to someone that something like the Art Police should be established to deal with that sort of thing.

Braudy, however, did not care for my paper. Although it received a high grade, and he again acknowledged my ability to write, he remarked that, for all its acuity, it was "vitiated by moral sniping." This meant it included less than respectful remarks about sacred cows like Burroughs, who strikes me as little more than a literary con man, an assessment he would most likely have appreciated. (After all, his "cut ups" are made from other people's work—Burroughs merely snipped them from a book or magazine, hence their name. So, he is guilty of a form of plagiarism.) Likewise, Kerouac's advocacy of leaving the straight life behind and heading out "on the road" seemed to me to celebrate a philosophy of irresponsibility and aimlessness, one that led to Kerouac's early death at the age of forty-seven.

Vitiated by moral sniping or not, the ideas and insights behind the paper had a longer life than my involvement with Braudy's class or with the department. Not long after the course, some of the paper found a home in "World Rejection and Criminal Romantics," one of the *Two Essays on Colin Wilson* that Colin Stanley would publish with his Pauper's Press. And some years after that, it would also provide material for the sections on Henry Miller, Kerouac, and Burroughs in my book *Turn Off Your Mind*. In fact, the notion of "giving way to strange forces" (*sich einlassen mit fremden Mächten*) which I borrow from Hermann Hesse and which runs as a leitmotif throughout the book—and which Mailer advocates in "The White Negro," although, of course, he doesn't use those words—first made its appearance in my paper. The book's revisionist look at the 1960s, which turns on its head the liberationist philosophy that informed that decade, had its origins in the paper. Not bad for moral sniping.

AT THE END OF THE FIRST TERM at USC, I thought about the future and whether or not to continue with the MA. I did well in my grades, even with the friction between myself and some of my professors. But I had not made a single acquaintance, let alone friend, among my fellow students, and there did not seem much chance of that changing. I also had to admit I did not enjoy teaching as much as I'd thought I might. This was mostly because of the tepid response from the students, who only wanted to know what would be on the exam.

But, more important than this, it was clear I was once again swimming against the current. I rarely back down from a challenge, but some walls are worth batting your head against and some aren't. In terms of general demographics, I was a white, straight male in his late thirties, who would most likely be in his early forties by the time he could apply for a position at a university. That was handicap enough.

Added to this was the fact that I had no interest in any of the fashionable critical schools, all promoting their own "theory" about literature. I had read quite a bit of literary theory and, while I found some of it of interest, on the whole it bored me. I wasn't interested in applying one theory or another to a writer's work in order to uncover what he was "really saying." I wanted to know what that writer had to say, what led him to say it, and what it meant. I belonged to the old school who believed, against the advice of my professor, that literature was an aid in understanding life, as well as a series of experiments in how it could be lived. (Hence existentialism, the most literary of philosophical movements.) George Steiner, whose work I read avidly throughout this time, once made a distinction between the reader and the critic. I certainly felt more at home as a reader than as a critic—certainly more than as a theorist—and the idea of ferreting out the hidden meanings in some text by applying the solvent of some theory left me cold. I was, and remain, an unrepentant romantic.

If so, where did this leave me? The more I thought about it, the more the answer became clear. Given who I was and my ideas about literature, writing, philosophy, and everything else, once I earned the degree, would I seriously have a chance of getting a job somewhere? The answer was: no, or at least, not much of one. But that was the reason I was taking the course. This only raised the real question. Did I really want to teach? Or, more specifically, even if I did get a job teaching somewhere, was it *really* what I wanted to do with my life? If, at the end of another few years of studying ideas in which I had no interest, I might find a job teaching them to students who most likely wouldn't be interested in them either. I would not be very happy doing this. So, the answer to that, too, was no.

Would I find myself like David Ray Griffin, who struck me as something of a dissatisfied if not sad figure? And would I ever have the time to write, which was still what I really wanted to do? I hadn't written anything in a while, having to devote most of my time to producing papers for the course. But if I dropped out now, what would I do? Go back to the bookshop? Look for yet another job? Apply to another university?

The idea of destiny or fate has turned up a few times in these pages. At this juncture in my life one or the other made a very much needed and appreciated appearance.[5] Every six months, I received a royalty check for the songs of mine that Blondie had recorded. For some years, they had been minimal, a welcome addition to what I was earning at the bookshop but not particularly substantial. Seeing that one had arrived, I opened it and at first thought there must have been some mistake. I had to count the number of figures to be sure. I had not seen that many on a royalty check for some time. But there they were.

In 1991, Blondie released one of several compilation albums of their work that would be put out over the years. *The Complete Picture: The Very Best of Deborah Harry and Blondie* was a collection of tracks from Debbie's time with Blondie and from her later, less successful solo career. Among the tracks on it was "(I'm Always Touched by Your) Presence, Dear." The album went gold in the UK and Australia, and platinum in New Zealand. It reached No. 3 on the UK charts, and did equally well elsewhere. (It did less well in the States, but Blondie had always

5. For the record, my distinction between the two is that destiny is something we fulfill, while fate is what happens to us. So, we struggle to fulfill our destiny against the backdrop of our fate.

been more of a UK success.) Evidence for that was the very substantial royalty check I held in my hand and looked at in disbelief. Touched by the presence, indeed.

Well, I thought. I won't have to worry about finding a job anytime soon. I then decided to let my advisor at USC know that I wouldn't be returning in the new term.

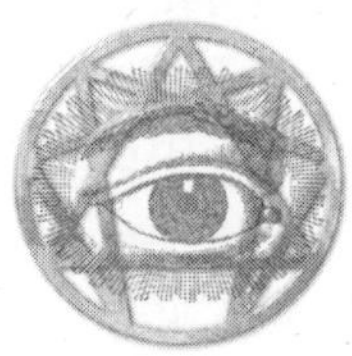

13
The Crack Up

Just how long I lived on that royalty check I can't remember, but it must have been for some months. And exactly what I did during that time is also vague. For the first time in many years, I was a free agent. I didn't have to be at work or at university or anywhere in particular, and I must have gorged myself reading and going to bookshops. I imagine for a while I was a "house husband," taking care of the flat, getting the groceries, and performing other domestic chores, my windfall covering my share of our expenses. Many men abhor housework, but having disciplined myself to be neat during my time living in squalor, I came to appreciate a tidy home. I also turned it into a kind of meditation. Wilson had written that if you purposely set out to take a positive attitude toward something you'd rather avoid doing, you soon discover that you enjoy doing it. I looked at cleaning the flat as I had the exercises I was given during my time in the Work, and tried to remember myself as I got through it, a practice I continue today.

I also had the time to write, and I did. I went about it methodically. I invested in a copy of the *Writers and Artists Yearbook*, a helpful reference work that comes out each year, and followed its advice. Beginning writers may dismiss the idea of getting help from reference books of this sort, preferring to rely on their native genius, but at the time I found it invaluable, and I always suggest getting a copy when anyone asks me for tips about writing. Articles on "How to Write A Book Proposal" or "How to Pitch an Idea Successfully," and others of that sort, were like recipes one could follow. Over time and with practice you can add an additional spice or two and make it your own, until writing them becomes second nature. It is also helpful in finding what magazines or journals might be interested in your ideas, which publishers accept unsolicited manuscripts, which ones published the sort of thing you want to write, what agents might be interested in you, and other necessary things one needs to know about the mechanics of the business.

I said "business," not "art." I had no pretentions that I was writing anything more than informative, readable articles. Nevertheless, I wrote as well as I could. I was not writing to express myself, but to explore and convey ideas.[1] If anything, I thought of writing as a craft, and a writer as a kind of carpenter. My job was to turn out a good article that was enjoyable and informative, in the same way that a carpenter aims to make a chair that is comfortable. (Ironically enough, this is rather close to the Marxist notion of the writer as proletarian.) I learned early on not to be too precious about anything I had written. If a particular phrase struck me as a bit of fine writing, and I found I was pleased with myself about it, more times than not it would wind up deleted. I found it a good practice to be able to delete anything that did not contribute to the piece as a whole; this, in some way, was rather like my attitude toward writing songs. I was not writing for myself. I wanted to be read and that meant I needed to be published, so I took the trouble to know what I needed to do in order to be. I did my homework and pitched ideas to the right places. More times than not, they were accepted.

I wrote more articles for *Gnosis* and *Quest*, and for another journal, *Lapis*, that was put out by the New York Open Center, a venue for holistic and alternative ideas in New York's East Village that had started up in 1984. I wrote for others, as well, journals and magazines whose names I've forgotten. I wrote about Rudolf Steiner, the I Ching, Swedenborg,

1. An invaluable aid in this is Jacques Barzun's short but extremely helpful guide, *Simple and Direct* (1975).

hermeticism, the Russian Silver Age, philosophy, Faculty X, the then-adolescent "information age," and anything else that I thought the journals I had in mind would be interested in. Most of the material later found a home in some of my books. I worked on book proposals and even considered writing about my rock and roll past, which I would do some years later. Among other things, I know that I worked my morally vitiated paper for Leo Braudy's class on Mailer, Burroughs, and others into my essay on "World Rejection and Criminal Romantics," and sent it to Colin Stanley, Colin Wilson's bibliographer in England.

I had heard about Stanley's work and his Pauper's Press, which put out short books on topics related to Wilson's work, and had corresponded with him. I had heard about him from Wilson himself during a visit we made to his home, Tetherdown, in Cornwall sometime in early 1994. F and I took a European holiday, part of which was spent in Palermo, Sicily, visiting friends.[2] Another leg of it was spent in London, from where we hired a car and made the journey to the West Country. What I remember most about that visit now is that Colin made a concerted effort to get us drunk, offering us several glasses of some exotic liqueur he no doubt received as a gift and would never drink himself. He would feign deep offense if we refused, so we didn't, and went off to bed in the chalet I had slept in a decade earlier about as tipsy as I had been then.

What I also remember from that trip is the peak experience I had watching smoke rise out of a chimney near the service station we stopped at to use the toilet. As I waited for F to return to the car, I noticed the chimney and became entranced, watching the smoke float up and dissipate in the cold winter air. Everything seemed crisp, clean,

---

2. It was on this trip that we took a day excursion to Cefalù, where in the 1920s, Aleister Crowley had established his notorious Abbey of Thelema in the hills above the town. My interest in Crowley was practically nil at this point, so, although I knew the remains of his abbey were there, I made no effort to visit them. I believe, though, that we passed near it, as we did see the ruins of the Temple of Diana which I believe Crowley mentions in *Diary of a Drug Fiend*.

and hard edged, like one of the paintings of the Japanese artist Hokusai, so much so that I felt I could hold the smoke in my hands. I have not had the full-blown mystical experiences many people tell of, nor any of the kinds of visions one hopes to receive via psychedelics or other means. But I have, once or twice, seen my everyday reality with such piercing clarity that its preciousness has been brought home to me unmistakably. Watching the smoke rise into the pristine air then was a moment of being, of wakefulness, of life lived without the robot. Remembering it now in its clarity—what else could it have been?

IT MUST HAVE BEEN around the early summer of 1994 that F began to feel it was time for me to get a job. The idea that I was using the windfall from "Presence, Dear" to live on did not sit well with her. We had shared the expense of living together all along, so that was not an issue. F did not want to be a housewife—although I think the Japanese part of her would not have been uncomfortable in the role—and she enjoyed her work at Sony Studios. Yet, though from the conventional point of view she was the breadwinner, I was not being kept. I may not have been earning much from it, but I did work at writing, sitting at my desk in front of my computer—they had just become widely available—every day. Articles appeared, book reviews, too. But ideas for a book did not pan out, and by this time the occult thriller I had been working on had ground to a halt somewhere after fifty thousand words. By then, the blank page had become the blank screen, but it was blank all the same.

Conversations about the future became more frequent. During one of them, F, impatient with my vague assurances that everything was fine and that I would come up with an idea for a book soon, let me know what she thought of that.

"The money you've been living on," she said. "You've wasted it! We could have used it to get a house!"

A house? What did I want with a house? "I don't want a house. I want to write a book."

"Ha! You need a job."

I corrected her. "I don't need a job. I need money."

Although my logic was impeccable, that did not go down well. Similar storms and sudden squalls appeared with greater frequency. Conventional thought sees woman as the dreamer and man as the practical one, but in many instances—at least in mine—it was the other way around; this was something that Bernard Shaw, of whom I was a great reader, knew well. Given that women need to secure a home and the wherewithal to raise their children, and that men have a disreputable taste for freedom, this makes sense—even if, in our case, there were no children. To appease F's righteous anger, I started to look at the want ads in the *Los Angeles Times*; aside from the film listings, this was about the only thing I read in the paper (I have never been a newspaper reader).

My mixed bag of qualifications did not immediately suggest anything in particular. I had several years of retail experience, but the idea of working in a shop of some kind again, even a bookshop, did not appeal to me. My degree in philosophy and one year's worth of English MA studies did not amount to much. I could write, but until I could produce something more than articles on abstruse philosophical, mystical, and esoteric subjects, I couldn't count on that just yet. The fact that I had written a hit song and received gold records—where did that fit in? And my age (I was thirty-eight) did not help. But, of course, F was right. I couldn't live on that royalty check forever, although its size suggested there was a good chance the next one would be similar. Soon, I would have to secure some form of steady earning.

For a brief time, I did earn some money at some work that, while not exactly writing, did involve my sitting at a keyboard. I can't remember exactly how it came about, but I learned that an English professor at UCLA—a campus I would shortly get to know quite well—named G. B. Tennyson was making a documentary about Owen Barfield, one of the "late bloomers" with whom I had come to identify. He had several hours of taped interviews with Barfield, and was looking for someone to transcribe them. I met with him, explained that I was a reader of Barfield and knew his work, and said that I needed the job.

Not long after that, I found myself sitting in front of my computer for hours at a stretch, starting and stopping the tape recorder, trying to make out exactly what Barfield, a man in his nineties with an old-school, upper-class, BBC English accent was saying. Having transcribed twelve hours of Barfield speaking about his long life, his friendship with C. S. Lewis and his association with the Inklings, his relationship to Rudolf Steiner's ideas, and his own ideas on language and the evolution of consciousness, I came to feel that I knew him although we had never met. That experience, however, primed me for our actual meeting, which took place soon after I came to London, and in the same location as the documentary, his flat in Forest Row. The documentary, *Owen Barfield: Man and Meaning* was released in 1996 and can be found on YouTube. An attentive viewer will see that I get a credit for "Interview Transcript" at 37:58.[3]

I enjoyed transcribing the interviews and wondered if I could find any other similar work, but nothing surfaced. Soon I was back at the want ads, fighting off the sinking feeling that anyone confronted with the situation I was faced with knows well. It was, it seemed, only a matter of time before I had to give up my precious if unproductive freedom and capitulate.

But I didn't want to give up yet. Desperate straits require desperate measures. An idea came to me. I devised a plan. I would apply for positions I would never get. That way, I would appear to be taking F's concerns seriously and still have time to write. If this sounds like the formula for a comedy, it was—although the ending was no laughing matter.

---

3. It was through G. B. Tennyson that I was put in touch with Marcus Welby, who ran the Wellspring Bookshop in Holborn, London. Welby knew Barfield, and told me he enjoyed receiving guests. I trust that he enjoyed my visit. Sadly, some years later, I learned that G. B. Tennyson had died in a fire in his home, which I'd visited once or twice while transcribing the interviews.

I CAN'T NOW REMEMBER many of the positions I applied for. I know I saw an advertisement for one at the Los Angeles Music Center, in downtown. I had gone there many times for performances, as I had to the Hollywood Bowl and Schoenberg Hall at UCLA. Exactly what the position was escapes me now, but I thought my love and fair knowledge of classical music in some way made applying for it not absolutely ludicrous. The reader will appreciate that I had a very fine balance to maintain: I mustn't apply for jobs that I obviously would never get (say, as a brain surgeon), but at the same time I had to apply for ones that I *could* get but wouldn't, lacking one or two absolutely essential requirements.

I must have written a good letter. Although I was not offered the job, the person in charge of finding the right applicant replied to me personally, letting me know she was sorry she had to turn me down, simply because another applicant had more background in the position.

For someone with low self-esteem, such a reply would be a tonic. Even I began to feel that maybe I was selling myself too short. Maybe I was more qualified than I thought? If so, I had to watch out.

At one point, I even condescended to spending two afternoons at an Evelyn Wood Speed Reading training course, having gotten it into my head—put there by F—that teaching that system wouldn't be too bad. What I remember now is the long drive out to San Pedro, where the course was held, and the area around the waterfront, which looked like it hadn't changed since the 1950s. Whatever possessed me to think I could teach people to read faster than was good for them soon passed. After the second day, I came to my senses.

So far, my plan seemed to be working, even if I wasn't. I wrote more articles and book reviews. I applied for one or two other positions that I didn't get. Things seemed to have hit a calm spell, the turbulence had settled. Then F saw it. It was an advertisement in the *Times* that the University of California, Los Angeles, had put in. The university was looking for a science writer.

Science writer? What's that? Generally, it's someone with a background in science who can translate difficult specialized material into prose understandable by the average reader. A science writer can work for a newspaper or magazines; Arthur Koestler, one of my favorite writers, started out this way, writing popular accounts of the latest scientific developments for syndicated newspapers. Or, one can work for a corporation or foundation. Or, as the position advertised in the *Times* was, for a university. In that case, a lot of the work entails writing grant proposals, which are glorified begging letters, competing with other universities for money offered by different foundations, to fund projects that meet their specifications. This entails a specialized language and structure, rather as legal writing does. It is almost like having to learn how to write in a foreign language.

"Look at this!" F said, when she saw the ad. "You can do this! Here!" she added, and put the paper down in front of me.

Perfect, I thought. This fit the plan to a tee. I had no science background, but I had written quite a few articles and book reviews about the latest fads in pop science. At the time, these were "chaos theory" and "complexity," two approaches that shared the theme of an unexpected "order" rising out of what, to all appearances, was random disorder. (Nietzsche had said that one needed chaos within oneself to give birth to a dancing star. Apparently, he was right.)

It was a very popular topic, with bestsellers like James Gleick's *Chaos: Making a New Science* (1987) bringing the latest discoveries into millions of households. I had read *Order Out of Chaos* (1984) by Ilya Prigogine and Isabelle Stengers, their work on "dissipative structures," thermodynamics, and non-equilibrium systems. The idea was that certain processes we consider to be chaotic and random actually display a much more subtle order than we are used to grasping. Prigogine and Stengers's work was fairly tough going, requiring more familiarity with physics than the average reader possessed. But some other works were more accessible, such as F. David Peat's *The Philosopher's Stone: Chaos, Synchronicity and the Hidden Order of the World* (1991) and *Turbulent Mirror: An Illustrated Guide to Chaos Theory and the Science of Wholeness* (1989), which he had written with John Griggs.[4]

It was the time of fractals, the Mandelbrot set, and the odd pairing of the new science with the rising psychedelic revival—witness the trialogue among Terence McKenna, the then-reigning psychedelic guru; the biologist Rupert Sheldrake, of "morphic resonance" fame; and mathematical chaotician Ralph Abraham, in *Chaos, Creativity, and Cosmic Consciousness* (1992). With Stuart Kaufmann and the Santa Fe Institute, chaos jumped the border from physics and entered biology, and was renamed as "complexity." Disorder, it seemed, was turning up everywhere. People were even going out of their way to find it.

Chaos, complexity, fractals, and the rest became the hottest pop science fare since Fritjof Capra's *The Tao of Physics* (1975) introduced the idea that there were important similarities between ancient Eastern ideas about the nature of reality and the reports about it being received from quantum physics. Along with writing about it all, I had also reviewed *Bright Air, Brilliant Fire* (1992), the Nobel Prize–winning biologist Gerald Edelman's book about the brain, for the *San Francisco Chronicle*, work that had been passed to me by Richard Tarnas. So, although I had no academic background in science, I had enough familiarity with some of its more accessible concerns to write about them and review books about them for a popular audience.[5]

---

4. I would meet F. David Peat in London in 1997, when I was hired to research material for a documentary on art and science. I attended a performance art event in which he was involved. The artist entered a black box in the same way that Schrödinger's poor cat had, and we wouldn't know if he was alive or dead—or both!—until it was opened.

5. My work as a science writer helped when I first arrived in London. One of the first pieces of writing I had published in the UK was a review in the *Times Literary Supplement* of Steven Rose's *Lifelines* (1997), a book arguing against determinism in biology, and Ian Stewart and Jack Cohen's *Figments of Reality* (1997), about the evolution of consciousness and intelligence in the human mind. I reviewed a few more books for the *TLS* that were not particularly pop science, such as Paul Rabinow's *French DNA* (1999), a study of the politics of genetic profiling. Eventually, although the reviews were well written, the fact that I also wrote about disreputable subjects like the occult suggested to the science editors that I was not quite the right man for the job, and that was that. It was just as well, as I found reviewing science books rather a chore.

When I reminded F that I had no qualifications in science, she shook her head. "Just send them some of your stuff," she said. So, I did. I dutifully Xeroxed copies of my articles and book reviews, wrote a cover letter explaining that, while I had no academic background in science, my training in philosophy and English would help in translating difficult, specialized language into something more approachable to the average reader, and added a few phrases about how much I would enjoy working in close proximity with scientists who were on the cutting edge of their fields. The last, of course, was pure window dressing, but it was the kind of thing I knew one should do.

I did not want the job, but I have to admit the salary offered was attractive. In any case, I was certain I wouldn't get it. However, I thanked F for spotting it at the same time that I looked forward to feigning disappointment when the rejection letter arrived. I would have sincerely tried my best, but . . . and perhaps I *could* hold out until the next royalty check turned up.

I don't remember how long it was before I heard from them. F's experience in landing her job at Sony Studios suggested I keep after them for a reply. I sent an email or two inquiring as meekly as possible about my application, and was happy when time passed without a response. But then one morning, there it was—something I never expected nor wanted to see—an official letter from the UCLA College of Letters and Science, asking me to come in for an interview and letting me know that the pre-semester training week for new staff was in mid-August. My plan had backfired. I had outsmarted myself. I had gotten the job.

F was delighted. "I told you you'd get it," she said. I may have said "Wow," but it wasn't what I was thinking—that was something much more unprintable. Anyone else in my position would have shared in F's delight. I've mentioned that the salary was quite substantial. Part of me must have felt as I did when I heard back from the Music Center: that I was more qualified than I gave myself credit for. Looking back on it now, it strikes me as a form of what the psychologist Victor Frankl called "paradoxical intention," when one purposely tries to do something one doesn't want to do. Frankl gives the example of a stutterer who was given the part of someone who stutters in a play, and when it came time for him to stutter, discovered that he couldn't. Consciously trying to stutter prevented him from stuttering.

In my case, consciously trying *not* to land a job nailed it for me. There is some wisdom here. It seems that not caring whether you get something or not may be the best way of getting it—even if you don't really want it.

My interview was with the dean of the College of Letters and Science, and as I drove out toward Westwood—where, years earlier, I had discovered *The Outsider*—I didn't know what to expect. The butterflies in my stomach were fluttering, and I had to fight down a powerful urge to run away. I didn't want the job but, having gotten it, I felt I couldn't back out. And who knows? Maybe it would turn out to be not as bad as I feared. Similar thoughts ping-ponged in my head as I made my way from the parking lot to the dean's office.

The dean then was Brian Copenhaver. His background was in philosophy and the history of science. I didn't know it then, but one of his areas of interest was hermeticism. Years later, I would make good use of his edition of the *Hermetica* (1991), his translation of the *Corpus Hermeticum*, and the *Asclepius*—the founding texts of hermetic philosophy—when writing my book *The Quest of Hermes Trismegistus*.[6] When I saw his name while referencing the book, and remembered who he was, I had to laugh. But back then, I knew nothing about him except that I had to get his approval to be hired. Exactly what I had to do to get that was unclear.

The interview, however, proved perfunctory. What I remember now is that he seemed rather impatient, gruff, and preoccupied with something else. Perhaps the fact that I didn't have a science background made him suspicious of me. At one point he quickly flipped through

6. *The Quest for Hermes Trismegistus* (Edinburgh: Floris Books, 2011).

the copies of my articles I had sent, then tossed them on his desk. "So, this is yours?" he asked. He looked at me and shook his head. "How do I know you wrote them?" he asked. "How do I know you didn't copy them from someone? How do I know they're really yours?"

Either Copenhaver was a very paranoid person or he'd had years of dealing with plagiarism when teaching his classes. There wasn't much to say to his remarks—maybe "I guess you could check with the editors"?—so I didn't reply. Which was just as well, as it was clear he didn't really want an answer. In any case, there wasn't much of an interview after that. With a gesture that said "We'll see," I was dismissed.

He may have been the dean of the college, but the department I later worked in was run by women. Besides myself, there were three other males. One was an older gentleman who was doing his best to hold on in order to collect his pension before the illness he was suffering from did him in. Another was a young Hispanic, somewhere in his twenties, with whom I got on. The third was in his forties and had been working there for a while. He was a pro, knew the ropes, and could navigate the obstacle course that working in the place turned out to be. He struck me as a rather depressed type.

Names escape me once again, but the head of the department was a woman in her fifties. She was one of those professional types who put on the charm when needed but whose natural demeanor was rather less friendly. At our first meeting she told me how glad she was that I would be working there. I got the position, she said, because what she thought the department needed was someone who could *write*, not just a grant writer (this, I suspect, was the argument she had made to the dean). They had those already. Her second-in-command, as it were, was one. She was another woman, younger but of the same mold, very sharp, dressed in a power suit, whitish-blonde hair pulled back in a tight bun, a single loose lock giving an impression of youth. I was such an innocent—in many ways, I still am—that, at the time, I didn't detect the subtle gestures of dominance that went on around me. These two were the bosses, but several other women filled out the rest of the ranks.

What I remember from the training week we attended before the real work began in September was being introduced to the other members of the staff, some talks about grant writing and what that involves, a tour of some of the new facilities in the college—I remember they were proud of a new addition to the molecular biology department—and a general tour of the campus. I had been to UCLA to visit the bookstore, and one of the perks of the job was that I would be able to use the library. That was one extra I certainly made use of.

One other thing that stands out from that first week was being shown the files on the alumni that the college kept. Along with writing grant proposals—which I soon discovered was about as interesting and satisfying as I imagine selling life insurance is—part of our job was to keep in touch with past students and faculty members, and to let them know about the important and valued work (there's grant proposal speak) being carried on in the college, with the aim of leading up to what was known as "the ask." This was one's pitch to get alumni—or whatever foundation you were writing to—to give you money. This was *raison d' être* for the whole business, but in each case, there was a special language one had to use. Making "the ask" with an alumnus was a different affair from petitioning a foundation, and neither had anything to do with how one would ordinarily speak or write.

The alumni files provided information about past donors, and helped one to make one's pitch with the right tone and at the right level, and to locate donors for specific projects. As we were walked through the room where they were kept—it was, as I recall, a rather large space lined with wooden filing cabinets—at one point, the head of the department stopped and gestured for us to come closer.

"Here, "she said, "is the file on a very special alumnus. It is one that under no conditions should ever be taken from this room. And it concerns an alumnus that under no conditions should anyone think of approaching for a donation." Having sufficiently aroused everyone's interest, she let us know whose file it was.

"It's the file on Carlos Castaneda." A collective "ooh" emerged from the group. As mentioned, I had read Castaneda's books in high school. More recently, I had sold quite a few copies of them during my tenure at the Bodhi Tree. Throughout his career, Castaneda had been something of a mystery man, avoiding publicity and photographs while still producing bestselling books about shamanism and native Indian spiritual practices. One imagined that the edict on not contacting him or allowing any of his information to leave the premises was a gesture of respect to his privacy. But one wonders if UCLA, who granted him a degree in anthropology based on his first book, *The Teachings of Don Juan: A Yaqui Way of Knowledge* (1968), was a bit embarrassed by the fact that there is good reason to suspect that Castaneda's Don Juan was little more than his own invention? Or that the anthropological "structural analysis" appended to the much more readable narrative of his adventures with his *brujo* was a piece of academic fraudulence, a bit of window dressing in fluent but meaningless academese? Suspicion that Castaneda had made up pretty much all of his encounters had started up in the late '70s, and by the time I got a peek at his alumnus file, many authorities on Indigenous drug use and other practices he wrote about took it as a given.[7]

Oddly enough, Castaneda, who was still alive then, lived not far from the university campus. He died in 1998. Events following his death eventually led to the suspicion that several of his female followers, who mysteriously went missing, never to be found, had committed suicide in order to join their guru in the "nagual," the spiritual dimension he had entered, himself. A few years after Castaneda's death, I would write about him and the mystery surrounding his followers in *Turn Off Your Mind.*[8]

It took a while to get used to my new environment. Along with the hefty salary, I had my own office and secretary—as someone who

7. See Richard DeMille, *Castaneda's Journey* (1976).

8. See the UK edition of *Turn Off Your Mind: The Dedalus Book of the 1960s* (2022).

does practically everything himself, having someone there to help was at first disorienting. I didn't know what I should have her do. Grant writing, as mentioned, proved a chore, although after a time I got a grasp on it. I worked on getting funding for a new mathematics program and some other academic projects, one of which included the development of an earthquake early-warning system, something very much in need in California. Something more concrete was the aquarium at Santa Monica Pier that I helped get the funding for. It was known as the Ocean Discovery Center until it changed hands in 2003. It still stands today, and is known as the Heal the Bay Aquarium. Odd to think that something I helped to make possible is still running and is visited by more than a hundred thousand people each year.

My real work, however, was less in writing grants, as the pros in the department could churn those out by the dozen; I was there for the "real writing"—the newsletter I put together for the department and which was sent to the alumni. I called it *The Basics*, and its tag line was "Science Without Frontiers," taking a cue from *Médecins sans Frontières*. I wrote and edited it, designed the layout, and interviewed various faculty members about their work.

In the first issue, I wrote an article about chaos theory and the butterfly effect, the notion that a butterfly fluttering its wings in one part of the world can start a chain reaction that leads to a tornado in another. This was a phenomenon known as "sensitivity to initial conditions," the recognition that what may seem to be small, insignificant changes can produce very significant effects. If I remember correctly, I used this as a metaphor for science itself—how seemingly unimportant observations often lead to remarkable discoveries, or something like that. In the second issue, I took on "dark matter," the idea proposed by some physicists of the necessity for some kind of invisible matter to account for certain characteristics of the universe. What I made of that I don't remember.

Something I did enjoy about the work was interviewing some of the faculty, on campus and off. I sat in on a class on the "origin of life," given by a popular biology professor who had some of his students come for an evening gathering at his home once a week. They made jokes about being served "primordial soup." I interviewed an astrophysicist about the odd "cosmic coincidences" and "just rights" that enabled life to develop on our planet. We are apparently very lucky to have gas giants like Jupiter and Saturn where they are in our solar system. Their gravity captures asteroids and meteors that might otherwise reach us. Our humble, pockmarked moon plays a similar role, intercepting much of what gets past the first line of defense, as it were. We, ourselves, are placed in what I can only call a kind of nexus of "just rights," in the way that Goldilocks, in the fairy tale, finds the bed and porridge "just right"—not too hard or cold or soft or hot. If our own position in the solar system was nudged a cosmic smidgen, life would not have been possible.

Various other astrophysical "coincidences" have led some cosmologists to speculate on what became known as the "anthropic cosmological principle." Simply put, this states that our universe is one in which intelligent life forms, like ourselves, not only can come into existence—which seems obvious—but *must* come into existence. In other words, the universe is designed to create intelligent beings like ourselves.

The scientist I interviewed would not agree to this, no doubt mindful of his tenure, but the coincidences he pointed out were nevertheless compelling. Years later, I would refer to this interview in a section of *The Caretakers of the Cosmos*. I do remember asking him a personal question: How did looking into the depths of space and time make him *feel* about life on Earth? I may have hoped for some existential awe or some of the disquiet the seventeenth-century French religious thinker and logician Blaise Pascal expressed when, reflecting on the new Copernican universe, he said, "The eternal silence of these infinite spaces terrifies me." But his response was more earthbound: "When I go home to my family, I forget all about this."

For one interview, I went out to the marine biology laboratory on Catalina Island and talked with the scientists and researchers there about their work. I remember seeing several dolphins popping through the water as they followed us out from Long Beach. On another outing, I went to the Mount Wilson Observatory, in the San Gabriel Mountains, and interviewed a solar physicist who had been studying sunspots for fifteen years. Along with taking a peek through the specialized telescope needed to observe the sun, I was given a tour of the grounds. Later, over lunch, we were told stories of some of the famous visitors, like Albert Einstein, who was there in 1931, and Harlow Shapley, who in the early twentieth century, using the observatory's instruments, calculated the size and shape of the Milky Way and determined that it was only one galaxy in a universe containing millions.

Yet, while I enjoyed the journalistic side of the job, the corporate part of it soon began to be a strain. The two women running the show soon made it clear that they played hardball. Signs that I was perhaps not really suited (certainly not power-suited) for the job began to show. I forget exactly what it was, but some department fete required that I rent a tuxedo. I had never worn one, and discovered why they are called monkey suits, but etiquette demanded it and I submitted. I had some articles published, and remember an awkward conversation, trying to explain to my boss what "transpersonal psychology" meant. I did not show the usual signs of someone eager to impress and move up the department ladder. Although I tried my best to disguise it, that I was constitutionally incapable of kissing ass must have come through. I suspect she was an old hand at detecting this character trait.

I was conscientious about my work, but didn't care for it to be corrected by her second-in-command. There were more than a few mixed messages, the kind that contribute to the lose-lose scenario of the "double bind." An article about writing we were required to read suggested, among other things, not to rely on the spellcheck function. This would make us lazy; we should only use it when a piece of writing is done, to find typos we missed, and so on. In some department meeting I mentioned this, and said I was following the advice.

"You're not using spellcheck?" number two boss asked.

"Only at the end."

"What? Use it all the time."

"But the article said—"

"I don't care what the article said, use the damn spellcheck!"

The real rift opened at another meeting. I mentioned the older gentleman in the department, who was ill and hanging on so he could collect his pension. I forget what the issue was, but at some board meeting the two bosses ganged up on him over some trifling mistake he had made. I'm not sure what his illness was—possibly multiple sclerosis—but it was clear he had difficulty completing his work; I had, in fact, finished a few things for him, and he asked me to look at some others to see if he had missed any mistakes. He may have been a weight the department was carrying, but he was ill and would be there only for another few months. But this didn't stop him coming under attack. Whatever his mistake was, when boss number one had finished admonishing him about it, number two took over until number one decided to continue. It was brutal, and I could see him shrink back from their criticisms.

"If you can't do your job you should leave." "Do you expect me to accept substandard work?" "What do you call this rubbish you handed in?" I'm paraphrasing—I recall the remarks being more stinging and not bereft of expletives. At one point I couldn't bear the browbeating they were handing out and let them know. "Stop it!" I said. "Leave him alone. You know he's ill." If I had said "pick on someone your own size," I would have meant it. Two pushy alpha women were ganging up on a weak, ill, old man while everyone else sat there and listened.

My outburst did end their abuse, but it did not help my own reputation. After the meeting, the fellow who had been working there for some time came up to me and asked me to step into his office. "You better watch yourself. You lost it there. If you want to keep this job, take my advice and never do anything like that again."

I nodded. But he was wrong. I hadn't lost it. I had found it.

But in the process of holding on to it, I would lose practically everything else.

Although I felt increasingly out of place with my work as a science writer, I did try to have a positive attitude. I remember emailing Colin Wilson, letting him know that I had taken the job and offering to do any research for him the position might make possible. I'm not sure what I had in mind, but the gesture was really a way of somehow maintaining contact with him and putting a purposeful gloss over something I was beginning to dread. I kept up my reading. One book about science that I found very important at the time—although how popular it was with scientists is debatable—was *Understanding the Present* (1994) by Bryan Appleyard.

Appleyard was a British popular science writer who took a very critical view of its effect on the modern world; his book was a deeply-felt analysis of the loss of the soul in a universe empty of meaning and purpose, such as the one science tells us we inhabit. Another book I read at the time was entitled simply that, *Book* (1992), by Robert Grudin.

Book is a brilliant "metafiction" about the attempted murder of an academic by another, who is out to destroy all copies of one of his books. I remember it being very funny, a biting satire on the world of literary theory and academic careerism from which I had only recently escaped. Its send-up of deconstructionism, postmodernism, and the ideas of literary theorists like Stanley Fish would have been welcome had I known of it during my time at USC.

I had read some of Grudin's other books and, like most aspiring—or, in my case, wannabe—writers, I wanted established writers to see my work, and to have some kind of contact with them. I wrote him a fan letter after reading *Book*, and included some copies of my articles. He replied very graciously, but the correspondence went no further than that.

As my time at the office slowly wore away the coating of optimism I had given it, my home life was showing its own signs of strain.[9] F hadn't lived with someone before, and I was probably not the best person to start practicing with. I can be difficult, and I was. For much of our time together, she had one hand on her suitcase and the other on the doorknob. My frustration at not fulfilling my ambition to become a writer took its toll on her as it did on myself. Marriage, unfortunately, can bring out the worst in people. Minor things became irritants which soon grew into major issues and, for much of the time, we argued. We had a very comfortable, spacious flat in about as central a location in LA as you could get, were both earning substantial salaries, were in good health and still relatively young, and had a circle of friends and the means of taking holidays if we wanted. But, as Lord Pentland had said long ago, something was "missing." I think we truly liked and cared about each other. But we nevertheless got on each other's nerves.

I found her a bit too simple and unable to understand the difficulties I was facing. She thought I was depressed and neurotic. Most likely she was right, but my concerns were nevertheless real. It is difficult to try to explain to someone that you feel—*know*—you are capable of much more, that there is something inside you that needs to emerge, to come out, and that nothing else is as important as this. Long ago, I had learned the truth of the Gnostic maxim: "If you bring forth what is within you, what is within you will save you. If you do not bring forth what is within you, what is within you will destroy you." Whatever it

---

9. The marriage was most likely doomed from the start. We got married during the Rodney King riots of 1992, when police officers were acquitted of charges of police brutality in the savage beating of an African-American in their custody. My parents came for the wedding, which was held in a friend's garden, the service performed by a colleague at the Bodhi Tree who was an ordained priest in some New Age church or other. It was their first visit to Los Angeles. The day of the wedding, the city was in flames. My parents watched the news coverage, not aware that many of the fires and much of the looting were taking place not far from our neighborhood. There was a curfew in effect. When I asked F if she thought it might be best to postpone the ceremony until things quieted down, she literally stamped her foot and said "No! I'm getting married!" If "initial conditions" are anything to go by, it isn't surprising that the ones at the start of our union seemed to fate it for chaos.

was inside me had yet to come out and it was not very happy about that.

I wanted to self-actualize, and felt that I wasn't. If I tried to talk about Outsiders and their problems, it invariably sounded like I thought I was some kind of repressed genius, or that I was somehow different and better than other people. She resented this, and asked why I couldn't be like other people and just get on and enjoy life? A good question. She was spiritual, embraced some New Age ideas, read Jung—some of her friends were psychotherapists, or were in training to be—but at heart she was normal, ordinary, everyday, and what she wanted were normal, ordinary, everyday things, as most people do. Many people who adopt a spiritual lifestyle are the same—take away the crystals and incense and they are fairly standard issue.

I don't blame her for this, although at the time the idea repelled me, and I am sorry now for the pain I must have caused her. But I didn't want the things she wanted and never did. I wish I did want them. My life would have been easier if I had. But maybe I didn't want an easy life.

Even now, as I write this, part of me cringes at the hints of "tortured genius" and tones of "no one understands me" it gives off, and wants to shrink back from it, to disown it. Is this the "voice of the herd," as Nietzsche would have said? Or fear of the hard road of individuation and the loneliness it demands, as Jung might have suggested? Or an expression of Maslow's "Jonah complex," our timidity and reluctance in the face of the challenge of truly being ourselves? The weariness of the Outsider, tired of being outside? Or is it simply a reaction to the fact that, just like everyone else, I have to go to the supermarket to get my groceries? All I know is that my life has been driven by needs most of the people I have known do not suffer from, and which in me, if they recognized them at all, they thought of as problematic at best. At the start of my aware, self-conscious life, I asked the question that troubled Hesse's Emil Sinclair: Why was it so hard to be my true self? Decades later, I was still asking it.

When the time approached to renew our lease on the flat, we decided a temporary separation might ease our troubles and help us get past this bad patch. Of course, such separations never do, and these kinds of compromises are merely ways of avoiding the real issue—that we were not suited for a long-term commitment such as marriage entailed, or used to at least. For a time, the separation did seem to work. But not for long.

IT'S OFTEN SAID that a man must hit rock bottom before he can work his way up again. I can say that in my case this was true. The rock bottom I hit and what brought me there, however, was not a financial crisis, nor drug addiction, alcoholism, or homelessness. Although it led to quite a bit of drama, it was much less dramatic than that. What was it? It was simply accepting that, after all, perhaps I wasn't going to be a writer in the way I wanted to. It was accepting that perhaps I needed to give up that dream and finally find some place in the "real world." I had given it a shot and hadn't succeeded. But wasn't there more to life than that? Everyone else told me there was, and they seemed to be happy.

My thoughts followed this theme, and seemed to lead to only one conclusion. I reached it as I was walking across the campus one day in early spring, 1995. By this time, we had each found our own flats and, strangely enough, there was a feeling, or at least the hint of one, that we might be able to repair the damage to our marriage. What precipitated my reflections, I can't recall. But I began to think along these lines:

"I *should* be happy, shouldn't I? I mean, here I am, with a very well-paying job. It's not what I *really* want to do, but at least I am writing and using my intelligence. And look at what comes with it—an office, a secretary, contact with scientists working (as I had pointed out to the alumni ad nauseum) at the cutting edge of their fields. I'm heading for forty but still young. I can still establish myself and have a career. F and I can patch up our differences and enjoy life . . ." And so on.

I went on with my inner monologue, doing my best to sell myself on this change of heart, and determined to work hard to make it real. That enthusiasm, however, did not last. Suddenly it fell away, producing the psychic equivalent of the shock we feel when a plane drops several feet during a flight. Or when we see that the ice we are skating on has cracked. I *should* be happy. Yes. But *am I*? From somewhere deep within me, from the dwelling place, no doubt, of whatever it was in there that needed to come out, a single word rose up and gave me the answer. It was "No." I wasn't happy, no matter how many times I told myself that I should be. I could do all the things I just told myself I would do, but it wouldn't change a thing. The part of me that really mattered, that was involved with what I valued most, the part that wanted above all to become itself most intensely, rebelled against my capitulation. I knew then that if I did this, I would be miserable for the rest of my life. I also knew then that I couldn't do it. If I did, I would, as the existentialists say, be living inauthentically. And that was no life at all.

Hesse says somewhere that if we cannot make the changes needed to follow the promptings of our true self, they will be made for us—and not always with our comfort in mind. Jung makes the same point when he tells us that if we do not consciously heed the needs of the unconscious, they will nevertheless be met, in ways that most likely will not be pleasant. Goethe tells us that a decision made with true resolve puts forces in motion that will have a tangible effect on our lives. I do not know if the moment of doubt I experienced, and my subsequent revulsion at the idea of giving up my dream, put into motion forces that led to the complete breakdown of my life. But the "sensitivity to initial conditions" that can transform the gentle flutter of a butterfly's wings into a tornado operates not only in the physical realms but in the psychic ones too. The rock bottom of despair I hit on that walk across the campus may very well have signaled to whatever it was inside me that, if it wanted to come out, it would have to resort to some desperate measures. Was it destiny? I don't know yet. But from that moment on, everything changed.

The central change was that any idea of a reconciliation with F went out the window. She had met someone else. And with the impulsiveness of someone whose life no doubt needed to change as well, she had run off with him. The details are irrelevant. What matters to this story is the effect her sudden disappearance had on me. One might think that, given we were separated and that I had come to see that I wasn't happy with my life, I would accept her freedom to act as she chose and concern myself with what I needed to do. Such logic, however, escaped me. The fact that she had run off with another man wounded my *amour propre*—my self-esteem—and my ego. But there was something else.

The crack in the psychic ice I had felt when the reality of my unhappiness was made clear to me widened. To continue with the metaphor, I suddenly felt as if I were stuck on a very small chunk of the stuff, and was quickly floating away from any sight of land. Or that the plane I was flying on dropped about a thousand feet in a second. All the moorings, all the supports, all the ties that bound me to life—the one I had been living—were gone. I was on my own and I was terrified.

I plunged into a depression that lasted several months. Was it technically a depression, in the pathological sense? I don't know. I can say that I took no antidepressants and when the therapist I was seeing offered to refer me to someone who could prescribe them, I declined. I told him that taking antidepressants would only make me more depressed, and I can mark my slow emergence from the black hole of pain I had found myself in from that moment. But before then, and for some time after, I do know that I found it impossible to stop weeping or sobbing or feeling utterly lost. Perhaps the fact that I had left home at an early age and that I had already been uprooted a few times, shuttling back and forth across the country, had something to do with it. Perhaps the fact that, when young, I didn't receive the kind of unconditional love we all need to receive made me more prone to this sense of desolation and cosmic loneliness. Whatever it was, my waking life was little more than a consciousness of pain.

I couldn't read. I couldn't watch television. I couldn't listen to music. Writing anything was out of the question. It may sound melodramatic, but I did think of suicide. At least, the idea of smashing my skull in with a hammer seemed attractive if it would get rid of the pain.

Nothing distracted me from the feeling of complete and total isolation from everything. Heidegger speaks of *Geworfenheit*, the sense of being thrown into existence. The way I felt, it seemed I had been thrown out of it.

As can be imagined, my distraught state did not help at work. I did my best to keep myself together, but it cost a tremendous effort to keep my mind focused on whatever grant I was working on. One of the other grant writers, a woman a few years younger than myself, saw the wreck I was and brought me home one evening, where she and her husband babysat me. I can't remember her name but she showed true compassion and sympathy, and I thank her for it. The young Hispanic fellow did something the same, inviting me to his flat for dinner. The pro who had counseled me on "losing it" told me to get some drugs and take a few days off to pull myself together. Other than this, he had nothing much to say.

When I learned of a seminar on science writing taking place in Portland, Oregon, I was told the department would take care of my expenses if I wanted to go. I decided I would, thinking a change of scenery might help. Attending the seminar actually did. The lectures were interesting and I learned more than a few things about writing. But whenever I was on my own, the pain returned—or rather, I remembered it or remembered its cause, as if I had forgotten about the death of a close friend until something suddenly brought it back to mind. I had a very bad spell while driving on a freeway from my hotel to the conference center where the seminar was being held. I was too thoughtful of others to give in to the impulse to drive into a wall. But had I been on a road less traveled . . .

When I returned from that seminar, the head of the department asked if I would like to talk to one of the counselors on campus. I took this as a sign that she understood what I was going through and wanted to help. I soon learned that her motives were less altruistic.

I went and had a tearful fifty-minute hour with one of the campus shrinks, a very considerate and understanding individual. She, too, asked if I had considered taking antidepressants. I told her that I had an opportunity to, but turned it down.

Looking back now, I see that if I wanted to keep the job, I should have accepted her offer. I suspect that the head wanted to get the counselor's assessment of my state, and that the verdict was that I was unstable and most likely unable to perform my duties with the required dispatch. In any case, not long after seeing the campus shrink, the head came into my office and let me know that my services were no longer required. My psychological state was preventing me from performing my work and she had no option but to let me go.

"Oh no!" I thought. "I lost my wife, my life, and now my job." This was, of course, exactly what I wanted to happen. I just didn't know that. I had dawdled, and fate, impatient with my dithering, took things in hand. Yet, the gumption that had me stand up for my elderly colleague did not desert me. "Screw this," I said, if not to my ex-boss then certainly to myself. "You're not getting rid of me that easily." I didn't want to stay, but I wanted to leave with something more than what I had arrived with. In the end, this meant three months' severance pay and a guarantee of several months of unemployment benefits. I may have been depressed and suicidal, but I wasn't stupid. I knew that wherever I was heading, I may not need a job—but, as mentioned, I would certainly need money.

BEING FREE OF MY CAREER as a science writer was some relief. But it also meant I had time on my hands and nothing to do with it except be miserable. Friends took turns minding me, offering distractions. I must have been a tiresome bundle, and I thank them for their kindness. For a while I fell into a routine of sorts. I took to sleeping on the floor; I associated my bed with sleepless nights and tried to trick myself, to upset habits and expectations. I grew fond of warm milk flavored with orgeat, an almond syrup. I frequented an Italian restaurant in my neighborhood and allowed myself a glass of expensive red wine with my dinner. And I began to be able to read—but only what is called "escapist" fiction. I needed to forget myself, and I found that this helped. Gradually, I was able to return to life.

Sometime in early summer, I saw that *Gnosis* magazine and the Open Center were co-sponsoring an event in the Czech Republic that September. An essential item for getting yourself out of the sort of slough of despond I had been wallowing in is having somewhere else to go. "The Rosicrucian Enlightenment Revisited," as the conference they were presenting was called, seemed like a good destination. By this time, the esotourist business started up by the Harmonic Convergence had been well established, and conferences on some esoteric subject or other could be found at quite a few exotic locations.

This particular conference was in honor of Frances Yates, the twentieth-century historian, and her book, *The Rosicrucian Enlightenment* (1972). The Rosicrucians were a group of radical German Protestant intellectuals in the early seventeenth century who created a "furore" throughout Europe by posting a series of manifestos declaring the start of a "universal reformation" and the dawn of a new age. Much of this was directed at breaking the hold the Hapsburgs had over Europe. They professed to be the followers of the mysterious Christian Rosenkreutz, a traveler in search of lost knowledge who they claimed to have lived to the age of 106, and whose hidden tomb they discovered decades after his death.

The Rosicrucians combined hermetic wisdom with natural science, and their influence on Western history is considerable, if little known. (I write about them in *Politics and the Occult.*) Yates was responsible for bringing much of this to light, as she had already done with her books on Renaissance hermeticism (which I plundered years later, writing *The Quest for Hermes Trismegistus*).

The location for the event was attractive. Cesky Krumlov is a UNESCO world historical site, a small, medieval, postcard-perfect town a few hours south of Prague, near the Austrian border. It escaped bombing in WWII, and so was in chocolate-box condition and only recently opened to tourists, the once-formidable Iron Curtain having kept them away. (Prague itself was not yet Westernized.) My attraction to *Mittle Europa* alone would have suggested a visit, but the lineup of speakers for the event was impressive indeed: The historian of esotericism Joscelyn Godwin; the alchemist Adam McLean; the writer on the Grail legends John Matthews; the Kabbalist Z'ev ben Shimon Halevi; John Michell, whose books on ley lines I knew well; Nicholas Goodrick-Clarke, the expert on Nazi occultism, and his wife, Clare Goodrick-Clarke, a specialist in Renaissance Platonism; Christopher Bamford, the Rudolf Steiner scholar; Christopher McIntosh, whose books on nineteenth-century French occultism I had enjoyed; Robert Sardello, the anthroposophical psychologist; R. J. Stewart, an expert on the magician Merlin; and—top of the bill—the poet Robert Bly. I had read the work of many of the speakers, and in years to come would get to know a few of them relatively well. Right then, the prospect of spending a week in a beautiful medieval Bohemian town, attending lectures on hermeticism, alchemy, and various other arcane subjects, was the main attraction.

I thought, "Right. Whatever happens, I'm going to this." It was a few months down the line and the bad days still outnumbered the good, but having a goal to look forward to making possible helped to gather my forces. I paid for my place at the conference and did some homework on the Rosicrucians. I decided that I might as well take in Prague, too, and arranged for a place to stay there for a week after my time in Cesky Krumlov. In the meantime, I did my best to get through the rest of the summer until it was time to embark on my Bohemian adventure. It was a trip that would change my life.

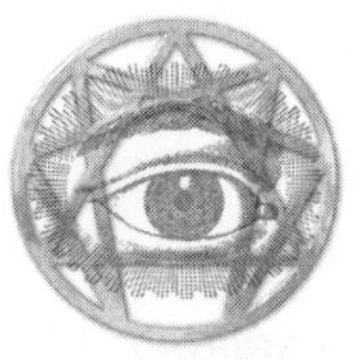

14
London Calling

My route to London and a new life led through Cornwall by way of the Czech Republic.

Let me draw you a map.

I arrived at the central station in Prague on September 8, lugging an overstuffed suitcase and wondering if the little German I knew would be of any help in getting around. (I later learned that, although they speak it well, most Czechs dislike German, a leftover from the Nazi occupation.) My stay at that point would be brief, just long enough to meet the others who, like myself, were on their way to Cesky Krumlov. A crowd of individuals looking as displaced as I did had gathered outside near the coach that would take us there, and I joined them. We hadn't yet met, but I recognized Jay Kinney, one of the editors of *Gnosis*, among the faces, and introduced myself. He then introduced me to some of our travel companions. Then, after the usual muddle and delay that comes with traveling by coach, our luggage was stored and we boarded. Three hours or so later, we arrived at our destination.

My suitcase was packed with more than I would need for the two weeks of my original trip. Before leaving Los Angeles, I received a surprise telephone call. It was from the United Kingdom. Cornwall, in fact. The caller was Colin Wilson. He had heard that I would be in Europe and said he would be delighted if I would extend my travel plans and come visit him and Joy at Tetherdown. How he had heard that I would be "on the continent," as the Brits like to say, I don't recall, if I ever knew. I must have mentioned it to Colin Stanley in some correspondence. I must also have mentioned the breakup of my marriage. Although Colin himself said nothing of this, I soon realized that the invitation to visit was his means of helping me out of my rut.

When I mentioned seeing about the extra charges that detour would incur, Colin interrupted. "It would be my pleasure to pay any fees," he said. When I tried to decline his offer, he insisted, and informed me that he would be terribly offended if I didn't accept—much as he did when I tried to avoid another glass of that oversweet liqueur during my last visit.

Wilson was not the most gregarious person. If not a recluse, he certainly did not enjoy being in the company of too many people for too long. He claimed it induced in him what he called "people poisoning." So, for him to go out of his way and personally call me to insist I fly from Prague to London and make my way down to him was practically unheard of. And that he would pay for me to do it—well, that was nigh unbelievable.

But there was more. Another Wilsonian—an American interested in Wilson, Abraham Maslow, and Henry Miller—was heading to Gorran Haven, as well. M—as I shall call him—was collecting Wilson's letters to various correspondents with the intent of publication, and he intended to visit some of Wilson's UK correspondents while in the country. Why didn't I speak with him and arrange to meet in London? Colin suggested. M and I could hire a car and make a road trip of it.

That was exactly what we did. But first, there were the Rosicrucians.

CESKY KRUMLOV, AS MENTIONED, is a small Bohemian town known for its medieval, Renaissance, Baroque, and Gothic architecture. The fantastic Renaissance-era Krumlov Castle rises from a promontory overlooking the Vltava River, which encircles it as if it were an island. It would be a cliché to say that it looks like the setting for a fairy tale, but during my week there, it did in fact become this. While we were there to attend lectures on hermeticism, alchemy, and other forms of magic, a production team was in town as well, using the location to make some magic of their own. They were shooting scenes for the film *The Adventures of Pinocchio* (1996), starring Martin Landau. The film was a flop (I never saw it, but that's what I've heard), but it was a delightful surprise to turn a corner when out for a stroll through the winding cobblestone streets and bump into a scene from the nineteenth-century fantasy about a wooden puppet that comes to life—a very hermetic theme in itself. To a tourist like myself, it was difficult to tell the difference between what was put up for the film and what was there all the time. For the few days I was there, it didn't matter.

But the picturesque beauty of the place wasn't why it had been picked for the conference—at least, it wasn't the central reason. As Frances Yates made clear in her book, Bohemia in the early seventeenth century was the setting for an esoteric Enlightenment, a burgeoning of hermetic wisdom and knowledge that, in its way, rivaled its more well-known scientific and rational counterpart which began later in the century. Much of the esoteric Enlightenment took place in Prague, where in the previous century, Rudolph II, the Holy Roman Emperor, drew alchemists, Kabbalists, magicians, and other delvers into the arcane arts to his court in his search for "the philosopher's stone" and hidden knowledge. One of the many masters of the mystic arts that Rudolph drew to Prague was the Elizabethan magician and mathematician John Dee, who for a time was Queen Elizabeth I's astrologer. Part of the conference involved a visit to Trebon, another small Czech town where Dee spent some of his time in Bohemia. More locally, the esoteric Enlightenment was represented by Count Wilhelm Rozmberk, who was Dee's host for his stay in Trebon. Like Rudolph, Count Rozmberk was a keen student of hermetic and alchemical knowledge, and used his immense fortune to further his studies.

But the Rosicrucian experiment, as we might call the attempt to unite hermetic wisdom with the rising "natural philosophy" that would eventually become what we know as science, was not confined to arcane knowledge. There was a political wing to it as well. The "universal reformation" the Rosicrucian manifestos spoke of would involve breaking the hold the Catholic Hapsburgs had over a Central Europe weary of their tyranny. Sadly, this liberation did not happen. The hopes of freedom from the Hapsburg yoke were pinned on the young Frederick V, the Elector Palatine and brief King of Bohemia. These hopes were dashed, however, in 1620, at the disastrous Battle of the White Mountain—one of the sights of the conference—when the anti-Hapsburg forces were soundly defeated by the Emperor's army. The short-lived Bohemian Revolt was over, and the Hapsburgs remained in power for another three centuries. What immediately followed was the Thirty Years' War, which devastated Europe and put an end to the Rosicrucian Enlightenment.

Yet, the Rosicrucian experiment was not a complete failure. As Yates points out, its influence reached far into the modern world, among other things, informing science through its involvement with the Royal Society—the world's oldest independent scientific academy—and social life through its promotion of universal education.

Nearly thirty years on, I can't say that I remember many of the details of the conference. And since that time, I have gone on to write about many of the themes it addressed, and so what was new to me then and what I subsequently learned are not easily separated. The talks were held at the courtly Hotel Rose—once a sixteenth-century Jesuit dormitory, now a huge luxury spa overlooking the Vltava. I don't think the attendees stayed there, or at least what I remember of my accommodation doesn't suggest it. Wherever I stayed, my room was spacious enough, but fairly soon after settling in, I discovered I was sharing it with a bat. It was flapping around, bumping into the walls and ceiling. When a porter finally came to shoo it away, I expressed surprise at it being there. "Oh, we get them all the time," he let me know. Well, it was Bohemia.

The other location for many of the events was the Krumlov Castle. Among other talks, this was the setting for a candlelit evening of music and poetry, with Robert Bly reading works from Renaissance poets, accompanied by music from the period—a performance to cap the event. I can remember attending several other talks there, but honesty compels me to admit that I have had to remind myself of them by looking at the brochure for the conference.

The following is not a full account, but it should give the reader a taste of what went on that week. So, we had Joscelyn Godwin speaking about the marvels of the Renaissance gardens, many of which included pagan motifs, a theme which informs his book *The Pagan Dream of the Renaissance* (2002). He also gave a workshop on Michael Maier, whom Frances Yates considered the "deepest of the Rosicrucians." Nicholas Goodrick-Clarke lectured on the mysterious "Bohemian mission" of John Dee and his scryer Edward Kelley, a diplomatic excursion thought to inspire the Rosicrucian Enlightenment that followed. He also gave a talk about the last work of the Austrian occultist and fantasist Gustav Meyrink, *The Angel at the West Window* (1927), in which Dee is a central character. Christopher McIntosh spoke on the legacy of the Rosicrucians, how it informed Freemasonry, alchemy, and other arcane pursuits in the courts of Prussia's Frederick Wilhelm II and Russia's Catherine the Great, something he wrote about in *The Rosicrucians* (1987). Christopher Bamford led us through a close reading of the Rosicrucian manifestos and how their ideas have been adopted by various contemporary Rosicrucian groups. Z'ev ben Shimon Halevi (otherwise known as Warren Kenton) spoke about the influence of Kabbalah on the Rosicrucian experiment, the centrality of Prague in the hermetic Renaissance, and the work of Rabbi Judah Loew, who is said to have created a golem—a human figure of clay brought to life by magic. And Clare Goodrick-Clarke lectured on the work of Jan Comenius, the Rosicrucian responsible for the promotion of universal schooling, and who is honored by the Comenius Medal awarded by UNESCO to individuals and institutions for outstanding service in education.

There were other talks, and some of the most lively discussions—at least, that I heard—were about the differences between what we can call "physical" or "material" alchemy and the more "spiritual" or "psychological" brand associated with the work of Jung. "Real" alchemy, at least according to those who practice it, may not be about turning lead into gold, but it is certainly concerned with actual, perceptible changes in the substances alchemists work with. This may take the form of extracting "essences" from certain plants or other organic substances. The Jungian sort sees alchemy as a form of what we might call "unconscious individuation"—that is, according to Jung, the alchemists of old were really practicing a form of what he called "active imagination." Jung believed that, when performing their operations, the alchemists of the Middle Ages and Renaissance projected unconscious contents onto the substances they worked with, and that the philosopher's stone and other alchemical objectives were symbols of the unification of the conscious and unconscious minds. A third approach to alchemy rejects Jung's psychological approach and sees it as a true spiritual discipline, raising the alchemist's consciousness to a higher metaphysical level.

As I recall, the "hard" and "soft" alchemists at the conference—the physical and the spiritual ones—did not have much good to say about each other. If I remember correctly, Adam McLean leaned more toward the "hard" school than toward the Jungians. After one of his talks, I spoke with a Dutch journalist who was writing about the conference for some magazine. He said he found McLean's talk interesting, but that he was more interested in the spiritual approach to alchemy than in the more "hands-on" method. At the time, I agreed with him. Years later, though, when I met a practicing "hard" alchemist in Devon, I had to admit I was impressed with the results of his work.

Other stray memories come to mind: of discovering the small but impressive Egon Schiele museum, one of the major figures of Viennese expressionism, who lived in Cesky Krumlov for a brief time; of wandering along the riverfront and coming upon a café frequented by members of the local avant-garde; of drinking *pivo* (beer) rather than wine, because that's what you do in the Czech Republic. But, although the conference and the talks were certainly memorable, what stands out most for me were some of the people I met—because, it was through meeting them that, a few months later, I would pull up stakes in LA and make my way to the UK.

As coincidence would have it—or fate, or destiny—almost as soon as I arrived at the conference, I bumped into someone I knew from LA. S was a friend of X, and over the years X had mentioned a few times that the two of us should get together, as we seemed to have many interests in common. Aside from one or two brief encounters, this meeting of minds did not take place. Now, some six thousand miles from home, it finally did. When we saw each other, we had to laugh. If we didn't say "Funny meeting you here," it would have been absolutely appropriate if we had.

Like myself, S had an interest in esotericism—but, also like myself, he was a fan of Lovecraft and the *Weird Tales* set. He was a screenwriter and director with a few cult horror films under his belt; in the years following the conference, he subsequently went on to greater glories. He knew about my pop star past, but he had also read my articles in *Gnosis*. After missing each other over the years in LA, we made up for lost time at the conference. Conversation ranged far and wide, from the horror films of the 1940s to my experiences in the Work. I started to get the odd feeling that I had found myself at one of those turning points in life, and that the peculiar "initial conditions" of finding myself at an esoteric conference in the Czech Republic would, like the gentle wings of that overachieving butterfly, lead to some curious results.

S had spent time in London, and had made some friends. Like him, they worked in media—some in music, some in film, some in rock videos, and the relatively recent form known as the "graphic novel," a more sophisticated and adult kind of comic book, which, I have to admit, I never quite took to. They also had an interest in the esoteric. Some of S's London friends had come to Cesky Krumlov for the conference, and at an outdoor café over some *pivo* he introduced me to them. I liked them immediately. They were intelligent, well-read, and their conversation had a harder edge to it than some of the more "spiritual" exchanges I'd had so far.

Some of them were involved with a magazine I had heard of but didn't know well until I moved to London and starting writing for it. This was the *Fortean Times*, a journal dedicated to "strange phenomena," inspired by the work of the American writer and collector of anomalies, Charles Fort. I had read about Fort years ago in *The Morning of the Magicians*, and Colin Wilson had written about him in some of his books. What attracted these people to Fort and the conference was their predilection for the weird and strange. They were not spiritual but they were spirited, and when one of them—who went on to become a good friend in London—told me that he had been at the Blondie–Television concert at London's Hammersmith Odeon in 1977, and saw me hopping around on stage, I felt I had fallen in with the right crowd.

I told S the sad story of the breakup of my marriage and the crack-up that followed. He was sympathetic and said what I needed was to get away from all of that. When I mentioned I would be heading to Prague for a week after the conference, and that after that I would be going to Cornwall to visit Colin Wilson, he said he would be in London for a while himself. Why didn't I catch up with him there before I flew back to LA? S's friends—slightly impressed that I would be visiting Wilson at his invitation—suggested the same. So, we arranged for us all to meet a day or two before my return flight. S also let me know that he was considering relocating to London for a while. His plans were still fluid, but maybe I should think about that too? In any case, we could talk about it.

I HAD ARRANGED FOR A PLACE to stay in Prague through an agency in LA. This was long before the time of Airbnb, and at that point there were not many hotels in the city—at least, that's what I was told. By now I suspect that has changed, but in 1995, Prague had yet to be Westernized—the first McDonald's there had opened only a few years earlier. Instead of a hotel room, I rented a small flat for a week. It was out of the city center, far from the tourist sights, in a working-class district—a rather drab, nondescript neighborhood that suggested more the country's recent past under communism than anything Rudolf II might have had in mind. The Velvet Revolution of 1989, following the collapse of the Berlin Wall, may have ended communist rule, but its ghost had yet to be exorcised. I can remember passing by large, empty plazas, with sculptures of rocket ships commemorating great Soviet advances in the "space race" of the 1960s. The newspaper flapping in the wind along the paving stones somehow seemed an appropriate commentary on these past glories.

Something else I remember from one of my tram rides back to the flat was the lovable, cute street urchin who tried to steal my wallet. There was a slight tug at my back pocket, and I could feel the wallet move. When I turned around, the boy (he couldn't have been more than ten or eleven) gave me a look that said, "So? What are you going to do?" He glared at me for a moment, then got off at the next stop.

My impressions of Prague before my visit had come from reading Kafka. As I walked around the city, which, like Cesky Krumlov, had been untouched by the war—so the architecture was just as fantastic and dreamlike—I saw shops selling Kafka T-shirts, cafés selling Kafka coffee, *hospodas* (pubs) selling Kafka *pivo*, and different locations announcing that Kafka had lived, worked, ate, drank, or slept there. For someone who felt absolutely crushed by the city, as Kafka had, for whom depression was a way of life and who had asked his friend, Max Brod, to burn his work, the impression this Kafkamania produced was anything but Kafkaesque. What would Kafka have thought to discover that, years after his death, a city that overwhelmed him and induced a sense of perpetual paranoia now celebrated him as one of its greatest citizens?

My more recent reading in Czech literature included some of the novels of Milan Kundera and those of Josef Skvorecky, whose detective stories about Lieutenant Boruvka of the Prague Homicide Bureau I had come to enjoy. Skvorecky, who for many years taught English at the University of Toronto, was a reader of Colin Wilson and Lovecraft, and wrote introductions to many of Lovecraft's works that were translated into Czech. One work I wanted to read but found difficult to get through was Jaroslav Hašek's classic *The Good Soldier Svejk* (1921), a satire on WWI in which, through a series of misadventures, a simple "common man" wreaks havoc on the Austria-Hungarian army. I found the humor ponderous, and lost interest.

Another book that prepared me for the visit, and made a greater impact, was *Magic Prague* (1978) by Angelo Maria Ripellino. This dense, erudite, complex, and often obscure work is something like a travel guide to Prague's less-known mysteries. As some have suggested, it is an early entry in a genre of writing that would become more popular in decades to come: psychogeography. Ripellino, an Italian who lived in Prague for many years, stalks the streets of *Stare Mesto* and *Nove Mesto* (the Old Town and New Town), *Mala Strana* (the "Little Quarter"), *Josefov* (the Jewish Quarter), and other parts of this haunted city, taking his cues from monuments, cafés, street names, and other urban features for tales of magic, mystery, and the peculiar states of mind this ancient capital can induce. Its curious blend of anecdote, historical fact, biographical detail, and poetic invention makes for a very heady read.

One Prague staple—almost as ubiquitous as Kafka and *pivo*—that Ripellino returns to often is the golem, the fantastic man of clay brought to life by the Kabbalistic magic of Rabbi Loew. I had read Gustav Meyrink's atmospheric expressionist work on this theme, *The Golem* (1913), some years back, but brought my copy along to reread in the city in which it takes place. I brought it on my long, meandering walks, and indulged in some psychogeography of my own. One obvious location was the ancient Jewish cemetery where Rabbi Loew's gravestone still stands. The cemetery goes back to the 1400s, and was in use until 1787, when the Holy Roman Emperor Josef II banned burials within the city's walls. Thousands of gravestones crowd the small burial ground—jutting out at odd angles, they give the impression of a weird, megalithic sight. Many are adorned with small stones, what are known as visitation stones, a sign of respect and remembrance for the dead. Rabbi Loew's gravestone had more than a few.

Other vagrant memories come to me. Prague is home to a number of buildings created according to the designs of cubist architecture, rather as if a Picasso or Braque had leaped off the canvas, grown a few stories, and become 3D. I sought these rare structures out, visiting the House of the Black Madonna in the Old Town, originally the site of a Baroque mansion; the Diamant House in the New Town; and an area known as the Cubist Island, which features some of the best examples of this little-known architectural style.

These last homes are in the Vyšehrad district, along the river, not far from another cemetery. The Vyšehrad Cemetery, near the Vyšehrad Castle, is the final resting place of some of the greatest Czech artists, writers, and musicians. I wandered through the spacious grounds—rather different than the small confines of the Jewish cemetery—finding the graves of the composers Dvorák, Smetana, and Josef Suk, the conductors Rafael Kubelik and Karel Ančerl, and the writer Karel Capek (who gave us the word "robot"), among others.

Other excursions took me to a museum dedicated to the work of the artist František Kupka, whose paintings I had first seen years ago at the *Spiritual in Art* exhibition at the Los Angeles County Museum of Art. Another took me to the heart of the city and the center of the esoteric Enlightenment that came to an end with the Battle of White Mountain and the collapse of the Rosicrucian dream—this was Prague Castle, home of the hermetic Holy Roman Emperor, Rudolf II.

What I remember most about the castle is Golden Lane, a narrow street lined with small houses that some believe were occupied by Rudolf II's alchemists, busily at work turning lead into gold. This, I discovered, is more legend than fact. The houses were occupied by Rudolf's goldsmiths, fashioning ornaments and decorations with gold obtained, one suspects, through normal routes—although one can't help but think that an alembic or two must have been part of their furnishings. (Rudolf's alchemists, among them Edward Kelley, did live and work in the Mihulka Tower, now known as the Powder Tower because it was later used to store gunpowder.) Kafka lived in one of the tiny houses on Golden Lane for a short time, and their brightly colored facades, which give the street a Disneyesque character, were only painted in the 1950s. (Thinking of it now, the impression is rather like a condensed Cesky Krumlov.) Shops, cafés, and other tourist spots have taken over, and the magic associated with the place these days stems more, it seems, from Harry Potter than any esoteric Enlightenment.

Rudolf II was as interested in the nascent science of the time as he was in alchemy and, along with Kelley and Dee, drew more reputable figures to his court—among them the astronomers Johannes Kepler and Tycho Brahe, whose work laid the foundations of our modern view of the cosmos. There is a story that Tycho died of a burst bladder because he refused to relieve himself during a royal banquet—a caution to the overly etiquette minded. Rudolf was also an obsessive collector of paintings, objects d'art, and natural curiosities, and during his long reign he amassed a remarkable collection that he housed in what was known as his *Kunst und Wunderkammer* (his "art and wonder chamber"), what today is called his "cabinet of curiosities." "Cabinet," however, does not relay the size of Rudolf's collection, which required serious additions to the castle in order to contain it. It was the sort of place Huysmans's decadent Jean des Esseintes would have spent days reveling in. For the afternoon I spent wandering within it, I did myself.

I HAD ARRANGED TO MEET M, the American collecting Colin Wilson correspondence, in London, at a hotel on Villiers Street, near Charing Cross. I had hired a car at Heathrow, and recall that it took some time to find a parking space. I finally did, somewhere on the other side of the river. Although I have lived in London now for twenty-seven years (as I write, I am about to start my twenty-eighth), and have driven in the UK many times, I have never gotten used to being on the wrong side of the road. I can remember walking back across the old

Charing Cross Bridge—replaced in 2000 as part of London's millennium makeover—stopping, and looking at the Thames, with St. Paul's in the distance. It had been a very packed two weeks. I had seen and done quite a bit, and now I was about to embark on another leg of my journey.

While in Cesky Krumlov, the talks, the fantastic setting, and the new friends I had made kept me occupied, and for a time I had forgotten why I'd made the trip in the first place. Alone in Prague, it began to come back to me. I began to miss F, and the pain and disappointment of our breakup returned. Now, in London, I found myself thinking, "What am I doing here?" The lost feeling that had overcome me in LA took hold, and for much of that part of the trip it remained in the background, like a nagging awareness that I had left some unpleasant but unavoidable business undone and that I could put it off no longer.

It was not the best state of mind in which to meet someone I didn't know, and travel with them. When I got to the hotel, I discovered that M had booked us into a shared room, rather than separate ones, as I had asked. "It was cheaper," he said. It was not the best way to start the trip, and marked the first of a few dissonances between us that came up along the way. It was not M's fault—I was not in a mood for company, at least not yet. But, soon into our road trip, it was clear to me, at least, that our journey would be a bumpy one.

Perhaps because it was, I find it difficult to remember much, prior to our reaching Cornwall. I know we drove to somewhere in the north, so M could meet with one of Wilson's correspondents, a crime writer he had helped get published, if I recall correctly. His name escapes me now. I have a vague memory of a rather grim, nondescript town and the small terraced house where he lived. Aside from London and Cornwall, and tourist cities like Bath, I had not seen much of England. (I had, of course, been on tour there in 1977, but we stayed at hotels and saw little aside from them and wherever we were playing.) Wherever it was that I had driven to, it was not part of the holiday route.

It all seemed rather depressing. We sat in a small kitchen, drinking tea while M and our host talked about Wilson and the plans M had for publishing his correspondence. I enjoyed meeting our host, but for some reason found the talk about Wilson boring. Perhaps because his work meant so much to me, I didn't care to hear someone else go on about it. I had no proprietary claim on it, of course, but I didn't like feeling that I was a "fan," in the same way M or others of his readers were—ego, of course, and my own bad mood. But even then, I was determined to be something more than that.

Another stop I recall before heading to the West Country was Nottingham, where we visited Colin Stanley and his wife, Gail. We had been in correspondence but had yet to meet—the same I think was true of M—and I found Colin and his wife very warm, charming, and inviting. What comes back to me now, as I try to picture our visit, is the huge and pristine collection of Wilson's books adorning practically one whole wall of their house, if I remember correctly. It made even me, who had no small Wilson library, envious. Colin Stanley later donated this collection—which by then had grown in size, Wilson being something of a writing machine—to Nottingham University, laying the foundation of the Colin Wilson Archive established there in 2012, a year before Wilson's death.

At the time of our visit, Stanley was a librarian at the university, and what I saw on the rest of his bookshelves suggested wide and serious reading. He had been a reader of Wilson since the early '70s, and since 1983 had been publishing short works by or about Wilson in his Pauper's Press Colin Wilson Studies series, to which, as mentioned, I had contributed a title, and would contribute another a year after my visit. He, along with Paul Newman, who published the Wilson-themed fanzine *Abraxas*, kept a small but dedicated cohort of readers informed about new books and other publications of Wilson's, and also provided them with a means of sharing their own ideas and creative efforts. I would meet Paul and his partner Pam on this trip, during a brief stop in St. Austell, where they lived, and would later contribute more than a few articles to *Abraxas*, until it stopped publication with Paul's death in the summer of 2013, six months before Wilson himself passed away. My book on Crowley is dedicated to him.

Unfortunately, what also comes back to me as I write is the row M and I got into during our visit to the Stanleys. I don't remember what it was about, but I'm sure that, given my mood, it wouldn't have taken much for me to overreact. I remember trying to talk with him about something *other* than Wilson while driving through the English countryside—the scenery, for example—and not getting very far. Again, it was not his fault I couldn't shake the unhappiness that was like a background radiation in my mind, the sense of being lost and the loneliness that came with it. He was under no obligation to make allowances for my mood, even if I felt he could have been a bit more aware of what was behind it.

I am more understanding of this now than I was then, though. At one point during our stay, I told M that I would make the rest of the journey on my own. I had hired the car, after all, and he could just as easily take a train to Cornwall. I was taking this trip, I reminded him, to get over the breakup of my marriage, not to chauffeur him around England. As you might suspect, this did not go down that well, and it took considerable peacemaking efforts by Colin Stanley to defuse the situation and get me to be reasonable.

From Nottingham to Gorran Haven, where Wilson lived, is a journey of some three hundred miles, just a tad short of my LA-SF jaunts. We—or, I should say, I (M didn't share the driving)—had already driven the one hundred-plus miles up from London. If we stopped anywhere along the way to meet another Wilson correspondent, I can't remember it. The last time I had driven to Cornwall—from London, not Nottingham—was a year earlier, when F and I had visited Colin and Joy at the beginning of 1994. Here, I was making my way there again, this time on my own—or, at least, without a partner. M and I had reached some understanding. At least, we didn't argue again. I can't remember what we talked about along the way. I didn't have much to say, and may have let him carry on as he liked while doing my best to ignore it.

This would be my third visit to Wilson's home. I've mentioned the musty smell of paper slowly giving way to damp that I remember from the chalet where I would stay. Providentially, M was given a different guest space, a slowly disintegrating caravan that was itself packed with books, parked on the other side of the house. Whether by design or chance, having the chalet to myself was welcome.

Another smell that greeted me, and I remembered, as Joy let us into her home, was that of toast. I suspect it is a common aroma in many English homes, and it is, of course, not unknown in the States. But the English seem to have a peculiar predilection for toast, which seemed certainly true in this household. It was a warm, homey fragrance that somehow seemed to go well with the slight doggy scent their pets provided. Over the years I have seen dogs, cats, and parrots on my visits to Tetherdown, making their way through the stacks of books, videos, and cassettes, and the occasional empty wine bottle or half-finished cup of tea that found a place on the living room floor. My own tendency to neatness wouldn't have allowed it at home, but here it seemed perfectly natural, as did the overstuffed bookshelves covering practically every bit of available wall space.

We had arrived for dinner, which we had eating off plates on our laps in the living room, sharing a sofa while Colin, who had spent the day, as he always did, sunk in his basement workroom, sat in a huge recliner, the television remote control within easy access. The dinner started, as it usually did in the Wilson household, with a serving of smoked salmon and avocado, and glasses of chilled white wine.

I've mentioned that Wilson was not the most gregarious individual. He was prone to watching the news while chatting, and his usually brief replies to any questions we had were often interrupted by a shout of indignation at some stupidity on the screen. I can remember a particular advertisement for an energy company that sponsored the weather report. It informed its viewers that the company—I can't remember its name—brings them energy "whatever the weather." The idea that the weather had anything to do with the electricity supply elicited an unprintable remark from Wilson. He was not the most tolerant person.

At the time of our visit, the O. J. Simpson murder trial was dominating the news. Simpson, a football and film celebrity, was charged with the murder of his ex-wife Nicole Simpson and her friend Ron Goldman, who were found stabbed to death outside Nicole's home on June 12, 1994. I can remember watching the television coverage of the low-speed car chase in which Simpson, who had failed to turn himself in as he had promised, forced a friend to drive him to his Brentwood estate.

Simpson was arrested, and the subsequent trial came to an end during our stay at Tetherdown. On October 3, 1995, Simpson was acquitted of the murders, a decision that "split the nation," as the cliché goes, with many people believing that racial concerns played a part in it. I can remember Colin shaking his head and saying, "he did it." With all he had written about the psychology of murder, he may have been right. Some years later, Simpson, who had been a football hero while I was first living in New York, was arrested for armed robbery and given a thirty-three-year sentence; he was released on parole after serving nine years.

Colin was usually invisible during the day, sequestering himself in his workroom and banging away at his typewriter (it would be some time before he upgraded to a computer). I spent most of my time on my own, walking along the cliffs or beach. I can't remember if his sons were there that visit, but his daughter, Sally, was, and I met her then for the first time. I had read about her in some of her father's books, and we got on well, mostly because, unlike M, I didn't pester her with questions or what I understood were some unwanted attentions. She was a few years younger than me, intelligent, well-read, and with her mother's looks. In subsequent years and over other visits, I got to know her fairly well and we became friends.

As mentioned, Colin spent the day huddled in his workroom. He usually went off to bed fairly early, around nine p.m., leaving Joy in charge of the guests, and woke up around six a.m., when he read for an hour or so with his morning tea. Then, he was at the keyboard until around four p.m., when he took the dogs for a walk. One afternoon, I was there as he was about to set off, and he invited me along.

Although very affectionate and demonstrative with his family, with others he was less emotional—a not uncommon trait among the British. (I find that this is true even of Brits I have known for many years.) I wasn't looking for any sort of "male bonding"—I am not particularly demonstrative myself—and in fact felt that I had outgrown whatever need Wilson may have filled as a "father figure" for me. After all, I was nearly forty. This didn't mean that I found his ideas any less important—quite the opposite. What I wanted to do was explore those ideas and put them into action, to write about them in the context of other ideas about consciousness, life, reality, and the other fundamental questions about existence.

We walked along the cliffs for a while. I asked about what he was working on at the time. I believe it was what became *Alien Dawn* (1998), his book about UFOs. Or possibly *The Atlantis Blueprint* (2000), one of his entries in the ancient civilization genre that Graham Hancock had massive bestsellers in. He had also just finished a sequel to his science fiction novel *The Space Vampires* (1976), the still-unpublished *Metamorphosis of the Vampires*, a manuscript copy of which I started reading during my stay and which Colin allowed me to keep. It is resting in a box in my closet somewhere, and I wrote about my visit and the manuscript in a short article about my trip for *Gnosis*.

After a while he asked how I was keeping and said that he had heard about the breakup with F. He had met her twice, first years ago when he stayed with us in the Zen castle in Laurel Canyon, and then during our visit in 1994. He said he was sorry to hear about it, and that he liked her. When he asked if there was any chance of a reconciliation, I mentioned she was with someone else already. Maybe after she tired of him, there might be a chance, I said. His response was sharp. "What? Are you going to wait in the queue?" It was as if he had heard something stupid on the telly. It was also the best thing he could have said.

After that, he asked about my writing. Did I have any ideas for any books? When I said that I wanted to write about him and his work, he said, "Forget it. No one will buy the book. No editor will commission it. I have a hard enough time getting my own books published. Anything else?"

I said I thought there was a need for a good, popular book—a biography—on Rudolf Steiner.

"That's a better idea. Steiner could use a good biography. The ones that have been written are hagiographies, or dismiss him outright. I bet you can find a publisher for that."

He was right on that account, but wrong on the first. A publisher did commission my book about him, which I wrote some years after my biography of Steiner.

I CAN'T RECALL EXACTLY HOW LONG I stayed at Tetherdown that visit. As I mentioned, I spent most of my time alone. I would find a quiet spot along the cliffs looking out over the channel, sit and read, or simply look at the waves reaching the shore. I loved finding some huge rock jutting out of the ground dramatically, covered in lichen, and would spend long stretches looking at the discoloration in the stone. I have been to Cornwall many times, but on each visit I am reminded of the peculiar atmospheric effects that are common to the area—sudden downpours or cold mists, followed by brilliant sunshine, and clouds so low in the sky one expects them to land. It's no wonder the terrain there is associated with magic.

When it came time for me to leave, so I could make my return flight—M had booked a different one—I mentioned to Colin that I wanted to drive through Dorset, John Cowper Powys country, the setting for *A Glastonbury Romance* and the other novels of his "Dorset Quartet." I had learned that there was a bookshop in the area, specializing in his work, and wanted to stop there on my way to London. Colin said he would get a map and show me the route. It would take me to where the flood that ends the novel breaks out. He fumbled around in a drawer, shoving its contents aside, then pulled out a West Country roadmap. He opened it, and held it up against the kitchen wall. As he looked for the route he wanted to show me, he began to get frustrated. He knew it was there, but the stupid map didn't show it.

"Where's the bloody route?" he said impatiently, as much to the map as to anyone else. Joy, hearing the urgency in his voice, came over. She took one look at the map Colin still had pinned to the wall with his hand, took his hand away from it, and held the map in place. Then she turned it right side up.

"Colin," she said, "you had it upside down."

As Wilson himself told me and his other readers many times, it is the "trivialities of everydayness" that are the Outsider's worst danger.

I GOT TO LONDON a couple of days before my flight, and took a room in an old-school bed-and-breakfast in Bloomsbury, near the British Museum, not far from where Lisa and I stayed ages ago on our trip at the end of 1980. S had given me the phone number of where he was staying. I called, and he was glad to hear from me. He said he would get in touch with some of the friends he had introduced me to in Cesky Krumlov, and we could catch up at a pub. We did. We also arranged to take in the fantastic art installation, *H.G.*, by Robert Wilson and Hans Peter Kühn, based on the work of H. G. Wells. It was held at the Clink Street Vaults, in a very old part of London, in Southwark along the Thames, an area I came to love. We walked through rooms done up as sets for *The Time Machine*, with a Victorian dinner table from which the guests have disappeared, to a vision of a bleak dystopian future.

At another pub, S and I talked about his plans. He intended to stay in London for a few months at least, possibly longer if he could find work. He was tired of the Hollywood grind and found that the film industry in London was more open to unusual ideas. Another factor informed his decision. He had met a woman, the sister of a friend, and had hopes that something would work out between them. British women, though—he informed me—are odd, unlike the women he knew in LA. Exactly what he meant by that wasn't clear. In any case, if I felt like having a change of scenery for a while, the two of us could, he said, find a flat to share. What did I think?

I had just spent the past few weeks having nothing but a change of scenery, but his idea sounded good. There wasn't much waiting for me in LA, but starting over once again—this time in a foreign country—required some consideration. I said I would think about it and let him know as soon as I could.

WHEN I GOT BACK TO LA, it didn't take long for me to reach a decision. I had lived there for fourteen years—sixteen if you counted my early stretch with The Know. I had a failed marriage, some bouts of depression, a career as a rocker, an aborted one as a teacher, another as a science writer, long years in retail selling crystals and self-help books, some good friends, several affairs, a degree in philosophy, and a handful of articles and book reviews to show for that time. A mixed bag, indeed. I would turn forty in two months and had enough money in the bank to support myself while I wondered how I would get more. Once again, the truth came back to me—I didn't need a job, I needed money.

I called S and asked if he was still interested in sharing a flat in London. He was. I told him he was on. It would take me a couple of months to set things in order here. Could he wait until the new year? He could, and was excited I had decided to make the move. I booked a flight for the first of the year, and would see him in January.

I decided that if I was ever going to be a writer, now was the time. My plan would be simple. I would give up my flat in LA, ask Lisa if she could rent me a room (which she did, in a house she had recently purchased), sell everything I didn't want, give away what I couldn't sell, and find someplace to store the rest. This, of course, meant my books. Once again, I would pack them in boxes and, once again, they would follow me as soon as I was settled. Only, this time it would be not only across the country but the Atlantic as well.

At the beginning of *The Invisible Writing*, one of his volumes of autobiography, Arthur Koestler has a quotation from the poet Dylan Thomas: "When one burns one's bridges, what a very nice fire it makes." Indeed. "The invisible writing"—written, as mentioned, in invisible ink—is the name Koestler gave to the hidden meaning, the unseen order, that informs the everyday world, to which reductive science and gloomy existentialism limit their perspective. Fate and destiny make appearances in Koestler's story, just as they have here. At our last session, when I told my therapist that I had decided to pull up stakes and head to London, he said, "Good luck." To throw yourself, at forty, into a foreign country and make a fresh start with little more than a wing and a prayer took guts, he told me.

Maybe it did. Or maybe it was an act of desperation. Whatever it was, making the decision was a relief, as it had been when I decided that, whatever happened, I would go hear about the Rosicrucians in Cesky Krumlov.

Once again, Lisa proved an extraordinary friend. She, too, had been through more than one wringer, and I think we were neck and neck in the broken relationship race. She and D—whom I mentioned earlier in this account—had separated long ago, and the tribulations of the acting life provided their own difficulties. After giving my notice at my flat—a lovely place, with a rooftop patio, avocado and olive trees, in an architecturally interesting part of the city, rare as they are—I had a yard sale. I priced everything low, so it would sell—and it did. My books found a harbor in another friend's garage, where they would stay for some time. It would be some years, in fact, before I could afford a place large enough for them to join me, and I offer belated thanks to the friend who let them take up space she might have used for something else.

What I did between packing up my life and leaving for the UK is something of a blur now. One thing I did was arrange to sell the last of my four 1966 Volvo 122S sedans. I placed an ad in a local paper—again, this was long before internet markets—and wound up selling it to a young couple. It struck me that they would appreciate it. A dealer who exported them back to Europe, where they were popular, offered more money, but I didn't like his attitude, so I passed. The idea that someone would be driving it along the PCH or the Hollywood Hills, as I had, seemed somehow fitting. At least it would get to stay in the old neighborhoods.

I took one last drive in it, out to the ocean and up to the hills. I am something of a fetishist—not in the sexual but in the mythic, one might almost say religious, sense. I collect odd bits of things and endow them with magical properties. I imagine Jung would say I am participating in ancient, collective rites. I do it still today, and my closet has more than one box filled with the *objets trouvés* collected while scavenging along the windrow—a very Powysian word—left by the Thames. These have made up what we might call shrines in different places I have lived in London. On that last drive, I had with me some stones that had served a talismanic purpose and a walking stick I had metamorphosed from a fallen branch of a tree. It, too, had served some mythic, magical need.

Somewhere along the coast highway, I pulled over and walked out to the beach. I can't remember what I did, but I performed some sort of spontaneous, impromptu ritual. I looked at the sun and then out to the horizon, then threw the stones as far as I could into the Pacific. Then I drove out to Griffith Park. I parked near the observatory and took one of the hiking trails I had followed many times over the years as a Californian. It would be some time before I would walk them again. I found a spot I knew, where I would often sit and meditate—which really meant trying to feel that I was *there, then*, as Gurdjieff taught was the formula for life being "real." Then I took the magical walking stick, left it on a large stone on which I'd often sat, walked back to the car, and drove away.

I turned forty on December twenty-fourth, 1995. I can't remember if I did anything special. Twenty years before that, on my twentieth birthday, I had stayed warm in the freezing Blondie loft on the

Bowery by burning Jimi Hendrix posters. Now, I was leaving the warm California sun for colder climes. They say life begins at forty. The one I've been living for the past twenty-eight years certainly did.

I did do something special on New Year's Eve. Lisa invited me to go with her and another old boyfriend to a karaoke bar on La Brea Avenue, to sing out the old year and sing in the new. She knew her other ex before she met me, but I knew him, as well, from our New York days, and we were friends.[1] Why not? I thought. It could be fun.

It was. I don't remember what her other ex sang. But I know Lisa sang "Sugar Sugar," an appropriately sweet pop tune by The Archies that was a massive hit in 1969. I remember watching the Saturday morning cartoon show it came from. I sang The Animals's song "Don't Let Me Be Misunderstood," a hit from the British Invasion in 1965. Has that request been granted? These days, hearing from some of my readers, I sometimes get the impression it has.

The next day, January 1, 1996, I boarded a jet at LAX en route for London, with a brief stopover in New York. What happened next? Plenty. But that, as they say, is another story.

The British Library
January 2023–January 2024
Completed on the twenty-eighth anniversary
of my relocation to London

---

1. This was Grant Loud, brother of Lance Loud, the singer in the Mumps. Both came to media attention as siblings in the early "reality TV" documentary *An American Family* (1973).

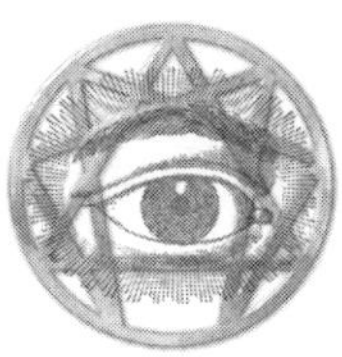

Acknowledgments

This memoir was written during an extremely difficult time in my life quite literally to keep me sane. How well it has succeeded at that is debatable, but I survived the writing of it and am genuinely surprised it has seen print, a sentiment some of its readers may share. More people need to be thanked for their part in this account than I can do justice to; my only excuse for their absence in the narrative is that the necessities of composition demand a certain economy: the need to tell the story overruled everything else. Some people, though, must be mentioned here, for their contribution was absolutely essential. I must once again thank the staff of the British Library, where I practically lived while writing this book, for their always congenial and excellent service. Without the library, I could not have written it. I do not know if he is still among us, but my thanks goes to my high school teacher, Mr. Daler, for handing me Sartre while teaching the rest of the class whatever was on the syllabus. He had no idea what he had started. My thanks goes to the late Clem Burke, who passed away while I was editing this book, for inviting me to audition for a fledgling Blondie, to Debbie Harry for taking me in when I was two steps from homelessness, and to Chris Stein for pulling the plug on that faulty lamp fifty years ago. My thanks goes to Tommy Ramone, for letting me borrow *The Occult*, and to Benton for introducing me to magick. Great thanks and fond memories go to Richard D'Andrea, Joel Turrisi, and

John McGarvey for making The Know possible. I have to thank my professors Henry, Joseph, and Daniel for infecting me with the love of wisdom; the responsibility for the use I have put it to rests solely with me. More thanks than I can express goes to Colin Wilson, for writing his books and for giving me the inspiration to write my own. But my greatest thanks must go to my best and oldest friend, Lisa Jane Persky, without whose presence you would not be reading this.

ALSO BY GARY LACHMAN

Maurice Nicoll: Forgotten Teacher of the Fourth Way

Dreaming Ahead of Time

Introducing Swedenborg: Correspondences

The Return of Holy Russia

Dark Star Rising: Magick and Power in the Age of Trump

Lost Knowledge of the Imagination

Beyond the Robot: The Life and Work of Colin Wilson

The Secret Teachers of the Western World

Revolutionaries of the Soul

Aleister Crowley: Magick, Rock and Roll, and the Wickedest Man in the World

The Caretakers of the Cosmos

Madame Blavatsky: The Mother of Modern Spirituality

The Quest for Hermes Trismegistus

Jung The Mystic

Swedenborg: An Introduction to His Life and Ideas

The Dedalus Book of Literary Suicides: Dead Letters

Politics and the Occult

Rudolf Steiner: An Introduction to His Life and Work

In Search of P. D. Ouspensky

The Dedalus Occult Reader (Ed.)

The Dedalus Book of the Occult: A Dark Muse

A Secret History of Consciousness

Turn Off Your Mind: The Mystic Sixties and the Dark Side of the Age of Aquarius

Two Essays on Colin Wilson

As Gary Valentine

New York Rocker: My Life in the Blank Generation

BOOKS OF RELATED INTEREST

Maurice Nicoll
Forgotten Teacher of the Fourth Way
by Gary Lachman

Gary Lachman draws on recently uncovered diaries to explore the unusual, syncretic approach Maurice Nicoll (1884–1953) brought to his teaching of the Fourth Way. He shows how Nicoll is unique in having Jung, Gurdjieff, and Ouspensky as teachers and incorporated Jungian psychology and Swedenborg-inspired mysticism into his sharing of Gurdjieff's and Ouspensky's ideas.

The Occult Elvis
The Mystical and Magical Life of the King
by Miguel Conner

Miguel Conner presents accounts from Elvis's wife, his friends and family, the Memphis Mafia, and his spiritual advisors to reveal Elvis the mystic, occultist, and shaman. By examining Elvis's efforts as a natural healer, his UFO encounters, and his telekinetic, psychic, and astral traveling abilities, Conner argues that Elvis was America's greatest magician.

Jim Morrison, Secret Teacher of the Occult
A Journey to the Other Side
by Paul Wyld

As author Paul Wyld reveals, despite Jim Morrison's reputation as a lewd, drunken performer, he was a full-fledged mystical, shamanic figure, a secret teacher of the occult who was not only central to the development of rock music, but to the growth of the Western esoteric tradition as a whole.

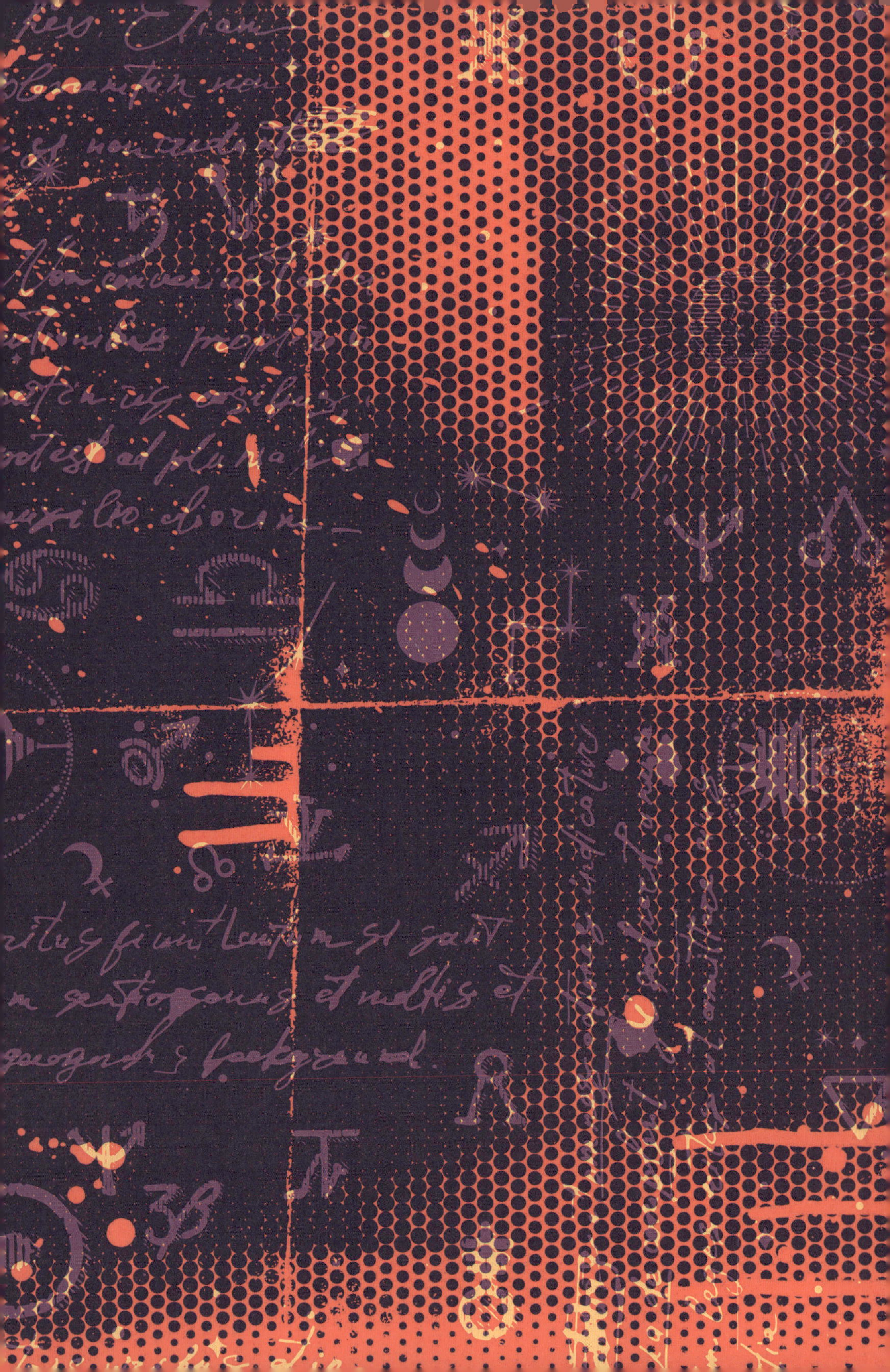